C. WRIGHT MILLS
An American Utopian

C. WRIGHT MILLS
An American Utopian

Irving Louis Horowitz

FP

THE FREE PRESS
A Division of Macmillan, Inc.
NEW YORK

Collier Macmillan Publishers
LONDON

Copyright © 1983 by The Free Press
A Division of Macmillan, Inc.

The Free Press
A Division of Macmillan, Inc.
866 Third Avenue, New York, N. Y. 10022

Collier Macmillan Canada, Inc.

Printed in the United States of America

printing number

1 2 3 4 5 6 7 8 9 10

Library of Congress Cataloging in Publication Data
Horowitz, Irving Louis.
  C. Wright Mills : an American utopian.

  Includes index.
  1. Mills, C. Wright (Charles Wright), 1916–1962—
Biography.   I. Title.
HM22.U6M427   1983   301′.092′4 [B]   83-5619
ISBN 0-02-914970-3

√ wl   11-21-83

God bless the children,
especially
Joshua, Jeremy, Emma, and Zoë

Contents

Preface

Biographers usually complain about the tedious nature of their efforts—and not without considerable justification. The amount of work required to gather even minimum information is great, and as Samuel Johnson observed: "The incidents which give excellence to biography are of a volatile, and evanescent kind such as soon escape the memory." The tendency therefore to reinterpret events from fragments, to force one's way through a confused jungle, as Lord Keynes would have it, is irresistible. The hard work comes in assembling information gathered from the many people who have been involved with the person who is the subject of the biography.

In the case of my work on C. Wright Mills, the burdens were made less onerous by the support colleagues provided. Johnson's concerns that time would cool the passions of those who had been involved with the biographical subject and lead to much impartiality and little intelligence were not borne out. Here one must be blunt and plain-spoken: my greatest difficulty was getting people who knew Mills to speak about him in a calm and reasoned manner. Although more than twenty-one years have passed since his death, and much more time than that has elapsed since people actually knew, saw, or corresponded with him, the sense of his presence was so imminent that old arguments were often rekindled rather than dampened at the mention of his name.

These problems acknowledged, I have tried to contact every living person who has firsthand information on Mills. Clearly, I have fallen short of this goal. Still, by referencing people mentioned in his correspondence, a powerful cross-section of opinion has been obtained. I must apologize for the inevitable omissions. Whether they were favorably or negatively predisposed to Mills, people have for the most part responded fully and enthusiastically to any questions I put to them, even those on embarrassing and difficult issues. So, without further ado, and to express my deepest appreciation, I list the following people and thank them for their help.

From the first, or Texas, phase: David L. Miller, Clarence E. Ayres, Carl M. Rosenquist, Ronnie Dugger. From the second, or Wisconsin, phase: Donald Bogue, Merle Curti, David Mechanic, Eliseo Vivas, Don Martindale, Alan C. Kerckhoff. From the third, or Washington, D.C./Maryland, phase: Richard Hofstadter, Herbert Blumer, George H.

Callcott. From the fourth, and quite lengthy, Columbia phase: Daniel Bell, Robert King Merton, William J. Goode, Jacques Barzun, Seymour Martin Lipset, Helen Merrill Lynd, Alvin W. Gouldner, Rose K. Goldsen, Meyer Schapiro. There was, in effect, a fifth period, covering people and events quite beyond the Columbia connections, when Mills became deeply enmeshed in world events. For help in dealing with this period I am grateful to Gino Germani, Tom Bottomore, David Riesman, Richard H. Rovere, William Appleman Williams, Theodore Abel, Pablo Gonzalez Casanova. It is, I believe, appropriate to mention that many of the people who gave me advice and information on Mills knew him across academic and even geographic boundaries; hence the five phases listed here are only intended to emphasize the core period of interaction.

Other people, who transcend such categorization, gave of themselves and imparted to me their knowledge of Mills's work without constraint; sometimes they even shared memoirs and other works in progress. First and foremost is Wilson Record, whose lengthy taped discussions with me about Mills remain a veritable gold mine of information, especially about Mills in his early years. Kenneth W. Wheeler, of Rutgers University, shared observations on the Texas milieu, and his comments on the organization of the manuscript as a whole were most supportive. In fact, it was his stimulating intervention that forced me to complete the manuscript at a critical juncture. Mary E. Curtis again proved to be an invaluable support and assistant. She helped me think through problems chapter by chapter and helped with the editing page by page. She good-naturedly shared in the toughest work of all. Hopefully, the opinions registered by each of these three former southerners are adequately represented in this work. I believe that they felt the calling of this book, the social need for it, and helped transform what began as a self-imposed duty into a labor of love.

My editor at The Free Press, Joyce Seltzer, faced the less than enviable task of making sure that the staccato efforts of more than two decades were unified and synchronized by the final version. She also fought hard for a clarity in presentation and a fairness in analysis, which, alas, I was not uniformly able to achieve. Still, it was her insistence on a consistent narrative thread that made me think through anew the problem of sociological biography in general and the problem of C. Wright Mills in particular.

Princeton, New Jersey
September 1, 1982

1

Introduction to an American Utopian

Sometimes a soul is sent down from Heaven which has to fulfill its mission in a hurry.

Isaac Bashevis Singer, *Short Friday and Other Stories*

A CURIOUS FACT about social science biographies is how few of them there are; even more surprising is how few good biographies have been written about leading American sociological figures. There are, of course, some extraordinary books on European intellectual figures: Marianne Weber's biography of her husband Max,[1] Steven Lukes's austere treatment of Emile Durkheim,[2] the venerable classic biography of Karl Marx by Franz Mehring,[3] and several outstanding intellectual biographies of LePlay,[4] LeBon,[5] Sorel,[6] Scheler,[7] and Gobineau.[8] Interestingly enough, in only a few of these cases have the biographies been written by other social scientists. More often, they have been written by widows, historians, and professional biographers. Even the fine memoir by Margaret Mead on Ruth Benedict is more in the nature of a personal reflection than a professional assessment.[9] The question thus becomes: Why do so few biographies exist about the major shapers of American social science?

The most significant factor appears to be the absence of a tradition of writing biographies on sociological figures. Biography, as a tradition, is closer to literature and politics than to the exact or inexact sciences. People whose habit of mind is the literary tradition tend to write biographies on literary figures they have known or by whom they have been influenced. Thus we have large numbers of biographies on poets and novelists, oftentimes multiple efforts on the same person. Such biographies make for good reading; they are the product of a literary grace that has

1

not gone into the manufacture and installation of a parallel tradition in sociology.

There is also the extremely powerful reluctance to appear as a follower, or an epigone, or an emulator of anyone else in social science. The tradition of individualism, or at least the appearance of uniqueness, is particularly powerful in American sociology. In point of fact, slavish imitation is nowhere greater than in social science. Witness the repeated, often exaggerated references to a select few names who wield high amounts of professional power during their careers. With their deaths comes a sharp decline in being referenced.* It may be not exactly a fear of following, but a fear of being found out as a follower, that inhibits sociological biographies. In a field as yet insecure as to its lineage, parentage, and even its future—as is sociology—there will always be a great dispute as to who warrants biographical treatment, and in turn, who should be the biographer.

In American sociology there has been an emphasis on strict methodological and empirical requirements, but without any corresponding discoveries or explanations found in the physical and biological sciences. The field does not easily lend itself to biographies, since a sense of unique achievement based on discovering the new is rarely found. John Madge came closest to communicating this impulse to empiricism in his work *The Origins of Scientific Sociology*—but his efforts were less biographical than methodological.[10] So much sociology depends on the reinterpretation of inherited theories, or the application of such doctrines to new situations, that the sense of discovery is somewhat muffled. Few reputations depend on actual discovery. Thomas Edison, Henry Ford, and Andrew Carnegie made discoveries, at least of a technological sort. Newton or Einstein can be said to have discovered fundamental theories and laws of nature in motion. But it is hard to claim a sociological equivalent of the discovery of an electric light bulb. Certainly, a general theory of social structure having the same simple elegance as Newton's laws of motion or Einstein's laws of relativity remains as elusive as it did in Comte's time. In the face of practical achievements in the engineering and physical sciences, the lack of celebration of even eminent social scientists is entirely understandable.

American sociology after the Second World War, in particular, doggedly entered the path of professionalization, refusing to acknowledge individual or occupational explorations that strayed too far afield from disciplinary horizons. Whatever else professionalism has produced, it has created a sense of commonality rather than personalities in Ameri-

---

*I am grateful to my colleague David Mechanic for this observation as it pertains to Howard Becker. Having gone to Wisconsin during the "transition period," he observed first how everything from course outlines to deference behavior changed with Becker's death.

can sociology: a focus on the facts rather than on an individual who identified events. The growth and development of professionalism has tended to make the field less individualistic or idiosyncratic. Organization men, rather than scientific or cultural giants, have emerged as central. Professionalism, whatever its blessings to the membership-elect, requires a high sense of organization and a necessary intellectual accommodation in the face of organizational responsibilities.

One would also have to add that in some respects sociology lacks a consensus about who the important figures are. Mills, for instance, was quite willing to describe Auguste Comte as both derivative and superficial; but there are those who have spoken (and written) about Mills in a similar fashion. Although there is a feeling that within the "classic" tradition, basically the European tradition, we know who the important figures are, the closer we come to American shores, and to contemporary sociology, the less apparent is any corresponding agreement about what constitutes real talent.

Because of the preceding reasons, or simply as an accident of the field itself, sociologists rarely are public figures. They tend to be identified by the tasks set for them, rather than those set by them; and they have a sense of reserve befitting scholarly research activity. Biographies, however, generally concern a public figure, or a quasi-public figure. One wants to read a book about someone who is at least distantly and vaguely identified by public achievement and public accountability, rather than by a professional job well done. As a result, the number of possible candidates for biographical treatment is instantly reduced to a select few. Becoming a public figure entails an enormous risk for the sociological professional. It is axiomatic that the more "popular" a sociological figure becomes, the more "unprofessional" he or she correspondingly has become. Thus, the price of public fame may often be professional isolation. This is itself a considerable deterrent in seeking wider public acclaim, and an even greater deterrent to becoming a subject for biography.

Writing biography is a creative act distinct from doing sociology. It is one thing to share a theorem, or a piece of new research data, or a survey technique, and give attribution to or even celebrate their discoverer. But to write an extended biography is quite another thing. It involves one in a world of persons and personalities, intimacies and privacies, private correspondence as well as public lectures, personal recollections as well as scholarly monographs, deeply felt passions as well as carefully stated reasons. The living polarities which I encountered in this work enhance my respect for the art of biography. It is an independent craft not usually undertaken by one sociologist writing about another sociologist.

These reservations and trepidations stated, it was, and remains, my feeling that C. Wright Mills is a worthy subject for biography. To begin with, Mills was an imposing physical specimen by any standards. He was tall (about six feet two inches); he spoke in a thundering drawl that marked him as a native American even if one did not identify his Texas origins; he smoked much, laughed easily, and angered many—although more often over abstract ideas than personalities. In fact, he heartily disdained professional shoptalk as "gossip." His carefully cultivated populist image notwithstanding, he remained throughout his career a hopeless academic, down to the pipe. He argued for the sake of scoring points, accepted eccentricities just within the boundaries of prevailing taste, and believed in the life of the mind even if he spiked metaphors with slang and curse-words. Mills presented himself as someone for whom mannerisms excluded manners, civic concerns excluded polite behavior, and personal style excluded conventional dress.

His personal demeanor was carefully contained to fit the outer limits of deviant academic thinkers (especially those who aspired to importance beyond university settings) but not to transcend university boundaries. He was the model Schumpeterian professor: an individual whose well-modulated levels of deviance were in perfect accord with cosmopolitan university settings. He well appreciated the fact that society creates a university environment precisely because it lacks other methods of receiving criticism without risking damage to the social order. This special set of circumstances gave Mills a sense of ease and intimacy with certain people if they perceived his manipulation of deviance as a device to stretch professional discourse to its limit. It was clear that the contradictions which Mills wore on his sleeves like a badge of honor were the essence of the man.

Mills was a strong character. He disguised his faults by admitting to even worse faults. He responded to others' claims that his behavior was boorish by behaving even more outlandishly. Critics were disarmed when he admitted to worse character flaws than he in fact possessed. It was a strategy dictated by his belief that the vocabulary of motives is nearly infinite, and hence the ability of any individual to make appropriate responses to others' interpretations is limited.

Mills's quite personal style led to a near-unanimous negative consensus about him. However much those who knew him firsthand differed about the quality of his work, they were unanimous about his personality. Of the many people I met, talked with, and corresponded with, very few mustered positive sentiments toward Mills. That in itself should occasion some pause. Anyone who, in effect, announces with Gide "I am the last great immoralist" is precisely the sort of individual for whom the moral situation is central, and his own moral demeanor critical. Thus, Mills never denied charges that he was a sexual athlete, a paramour at times and a lover on other occasions. Quite the contrary, like Benjamin Disraeli before him, Mills simply exaggerated all reports to the point of disbelief.

This style of self-deprecation, this higher form on one-upmanship, creates difficulties for the biographer, which I have by no means resolved. My own approach has been to minimize the significance of these personal elements, to ignore rather than affirm or deny their importance. The justification for this approach, apart from a deep belief that often apocryphal stories add little to our fund of information on Mills, is that they may actually detract from our sense of Mills as social scientist, political actor, and American utopian.

Support for this approach, albeit of an indirect sort, is that Mills only infrequently mentioned any of his three wives, Freya, Ruth, or Yaroslava. They seemed to enter into his consciousness only at the work level. Early in his career, Mills's correspondence does provide some insight into how the troubles in his first marriage impinged upon his intellectual output. But invariably he mentions external impediments rather than organic inspiration. It is true that his second wife, Ruth, is mentioned at times as a co-worker and junior partner. And it is probably true that Mills was happier with Yara than with his previous two wives, but the problematic nature of that final marriage is not discussed in his correspondence. In the main, Mills's personal relationships with his wives and friends were not part of his public or professional world. He had a keen disdain for "gossip," for those who converted private ills into public discourse. Insofar as possible, I have respected these feelings in the making of this book.

Because he tended to engage in self-glorification through self-deprecation, Mills gives any interpreter trouble. For example, he often boasts in his correspondence of his opposition to military service, implying that he hustled a permanent deferment status. In fact, as he let slip in person, he was medically diagnosed as having a severe heart ailment as early as 1942, his first full year at the University of Maryland. This is one of many cases where not only his critics must be taken in small doses, but he himself must be taken with a grain of salt. He did not so much fend off criticism as incorporate it as part of his mystique.

C. Wright Mills was born in Waco, Texas, on August 28, 1916. He died in Nyack, New York, on March 20, 1962. In his forty-five years he packed in a career worthy of the best, in both quantity and quality. If he wrote things in a hurry, if he accelerated the pace of personal events dangerously, it may have been due in no small measure to his awareness that he might have a short life. Certainly, from the time he was twenty-five, and received the first medical report that he had a heart condition, to his fourth and fatal heart attack twenty years later, Mills worked at a fevered pace; he was a man in search of his destiny.

Mills's religious life included a youth as a choirboy in the Catholic church of Waco, a lifelong resentment of Christianity, appeals to the clergy to oppose rearmament, and a funeral in a marvelously nondenominational church called Columbia University Chapel. His personal life included three wives and three children—one by each wife. He offered pious pleas about the sanctity of marriage to those living out of wedded bliss while making self-aggrandizing claims to having more women in one month than Don Juan could boast in a lifetime. His was a life of assault on the bastions of power and the notions of power, counterbalanced by work for the War Plants Administration during the Second World War and, later on, lectures to many senior military academics. Mills's style was individualist, flamboyant, and antiauthoritarian; but he found no difficulty in taking a post as director of the Labor Research Division at the Bureau of Applied Social Research. He was generous to intellectual opponents, but punitive to personal associates.

These contradictions and many more are the stuff of everyday mortals. They serve to enhance a sense of wonderment at Mills's significant intellectual accomplishments. No other figure in American social science until Margaret Mead developed such a powerful appeal to the public conscience, or at least the educated public of the day. Like Jean-Jacques Rousseau before him and countless other figures since, he was emotionally a gnarled bundle of twine and intellectually a beacon of rational judgment. Life is contradiction, only death is resolution. Mills did not progress far enough with the former to reach the sort of synthesis characteristic of the mature, the old, or even the genius. But it must also be said that if a touch of immortality rubbed off on Mills, it was not because he sought a dialogue with angels, but because he was immersed in the everyday dialogue of people and institutions. This biography is, in short, not so much about a great man as it is about a man who understood the parameters of greatness.

Utopianism is a notoriously ambiguous concept—made so by its dual nature. On one hand, individuals like Plato, More, Campanella, and Bellamy are defined as utopian because they spent much effort in fashioning a more or less precise image of future social and political structures. On the other hand, there are those individuals whom Marx had in mind when criticizing "utopian socialism," such as Saint-Simon, Fourier, and Babeuf, aptly named the "prophets of Paris." These thinkers were much less concerned with locating the secular garden of Eden than with ridding mankind of the scourges of oppression associated with civilization. It was the process rather than the outcome which fascinated these "scientific" utopians. Mills shared much in common with this latter vision. His statements about a higher civilization were cloudy, brought secondhand from utilitarian and pragmatic views of a rational world order. His statements about social development, to the contrary, rested on the belief that the data of one age leads inexorably to the eruption of all contradictions within it, and hence already contains the materials for a movement to a higher epoch. Mills was too exacting a student of the classical sociological tradition, with its dire warnings against utopianism, to fall easy prey to asserting a complete model of a good society. Besides, he was too out of sympathy with model building to strike such a pose. Still, in the broad sense that he continued, against all odds, to believe that social theory must contain a moral edge, and that such an edge was locked into the primal belief that change in human beings can be for the better and not just random, the utopian spirit is deeply embedded in Mills's work. Indeed, as his work became more strident, losing sight of the distinction between analytical research and journalistic blandishment, the turn toward the utopian became ever more manifest in his writings. Immanuel Wallerstein, in his notice on Mills in the *International Encyclopedia of the Social Sciences*, nicely appreciated this element. "In a basic sense, Mills was a utopian reformer. He thought that knowledge properly used could bring about the good society, and that if the good society was not yet here, it was primarily the fault of men of knowledge."[1]

"American," too, is a word which requires some justification for its use in the title of this book. Mills was so vociferous in his opposition to specific government policies and social mores that one might be tempted to claim that he was more anti-American than American. Yet that would place far too narrow a construction on what it means to be an American. Testing the outer limits of civility no less than of ideology is an ingrained tradition from Samuel Adams to William James to Randolph Bourne. Testing the American grain may mean—and often has—taking on the giants of industry and the leaders of intellect. Mills was definitely of such a persuasion, but it would be ingenuous to see Mills's Americanism as a simpleminded negativism. He had an unyielding commitment to speaking directly to his fellow-citizens. In his near-total incomprehension of foreign cultures and languages, in his insistence on a broad style of do-it-yourself clothing design and housing construction, and in the thousand smaller ways from swagger to sentiment, Mills emerged as a quintessential American. Without unduly belaboring the point, it is entirely warranted to see Mills as an American utopian: a sociologist for whom morality was a centerpiece, a political theorist for whom the sensuous feel of events was a necessary way of avoiding the twin European curses of "grand theorizing" and "abstracted empiricism." As long as America was worth reforming, it was the new Utopia rather than the old Atlantis. The European world was tired, even exhausted, a past; the underdeveloped Third World was angry, a possibility, a future. But America was the present; and Mills liked living in the present, even if he spent his waking hours and sleepless nights fashioning a vaguely better future.

I have tried to write a sociological biography. By that I mean that the volume is clearly divided into three sections corresponding to three distinct perspectives. The first section traces Mills's progress through academic milieus in chronological order. I have long held that professionals who work at universities must be studied within that context, or their intellectual development will make little sense. By charting Mills's movements from Texas to Wisconsin, to Maryland/Washington, and to Columbia/New York, I have also been able to illumine the varieties of his sociological experience.

The second section of the work is written in the history-of-ideas tradition, in which the major intellectual influences on Mills's career, including Karl Mannheim, William James, John Dewey, Max Weber, and Karl Marx, are explained, not so much in any serial order—the movement of ideas is epiphenomenal and not sequential—as in a sequence meant to establish an intellectual and emotional context for understanding Mills. Mills wrestled deeply throughout his life to locate himself in a social science and philosophical galaxy. Interpreting how well he achieved his goals, by borrowing from the ideas of others to create his own new mix, is the burden of this central section of the book.

The third and final section addresses directly the major works Mills produced. Here it will be seen that, in my judgment, the central core of his contribution was less the style of sociological performance than the substance: the analysis of social and political stratification in the United States. I deal with Mills's later, more pamphleteering efforts less for the ideological statements he made there than for his desperate attempt to move beyond an American into a global vision.

Both the opening and closing chapters address the issue of utopianism directly. Anyone attempting to bite the world whole, rather than be content with chewing at one small piece, represents, by that effort, something of a utopian. However, it was not simply his holistic vision but his movement among philosophical, sociological, political, and cultural themes that stamped him as a utopian. The boundaries of intellectual space were made to yield to the outer limits of big pictures and even bigger visions. The private person and the historical epoch were part of the same fabric, and that fabric was made up of an admixture of scientific evidence, ideological sensation, and utopian imperative.

There are doubtless other, simpler ways of organizing such a volume. And just as plainly there might be other points of emphasis. There could have been greater attention to Mills's indebtedness to Veblen, more study of his trips to England, a further appreciation of his contributions to the profession of sociology. To this I can only respond in the words of Marianne Weber concerning her own efforts to chronicle Max Weber's life: *Was ich nicht mache, machen andere*. Which simply means: What I fail to do, others will.

REFERENCES

1. Marianne Weber. *Max Weber: A Biography*, translated by Harry Zohn. New York: John Wiley & Sons, 1975.
2. Steven Lukes. *Emile Durkheim: His Life and Work*. New York: Harper & Row Publishers, 1972.
3. Franz Mehring. *Karl Marx: The Story of His LIfe*, translated by Edward Fitzgerald. London: John Lane/The Bodley Head, 1936.
4. Michael Z. Brooke. *LePlay: Engineer and Social Scientist. The Life and Work of Frederick LePlay*. London: Longman Group, 1970.
5. Robert A. Nye. *The Origins of Crowd Psychology: Gustave LeBon and the Crisis of Mass Democracy in the Third Republic*. London and Beverly Hills: Sage Publications, 1975.
6. John L. Stanley. *The Sociology of Virtue: The Political and Social Theories of Georges Sorel*. Berkeley and Los Angeles: University of California Press, 1981.
7. Jean Raphael Staude. *Max Scheler: 1874-1928*. New York: The Free Press/ Macmillan, 1967.
8. Michael D. Biddiss. *Father of Racist Ideology: The Social and Political Thought of Count Gobineau*. New York: Weybright & Talley, 1970.
9. Margaret Mead. *An Anthropologist at Work: Writing of Ruth Benedict*. Boston: Houghton Mifflin Co., 1959.
10. John Madge. *The Origins of Scientific Sociology*. New York: The Free Press/Macmillan, 1962.
11. Immanuel Wallerstein. "C. Wright Mills." In *International Encyclopedia of the Social Sciences* vol. 10. New York: The Macmillan Co. and The Free Press, 1968, p. 364.

PART

I

∽∽∽

Settings

2

Texas Cosmopolitanism

A university is a city for the freedom of the mind, full of homes for thinking, shops for finding truth, and meeting rooms with windows. A university is a place for Emerson's man thinking and for woman thinking too. A university is a city of the people working together within our own and all of nature to make our freedom and our structures with our ideas. A university is a city of sunlight streaming into the naked minds of the citizens. A university is a place of reflection in the universe of mystery. A university is a city of the human kind that is worthy of the universe. A university is a universal city. And what is a state university? It is the same.

Ronnie Dugger, *Our Invaded Universities: Form, Reform, and New Starts*

A UNIVERSITY IS a special institution. Although it is linked to industry, the military, or the polity, it retains a peculiar resilience which keeps it from becoming captive to other agencies of power. Partially, this is because the university is concerned with knowledge, and knowledge does not respect boundaries invented by politicians or enforced by militarists. A university is also a source and not just a reflection of power.

The University of Texas ranks as a major institution. Texas historians emphasize local or parochial events so often that it is tempting to think of that university as simply a provincial outpost of the Lone Star State and overlook the national, even international, context in which it operates. During Mills's student years at Texas, between 1935 and 1939, the university sought and achieved its wide-ranging reputation, bringing in first-ranking scholars in many fields. In a sense Mills's mentors were more attuned to events in Chicago, Ohio, or Wisconsin, where they had taken their degrees, than to local events.

Texas has so often been entombed in its past by the rest of the United States, however, that even Texans sometimes put on their broadbrimmed Stetsons and reenact parochial cowboys-versus-Indians scenarios. Mills never really escaped his birthplace, certainly not in the minds of his commentators. More than once, and even by associates, he was described as a Texas cowpuncher who headed north via pony express to carry the message of radical sociology. There are several myths involved; one is small-scale and personal. Mills never rode a horse and never cared to, and except for two lecture engagements he never even returned to Texas once he left for the University of Wisconsin. The larger myth concerns Texas itself. Even the crudest demographic information reveals that Texas has been one of the most rapidly urbanizing and industrializing (as well as one of the most culturally diverse) states in this country during the twentieth century. The Hollywood dream factory perpetrated the notion that Texans have not yet given up the horse and saddle for the automobile. This was as inaccurate in the 1930s as it is in the 1980s.

Mills himself was typical of the new Texan: His parents were pious, middle-class, Irish-English in background. His father, Charles, was an insurance broker in Waco, where Mills was born; and his mother, Frances, was a housewife. His background was rooted in the smaller, frontier cities of Texas. From Waco, the Mills family moved to 3600 Lovers Lane in Dallas, where they remained during his high school career, to Milan Boulevard in San Antonio in 1938, to 2610 Salado Street in Austin in 1939. In addition to his city upbringing Mills was typical of the new Texan in that he went to Dallas Technical High School in anticipation of a career as an engineer. Beyond required courses in civics and history, Mills took no social studies courses. His areas of concentration in high school, beyond the standard majors, were algebra (two years), physics (one year), and mechanical drawing (four years). In these early years Mills was clearly an urbanized youngster, being prepared by his parents for a practical career in a rapidly industrializing environment.

Mills's interest in a technical career did not cease when he left for college. Like so many other young people experiencing the aftershock of the Great Depression, his concern with making a living prevailed over any articulated intellectual instincts. He first went to Texas Agricultural and Mechanical College. He managed to get A's or B's in just about all of his courses, including general zoology and inorganic chemistry. His poorest area, oddly enough, was physical education. Everyone managed to confuse his size with physical prowess. He was constantly being goaded to try out for football, basketball, and wrestling. Apparently, most students at Texas A & M were first and foremost athletes, and only secondarily students. The year at Texas A & M was a fiasco. Apparently Mills did join the wrestling team, and was promptly accused of needlessly injuring another student during a match. His punishment was that no one was to speak to him.[1] Just how apocryphal this story is remains to be established, since other classmates raised some doubt that he ever wrestled at all.[2] But one item is certain: that he soon transferred out of Texas A & M and into the University of Texas.

The University of Texas was, for Mills at least, a veritable oasis surrounded by an educational desert, exemplified by Texas Agricultural and Mechanical. Like many youngsters of his background and financial circumstances, his sense of college and university choices was circumscribed by state boundaries. Preferential tuition rates for state residents reinforced this spirit of insularity. Texas was large and buoyant enough to create a self-image approaching national rather than state proportions. The collapse of Mills's engineering ambitions, or simply the feeling that Texas A & M was not what he wanted, inevitably meant a move to Austin and the state university, the pinnacle of student ambitions.

The University of Texas was an exciting place to be during the 1935–1939 period: a school in turmoil and transition in sheer size and numbers, as well as in political orientation. The modern history of higher education in the South begins only in the second or third decade of the twentieth century. What provided particular impetus to higher education in Texas during this period was the legislative provisos which channeled the tax revenues from petroleum sales largely into the state educational system. The unique contribution of the University of Texas to this break with conservatism was the development of strong departments of graduate instruction in both the physical and social sciences. Mills benefited greatly by this unique break with gentlemanly collegiate tradition in southern education—a tradition that emphasized teaching to the exclusion of research.[3] However, despite this growth of Texas education during the period Mills went to college, other aspects of southern education in the mid-1930s, as outlined by Howard Odum, were scarcely inviting:

> It is not only that the region has no university of the first ranking, but it lacks college and university scholars and administrators of topmost distinction, measured by the usual standards of achievement and recognition . . . it lacks a reasonable number of endowed institutions sufficiently free from state or church dominance to function independently in the best manner of university standards and sufficiently well endowed to set the pace for other regional universities and to keep interregional and national influences and participation constantly on the scene. . . . The region has no educational administrative leaders who participate freely in the nation's councils of learning or who have access to its larger sources of endowment and support.[4]

If the lack of independent and vigorous universities was a problem in southern education generally, problems in Texas were compounded by a state Board of Regents more politicized and powerful than in nearly any other state of the union. The history of the University of Texas in the thirties, and every subsequent decade, can be summarized as a struggle between the Board of Regents, controlled by state industrial and political leaders, and a faculty with national aspirations and radical inclinations that rarely got much administrative support; the latter was enfeebled by the Board of Regents and the diffuse political forces responsive to its wishes. Texas, after all, is the only state in the union which enacted legislation, with only one dissenting vote, "that no infidel, atheist, or agnostic be employed in any capacity in the University of Texas, and . . . no person who does not believe in God as the Supreme Being and the Ruler of the Universe shall hereafter be employed." If this proclamation was more often violated than enforced, the fact is that it remains a painful reminder of the legacy of a rural South and, just as much, of an anti-Darwinian intellectual environment dominated by religious fundamentalism. A description of the university proffered anonymously in 1937 and repeated by Ronnie Dugger summarizes the general feeling toward the university among both its outcasts and its proudest sons and daughters.

> The University of Texas is in many ways a microcosm of the state—a vast, amorphous, gelatinous sort of institution, where skeptical professors of philosophy and cynical workers in the sciences rub elbows with Baptists who believe that a smoking hell lies three miles underneath their brogans. It is populated, yearly, by some six thousand bewildered boys and girls who are far less interested in the chase after the Higher Learning than in the pursuit of their own adolescent amours. Plucked from the bayous, the buckbrush, and the bulrushes of this far-flung commonwealth and dispatched to the Pierian Spring, they decline almost unanimously to drink of the founts of learning. They would rather see a football game. They would rather go to a movie. They would rather make passes at their girl friends.[5]

The passions concerning the Univesity of Texas have hardly lessened over time; only slight changes in the mores of the state's residents are discernible. In a recent article by Alan Grob, a professor from Rice University (also very much in Texas), in the official publication of the American Association of University Professors, Texas is described as follows:

> Higher education in America is strewn with incidents of political interference and violations of academic freedom much like those that have occurred at the University of Texas, and we must be vigilant both to prevent such intrusions and to resist them when they do take place. But if it is our duty to be vigilant, it is also our duty to be honest and fair. Though episodes resembling those at the University of Texas have occurred elsewhere, no comparable institution, that is, a major state university with significant academic credentials, can lay claim to a history of regental misgovernment and intellectual oppression remotely approximating that of the University of Texas.[6]

Grob goes on to shrewdly observe that the University of Texas should not be compared with Ivy League schools because such comparisons make little sense. Even excluding factors such as regional late starts and cultural differences, any effort to compare Austin, Texas, with Cambridge, Massachusetts, would falter because of structural differences between public and private universities. Comparisons of Texas with other state universities are more convincing, and at the same time more damaging.

> The question is not why the University of Texas is so unlike Harvard or Columbia in its history, but why it is so unlike Wisconsin or Washington. Some thirty years after the regents of the University of Wisconsin had proclaimed as an article of their academic faith and, more important, had established as a guide to their academic practice and principle that "the great state University of Wisconsin should ever encourage that continual and fearless sifting and winnowing by which alone the truth can be found," the regents of the University of Texas were implementing . . . an impromptu inquisition conducted to ferret out the suspect religious opinions of the dean of the college of arts and sciences.[7]

Yet, after all just criticisms are registered, the University of Texas was and remains an exciting institution. It is a center for research on everything from cancer to Latin America; it is a university that continues to boast a remarkable group of faculty members despite, rather than because of, boards of governors and state regents.

The period when Mills was at the university corresponded with the high point of New Deal sentiments and passions. The progressive governor of Texas, Jimmy Allred, changed the complexion of the Board of Regents and in so doing the structure of the school. The governor was himself both a rich oilman and a New Deal Democrat supportive of Franklin Delano Roosevelt, and like the president, he was conservative in personal matters. He managed to find a Texas-born-and-bred intellectual, Homer Price Rainey, born in Red River County, to appoint as university president. This in itself helped to allay conservative fears, since East Texas traditionally has been viewed as southern whereas West Texas is identified with the American West. Rainey was trained in education at the University of Chicago. He, in turn, appointed as his associate Chester Rowell, who had served him on the American Youth Commission in Washington, D.C. Rowell introduced ideas which must have been as shocking to Texas conservatives as anything heard before or since, including an attack on totalitarianism and a defense of the unfettered search for truth. He steadily emphasized that the anti-intellectual compulsions of Nazism did violence to the spirit of freedom and ended by closing every field of inquiry deemed dangerous to the regime.

Rainey's positions derived their energies from the New Deal. He set the tone for a struggle in the late 1930s in Texas that ultimately resulted in political turmoil. Mills heard liberal doctrine derived almost directly from the New Deal, and intellectually from the pragmatist movement as it found its way to Chicago and back down to Texas. Here is Rainey speaking at his inaugural:

> We are making, or are about to make, here in Texas, a momentous decision. The regents have set out to take literally the requirements for a university of the first class. But the people would decide whether it would be allowed to run free. It is their wish to remove as far as practicable all hampering restrictions. Do not keep too close a control. Provide freedom of action and the university could be great.[9]

The faculty boasted some extraordinary people, including one of the great historians of American civilization, Walter Prescott Webb. Jess Walker graced the School of Law. Henry Sheldon, Clarence E. Ayres, and Wendell Gordon gave Texas a first-rate institutional economics department. Carl M. Rosenquist and Warner E. Gettys in sociology provided a range of courses from survey research to ethnography. David L. Miller and George Gentry in philosophy also provided a strong base in social theory. The strength of the social science departments thoroughly aroused and alarmed the Texas Liberty Leaguers and Christian fundamentalists of various sorts. "The son of a University of Texas professor during this period remembers a wealthy old lady snapping to his father, 'I can't stand the University of Texas. It's full of sociology and sodobottomy!' "[10]

This malapropism aside, the impact of the "Chicago school" of sociology is attested to by the fact that Warner E. Gettys, the dean of sociology at Texas, felt it necessary to spend three summer quarters between 1920 and 1922 at Chicago for the purpose of studying under the tutelage of Professors Albion W. Small, Robert E. Park, Ellsworth Faris, and Ernest W. Burgess. Further, Carl M. Rosenquist, who was Gettys's protégé, received his doctorate at Chicago in 1930. Robert Lee Sutherland, the Texas expert on race relations, was also a graduate of the Chicago program in sociology. Indeed, in his brief history of sociology at Texas, Gettys notes that "it was an interesting coincidence that brought the first three full-time sociologists to the University of Texas from graduate study at the University of Chicago."[11] With people like Max S. Handman and Albert B. Wolfe, the post–World War epoch at Texas was cosmopolitan by any standards, with courses in socialism being standard.

The impact of Chicago-style work in philosophy, sociology, and economics at Texas reached from President Rainey down through the spine of every department: Ayres in economics, Gettys in sociology, and Gentry and Miller in philosophy all held doctorates from the University of Chicago. Typical was its influence even on nativists like Walter Prescott Webb, author of such classics as *The Texas Rangers, The Great Plains, The Great Frontier*, and also a New Deal economic tract, *How We Stand*, that went far beyond conventional Texas nationalism. His central role was bringing cosmopolitans like John Dewey and the pragmatic tradition to the attention of youngsters like Mills.[12]

The university which emerged during this period reflected the large-scale impact of the New Deal on Texas politics generally. The New Deal helped Texas break away from the South and move toward the creation of a new category: the Southwest. The state and its university reflected the pulling power of that new frontier rather than an old structure. Mills was part of that wave. His cultural roots were very much with the Southwest. In speech, habits, and manners, Mills was western and not southern; expansive rather than reflective; effective rather than sardonic.

In trying to get a handle on Mills as a Texan, one could do no better than to recall the observation made by Eric F. Goldman in his biography of Lyndon B. Johnson, comparing Johnson with his predecessor, John F. Kennedy.

> The more he heard of the "great John Kennedy," the more he was driven to be "the greatest of them all, the whole bunch of them." The more Lyndon Johnson heard the cultivated Kennedy from Harvard compared with his boorish Texas self, the more he held back on occasion, at other times deliberately exaggerated Lyndon Johnson from Johnson City, drawl, boisterousness, banality and all.[13]

So it was with the later Mills in relation to his Columbia colleagues—particularly those from quasi–upper class backgrounds. His well-disguised animosities, which scarcely show up in his correspondence or even the critical essays, were manifested in personal contacts in his disregard for manners at the expense of frankness. But here comparisons with Johnson end: Mills never owned property in Texas, he had no wish to return, and he never minced his disdain for his middle-class parents in Waco. Johnson never left Texas, but Mills never returned.

Mills's official transcript from the University of Texas indicates that he graduated on June 5, 1939, receiving both the baccalaureate and master's degrees on that date.[14] As was so often the case in Mills's later life, he did things in his own way, and that meant rarely following the rules. Since he did not graduate on time, he fell between two cohort groups rather than being part of one. He was anxious to finish his coursework, clearly understanding the infantilizing nature of further schooling. But he was not anxious to leave Texas at the time, since he did not know where he was headed. Thus, he failed to obey the rules until disobedience would have endangered his graduation.

Mills was a good young scholar—as long as he took courses he liked from teachers he respected. He made top grades in sociology, cultural anthropology, social psychology, economics, and all his courses in philosophy. When it came to subjects he was not interested in, he quickly became a "gentleman C" student: these included French composition, algebra, and the mathematics of finance. Nonetheless, his work was sufficiently distinguished to merit his receipt of the Charles Durand Albright Scholarship for 1937–1938. He was also made student president of the Southwestern Social Science Association for 1938–1939. By the time of his junior year, then, there was no question that Mills was destined for an academic career.[15]

Mills was not alone as an outstanding student at Texas. The late 1930s produced figures who went on to make substantial contributions in sociology. Marion J. Levy, Jr., was a student in the economics department, William J. Goode came from the sociology department. Each went on to become a significant figure in the development of American sociology: Levy at Princeton University, and Goode as Mills's colleague in the Columbia University department before moving on to Stanford. Mills was controversial and scarcely universally appealing.[16] But if he was not exactly revered by his fellow students, he was extremely well regarded by the faculty, not just the faculty generally, but the avant-garde of the Departments of Philosophy, Sociology, and Economics. Transcripts containing letters of recommendation sent by his Texas mentors to the Department of Sociology at the University of Wisconsin attest to this regard.

The opportunity for remaining at Texas to do doctoral work was not available. It was not until 1941 that the university produced its first doctorate in sociology; interestingly enough the first dissertation was Mattie Lloyd Wooten's "The Status of Women in Texas." This was followed by one more dissertation awarded to Rex H. Hopper of Project Camelot fame,[17] who wrote "The Struggle for Independence in Latin America." Perhaps these two works were more than the authorities bargained for, since it was not until 1949 that the program genuinely got underway, fully ten years after Mills had left Texas. His choice at the time was to pursue advanced studies in another department or another university. His choice of Wisconsin, while at first surprising, is less so given the close ties of departmental figures like Gettys with E. A. Ross and John Gillin, his prewar mentors there, who in fact remained influential, certainly at the appointment level, when Mills was making his fateful choice.[18]

George Gentry, who introduced Mills as an undergraduate to Dewey, Mead, and Peirce, also supervised Mills's master's dissertation, "Reflection, Behavior, and Culture." Gentry was the kind of unheralded thinker who did little writing but much sound teaching. His remarks about Mills typify the sense of promise the faculty felt he had even at that time, and their expectation of a greatness to come.

As a result of conversations concerning theoretical and methodological problems in the social sciences some three years past, I was considerably impressed by Mr. Mills' acuteness, intellectual vigor, and driving interest.

He struck me as a young man of real potentiality. As a result I encouraged him to do work in philosophy. During the past two years and a half I have been very closely associated with him both in the lecture room and in more informal discussions. During this period he has taken a great deal of work with me: logical theory, general semantics, work on the pragmatism and social behaviorism of Mead as well as work on Dewey and Peirce. At present he is working out his master's dissertation with me. My respect for his abilities and possibilities has grown with time. He is head and shoulders above most graduate students I have known here and elsewhere. I have no hesitation in saying that he is one of the two most promising young men I have contacted in my eight years here. The other, Milton B. Singer, is taking his Ph.D. in philosophy at the University of Chicago this spring with high distinctions. If Mr. Mills doesn't go places in the academic world, I will be greatly surprised.[19]

Mills served as Gentry's teaching assistant; his fabled ability as a lecturer to large groups was apparently manifest as an undergraduate. Teaching was an adult role that Mills easily identified with, in contrast to his endless chafing in the student role. To quote Gentry again:

Mr. Mills has been my assistant from time to time during the last two years and has demonstrated his capacities along such lines. He gets along well with students and is very apt in handling the details connected with conducting under-graduate work. He has also handled my classes on occasion and proved himself to be a very capable and interesting lecturer and discussion leader.[20]

Another of his philosophy mentors, A. P. Brogan, who was not only a professor of philosophy but dean of the graduate school, mentions Mills's talent, but also his "arrogance" and "lack of discipline." It would be much too simple to chalk this up as a typical administrative response. In fact, he only articulated a general complaint. Yet even Brogan seems certain that Mills had a bright future.

I have been very much impressed by his intellectual ability and power. He is interested in the borderlines of philosophy and sociology or the theory of the social sciences. He is widely read. He speaks and writes clearly and forcefully. He has a great amount of energy and drive. Under the proper influences, he might develop into an unusually able student. In the past he has at times been somewhat temperamental, but he seems to be outgrowing that condition. His main source of trouble was formerly a certain arrogance that aroused hostility among the persons he criticized. I think he has overcome most, if not all, of this at the present time. He may still need a bit of discipline, but I think he might repay the effort.[21]

Another professor of philosophy, David L. Miller, gives Mills very high marks. Miller was an editor, along with Charles W. Morris, of George Herbert Mead's *The Philosophy of the Act*. Miller undoubtedly exercised a profound impact on Mills's continuing interest in pragmatism.

> Under the influence of myself, C. E. Ayres, G. V. Gentry (each of us having a doctor's degree in philosophy from the University of Chicago), Mills was introduced to Peirce, Dewey, James, and Mead. His interest in the sociology of knowledge is by way of American pragmatism, not from Scheler or Mannheim.[22]

Through Miller, Mills learned to use Mead to bridge the gap between sociological and philosophical understanding. Miller believed that Mills had developed tremendously during the three years of undergraduate education he had known him and said, "I see no signs of his letting up." Miller's support of Mills remained unstinting. Interestingly, Miller drew attention to an aspect of Mills's development that was never acknowledged by Mills, certainly not in his later writings: the role of Kimball Young.

> Mills is energetic, both physically and mentally. He is keen at analyzing, especially motivating social forces, and broke away early from superstitious beliefs common to many of our Southern students. Consequently, with this training and aptitudes, I consider him one of the most able prospective graduate students we have had in the past four years. He meets students well, has been unusually successful in tutoring them, does not assume the offensive attitude when students come to him for explanations about low grades, etc. Mills has been particularly interested in social psychology and has followed the behavioristic approach of such men as Dewey, Mead (especially) and Kimball Young. He is continually working in the Library, looking for new materials on problems, and usually comes out with good results, as is evidenced by his term paper.[23]

This term paper was published later in 1939 in the *American Sociological Review*, largely as a result of Howard Becker's support. Meanwhile, Mills's contact with the sociology department increased. He began to work with Rosenquist, Douglas W. Oberdorfer, and Gettys as often as with anyone in the philosophy department. Through this sociological connection the link with Wisconsin was made. Oberdorfer, an instructor in social psychology, was a graduate of Wisconsin who was conducting ongoing research with people at the university, particularly Professor T. C. McCormick, then chairman of the sociology department at the University of Wisconsin and supervisor of Oberdorfer's thesis. Stimulated by Miller, Mills's direct communication with Becker, the most esteemed of Wisconsin's sociological theorists, proved invaluable in getting him the Wisconsin appointment. The analysis of Mills given by Oberdorfer is itself interesting:

> While Mills' chief interest is in sociological theory and social psychology, he is well oriented in the entire field and is quite aware of the importance

of empirical research. Last year he worked for Henry Sheldon in connection with the latter's population research. Despite his youth, Mills has attained a degree of maturity in his work which is rare among pre-doctoral students. Knowing the high quality of work which is demanded of graduate students at Wisconsin, and realizing the breadth of training which its facilities provide, I strongly urged Mills to apply to the Department for an appointment. I feel sure that you would not be disappointed in him. He recently submitted a paper to Professor Becker, who recommended its publication in the *American Sociological Review*. Personally, Mills is well-adjusted; he is married to a charming girl. The two of them would be worthy additions to Wisconsin's sociological community.[24]

Carl Rosenquist, an early quantitatively oriented sociologist, was another important supporter. Rosenquist was respected within the profession as a technician and analyst, especially in areas involving the statistical study of social mobility. Mills studied social psychology under Rosenquist. Criticism of Mills for behaving with arrogance and cocksureness emerges in Rosenquist's evaluation. He softened the critique by a prediction that such behavior would not manifest itself in graduate school, where Mills presumably would come upon a higher caliber of professional students. This anticipated behavior modification never took place. Nonetheless, Rosenquist's letter, too, indicates the high regard in which Mills was held during his Texas years.

Coming here two or three years ago as a transfer from our A & M College (of all places) he has proved himself an excellent student, with a degree of intellectual curiosity and interest seldom observed in these parts. He has read widely, particularly in philosophy, in which he has taken many courses. He probably knows the philosophical field just as well as the sociological, but he quite definitely wants to continue with the latter. In the several classes of mine in which he has been a member he has always been outstanding as a student. He always knows more than he needs to and at once he sees the implications which the rest see, if at all, only after long explanations. This fact, his being so far ahead of the rest, has manifested itself at times in the form of a little impatience with the sophomoric mind and has given to his own utterances an air of cocksureness which might perhaps be misunderstood as arrogance, but which I think would never appear in a group of graduate students of the caliber he is likely to run into at Wisconsin.[25]

Although Rosenquist admitted that Mills did not distinguish himself in his statistics course, he was quick to add that this was not due to stupidity, but to Mills's desire to deal with statistics only if and when he needed to do so. Methodology was a tool rather than a way of life. He concluded by noting that "on the whole I believe Mills is a good bet. He is easily the best we have to offer. I hope you can do something for him."[26]

An extremely potent force in Texas sociology was Warner E. Gettys, part of that long connection from Chicago to Texas, extending from the administration into the professoriat. Mills took courses in urban sociology, and in sociological attitudes, under Gettys's supervision. In the first edition of *An Introduction to Sociology*, which he wrote with Carl A. Dawson, Gettys dedicates the entire first section to the "urban social world," which turns out to be the Near North Side of Chicago. One can only imagine how odd it must have been for native Texas students to find that the first thirty-seven pages of their sociology text studied the North Side of Chicago. So powerful was the Chicago influence upon Gettys that even the basic textbook in sociology by Park and Burgess contains fewer references to their own Chicago researches than the text of this usually reserved scholar from Texas.[27] Gettys undoubtedly had a major impact on the young Mills, especially in the area of social psychology. His letter of support was genuinely felt.

> Mills is a very promising young sociologist, well above the average in interest and ability. He has made a very fine scholastic record here both in the fields of sociology and philosophy, with some work in economics. He is a tireless student, widely read on many subjects, and a fairly clear, though not particularly mature, thinker. He has an abundance of self-assurance and a certain cocksureness, which tend to irritate some of those who come in contact with him; but these are qualities, which, if properly directed, may become assets, it seems to me. There is a confidence and a drive about him which should carry him a long way. He is very ambitious and I believe he should be encouraged to go ahead with his plans for the Ph.D. degree. I am pleased to recommend him to your department because I believe his major interests in theory and social psychology can find in your department their best chance for development.[28]

Mills had a penchant for courses that he was attracted to because of content or teacher, without much regard for departmental majors. As a result, he found himself moving into economics as well as philosophy and sociology. One powerful economist whose course he took was Henry D. Sheldon, who went on to become chief of the Bureau of the Census, and who was far more interested in sociology and demography than are most economists. Sheldon wrote two letters to Wisconsin: one to John L. Gillin, chairman of the sociology department, and the other to McCormick, while he was on leave at Stanford. His letter to Gillin, in particular, made mention of what had become a standard reservation about Mills: his pugnacious characteristics. Sheldon wrote that a general impression at Texas was that Mills was critical and aggressive. "He is inclined to take a rigorous and uncompromising stand on all issues that may arise—an attitude which has not contributed to his popularity in certain quarters there."[29] Like everyone else, Sheldon was convinced that Mills's aggressive manner would tone down. Given the sophistication of Mills's work style, his mentors undoubtedly understood that this was more a hope and prayer than a likelihood.

> My impression of him is that he is extremely competent intellectually and pretty original in his thinking. For a person just getting his B.A., which he was doing when I knew him, he seemed to have an unusually comprehensive grasp of the field of sociology. His interest is, I should say, primarily theoretical and in this connection he has done considerable work in philosophy. He writes me that this year he is doing some lecturing and quiz section work in that field. The general impression of him at Texas, I think, would bear out what I have said. . . . I feel that he is excellent Ph.D. material and that as he matures his aggressive manner will tone down somewhat. We are looking forward very much to being in Madison this summer. When does summer session start? We shall be able to leave here about June 16th which, if my impression is correct, should get us there in plenty of time.[30]

This letter to McCormick indicates not simply Sheldon's support for Mills but also the fact that Sheldon would be going from Stanford to Wisconsin to teach statistics in the sociology department there. Thus Sheldon also had a connection to Wisconsin sociology which made his support of Mills quite crucial.

> I was happy to learn [Sheldon wrote McCormick] that I was to fill in for you this summer in elementary statistics and also a little worried. Could you give me some notion of the ground you cover in the course and any ideas as to texts? I feel that it is of considerable advantage to the students if they expect to go on at all in the department to preserve a certain continuity.[31]

Sheldon's letter on behalf of Mills raises the question of bellicosity, but notes that he is remarkably original and well-grounded. None of the supporting statements quoted above hints at any concern over Mills's politics. If he had become radicalized at Texas, Mills kept it remarkably well hidden, even from conservatives like Sheldon. Mills had developed an idiosyncratic personal style, but it was socially deviant rather than politically radical. While highly critical of those involved in campus politics, he remained apart from any efforts at reform and did not engage in any of the larger causes, i.e., sharecropper education programs, widely current at the time. With the exception of a rare letter to the campus newspaper, he preferred the company of his academic mentors to that of his student peers.

The letter on behalf of Mills which probably carried the greatest weight was by the great institutional economist Clarence E. Ayres, who had already received many nonacademic as well as academic honors—including the distinction of being a target for dismissal by the Texas legislature. The vote went against him 130 to 1 because of his presumed advocacy of the destruction of free enterprise and support for a socialist system of government. This piece of premature McCarthyism was urged on the university to avoid "damage and detriment to the people of Texas." The House of Representatives went on to ask the Board of Regents to investigate Ayres and decide whether to fire him. "If the University does not do something we ought to knock out appropriations for the Economics Department," one representative said. "Too mild a remedy," said another. "I think we should run him out of America." And indeed, efforts to at least run him out of Texas were approved by the Texas legislature.[32]

In his letter, Ayres declared that he felt he knew Mills as well as "any but one or two of our advanced students in economics." This was one instance in which Mills's rambunctious, raucous style met with academic approval:

> Mills' character and personality are most unusual. In the first place he is a rather good-sized fellow. Indeed "strapping" would describe him and he looks much more mature than his years. His attitude and manner are those of a mature student, not to say scholar. For some years he has read voraciously. Every now and then he stops me in the hall and asks me what I think of something I have never heard of. Some of my colleagues regard this as a pose, but I think they are mistaken. Another quality that sometimes arouses slight antagonism is Mills's highly developed critical faculty which sometimes finds rather blunt expression. But my impression is that Mills' critical sense really is unusually acute and that however tactless his remarks may have been on occasion his opinions have been genuine, informed, and usually sound. He writes well and has already had at least one article accepted for publication as doubtless he has told you.[33]

Ayres was clearly more inclined to accept Mills's character for what it was than presume that it would be bleached and starched with time. Clearly, this is because Ayres, too, had many of the same characteristics. His letter continues: "My judgment is that Mills is not a crank nor a flash-in-the-pan precocity. In my opinion he is the real thing and undoubtedly 'going places.' Any university would be fortunate to number him among its Ph.D.'s."[34]

The picture that emerges is of nearly universal support from senior representatives of three extremely powerful departments. These letters, written on behalf of an aspiring graduate student, indicate how well Mills was regarded by his reference group. In the meantime, Mills still had to go through the personal travails of the student life.

Mills did not participate in social reform efforts at Texas, but he did maintain friendships with fellow students who did. He met his wife-to-be, Dorothy James, on a double date with Wilson Record and Jane Cassells, who, along with Dorothy, had strong ties to the Young Men's and Women's Christian Association at Texas. In the context of Texas in the mid-1930s, the YMWCA represented a forward-looking agency for social change. Pioneering in efforts to educate Negro sharecroppers and Chicano pecan pickers, the "Y" practiced nondiscriminatory hiring policies, which was quite rare for the period. While a student, Dorothy worked as a secretary at the "Y," under the supervision of Ida Mae Brandner, who was in charge of women's programs.

Compared to Wright, Dorothy seemed quiet, reserved, and frail. She suffered from a host of maladies during the Texas period, but none impaired her work efficiency or diminished her personal attractiveness, both of which were commented upon by all those who knew Wright. Wright chose the nickname "Freya" for her. The allusion to D. H. Lawrence's wife Frieda was presumably intended to heighten a sense of drama in the relationship. Dorothy may have seemed too ordinary for Mills's sense of himself. He did not express love and affection, and it is small wonder that those who knew both of them were surprised, even upset, by the marriage. At first Freya's secretarial skills and editing prowess compensated for the intellectual imbalance between the two. Mills was notoriously weak in spelling, syntax, and editorial matters of all sorts. As he began his professional career, Freya was able to be particularly helpful in typing and polishing his manuscripts. Beyond that, Mills poorly fitted into social occasions with a graduate peer group. With her winning, outgoing, and friendly disposition, Freya smoothed the way for Wright in these events as well.

Marriage at such a young age, while not unusual, was also not that common on the Texas campus. Freya was the breadwinner, and her earnings enabled Wright to satisfy some of his more expensive needs: from movies to books to fine clothes. Since Wright saw his reference group at Texas as the teaching community to which he aspired, being married at Texas made him undoubtedly feel older and more a part of that group. Not uncommonly, Wright had chosen a woman with many traits opposite to his own. He was barely able to express compassion for the less fortunate, had little regard for the weak, and became frantic and pugnacious under criticism. Freya was gracious and a model of support. She continued to work at the YMCA throughout the Texas period. But friends and associates make it clear that tensions developed when she asserted herself, or took a position on social questions different from her husband's. In short, it was a marriage which quickly moved from affection to convenience to despair.

The Millses had a baby girl in 1941. While this blessed event added personal stress to an already difficult relationship, it satisfied the young Mills's sense of academic propriety. Many of the letters of support for his appointment at Wisconsin mention Freya. Gentry noted that "Mills has married a very intelligent and charming girl. The two of them would make an excellent addition to a University group."[35] Miller commented that Mills was married to a most agreeable, nice-looking girl.

> I have had her as a student, and can vouch for her high degree of intelligence, her unusually fine character, and for her congenial attitude. Also, she is an excellent stenographer, and has done personnel work. Consequently, she will be a great help to Mills in gathering data, stenographic work, etc. I mention this also in order to justify recommending Mills and his wife to you not only as intellectually desirable young people, but also as worthy citizens of your community.[36]

Rosenquist exhibited a much more critical attitude toward the marriage—perhaps a more austere, Protestant view of what marriage is about and what is can do to careers. He wrote to Gillin, then chairman of the sociology department at Wisconsin, the following:

> Mills is married, which I think was a mistake for one who still has his education to complete. "He gives hostages to fortune." However, he does not let his domestic affairs interfere at all with his career so far as I can discover, and he has married a charming and talented girl. So it probably comes out even.[37]

Mills himself adds precious little to our understanding of Freya other than a rather sophomoric acknowledgment, in his master's thesis, of "her laughing courage in confrontation with unfunny personal circumstances."[38] The woman-as-handmaiden notion had already soured early on in the marriage. Freya's ability to compensate for his shortcomings did not, apparently, deter his continuing interest in sex outside the marriage. The picture of a desultory relationship, punctuated by exploitative attitudes on Wright's part and bitter acquiescence on Freya's part, is confirmed by all who knew them both.

An unusual fact about Mills is how little attention he paid to the formal amenities of higher education, including intellectual backscratching. Rarely are his Texas mentors cited in footnotes or references when such acknowledgment might well have been called for. As a result, it is difficult to judge the precise impact of each teacher or department. This, too, is a matter of reconstruction, but one that is warranted on the basis that Mills's formative years should not be disregarded. Even if talented intellectual mentors are not paid proper homage by intellectual offspring, that does not mean a relationship is absent.

David Miller introduced Mills to George Herbert Mead. But Miller also made him aware of the weaknesses of an analysis of pragmatism as a purely philosophical activity. He also made Mills aware of Mead as probably the most socially aware of the pragmatists.

Mead's social-symbolic theory of mind is certainly the most elaborated of all pragmatic theories of mind and is perhaps his most distinctive contribution. By regarding mind as the symbolic phase of conduct made possible by social participation, and by placing mind within the emergent process of nature, Mead makes provision within a naturalistic cosmology for the actual determination by mind of certain eventuations of natural processes. Final causes are thus reintroduced, but not in wholesale and non-empirical fashion. Through the symbolic indication of possible futures—a process whose conditions are traced in detail—natural terminations become ends-in-view, and the world gains new direction and new contents which without reflection it would not have had.[39]

Miller and his colleagues also pointed out that Mead introduced the notion of truth as well as experience into the pragmatic canon. Mead took the position that thinking is instrumental not only to action but to the attainment of objective values.

What we want are objects of such character that they not merely release but satisfy the blocked impulse or interest, and the whole context of Mead's thought makes it clear that action does not normally stop with the manipulation of objects but passes on to their consummatory use: in the last analysis the entire world of scientific objects is an elaborate instrumentation functioning in the service of social values. Instead of sacrificing value to action, Mead's variety of pragmatism proves at the end to be a value-oriented philosophy of a distinctive sort.[40]

This clearly is the posture that Mills adopts in his early published papers—particularly in his attempt to show that instrumentalism is not opposed to holding social values. This view is quite different from that of John Dewey and Percy W. Bridgman, who assert that values can be reduced to operations. It was Mead, through Miller, who made it possible for Mills to propose an objective, naturalistic interpretation of the mind in a social setting as well as a social act. Miller's own ideas were later formulated in an elegant, beautifully written book, *Modern Science and Human Freedom*, that has received much too little attention. As he points out, the main ideas of his work were developed as a graduate student at the University of Chicago, "where I was privileged to study under the late George Herbert Mead."[41] Miller claims that his thoughts existed in embryonic form even during the late 1930s.

Probably the most important influence on Mills was Mead's strongly sociological notion of the person as a self only in relation to an objective social perspective. Individual behavior is conditioned by other people, and only significant human interactions permit true frameworks. Beyond that, Mills's earlier views come down to the fact that the distinction between the individual and the social is largely arbitrary since objectively they entail each other. Miller's notion of a functional connection between self and society certainly forms the basis of the Gerth and

Mills volume *Character and Social Structure*. The very words used by Miller remind one of the early Mills.

> Those who assume that *society* is primary and that the individual is secondary, and on that assumption try to develop a theory of the social dimension of knowledge, will come out with a distorted view. On the other hand, if we conceive of the individual and society as separate but integrally related, and thereby recognize that the *condition* for (but not the determiner of) reflective thinking may be social behavior but that, nevertheless, the individual is necessary for reconstructing social behavior, we will be free to develop a theory of the functional relation between the individual and society.[42]

Beyond that, Miller hammered away at the sociological as well as philosophical style of the University of Chicago. Through him Mills learned to identify intellectual trends from faraway northern places. One might surmise that Rosenquist's direct impact was somewhat less, given the fact that Mills was not a world-class figure in quantitative analysis. This would miss the point. The early Rosenquist, who reviewed the Lynd and Lynd book *Middletown*, was clearly in tune with the new sociological emphasis on exactitude and ethnography. His evaluation of the book gives us some insight into his emphasis on ethnography and fieldwork: getting out there and doing work rather than thinking about doing work in a library or classroom. Rosenquist helped Mills distinguish between being a sociologist and teaching sociology.

> For many years sociologists and anthropologists have been deploring the lack of objectivity in their fields and giving wordy advice as to how this deficiency should be overcome. Very few of them have had the inclination or ability to put their preachments to the test of practice. Perhaps it is impossible for a man who knows only his own time and place to view them with the impartiality of an outsider. The first satisfactory objective studies of society were made, not of our own, but of distant, primitive societies whose cultures strongly contrasted with those of the investigators. Even these studies were in the beginning little more than evaluations and interpretations of savage customs in terms of civilized morality. However, the technique of observation has been developing, little by little, so that now anthropology can show numerous examples of accurate, unbiased investigation. Upon the broad base of a general understanding resulting from such considerations of many different societies, we can at least find a viewpoint from which to examine ourselves.[43]

Even the later Rosenquist, who worked on delinquency in different subcultures, paid serious attention to fieldwork. The conclusion of his main work was extremely important; he moved beyond the parochial vision that delinquency grows out of problems in the school, or is located exclusively in specifically Latin or non-Anglo cultures. Rosenquist is one of those sociologists who democratized the concept of ethnicity by showing how similar patterns of norms and deviance arose whatever the ethnic or racial characteristics of a culture. By the late 1950s, Rosenquist had become remote from Mills. While Mills was working on *The Sociological Imagination*, Rosenquist was writing on sociological investigation. But despite the fact that quantitative analysis was not Mills's sociological forte, it is how he made a living at Columbia, and his first mentor in this area was Rosenquist, the ex-chemist turned statistician.[44]

The work of Warner Gettys was important in its own right. His 1929 text on sociology reveals the basis of Gettys's ideology as well as his sociology. Not only is his text written in the Chicago style, but Chicago as an urban model is the content that Gettys brought back with him from his mentors Everett C. Hughes, Robert Park, and Ernest W. Burgess. In his co-authored textbook, *An Introduction to Sociology*, no fewer than three chapters are devoted to the theme of "conflict." It forms the intellectual spine of the book. An entire section is devoted to conflict related to race, and the book concludes with a chapter on conflict as an issue in social class. This was the essence of the Chicago style. Gettys not only wrote about these themes, but did so with a kind of blunt integrity that must have sounded an unusual note in Texas even in the mid-thirties. For example, terrorism is treated as

> a form of mechanism long employed by the whites in the United States in dealing with Negro criminals or suspects. The lynching of Negroes is rare in the North, but race riots with their reign of terror for both whites and Negroes are more numerous. Lynching is the method of dealing with the individual, rioting is the method of dealing with the mass.[45]

Even in talking about political party strife Gettys hits home, linking the Ku Klux Klan with the power of the fraternities in a general analysis of secret societies.

> In civilized secret societies the political function is more obscure, and in most cases where it exists its presence is not openly admitted. The Ku Klux Klan, however, is an example of one such secret order in which the political function was openly avowed in both declaration and activity. Every university student who has experienced an election for student offices or other political procedures in a modern university campus knows the power of the fraternities to swing things their way.[46]

Gettys was a political radical in sociological clothing. The basic lesson he drilled into his pupils was Park's life cycle, a cycle that extended from interaction through conflict, accommodation, and assimilation. Gettys's entire text is written to illustrate Park's life cycle hypothesis. One can see here the enormous, if indirect, power that the Chicago school exercised on Mills. In an odd way, Mills was the unique holdout against functionalism at Columbia, for he identified more closely with the midwestern emphasis on symbolic interactionism.

Gettys ends his text by noting that all scientific facts come in time to be employed by imperfect beings and, as a result, link science to ethics.[47] This idea, so often repeated in Mills's subsequent work, became commonplace. But what Gettys anticipated, and properly, was a period in which the preoccupation of sociology would be to *what* purpose it is used rather than endless questioning of whether it had any utility. Mills, in his own work, rarely credited this influence directly. Yet it was Warner Gettys who made possible Mills's appreciation of the linkage between the Chicago style as a way of doing sociological work and a style of thinking in terms of human actions and symbolic interactions.

It is hard to measure the influence of Clarence Ayres. Certainly Mills became a legatee to Ayres's political radicalism. But he provided more than that: a sense of social science as policy options. Specifically, this meant an understanding that capitalism and socialism were social systems, not divine emanations. Indeed, Ayres wrote an entire book, entitled *The Divine Right of Capital*, asserting the transience of economies. It was Ayres who may well have been the direct source of Mills's power elite concept by focusing on the "big three" of economy, polity, and military. Listen to Ayres's description of the United States.

> In our society money is power. This power derives from the institution of property which we have inherited from feudalism. In the feudal order control of property, especially property in land and in the means of working the land, was tied up with hereditary rank. But these two principles of property and rank were never absolutely inseparable. Even in feudal times some things were bought or sold, and some forms of property were disposable more or less regardless of rank.[48]

Ayres had a vigorous style and a populist bluntness that undoubtedly impressed Mills. He was the one figure at the University of Texas who actually transcended his own discipline. He was well known to people throughout the state and even the nation. This, too, undoubtedly impressed Mills. Like Ayres, Mills was a meliorist rather than a revolutionary: someone who wanted to preserve the democratic tradition even if it meant sacrificing capitalism, but who, on the other hand, preferred a democratic tradition to the totalitarian justice of socialism. This is also a Chicago-style theme: skepticism about all social systems, but a denial of none. It was a shopping-basket concept of purchasing the best in political systems rather than settling for an a priori commitment to only one political economy. "The present order of society can be saved, and there is much to be said for saving it. But it can be saved only by the abandonment of capitalism as it is conceived by capitalists and their spokesmen, present and past."[49]

Ayres gave Mills a profound insight into institutional economics that was later to be reinforced by Weber in sociology. It emphasized the importance of administrative techniques to technological development.

However, Ayres added that it was the relationship between man and man, not simply man and machine, that helped determine society's institutional arrangements.

> These institutional changes did not precede and "make possible" the technological development with which they coincide. They were not derived from preexisting institutions by the proliferation of the legendary mores of rank and power. What brought them to pass was rather the elaboration of administrative techniques along distinctively instrumental lines, and the gradual atrophy of whatever institutional considerations of rank and power failed to take this line. To speak of this process as having made possible the development of machine technology is to misconceive completely the essentially technological character of the process.[50]

Ayres went on to note that this kind of technological development may give rise to disorder, imbalance, and conflict, which are troublesome but inevitable.

> There is a sense in which technological development might be said to give rise to disorder. It has been recognized all along that technological development alters the physical habitat of a community in such a way that a shift in the institutional balance of power becomes inevitable. This shift may well be accompanied by disorder.[51]

This was written before the age of cooptation by government and industry of the findings of science, but again, Mills's *The Sociological Imagination* also reveals an emphasis on the hostility between science and power. The theme of community and power was constantly reiterated by the mature Mills. But, ultimately, it was Ayres as a macromethodologist of social science that most impressed Mills. The social impulse toward simplification and clarity was a theme Ayres struck often. What Ayres called "scholasticism" and what Mills called "obfuscation" became a prime enemy. "The progress of science is always in the direction of the simplification of what seemed complex before."[52] More than simplification, it was also a sense of partisanship that Mills derived from Ayres: the sense of an obligation not just to present both sides of every question, but to present essential truths. Interestingly, Ayres reverts to such an appeal to reality and not just opinion when he discusses the nature of science in his recommendation of Mills to Wisconsin.

> It is of course supremely desirable that students, and the entire community, should be "allowed to see both sides" of every picture. But whatever they are shown should be the real thing. I confess I have no patience with the notion that the business of teachers (and, I presume, writers) is to "present both sides" of any matter that is in dispute, leaving it to their students (or readers) to "decide for themselves" where the truth resides. The effect of this is to expect students and readers to do what the teachers and writers have seemingly been unable to do themselves.[53]

It would be erroneous to conclude that Mills left the University of Texas with no inkling of Marxism. A rather remarkable figure in the economics department, Edward Everett Hale, taught a course on Marxism which was taken by Mills.[54] The flavor of Hale's impact can best be ascertained by his reviews, since his larger writings were largely restricted to classroom notes. In reviewing Leon Trotsky's polemical tract of the later twenties, just after his exile, *The Real Situation in Russia*, Hale shows a moral preference for Trotsky but historical appreciation for Stalin. Not until the three-volume biography of Trotsky written decades later by Isaac Deutscher did a similar sense of the dualism between morality and polity in Soviet policy become apparent.[55] Hale writes:

> Trotsky is thoroughly convinced, in the light of the materialist interpretation of history, that communism in peasant and economically backward Russia is impossible of realization unless supported by working class revolution in the great industrial western countries. He is therefore intransigent, bitterly opposed to opportunistic concessions to individualist peasants or Nepmen (advocates of the New Economic Policy, or NEP). He has always regretted the substitution by Lenin of the New Economic Policy for war communism. Stalin, unfamiliar with western civilization, essentially Asiatic in viewpoint and temperament, is more Russian and more nationalist. He is less and less interested in the preservation of Soviet Russia as a workers' and peasants' state. He is a communist, he keeps the goals in view, but he would hasten towards it slowly. Above all, the Party dictatorship in Russia must be maintained, and the passive acquiescence of the peasants. Concessions and opportunistic deviations from the communist path are therefore inevitable. Trotsky is the better Marxian but Stalin is the better politician and strategist.[56]

One can here observe, in nascent form, Mills's very late writings on the Marxists—in which plain Marxism and pluralistic socialism became the order of the day. It was most probably Hale who first made Mills aware that Marx's method represented "a signal and lasting contribution to the best sociological ways of reflection and inquiry available."[57] And it was probably Hale who first opened a door to Marxism that made Mills receptive to Deutscher's heretics and renegades alike.

It is difficult to represent perfectly the impact of any of these Texas mentors on Mills. But the available evidence indicates that Mills did not come into the world as a full-blown, natural-born intellectual; nor was he simply a product of his parental upbringing or political training. The four years at Texas were a period of radical intellectual evolution, in which he developed an extensive vision of the world based on the wonders of social philosophy, sociology, and economics. It would be pleasant to report a similar emotional growth, but this was not the case. Like others since who have placed a high premium on pragmatic achievements, he became a sociologist of the chair; or, more bluntly, an armchair sociologist.

If the University of Texas is portrayed in the literature as being something less than in the first rank of intellectual freedom, for someone like Mills, coming directly from Texas A & M and from a provincial middle-class background, it was a thoroughly exhilarating environment. It made possible an understanding of a world far beyond the University of Texas and beyond the borders of Texas itself. Ayres and Sheldon taught him there was a place called Washington, D.C., while Gettys and Miller taught him there was a place called Chicago. Collectively, Mills's teachers taught him that there was a place called the United States of America which needed broad-ranging analysis. Mills started out not only as a student of philosophy but also as a student of social psychology. The great merit of his mentors in philosophy, as well as in economics and sociology, was that they moved Mills from philosophy to society, on one hand, and from the world of culture and mind to the world of power and matter, on the other. That was Mills's actual evolutionary path, in which his years at Texas played an absolutely paramount part.

REFERENCES

1. C. Wright Mills. Autobiographical fragment in "Contacting the Enemy" (unpublished). See, on this, Joseph A. Scimecca; *The Sociological Theory of C. Wright Mills*. Port Washington, N.Y.: Kennikat Press, 1977, pp. 8–10.

2. Wilson Record to Irving Louis Horowitz, February 20, 1978.

3. Alan M. Cartter. "The Role of Higher Education in the Changing South." In *The South in Continuity and Change*, edited by John C. McKinney and Edgar T. Thompson. Durham, N.C.: Duke University Press, 1965, p. 289.

4. Howard W. Odum. *The Way of the South: Toward the Regional Balance of America*. New York: The Macmillan Co., 1947, pp. 513–14.

5. Ronnie Dugger. *Our Invaded Universities: Form, Reform and New Starts*. New York: W.W. Norton & Co., 1974, p. 23.

6. Alan Grob. "Invasion in Austin." *AAUP Bulletin* 61, no. 1 (April 1975):6.

7. *Ibid.*

8. Dugger, p. 36.

9. *Ibid.*, p. 37.

10. *Ibid.*, p. 45.

11. Warner Ensign Gettys. "Sociology at the University of Texas: 1905–1958" (mimeographed and unpublished). Austin, 1959, p. 10 passim.

12. Dugger, p. 69.

13. Eric F. Goldman. *The Tragedy of Lyndon Johnson*. New York: Alfred A. Knopf, 1969, p. 20.

14. Transcript, The University of Texas at Austin, June 30, 1939.

15. David L. Miller to Committee on Graduate Awards, Department of Sociology and Anthropology, The University of Wisconsin, February 3, 1939.

16. William J. Goode to Irving Louis Horowitz, June 10, 1975.

17. On Rex Hopper's role as project director of Project Camelot, see Irving Louis Horowitz, *The Rise and Fall of Project Camelot*. Cambridge, Mass.: The M.I.T. Press, 1967, pp. 12–13, 39.

18. Gettys, "Sociology at the University of Texas," pp. 11–14.

19. George V. Gentry to Committee on Graduate Awards, Department of Sociology and Anthropology, The University of Wisconsin, February 3, 1939.

20. *Ibid.*

21. A. P. Brogan to John L. Gillin, February 2, 1939.

22. David L. Miller to Irving Louis Horowitz, July 22, 1975.

23. Miller to Committee on Graduate Awards.

24. Douglas W. Oberdorfer to John L. Gillin, February 2, 1939.

25. Carl Rosenquist to T. C. McCormick, February 2, 1939.

26. *Ibid.*

27. Robert E. Park and Ernest W. Burgess. *Introduction to the Science of Sociology*. Chicago: University of Chicago Press, 1921.

28. Warner E. Gettys to John L. Gillin, February 5, 1939.

29. Henry D. Sheldon, Jr., to John L. Gillin, February 4, 1939.

30. Henry D. Sheldon, Jr., to T. C. McCormick, February 4, 1939.

31. *Ibid.*

32. Dugger, p. 62.

33. Clarence E. Ayres to John L. Gillin, February 8, 1939.

34. *Ibid.*

35. Gentry to Committee on Graduate Awards.

36. Miller to Committee on Graduate Awards.

37. Carl Rosenquist to John L. Gillin, February 4, 1939.

38. C. Wright Mills. Acknowledgements to "Reflection, Behavior and Culture" (unpublished thesis). Austin, Texas, June 1939, p. iv.

39. Charles W. Morris, John M. Brewster, Albert M. Dunham, and David L. Miller. Introduction to *The Philosophy of the Act* by Geroge Herbert Mead. Chicago: The University of Chicago Press, 1938, p. lxxii.

40. *Ibid.*, p. lxvii.

41. David L. Miller. *Modern Science and Human Freedom*. Austin: The University of Texas Press, 1959, p. vii.

42. *Ibid.*, p. 172.

43. Carl M. Rosenquist. Review of *Middletown: A Study in Contemporary American Culture.* In *Southwestern Political and Social Science Quarterly* 9, no. 2 (June 1929); reprinted in *Social Science Quarterly* 50, no. 4 (March 1970), pp. 1080–1081.

44. Carl M. Rosenquist and Edwin I. Megargee. *Delinquency in Three Cultures.* Austin and London: The University of Texas Press, 1969, pp. 435–68.

45. Carl A. Dawson and Warner E. Gettys. *An Introduction to Sociology.* New York: The Ronald Press. 1929, pp. 381–82.

46. *Ibid.*, p. 417.

47. *Ibid.*, pp. 827–29.

48. Clarence E. Ayres. *The Divine Right of Capital.* Boston: Houghton Mifflin, 1946, pp. 7–17.

49. *Ibid.*, p. 197.

50. Clarence E. Ayres. *The Theory of Economic Price.* Chapel Hill: The University of North Carolina Press, 1944, p. 201.

51. *Ibid.*, p. 243.

52. *Ibid.*, p. 307.

53. Clarence E. Ayres. *The Industrial Economy: Its Technological Basis and Institutional Destiny.* Boston: Houghton Mifflin Co., 1952, p. ix.

54. Miller to Horowitz, July 22, 1975.

55. Isaac Deutscher, see especially vol. 3, *The Prophet Outcast—Trotsky: 1939-1940.* New York and London: Oxford University Press, 1963.

56. Edward Everett Hale. Review of Trotsky's *The Real Situation in Russia.* In *Southwestern Political and Social Science Quarterly* 9, no. 2 (June 1929); reprinted in *Social Science Quarterly* 50, no. 4 (March 1970), pp. 1079–1080.

57. C. Wright Mills. *The Marxists.* New York: Dell Publishing Co., 1962, pp. 128–29.

3

Ishmael in North Star Country

It has been said by some of our friends that the University of Wisconsin is in politics. If by this is meant that the University has ever been organized in the past or in the present, in whole or in part, in the interests of any individual or faction or party, the statement is absolutely false. If, however, it is meant that the University is attempting to lead in the advancement of our people; if it is meant that problems which relate to water power, to forests, to marketing, to public utilities, to labor, are legitimate fields of university inquiry and teaching, then the University is in politics, and will remain there so long as it is a virile institution worthy of the support of the people of this state.

Charles R. Van Hise, president, University of Wisconsin, May 23, 1913

MILLS'S MOVE FROM Texas to Wisconsin represented far more than geographical relocation. It permitted an enormous redirection personally as well as intellectually. His odyssey was not unlike that of many other bright young Southerners of the 1930s. Success was as much defined by getting away from the hometown origins as it was by financial reward or "making it" in conventional status terms. Leaving meant having a broader range of options than were available in a highly circumscribed environment.

Even at the close of the depression decade the South and the Southwest were a poverty belt still very much stamped by the economic backwardness of the post–Civil War period and the social and political traumas that the First World War left behind. The region had not yet discovered its independent sources of wealth and was still mired in agrarianism, single-crop cultures, and bitter segregation by race and by class that seemed destined to continue without change. When Mills left

Texas, he was never to return—again much like other bright young people of his generation.

Mills briefly considered going to the University of Chicago. The key contact was with Milton Singer, a young instructor in the philosophy of science, whom the philosophy department at Texas considered its finest product to date. He discussed with Singer the possibilities at Chicago for an assistantship, and Singer was keen on the superiority of Chicago over Wisconsin, but more specifically, the choice to continue in philosophy. But Mills decided otherwise. Since the "insider" connection at Chicago was through Gettys and Miller in philosophy, the decision to accept an appointment at Wisconsin was more nearly a commitment to sociology. Beyond that, the activist mood of sociology, its concern with broad social issues, seemed to make sociology a good choice. Anyhow, a Wisconsin group that could boast the likes of Howard Becker, E. A. Ross, and John Gillin was sufficiently philosophic to satisfy Mills's acquired taste for the big picture.

The move from Texas was marked by personal ambivalence. Mills had developed and cultivated allegiances and friendships at Texas. He was on a first-name basis with nearly all the senior professors. He was viewed as a campus intellectual giant, and hence was not subjected to the usual rules of departmental segregation. He took courses with all the great men at the University of Texas, and could hardly have cared less about professional affiliation. His nominal degree was in philosophy; his actual coursework ranged throughout the social sciences. This early disdain for professionalism was to remain characteristic of Mills—strongly influencing his later reticence to teach graduate courses or advanced students. Mills had a style of self-presentation that suited his Texas manner well.[1] Professors were simply older colleagues; and his sense of self-importance was fueled by the special relationships he was permitted to establish, particularly with some of the junior faculty at Texas. In fact, this junior faculty led him to consider Wisconsin.

The relationships which Mills established with Texas social scientists were especially strong: Following undergraduate work at Texas, Douglas W. Oberdorfer went on to take his doctoral degree at Wisconsin in 1939 when he recommended Mills to the department for admission as a Ph.D. candidate. Henry D. Sheldon of Texas's Department of Economics, another graduate of Wisconsin, went to Wisconsin from a visiting professorship at Stanford to do summer session work during the same summer Mills left for Wisconsin. Carl Rosenquist also had strong links with sociology at Wisconsin through his Chicago connection, a relationship which was quite strong especially in the era immediately preceding the Second World War. But it was Oberdorfer, with whom Mills had much in common in terms of age and interest, who was the essential catalyst.[2] And so, with some hesitation and trepidation, Mills packed his belongings and came north.

Mills had earlier made himself known at Wisconsin by an exchange of correspondence with John Gillin and Howard Becker.[3,4] He had sent his paper, "Language, Logic, and Culture," to Becker, and it was subsequently published in the *American Journal of Sociology*. Becker wrote to Mills, saying that "the paper impresses me very favorably, and I am forwarding it to Read Bain [then editor of the journal] with a strong recommendation that it be published."[5] For his part, Mills made certain to mention Becker favorably in the footnotes to the final version of that article. He had already learned enough about the academic game to realize the long-term advantages of such a short-term price. Between December 1938 and January 1939 it was clear that, except for the paperwork, nothing stood in the way of Mills's appointment as a graduate fellow at Wisconsin. He had secured strong support from both institutions. Mills left the University of Texas for Wisconsin having already published articles in the two leading journals of the profession: the *American Sociological Review* and the *American Journal of Sociology*. Little wonder that Mills considered himself the intellectual equal of his academic superiors at Wisconsin, who in turn viewed him as something of a wild card.

It should not, however, be thought that Mills's only, or even major, decision at the time was the choice between Chicago or Wisconsin, and philosophy or sociology. The larger choice was whether to continue on in academic life at all. There was nothing in Mills's family background to encourage his academic pursuits, and the thought of going north had the same terrors for Mills as it did for other Southern intellectuals. His conversations with his friend Wilson Record at the time are quite revealing on this score.

> In Dallas in the Spring of 1939 [Mills] was seriously debating whether to abandon academia altogether. He thought about going into business. He said his father would be quite helpful to him, since the elder Mills had a great many connections in the insurance business in Dallas. Mills would be taken into an insurance company, possibly his father's own firm. Mills said also that he was thinking about becoming a used car salesman. He expressed doubt about his ability to cut it at Wisconsin. I tried to reassure him, telling him I thought he would do extremely well, and that it would indeed be a tragedy if he did not complete his graduate work. Specifically, he discussed the possibility of going to work for the Singer Company, which was distributing small automobiles here in the United States during that time. During the two days that I spent with him in Dallas, he expressed great doubt about the future of his marriage. Her friends and relatives were there. She was quite ill. But apparently things got straightened out and they went on to Wisconsin together.[6]

Financially, the move meant very little. Mills held a departmental Fellowship at the University of Texas, which was worth $500, the best that Texas had to offer at the time. Mills's teaching assistantship at Wisconsin provided $600 annually in 1939–1940 and $650 the following year—which even in the halcyon days before the Second World War was not exactly a spectacular salary. Mills's financial needs, which were considerable, were largely met by Freya. She picked up the pieces at Wisconsin, doing free-lance work in Madison which helped cover their needs. She was an excellent stenographer, experienced in personnel work and management. Her previous involvement in YMCA affairs gave her the opportunity for employment just about everywhere. The decision to move also represented a renewed dedication to a marriage that had seriously eroded. Both had become disillusioned with the marriage by the time of the move to Madison, a disillusionment perhaps symbolized by an abortion that was only halfheartedly sought by Freya, but insisted upon by Wright. The fact remains, however, that Mills did not lack for adequate funds. He was able to live more in keeping with the style of a young instructor than with that of a graduate student, a role for which he developed contempt.

Freya was, by all accounts, as well liked at Wisconsin as at Texas. Her love for Wright, while sorely tested, had not been broken. She was not, however, an intellectual, and the very absence of references to her by Wright in correspondence or conversation indicates how remote Wright had become. If the doubts in his mind about the marriage were already well developing at Texas, they become even stronger at the Wisconsin campus. The Madison campus was a pioneer in graduate education for women, and its role served as a painful counterpoint to the academic weaknesses of Freya. His private life probably centered as much on the home of Hans Gerth as his own home. And from the fragments of commentary which exist on this period, one can only infer that Freya was odd woman out—a woman saddled with an infant daughter, interested in the Church's message on social justice, and not terribly concerned about departmental gossip. This was at a time in young Mills's life when he developed a powerful sense of his masculinity, a disdain for religious messages of any sort, and an intense involvement, however negative, with the sociology department.

Wisconsin was to become Mills's first real departmental affiliation, his first association with sociology as a profession. He presented a complex picture of a young man who is contemptuous of authority, especially of the academic sort, and equally contemptuous of a field that he only halfheartedly believes is capable of attracting the best or the brightest. Mills had chosen a school that probably best exemplified the democratic tradition in American higher education. Surely no university in America placed greater emphasis on interdisciplinary and innovative research while maintaining absolute adherence to academic and civil liberties. Perhaps the best illustration of this powerful Wisconsin commitment during Mills's stay is the case involving Stephen Ely and the so-called "Whitehead's God" decision.[7] Even the mildest reservations by a member of the Board of Regents concerning publication of a book with a theological theme created a campus incident of considerable proportions. The outcome of this minor flap was that the Wisconsin University Press achieved complete freedom from control of the Board of Regents—even though that control had never been much exercised to begin with.

For Mills, the contrast could hardly have been more vivid: the University of Texas is located in Austin, which is the capital of a state whose legislature had never had any problems in condemning and censoring faculty members; the University of Wisconsin, located in Madison, also capital of the state, had long-established traditions which made such interference impossible. In the words of then President Van Hise in his Commencement Address in 1912, the spirit of Wisconsin was outlined, one that was to guide that university throughout the remainder of this century:

> Whether the subject taught be the language or history of a people, knowledge of the universe without reference to the wants of man, or the applications of this knowledge to his needs, is a matter of indifference; provided only [that] this broad, inexorable, noncompromising spirit . . . to follow wherever truth may lead . . . be maintained. This spirit forever makes a university a center of conflict. If a university were content to teach simply those things concerning which there is a practical unanimity of opinion . . . there would be quiet; but it would be the quiet of stagnation.[8]

Sociology at Wisconsin goes back to 1893. During that year Richard T. Ely came from Johns Hopkins to give a course called "Charities and Corrections," followed a few years later by Frederick Howard Wines, who, appropriately enough, gave the companion course, "Punishment and Reformation." But the department developed after Edward A. Ross was brought from the University of Nebraska to teach sociology. Ross, along with Charles H. Cooley at The University of Michigan and Albion Small at the University of Chicago, formed the trinity of Midwest sociology for the better part of two decades. When sociology and anthropology were organized as a separate department at Wisconsin in 1929, it developed a full line of courses from social pathology to social statistics that positioned the department well for the depression era.

By the time Mills arrived at Wisconsin, its sociology department was already regarded as a premier entity in the field. "Two studies rating sociology departments in the United States in 1940 both gave the Wisconsin department high marks. The American Council of Education issued a 'distinguished' rating, while a second survey rated the department one of four in the country of 'high excellence.' "[9] But it was not

42

simply on objective criteria that Wisconsin was well rated. There was a sense of excitement and discovery, compounded by a closeness between faculty and graduate students that was atypical. John Useem, a contemporary of Mills in the graduate program, described matters thus:

> Despite the extraordinary differences in the personal styles and conceptions of how to "do sociology" among the faculty, the ethos of the department was characterized by respect for the various approaches and genuine openness for students to explore the range of sociological interests. Perhaps it is hard to believe, but in that time frame and setting there were no deep divisions nor factional alignments within the Department which touched the fragile lives of graduate students.[10]

Still, while emphasizing how "everyone contributed their knowledge in some way to the service of others," Useem could hardly resist mentioning Mills as someone whose contribution was to self rather than society, whose main concern was "becoming a sociological legend in our time."[11]

The students at Wisconsin, people like John Useem, and even more so Don Martindale, were hostile not so much to Mills's ideas as to his manner. That "certain arrogance" which A. P. Brogan spoke about[12] came home to roost. And his very physical and mental energies,[13] oriented as they were to cultivating the approval of the faculty, only served to alienate the affections of his graduate peers. But Wisconsin was not Texas. It had recruited assiduously and well for its sociology program. The easy camaraderie Mills had established with faculty at Texas turned fiercely competitive at Wisconsin. That Mills's relationships were with the most marginal member of the department, Hans H. Gerth, and with equally marginal faculty in other departments is a measure, not so much of his troubles, but of how poorly the Texas strategy transferred to Wisconsin. Mills never did acquire the same sense of ease at Madison as he had at Austin—indeed was never again to do so.

The Millsian tactic of studying with the best professors and taking the finest courses was modified but not entirely abandoned in graduate school. However it violated departmental mores, it did have great payoff in terms of future research and thought. One such course was the year-long course in the history of economics given by Selig Perlman, the successor and heir to the tradition established by John R. Commons. Perlman, while emphasizing Commons's belief that politics was not a mere reflection of economics, went one step further: the concrete person was not acting out a predetermined historical script, but was primarily concerned with day-to-day recognition and personal improvement both materially and spiritually. Specifically, Perlman focused on problems of labor, not class; on the struggle for trade unionism, not world communism. Commons's concerns with the history of American unionism were thus transformed into a larger concern of how the phenomenon of unionism helps to explain the durability of social systems no less than their transformation.

Perlman opened up for Mills the whole area of class analysis with a labor orientation, rather than stratification analysis without any real social foundations. Mills took Selig Perlman's great courses on socialism and capitalism, and although he was later very critical of Perlman's theory of unionism, the impact on him of the Commons-Perlman school of political economy was noticeable. For example, 1940 was the year in which Commons's volume on the American labor press appeared.[14] It was also the year in which Mills took the Perlman course on capitalism and socialism.

The special relationship which Mills had to Perlman is reflected in the fact that, other than a graduate course in statistics, Mills took only three courses outside of sociology—all in the economics department and all with Perlman. There was the full one-year sequence in the history of economics and his semester courses on socialism and capitalism. The impact of Selig Perlman on Mills is both unmistakable and direct. Now that these remarkable lectures have been put into print we can have a clearer idea of the extraordinary impact Perlman had. He introduced Mills to James Burnham and the managerial revolution; Lenin's theory of war and imperialism; the concept of job consciousness; and above all, in his person, an authentic Jewish intellectual.

"Revolutions are less dependent upon managerial personnel and their myths than upon those who bring to focus and legitimate the revolutionary activity of struggling classes."[15] Perlman's concerns were soon to be translated by Mills into a general concern with the militarization of revolutionary doctrines.

> A book I read said the Nazi is sent into the business corporation and gets the salaries and thus the business corporation rules the Nazi—this is silly. The book, by James Burnham—*The Managerial Revolution*—caused a lot of talk. I think it is not a managerial revolution that is the issue, but the organization of political power. Goering is at the top because he is a ruthless fellow and is clever. He is a politician. . . . Today we have a new phenomenon. It is a political military phenomenon—the modern Mongol theory of state. It is a pragmatic state. A state that does not operate on a particular theory. It has ideals, but on the instrumental side is flexible.[16]

The major lesson that Mills learned from Perlman was that politics did not merely reflect economics, but was a co-equal factor in determining the fate and fortunes of world societies and systems. This political emphasis, when linked to the strong sense of historicity which Perlman imparted to his students, clearly helped stimulate Mills's writings on labor and the working class.[17] What Mills was to say of Perlman in relation to Marx (namely, that Perlman "took something—in fact quite a lot—

from the theory at which it is directed''[18]) is surely no less true of Mills in relation to Perlman. Although Mills became strongly critical of Perlman's theory of unionism and job consciousness, he managed to take quite a lot from that with which he disagreed. That fifteen years after sitting in Perlman's class Mills found it necessary to come to terms with him is an indicator of how important Perlman became in Mills's thinking.

In an essay on Perlman he delivered at a conference on the sociology of labor and work at Wayne State University in 1955, Mills wrote:

> Professor Perlman's answers do not meet the questions to which I believe events force our attention. I am not saying that this theory is not interesting because it isn't addressed to problems in which I'm interested. That would be both foolish and unfair. I'm saying that it is a partial theory, that within a much larger and more imaginative scheme it is historically circumscribed, and that if we accept it and remain satisfied with it, we won't even raise the kinds of questions which I can't help but believe are now central for those who understand "labor problems." The Perlman statement doesn't meet those questions because it accepts the existent union context so fully—and so statically—that it doesn't see the relevance of such unionism only in a restricted context—the labor market—which the union closes for the occupational security of its members—and then derides as "intellectual's ideologies" all other attempts to examine functions of unions in larger contexts.[19]

Mills's continuation of the pattern of learning he had begun at Texas, which emphasizes broad interdisciplinary tasks rather than narrow disciplinary boundaries, could hardly have sat well with the Department of Sociology. To be sure, Mills maintained his Olympian view of philosophy and his criticism of sociology throughout the Wisconsin period, and derided the juxtaposition of rationality and action common to sociological theories of reason. In another unpublished essay, written just after he arrived at Wisconsin in the fall of 1939, Mills began to articulate his critique of social engineering and social technology; it reads like a sly judgment on the Wisconsin departmental offerings.

> The physical technologist is an accepted and sanctioned social type. He is so situated with reference to the ruling elite, the pyramids of power, of authority to act, to the human sources of social change that his work is effective in concrete change and in influence. The social technologist is not so situated. And so far, only in the realm of the physical is the demonstrable test of competitive efficiency of means unambiguous and accepted. I agree wholly with MacIver that this principle of efficiency has no one *clear* application in the realm of sociology. At the present time the great mass of sociological inquiry vibrates between gross empirical pointing and individual dialectics. It is these two models of rationality that have been built into the structure of the parliamentarian state, but social thinkers are striving to attain the technological model.[20]

He was still writing mainly from a philosophical perspective. His references were nearly all to philosophical figures, both European and American, or figures like MacIver who were comfortable with generalization. But he was beginning to come to terms with forms of rationality as they pertained to technology and ideology. It was the process of how people were socialized into roles rather than earlier problems of epistemology that began to grip his attention. That he recognized the authority of Weber and MacIver, who were at home with philosophical concepts, was natural, but the impact of the Wisconsin department was clear. Wisconsin forced Mills to consider sociology as a science of human values and what that concept demonstrates with respect to other types of learning. His philosophical training helped Mills avoid the hubris of manufactured discovery. It enabled him to appreciate the extent to which sociology was re-creating problems of the past rather than manufacturing solutions for the future.

His first sortie against academic sociology—made after a conventional attack on liberalism and the *Partisan Review* group—was entitled "Locating the Enemy." The "enemy" for Mills was very rarely exclusively political, and during these Wisconsin years it was almost inevitably intellectual. To quote from his early anti-academic polemic:

> Academic sociologists do not think in terms of classes, but in terms of stratifications—of economic goods, status deferences, safety . . . any value; and these diverse stratifications do not coincide neatly to spell out a political promise and a clearly visible social enemy. By fragmentalization or careful dimensionalism we lose the chance for vigorous political opinion. The transition "from Marx to Weber" is, in this connection, decisive. We have relativized and partialized ourselves away from a position permitting bold and clear political views, views permitting their diffusion as effective ideologies.[21]

But in this assault upon empiricism and academism in American sociology, as well as its practitioners' inability to think in class terms and their emphasis on stratification, Mills did manage to come up with an ally who also became a strong influence in his life: namely, Hans Gerth, who had immigrated from Germany. Gerth shared many of Mills's animosities toward American empiricism, but did so from a particularly Germanic background. There can be no doubt that Mills, in contact with Gerth, shared this faith in German social science. Having already discovered Marx and Mannheim at Texas, Mills was ready for Weber, and Gerth was ready to impart Weberian wisdom to Mills.

Gerth's reflections on his first impressions of Mills are touching and at the same time typical:

> Mills came from Texas University with Thorstein Veblen in one hand and John Dewey in the other. He was a tall, burly young man of Herculean

build. He was no man with a pale cast of the intellect given to self-morti-
fication. He was a good sportsman with bat and ball, a dashing swimmer
and boatsman, sailing his shaky dory on Lake Mendota. A slender white
birch tree here and there served to emphasize that somber quietude of the
majestic stems of coniferous bush. We would walk with machetes to make
our way to the boat. Mills dashed with his motorboat past the more imposing houses of midwestern corporation executives to the pier of the village store. Some poor Indians stood around as forgotten men to admire
the noise and the splash of swift cutters and motorboats, which had dis-
placed the silent glide of their ancestral canoes. A sky-writing plane left its
fading ad in the sky—the rest was silence. After a while Mills was bored
and we drove over to Madison.[22]

The volume of essays entitled *From Max Weber*, translated by Hans
Gerth and edited by Gerth with Mills, that was published in 1946 actually germinated during the stay in Wisconsin. The intellectual impact of
Weber and the personal impact of Gerth can be inferred from the biographical introduction to that volume. Mills began to see himself carved
in a Weberian mold. Like Weber, Mills saw himself as an "observant,
and prematurely intellectual boy"; like Weber, Mills responded harshly
and negatively to the patriarchal and domineering attitude of his father;
like Weber, Mills viewed himself as suffering from an ineffaceable sense
of guilt. As Gerth and Mills noted: "In the presence of his [Weber's]
mother and wife, he saw fit to hold judgment over his father; he would
remorselessly break all relations with him unless he met his son's condition: the mother should visit him 'alone' without the father. One may
certainly infer an inordinately strong Oedipus situation."[23] Weber's
personal feelings were reinforced by his love-hate relationship with
power: his special appreciation of Prussian values and his public assault
on Prussian militarism; his strong nationalism and his assault on all
forms of nationalism in his writings; his sense of the growing bureaucratization of life and his derision of those who retained individualist, anti-
statist values.

All of these ideas Mills clearly incorporated into his own sensibility.
Mills writes that Weber says in his autobiography that he made matters
of public concern his voluntary burden. And he finally concludes with
the following statement of Weber's life (on the basis of which it is hard
to avoid the judgment that Mills felt even more than Gerth that the
same antinomy in regard to authority was as true for him as it was for the
German master):

Weber's life illustrates the manner in which a man's relation to political
authority may be modeled upon his relation to family disciplines. One
has only to add, with Rousseau, that in the family the father's love for his
children compensates him for the care he extends to them; while in the
State the pleasure of commanding makes up for the love which the political chief does not have for his people.[24]

47

Mills's list of German heroes was now complete—Marx, Mannheim, and Weber. They were to be counterparts to his American heroes—Dewey, Mead, and Veblen.

During this period of work with Gerth, the idea came for his book on social psychology, ultimately entitled *Character and Social Structure*. Whether Gerth or Mills was the chief architect of the book must be discarded as irrelevant speculation. The book had a strong dose of Marxism, some conventional progressive ideas about the death of liberalism and the insipidness of conservatism, and plenty of good philosophical weltschmerz—indeed some of the best social theorizing produced at the time in sociology. Mills later in his life indicated that this was the book he was least satisfied with, the one least likely to succeed, and the book most in need of drastic revision. With characteristic flamboyance he dismissed the work as intellectual "crap," and he blamed his excessive reliance on Max Weber as the cause.

Character and Social Structure has many pages, many themes, many ideas, and—the kicker—many points of view. But it is so central to understanding Mills's Wisconsin period that the book deserves more than cursory treatment. The eclecticism of *Character and Social Structure* is extremely disconcerting. We are told that "we have no objection, if the reader prefers, to use the names George H. Mead and Max Weber although of course they differ from Freud and Marx in many important ways."[25] The "classic tradition" was used to cover a multitude of intellectual sins—as if these four names could be plugged into the same circuit without causing the most violent consequences. But the authors had little choice. They were confronted by a mélange of ill-shaped theories of social psychology, and they confronted each other as bearers of alien traditions of American pragmatism and European sociologism. One can go through the book and pick out passages and paragraphs which are characteristic of either Gerth *or* Mills. What is definitely more difficult to isolate are the characteristically Gerth *and* Mills portions. What compounded the difficulty is that by the time the book was readied for publication, the relationship between Gerth and Mills had reached a breaking point.

Gerth could use everyone from Kant to Weber in discussing symbol spheres. He wrote of social control and command in big international terms—dealing with the comparative social structures of Prussian Junkers, Japanese samurai, and British gentlemen. Gerth saw "collective behavior," the sociological term meaning uncontrolled or unstructured action, in terms of mobs of storm troopers hunting Jews in boulevard cafes or Klansmen beating up Negroes in race riots. Mills discussed symbol spheres in such terms as Mead raised: his concern was the motivational functions of language. He spoke of social control and command in terms of the administrative policies of the New Deal and the organization of a labor bureaucracy in the American Federation of Labor. Collective behavior did not mean much to Mills. Storm troopers and hunger riots were outside his empirical purview. And that which Mills did not experience he rarely appreciated. In addition to his honest-to-God pragmatism was his emphasis on structure, his fixation with it, so that spontaneous events hardly dented his sociological imagination.

There are powerful unifying themes and faiths in *Character and Social Structure*. Gerth and Mills shared a deep propensity to think in terms of conflict models, rather than any consensual scheme. Problems of social psychology were liberated from the ugly clichés of ''deviance'' and ''disorganization''—catch-all words which have little to do with science and a lot to do with sociologists' distasteful acceptance of official definitions of reality. Gerth and Mills were also committed to worldliness, even if that term were differentially understood. Gerth was cosmopolitan about the world. Mills at this point in his career had not gotten beyond American shores. But neither could be chased into using hapless slogans about the ''corruption of power,'' or the ''struggle between democracy and totalitarianism,'' or ''the human impulse to . . .,'' or such similar formulas. There are breathtaking passages about historical epochs, about Caesarism and sultanism, monarchism and Bonapartism, that both echo a Weberian past and remind the present generation of sociologists and psychologists of what would be lost in the way of historical insight in a sociology without a sense of real leaders and real dynasties.

The ultimate question about *Character and Social Structure* is: Why did such an invigorating text fall into total disuse? The answers are complex in the extreme. Gerth and Mills employed Freudianism in a more than fashionable sense. It was woven into the fabric of their work as no other American sociologist had yet dared to use it. However powerful Freudian thought was in a clinical, patient-analyst setting, it had yet to gain respectability in departments of either psychology or sociology. And without such academic respectability a text which used Freud so extravagantly, even lavishly, was doomed to academic oblivion.

Gerth and Mills used Freud and the psychoanalytic literature in a therapeutic way. In England, in such places as the Tavistock Institute, Freud was used in factory studies and experimental situations of all sorts. European social psychologists were exposed to Freud in a public, practical setting—which retained a firm grip on the therapeutic, applied side of psychoanalysis and its offshoots. In the United States, strictly Germanic impulses prevailed. Even a pragmatist like Mead was an impractical man, caught in the vise of abstract metaphysics. Freudians, separated from practitioners, became critics without portfolio, unable to translate theory into usable values.

To the degree to which criticism replaced construction, ideology replaced therapy. In the United States, Freudianism was cleaved: the ''analysts'' ignored the conceptual cutting edge of their master, while the "academics" ignored the therapeutic setting of Freudian analysis. And while there are some momentary flashes in *Character and Social Structure* that show some understanding of the issue, Gerth and Mills could not tackle the issue straightway. The two authors were poles apart methodologically, and moving further away from one another ideologically over time. This was early signaled by Mills's choice of American pragmatism as a dissertation topic. The career of an intellectually exciting book had such a short life because its authors no less than its readers were not sure what to make of its theories or how to translate them into an American context.

The clumsy confusion between social roles and institutional roles, the traditionalist, almost Parsonian, relegation of social change to a footnote to the "model of social structure" which anchors *Character and Social Structure* to the least viable part of Weber's *Wirtschaft und Gesellschaft*, clearly "date" the book. But this strange pairing of minds accomplished much within a theoretically loose framework. When Gerth and Mills speak of hypocrisy as "the stylization of self-presentations," they clearly speak of the status sphere in terms of "the claimant's side or the bestower's side." In so doing they anticipate a major element in game theory. While both were too enmeshed in the Freudian and Meadian approaches to symbols, language, gesture, and motivation to make any experimental psychologist happy, it cannot be said that they were ignorant of findings made by physiological psychology as it existed in the Wisconsin social science environment of 1940. At the macroscopic level, Gerth and Mills are eminently more sound on questions of economic development, dictatorship, psychology, or bureaucracy than are the thundering totalists. They see the double process of convergence and competition between East and West as a longstanding one. And if their lengthy statements on "sea power" and "land power" may appear obsolete in a thermonuclear epoch, their underlying appreciation of the role of militarization in differentiating democracy and totalitarianism is more welcome than denunciations of the modern world, or convergence theories about that world, which came to define the limits of radical ideology in the postwar American universities beset by a narrow materialism at home and totalitarianism abroad. *Character and Social Structure* is ultimately a forlorn statement of dissatisfaction with the modern world by two alienated figures. In this abstract sense, this clearly was Gerth's book rather than Mills's.

This analysis of *Character and Social Structure* may seem a needless digression, but in fact, since along with his dissertation it was Mills's crowing achievement at Wisconsin, it must be understood in its milieu. This is a case of a book being published many years after its gestation period. We see Mills extremely disappointed with the product as it appeared, almost embarrassed by publication of a work from a distant past, touched as it was by an earlier period of an older colleague's pessimism. The work appeared between *White Collar* and *The Power Elite*, and was completely asynchronous with his concerns in the mid-1950s. Still, the book commands as much respect as it does curiosity. It remains one of the few serious attempts by sociologists to examine and explain totalitarianism.[26]

With the exception of Gerth, Mills's professional relationships at Wisconsin were exceedingly argumentative and adversarial, not in keeping with the consensualism of the department. Even a person marked as a friend, Eliseo Vivas, was the object of harsh criticism and attack. In Mills's paper on Marcel Granet and the language and ideas of the ancient Chinese, one can detect a strong attack on Vivas and the "Greek way." Granet, a French ethnographer with a strong bent for the sociology of knowledge, had written two works of Chinese civilization and Chinese thought which showed how mastery of the environment was linked to political unification. Ever the foe of Western religion and theology, Mills was especially disconcerted by Vivas's emphasis on Greek ideals and the dualism which was said to exist between the political and the religious. The essay on Granet was significant in several respects. It separated the sociological from the philosophical in a very positive way. Mills used the term "sociotic" to show the need for sociological analysis of ideological and metaphysical thought. He used the occasion to attack all philosophical thinking which considers human beings to be independent from society and morality independent from sociology. And in a direct confrontation with an instrumental search for God, Mills used the occasion to review Chinese monistic thought as a rational system superior to Western dualistic thought:

> The Chinese never consider man as isolated from his society. And society is never thought of as isolated from nature. They do not dream of placing underneath them some vulgar reality, nor above them a world of purely spiritual essences. Nature forms a single realm. A unique order presides over a universal life. And it is this order which imprints itself upon civilization.[27]

Once and for all, Mills settled accounts with the Western concept of religion. He thundered against Original Sin and his Catholic background "There is no God, there is no Law!" and then concluded:

> In China religion is not a function differentiated clearly from the rest of social activity. The sentiment of "holiness" plays a large role in many sectors of life; but in none of them is the object of this veneration in the strict sense comparable to any gods of the West. There is simply no tendency toward a metaphysical spiritualism. Such beings as might be called thinkers are independently wise. Always they are humanistic. And they owe nothing to the idea of God.[28]

At the same time one could read the famous essay by Mills, "The Professional Ideology of Social Pathologists," as a critique of his departmental chairman, John Gillin. In fact, if one pays attention to footnotes one would be hard put to read it otherwise. Repeated references jibe at Gillin: his years of experience as a social worker; his subjective view of the depression; his belief in rehabilitation of individuals; his faith in the ability of society to alleviate social problems by a theory of multiple causation; his passion for social righteousness; and his rural bias against the city as a place of higher social disorganization than the country. The entire essay must have had a tremendously jarring impact on Gillin—the graduate student annihilating the department chairman. If Mills's critique of Vivas for intellectualizing pragmatism was indirect and obscure, the attack on Gillin could be missed only by those who pay no attention to footnotes. This particular essay has eighty-three footnotes—nearly half of them addressed to Gillin's work. The sting must have been direct, and the atmosphere in the department less than pleasant. What emerges is a picture of Wisconsin sociology as social pathology: small-minded, ruralistic, incapable of dealing with ethnicity; sociology simply living out the ideals of small-town America.[29] It is hard to know whether Mills was seeking ideological or political revenge on his senior sociologists. In any case, it certainly shortened his tenure at Wisconsin, making a permanent appointment impossible.

Another important figure in the department to whom Mills showed marked, in fact extreme, hostility was Howard Becker, who had sponsored some of Mills's earlier publications.

> During his Wisconsin years Mills had some extremely derogatory things to say about Howard Becker. He characterized him as a "real fool." Mills said he resented Becker because he was a Nazi sympathizer, and had said many very favorable things about the German Youth Movement. How much of this was true I don't know. I haven't read Becker's stuff for years, and I don't recall what he wrote that might justify Mills' accusation. Perhaps this wasn't the real source of Mills' distaste; possibly it was simply a convenient alibi. In my view, his relationship to Becker was strained because of the seemingly unequal positions in which they found themselves: Mills a student, and to a degree dependent on Becker, and Becker a professor in a position to judge and control things that Mills did. I am sure that the strain was due as much to personal clashes as to any political differences.[30]

In personal conversations in later years, Mills described how he taunted Becker by refusing to change the word "pragmaticism" to "pragmatism." He argued (with apparent success) that they were different words with a different meaning. Mills gave such considerable offense to the powers-that-be in the University of Wisconsin Department of Sociology that upon his return from Maryland, where he had already accepted a post, for oral defense of his dissertation Mills put the department in a quandary. Mills was unwilling to make the small changes asked of him and in turn had a dissertation committee unwilling to acknowledge his achievements. The defense became a standoff, and the dissertation was quietly accepted without ever being formally approved.

The actual granting of the doctorate was mired in formal requirements. As late as May 6, 1942, a secretarial note appended to Mills's transcript read: "Conference with Professor [Howard] Becker. He agreed that Mills may complete his residence with four weeks of pre-session work, with an additional eight weeks of summer session." An alternative that Becker suggested was "two summers of eight weeks each."[31] While Mills may have made side trips to Madison, he clearly was spending summers in New York during these wartime years. There can be little doubt that the bitterness which existed between Professor Becker and student Mills ripened over time; and as is so often the case in academic life, this led to sticking to, rather than waiving, administrative requirements. Despite Mills's deep belief that any further student role meant sheer infantilization, he was left in the uncomfortable position of needing to spend two summers in Madison, although the transcripts show no further graduate coursework, or whether in fact the residency requirement was met. Indeed, even the two incompletes Mills had with Becker were never removed. The resolution was simply to let matters rest, and in effect work around Becker—with the latter's tacit consent. This interminable episode unquestionably left Mills with a permanent bitter taste for sociology and its exaggerated professionalization.

⁓

The two years at Wisconsin could be summarized as a mixed blessing. Mills's personal relationships had turned sour; even his connection with Gerth had become strained. But the interval had permitted him the passage into sociology which enabled him to make a living as well as develop a work style. Hans Gerth perhaps never quite understood that Mills was more important to him than he was to Mills; even Gerth's very last sentence of tribute at Mills's death spoke patronizingly of him as being "my alter-ego." Whatever Mills was or was not, he was far removed from being Gerth's alter-ego by the time of the death in 1962; indeed, even by the time of his departure from Wisconsin in 1941 he had a very different sense of sociology and politics. As Mills's personal life changed with the dissolution of his first marriage and with a deepening commitment to research, the relationship between the two men tended to unravel, and increasingly they became not so much textbook interpreters of Weber's life and ideas as different individuals moving in profoundly opposite directions. Ultimately Mills remained the American sociologist, just as ultimately Gerth remained the German epigone. The bitterness, displeasure, and sense of frustration that gripped the older man counted little with Mills—although Mills paid his respects to Gerth by following through in later years with the essays on Weber and the volume of social psychology.

Mills's persistence with projects started at Wisconsin and concluded at a much later date was perhaps the one time when he permitted his sense of obligation to test and overwhelm his sense of sociology. By the time *From Max Weber* and *Character and Social Structure* appeared, Mills was well beyond the range of Wisconsin sociology, safely ensconced in New York City at Columbia. He was far removed from the democratic vistas of Wisconsin and settled into the elite private university which revealed the fact of power he both aspired to and loathed. Mills learned much at Wisconsin, but ultimately was untouched by the notion that a progressive democratic university had worth. Such a populist notion struck him as precisely the kind of academic celebration of the past that made him uncomfortable and from which he had dissociated himself. In his essay on the University of Wisconsin between 1925 and 1950, Mark H. Ingraham wrote that "the history of any period starts with chaos preceding creation and ends only with the last trump."[32] The same Hobbesian note of the certainty of the empirical importance of power but uncertainty as to the moral worth of power characterized Mills. Wisconsin gave him a sense of professional identity and resolved the chaos of the earlier period. But the "last trump" was still to be played out much later, far from the "Athens of the Midwest"—which was, after all, a way station toward the Mecca of the East.

REFERENCES

1. Don Martindale. *Prominent Sociologists Since World War II*. Columbus, Ohio: Charles E. Merrill Publishing Co., 1975, pp. 74–75.

2. Douglas W. Oberdorfer to Thomas C. McCormick, February 4, 1939.

3. C. Wright Mills to John L. Gillin, January 27, 1939.

4. C. Wright Mills to Howard Becker, December 18, 1938.

5. Howard Becker to C. Wright Mills, January 31, 1939.

6. Wilson Record to Irving Louis Horowitz, February 29, 1978.

7. G. C. Sellery. "Lee Ely and Whitehead's God." In *Some Ferments at Wisconsin, 1901–1947: Memories and Reflections*. Madison: The University of Wisconsin Press, 1960, pp. 103–11.

8. Charles R. Van Hise. In Sellery, p. v.

9. William Sewell. "Department's History: From 'Modern Sin' to Marx." *Wisconsin Update* (Newsletter of the Department of Sociology and Rural Sociology), Fall 1977, pp. 1–2.

10. John Useem. "Great Start Made by Small Group." *Wisconsin Update*, Fall 1977, pp. 3–4.

11. *Ibid.*

12. A. P. Brogan to John L. Gillin, February 2, 1939.

13. Carl Rosenquist to Thomas C. McCormick, February 2, 1939. A similar letter of support was sent on to McCormick by David L. Miller. Letter to Committee on Graduate Awards, February 3, 1939.

14. John R. Commons. *The American Labor Press*. Washington, D.C.: American Council on Public Affairs.

15. A. L. Reisch-Owen. *Selig Perlman's Lectures on Capitalism and Socialism*. Madison: The University of Wisconsin Press, 1976, pp. 146–50.

16. C. Wright Mills. "A Marx for the Managers." In *Power, Politics and People*. New York: Oxford University Press, 1963.

17. Reisch-Owen, pp. 135 and xv–xvii.

18. C. Wright Mills. "Selig Perlman's Theory of Unionism" (lecture delivered to the Conference on the Sociology of Labor and Work, Wayne State University, November 1955). In *On Social Men and Political Movements*, pp. 234–44. (This collection has appeared in Spanish only, under the title *De hombres sociales y movimientos politicos*; Mexico City: Siglo Veintiuno Editores, 1968.)

19. *Ibid.*, pp. 241–42.

20. C. Wright Mills. "Three Types of Rationality." In *On Social Men*, pp. 103–19.

21. C. Wright Mills. "Locating the Enemy: Problems of Intellectuals During Time of War." In *On Social Men*, pp. 134–37.

22. Hans H. Gerth. "On C. Wright Mills" (lecture at memorial meeting for Mills, held at Columbia University, April 16, 1962). *Transaction/SOCIETY* 17, no. 2 (January/February 1980): 71–75.

23. Hans H. Gerth and C. Wright Mills. Introduction to *From Max Weber: Essays in Sociology*. New York: Oxford University Press, 1946, pp. 28–29.

24. *Ibid.*, pp. 30–31.

25. Hans H. Gerth and C. Wright Mills. *Character and Social Structure: The Psychology of Social Institutions*. New York: Harcourt, Brace & Co., 1953, and passim.

26. *Ibid.*, pp. 405–59.

27. C. Wright Mills. "The Language and Ideas of Ancient China." In *Power, Politics and People*, p. 520.

28. *Ibid.*

29. C. Wright Mills. "The Professional Ideology of Social Pathologists." In *Power, Politics and People*, pp. 525–52.

30. Wilson Record to Irving Louis Horowitz, February 20, 1978.

31. Note on "Examiner's Report" of Departmental Fellows, The University of Wisconsin, Graduate School, May 6, 1942.

32. Mark H. Ingraham. "The University of Wisconsin, 1925–1950." In *The University of Wisconsin: One Hundred and Twenty-Five Years*, edited by Allan G. Bogue and Robert Taylor. Madison: The University of Wisconsin Press, 1975, p. 38.

4

Pacifism in Wartime Washington

Sometimes I'm not sure whether the presidency is a promotion or demotion from my coaching job. Ah, but it's all a game. You outguess him in this end of college work just as you outguess him in the sports end. Running a school is pretty much like deciding on a football system. You make sure you've got something that's right, and readily understood by the men you're aiming at. And then nothing can stop you.

Harry Clifton "Curley" Byrd, in George H. Callcott,
A History of the University of Maryland

MILLS'S YEARS AT the University of Maryland are a biographical mystery until one understands that his main orientation during this brief period was Washington, D.C., rather than the College Park campus. He thought of the University of Maryland as little more than a way-station to Mecca, meaning New York and Columbia. Practically from his earliest days at the University of Maryland he worked toward the time he would be moving along. Apart from some fine-etched essays that he completed there, most of his time was spent cleaning up work he had begun at Wisconsin: the dissertation on pragmatism, the edited volume on Max Weber he was doing with Hans Gerth, and the volume on social psychology, which was to take far longer than either Mills or Gerth expected. The Maryland years were transitional in intellectual no less than personal terms. It was only at Maryland that he made his final decision to move from philosophy to sociology.

The wartime years remain the most difficult and troubling in any effort to understand Mills's career, much less reconstruct it. What more exciting place could there have been than the nation's capital from 1942 to 1946, during the worldwide historic struggle against the Axis powers? Social science finally began to come of age as its methods and findings were put to use by the policymaking apparatus; many of its pioneering senior representatives were a very real part of the war effort. Studies of Nazi and Fascist propaganda techniques, analysis of American soldiers' behavior in combat and of race relations under stress, psychological profiles of enemy leaders—all manner of social science research became dramatically alive and in increasing demand. Funding for fledgling social science research institutes became available, even plentiful, in Washington, and research posts were created. For the first time in American history, the social sciences were an acceptable part of the "real world," rather than some footnote to theological disputation, social work, or metaphysics.

One would have expected young Mills to rejoice at the opportunity to participate in the gains and partake of the feast made possible by the miseries of world war. Wisconsin had become a contentious place. Mills had developed powerful enemies within the department and had precious few friends. Still, he clearly did not relish the idea of moving to yet another large state university like Maryland—one which, to his way of thinking, had neither the emotional grip of Texas nor the intellectual attractions of Wisconsin. It was his discovery of the District of Columbia that preserved his calm. Thus, instead of being years of pleasure, his first move toward academic independence from the mentors of his youth, the sojourn at Maryland turned out to be a self-perceived exile. Mills looked backward to what was left behind and anticipated what surely had to be in front of him.

The "farewell and have a good trip" letter from Gerth to Mills, sent in the first days of January 1942, had all the characteristics of Polonius's final words to Laertes when he departed from Denmark. It was filled with the sort of pomposity characteristic of advice given by the old to the young. Gerth envisioned Madison, Wisconsin, as the "Athens of America." What would Washington, D.C., boast to equal such a self-proclaimed plaudit? After noting but not explaining that "the war must have terribly shaken" Eliseo Vivas, the Wisconsin philosopher and close friend to Mills, Gerth concluded his letter:

> Now, finis and greetings. Hold your chin up young man and stick to the major guns with the "long range" and don't allow your ambition to do something right now to run away with you in the field of the freelancer and journalist. Write for decades, not for the week. Concentrate on the thesis and don't look right or left until it is done. Rest assured of both our best thoughts—and if things look bad or dreary remember that among the young men around here you are the most fortunate one. And with regard to money matters, learn to be self-sufficient and stoic and with good taste. . . .[1]

Mills came to the attention of the Maryland department as a result of an exchange of communications between Robert K. Merton, who had just moved from Tulane University to Columbia, and Carl S. Joslyn, the chairman of sociology at Maryland. The two had been close friends as graduate students in the early 1930s at Harvard. And when Merton was informed of the two new openings at Maryland by Joslyn, he did not hesitate to recommend Mills. Mills had written to Merton of his job availability, and while Maryland was not quite what Mills had in mind, its proximity to the District of Columbia was to prove a definite plus, giving him access to the sources of research funding that were to stand him in good stead in the years ahead. Joslyn was a mild-mannered and understanding man; and as long as he remained the helmsman of the Maryland sociology department, Mills remained relatively content with his situation. With Joslyn opting for early retirement, and moving from sociology to farming, Mills realized that his days at Maryland were numbered. Tenure notwithstanding, he early on viewed Maryland as an interim academic appointment.

Sociology was not one of the stronger departments at the university; it had only gained its autonomous state in the mid-1920s. The Maryland administration did bring in the anthropologist George P. Murdock to head up the department then, but his strong cultural interests clearly moved counter to the functionalist center of gravity emerging in sociology in the 1930s. But social science at Maryland, like the university as a whole, was a unique benefactor of the New Deal boom in higher education. Enrollments soared, funding quadrupled between 1935 and 1945, and a sense of being at the center of American politics and economics was instilled through the extraordinary leadership of Maryland's president, H. C. "Curley" Byrd.

Maryland was transformed into a populist alternative to the elitist Johns Hopkins; its emphasis on agricultural experiment stations, mechanical engineering, and a university hospital system betokened a trade-school thrust. In some curious way, Maryland was a living example of the sort of wide-open pragmatism which Mills had chosen to write about in his dissertation but did not especially delight in up close. George H. Callcott, in his fine history of the University of Maryland, makes this connection to the pragmatic impulse quite clear:

> Although many professors hardly realized it, the educational outlook of John Dewey was making headway in the colleges for the first time. Pleading for closer identity between education and experience, he urged schools and colleges to face forthrightly the questions facing society. He was less concerned with instilling a body of information, however sacred, than in helping man face the problems of life. He called for the breaking down of the traditional barriers between disciplines, focusing on the applicability of knowledge, emphasizing the contextual nature of truth and the gradual rebuilding of present day society by the application of intellect to social problems. . . . Although some of the concepts seemed vague

in theory and were easily perverted in practice, they had highly specific application in the individual schools and departments of the University.[2]

While one might have expected Mills to invoke his own allegiance to the pragmatic tradition as a step to job procurement, his actual interview for a post at Maryland was far more prosaic and amusing. Wilson Record reports this conversation with Mills:

> Mills learned that President Byrd was an ex-jock, and that he was particularly impressed by prospective faculty who themselves had participated in sports during their college years. Not far along in the conversation, "Curley" Byrd asked Mills what sports interested him. Mills responded that he had been a light-heavyweight boxer at Texas. As far as I know, Mills never put on a glove in his life. Mills went on to tell the President that he was a champion boxer and that he could take anybody on the Maryland squad at any weight. This made a great impression on the President. Mills told me later that this boxer pose was more responsible than anything else for his being offered the University of Maryland position.[3]

After the appointment was made, Mills did not participate very heavily in university affairs—either intellectual or recreational. Despite the presence of other young scholars, like William Form, who later became important sociologists, he tended to relate in professional affairs more directly to the Washington, D.C., area. Mills viewed Maryland as a place to get away from rather than to understand or enjoy. From the outset, he saw the appointment, tenure notwithstanding, as transitional. With respect to the situation at the university, Mills could hardly have been less accurate in his appraisal of the special character of its growth and prestige. And with an ongoing war, few students, and the specific situation in the sociology department brought about by the departure of Joslyn, Mills's evaluation of the condition of the university as a whole became increasingly critical. Writing to Merton in 1944 he states:

> The University of Maryland is a sinking ship. Since Joslyn left, matters have deteriorated to such an extent that were the war not underway as an excuse, I do not believe the University institution should or could be accredited. I will not bore you with the details, for I am sure these things follow regular patterns, and I am sure you are acquainted with the pettiness, the inequities, personal despotism and humour of such messes. Anyway, if you run into a decent job, I should appreciate your letting me know about it. I am on the market.[4]

That the University of Maryland had its share of wartime problems was doubtless true; but it probably had fewer than many other universities. Maryland was strategically positioned for a wartime environment. The College of Arts and Sciences doubled, even tripled, in enrollment during this period. Enrollments in economics, sociology, and political science also rose dramatically during the war years. The history department had such scholars as Frank Freidel, Kenneth Stampp, and Richard Hofstadter. Callcott, in summarizing the competitive nature of Maryland during this period, closes with a curious reference to Mills—one which suggests that Mills's negative feelings were reciprocal and mutually felt.

> While some full professors received $3,100 annually, others received as much as $7,000. During Byrd's first three years the University employed 48 new men with the Ph.D. degree. While the total number of full-time faculty members at College Park increased from 130 in 1934, to 263 in 1941, the number of doctorates on the staff increased from 44 to 119. A few years later an outside evaluating committee expressed frank surprise that the University ranked in the highest 5 percent of accredited institutions in the amount of graduate training possessed by its faculty members. The same report noted that the amount of scholarly publication by the faculty ranked among the top 15 percent of accredited institutions, averaging .364 books and 2.87 articles for each faculty member every four years. . . . Many outstanding men, of course, were not administrators. Far down in the ranks was the sociologist, C. Wright Mills.[5]

Mills clearly felt the pressures of a university on the make and on the rise. On the day before Christmas in 1941 he wrote to Vivas: "I have to get the degree or lose my job. They make a great deal of that sort of thing here."[6] The bureaucratization of graduate training was in part the focus of the first part of his dissertation. His definite feelings of being out of step with Maryland were, if anything, reinforced by his critical attitudes toward graduate training in general. Mills's deep ambivalence about doctoral training in sociology in particular had been reinforced by events in the Wisconsin department. Now he was writing a critique of the bureaucratization of the higher learning in America, as evidenced by the Ph.D. degree, and participating in that very network he so roundly loathed.

In terms of career management the Maryland years were indeed an interlude for Mills. He looked backward to Wisconsin and the friends he left behind, like Gerth and Vivas, while he searched for a permanent post. There was no suggestion of any self-awareness that the problems he was having with colleagues at Maryland were self-induced. But Mills did have an uncanny sense of the importance of Merton to his future well-being. His correspondence during this period was thin, but central to it all was Merton.

Mills's work at Wisconsin had been related to broad philosophic themes in the history of ideas. His dissertation on Peirce, James, and Dewey, and the collection of essays he and Gerth prepared (which were to become *From Max Weber*), were typical. A sharp break took place, and his work turned upon issues in social stratification such as *The New*

Men of Power and *White Collar.* The intellectual products of both the Wisconsin and the Columbia periods were in part taking shape side by side while he was at Maryland. Mills did not quite appreciate the dilemma inherent in moving in contrary intellectual directions during this period; and he continued to perceive difficulties as caused by the obtuseness of others rather than the shift in himself.

The years between 1942 and 1945 were a wartime period; and even though Mills may have perceived this fact through a glass darkly, the impact of the war was unmistakable. These war years added a specifically political dimension to his thinking. The myth of being a "Texas Trotskyist" notwithstanding, for Mills politics at Texas was a slender matter of ideological debate with his mentors, an entirely bookish affair that entailed no activism whatsoever.[7] Later, the situation at Wisconsin was only slightly different. The only radicalism of which he was aware was that related to a sociological interpretation of events. The "radical" or "conservative" dimensions of Weber became sharper as a result of the struggles between "old" Howard Becker and "young" Hans Gerth. The level of abstraction at Wisconsin made the debates quite removed from American political/intellectual debates; indeed they were heavily continentalized. Becker did write about the Hitler Youth movement; and Gerth, about the Nazi rejection of working-class organization and ideology; but the gathering clouds of war hardly seemed to affect Mills. Despite the furies of intellectual struggle about European political issues, the larger question of democratic survival barely provoked the young Mills. Mills himself confirms that before he moved to Maryland, he never had a theory of the good society because he never came to terms with real politics. Writing to Gerth in early 1942, Mills confesses:

> You see, as if you didn't know it, I am a political youngster. I never paid any attention to political affairs until last year, or better, until this year in Washington (you ought to see me clipping the *New York Times* now). Such training as I have had, has been concerned with the sharpening up of the intellectual apparatus, and I am quite weak in content: social and political history.[8]

That Mills speaks in terms of Washington, rather than Maryland, is instructive. It suggests the great importance of the District area as a whole on his thinking, and how little he felt a part of Maryland.

The war years were filled with intense personal as well as intellectual dissatisfaction. Mills did not live on campus, and his contacts with colleagues remained limited throughout his three-year stint at Maryland. He lived on the Maryland–Washington Beltway and spent much of his time with other "exiles" to the D.C. area during the war years. At first his associations were with small philosophical groups that Vivas had put him in contact with. But these individuals, largely drawn from Jesuit circles from Catholic University and Georgetown University, quickly wore on Mills and eroded his patience, already limited. He made contact with the editors of *The New Republic* in Washington and with those of *The New Leader* in New York. Increasingly he began to see himself as a commentator on world events, or at least national events, rather than as a teacher of sociology in a semirural state university. If anything, his brief encounters with the Jesuits ensured his final break with philosophy—not to mention solidifying his manifest disdain for his own childhood background in Catholicism.

> The other night I was out in a circle of philosophers in and around the Washington area. Jesus, it was awful; very dead and awful to hear grown up men talk that way. They talked about their feelings and about God's immanence in a good man's thinking. There was one sophisticated monk with his collar on backward who addressed everyone present as "my son." It was smelly and the whole thing gave me the creeps. I backed off about half way through the thing and ran at them full tilt with an extreme positivism which I no more believe than progress.[9]

Mills's reading habits also swung from the philosophical to the political in this period. *Darkness at Noon* by Arthur Koestler became a great favorite, as did other, lesser works of Koestler and writings by Hemingway. He began wrestling with the problem of socialism in earnest. Troubled by the war, by categories of nationalism, he began seeking alternatives to imperialism—American, European, and Soviet. Mills saw everything through the prism of the "intellectual": labor and the intellectuals, the Left and the intellectuals, liberals and the intellectuals. He was the perfect embodiment of the Jamesian parody: Intellectuals of the world unite: you have nothing to lose but your classlessness. His contempt for nearly every other class category, urged on by his strange love-hate relationship with university life and its denizens, led him to seize the silver lining in being at the University of Maryland, its proximity to the District; and the prospect—later capitalized upon—of avoiding the military draft. Writing to Vivas, he managed to let the war intrude only enough to say:

> About my draft situation: I think I am alright: married and still in III–A status to my knowledge. Freya hasn't worked in over a year. My department head will do all he possibly can to keep me. I am also trying to angle a part-time job in a government bureau—ideological monitoring. No leads, even, so far. But I am trying. I am not jittery. If they get me, I am gotten. I wiggle a while, all I can. But if I am in, well I am in.[10]

For Mills, the Second World War was neither a struggle for democracy, as it was seen in the West, nor a Great Patriotic War, as it was seen in the East, but yet one more instance of imperial redivision of the world. He always disliked discussing the war, even years later. His was no pacifist view, no remorseless criticism of war as simply a moral evil; indeed, in later years he came to identify with wars of national liberation. Mills sought to construct an "orientation" to guide him personally in a "time of crisis." But he was shrewd and aware enough to realize that his standing apart from the struggle of the time may have been "merely my little fence built around a nascent fear." He did not amplify what this fear might be. The atheistic Mills ended his epistle to Vivas with the Dickensian cry "God bless us all."[11]

With his belief system made irrelevant by the war, Mills could only fashion a personal environment in which past is prologue. He completed the dissertation on pragmatism and worked with Gerth on the Weber materials. Ever the observer of men and events, he could not quite avoid the present. That he looked at the war from a special perspective of an alienated young intellectual was less important than war's capacity to give him something to work toward. In a letter to Gerth he outlined his personal wartime agenda, one that occupied his writing for the duration.

> What I am trying to do is see a path for thinking and thinkers that avoids the bureaucratization of thought (the Chicago boys and half of Harvard are going through this in Washington now), and on the other hand, ranting and hortatory junk. Roughly, agenda should encompass the following: (1) the position and uses of intellectuals in this nation at war; (2) the debacle of "the left" during the latter 1930s; democratic revivalism and flirtations with the spiritual. Guilt dimensions. (3) The course of the liberal weeklies from pink to red, white and blue. (4) Where to look for promises and enemies, i.e., orientation for thinkers in time of war.[12]

Even in the gravest years, Mills saw the world in terms of intellectuals and their needs, friends, and enemies. The intellectual task he set for himself was to create a retrospective view of the 1930s, and a prospective view of the postwar 1940s and 1950s. These agenda items tell us much about his Maryland-Washington interregnum. Even more, they anticipate where his analysis was to lead in the postwar climate, which initiated his writings on labor and power. When he articulated this program, Mills's longstanding friend from Wisconsin, Vivas, made clear his own utter disenchantment with him. While Mills was talking about identifying postwar enemies and problems of intellectuals, Vivas was left with the problems of a "deformed face" and of "bayonets shoved into soldiers."[13] The ground on which the two men stood—teacher and student, metaphysician and sociologist—had grown too wide. The war tore apart past friendships as well as assumptions.

Mills's foray into his three-part mission of understanding the structure of events began with an overview of the period 1917–1940. Quite simply, it was a superficial and futile task. The effort had the effect of intensifying his animosity toward Stalin's bureaucratic effort to forestall the invasion of the USSR by Nazi Germany. But this exercise did solidify his growing conviction that the intellectual is not only a class in itself but for itself. The new class fueled his near-Platonic faith in "an intellectual as a person who concerns himself with the structure of events, and tries to alter and understand, through symbol manipulation, the course of those events."[14] Slowly, as the war progressed, and his professional commitment sharpened, Mills began to fuse his idea of intellect with the practice or craft of the sociologist. A sense of urgency about events, coupled with a recognition of the significance of hard data, was the most positive outcome of Mills's wartime flirtation with the physical center of American political power.

Mills was infused by a profound sense of the importance of power as the mediator of politics, business, and military affairs. During the war years he filtered everything through his sense of the role and position of the intellectual sector: its specific role during wartime; the collapse of its sense of specific mission in the prewar epoch; the liberal ideology and its cultural apparatus; the special place of highbrow periodicals in fostering intellectualist illusions; and the question of who are the friends and enemies of intellectuals in wartime. The war years represented not simply the conversion of Mills from a student of philosophy to an innovator in sociology, but more important, his conversion to a person for whom the traits of the intelligentsia as a social class, with its own personal life-style, became clear. However, it was not simply the study of intellectual life in general that began to gnaw at Mills, but its specific political forms, what was to be called its "cultural apparatus," that he started paying attention to during the Maryland interlude. In January 1942, we find him writing to Hans Gerth hinting at this revelation.[15] Mills revealed a strong dialectical inclination during the Maryland period which at times lapsed into literary mannerism: abstracted empiricism versus grand theory, the public against the private, the personal vis-à-vis the political. Whether this polarized vision derived from his early Catholic training or a later commitment to Marxism is really beside the point. His infusion of empirical life with moral meaning, with symbols of good and evil, is a characteristic of both traditions. In an essay written at Maryland, "The Personal and the Political," Mills views the polarity of experience and ethics as a problem in intellectual obligation: "The unmasking of lies which sustain irresponsible power is the political calling of the intellectual." He viewed "society" as a euphemism for America, a place where "much power and prestige are based on lies." In such a context, the intellectuals must develop "a genuine interest in truth," which becomes "one of the few possessions of the powerless."[16] In this Platonic vision, democratized by a vague commitment to the powerless, intellectuals were destined to "wield power" by being placed in the leadership of a "third camp" (presumably the leaders were the avant-garde sociologists). Mills even went so far as to speak of "a third party with a chance to influence national decisions."

Even during the height of the wartime policy efforts, Mills viewed his intelligentsia as a vanguard group, uniquely suited, despite all obstacles and temporary defeats, to engage in the politics of truth on behalf of the powerless, and to institute an ethics of responsibility which could dissolve the false dichotomies upon which modern life had come to be based. He kept it all quite abstract and attractive. In the world of the little magazines for which Mills was writing, the appeals must have been both electric and discordant. Gathered about these little magazines were clusters of intellectuals who deeply opposed the wartime effort, or tacitly denied its centrality to world history. In his review of Robert Brady's classic text *Business as a System of Power*, which first appeared in *The New Republic* in 1942, Mills went far beyond Brady in articulating a plague on both the Allied and Axis houses.

> There are structural trends in the political economy of the United States which parallel those of Germany. They are more important than the fifth column smallfry and as important perhaps as Nazi armies, for they have an objective chance to shape the societies we are going to live in. . . . The unmistakable economic foundations of a corporative system are being formed in this country [the United States] by monopoly and capitalism and its live political gargoyle, the NAM [National Association of Manufacturers] and its affiliates.[17]

Given such stark imagery of an America at war with an adversary no worse than itself, it is little wonder that Mills stood apart from the war not only personally but intellectually as well. He was already hard at work seeking the necessary class allegiances to cement his third camp. He located "this chief social power upon which a genuine democracy could come to rest" in the American labor movement. It alone could overcome the venal tendencies of organized business. Political democracy was a snare and economic opportunity a delusion, both of which were fostered by an older liberalism which contaminated a native Left movement in the 1930s.

It is in the context of his growing alienation from the American mainstream that an article, written at the height of the war, must be read. Seemingly incongruous and inconsistent with Mills's overall agenda for postwar intellectuals, "The Sailor, Sex Market and Mexican" was by no stretch of the imagination an area of primary (or even secondary) intellectual concern. His recommendation—to legalize prostitution around military bases—is hardly novel, even for that time; and his cool analytical response to Chicano youth, nativist sailors, and problems of deviance is part of the standard sociology of the day. Nonetheless,

Mills's unusual foray into the world of race relations and double-standard attitudes toward women—especially minority women—deserves mention. It is certainly his most forward-looking comment of the period, even if seemingly remote from his research agenda at Maryland.[18]

His article is not based on any firsthand interviews, but on the newspaper reports of the time. This was the first of many times to come in which sociology was converted into a journalistic framework. In his analysis of the "Zoot Suit" rioting, Mills argues that the sailor is no longer restrained by conventions, which "in a morally regulated sex market have slipped." The sailor "feels that his uniform affords him an exemption. The persons who stood for Morals are not immediately present." Military life involves "discipline punctuated by large freedoms." These must be used "to nurse away anxieties, to gain back a self subordinated by military anonymity." Mills was no Ernie Pyle. All of the deep animosities he felt toward regimentation and his ambivalence about having done everything in his power to escape military duty are evident in this essay. Mills's experience with "the night life of Mexicans and soldiers in San Antonio, Texas" was a prewar phenomenon—probably casual at best, given the distance from Austin.

Race and ethnic problems were real then as now, but such issues did not enlist Mills's attention either before or after the war. One suspects that the apparent concern he showed for the issue in his article was part of his ever-deepening alienation from the American mainstream. It enabled him to address the sociological problem of deviance detached from the much larger political and global considerations he was already exhorting others to account for. And yet, his article, written as breathless eyewitness journalism, betrays a dilemma which Mills never quite resolved: the tension between explaining behavior in terms of intimate factors of sentiment and impulses—often brilliantly, if intuitively, etched—and explaining it in terms of impersonal or historical factors. The uneasy intellectual alliance of Mills's social psychology and political sociology was oddly anticipated by another venture into journalistic sociology: "Sailors, Sex, and Chicanos." But it remains a footnote to his main agenda: the collapse of liberal ideology and the rise of intellectual power.

Whatever the personal sources of Mills's alienation, the fact remains that he was one of the first to come to terms with what he saw as the debacle of the Left in the 1930s. The Nazi-Soviet pact of 1939 shocked many intellectuals of the time into rethinking their premises—but almost all in retrospect, few in anticipation. One must remember that Mills was in his late twenties during the Maryland years, and his vision of the diplomatic debacle occasioned by the Von Ribbentrop–Molotov meetings was strongly tinged with an admixture of contempt for the betrayal of socialism by the Soviets, yet continued regard for the original aims of the Bolsheviks. In a reflective essay, Mills located the sources of the debacle in three elements: the nationalization of the Soviet Union, the privatization of the United States, and the establishmentarianism of Western European socialism:

> Today in the Soviet Union there is no real basis for opposition; opposition (or "revisionism") is disloyalty; political and cultural activities are embraced by the establishment of the Communist Party, which is nationalist, official, and, on due occasion, coercive. Today in the United States there is no Left; practical political activities are monopolized by an irresponsible two-party system; cultural activities—although formally quite free—tend to become nationalist or commercial or merely private. Today in Western Europe what remains of the older Left is weak; and its remnants have become inconsequential as a cultural and political center of insurgent opposition. "The Left" has indeed become "established." Moreover, even if the Left wins state power—as in Britain—it seems to its members to have little room for maneuvers—in the world or in the nation.[19]

Writing immediately after the Second World War, Mills still saw the problem in much more abstract terms, namely, as a disillusionment with reformism. For him, the New Deal period bolstered both a capitalist system and a liberal attitude of mind no longer valid. It simply maintained two-party politics intact, when what was needed was what Mills called, in an essay of that title, "the politics of truth"—or better, a conception of the world that moved beyond the established political consensus. He ended this unpublished essay with a cry: "We have to build a third party as far outside their social world as possible and still remain in communication with it." In a closing final sentence he announced the "happy alienated man" syndrome: "Being alienated we must act that way."[20] But although Mills had become far more political in the Maryland era than he ever was at Madison, Wisconsin, he was still operating within philosophical rather than participatory categories. The problem was posed in terms of the truth of change and the falsity of the social status quo.

> The formula for a third party is to tell the truth to the right people with the right words at the right time. Do not be alarmed at how simple it seems; and do not believe that it is naive until you think carefully about each of the several phrases that make it up. The truth is what we know of the happenings in the world, and of what these happenings are doing to man's chance to stand in full stature. The right people are those in whose interests the truth, if set loose into action, will work. The right words are those for which such people will replace apathy with the energies for action, which will locate a true center and focus for all the aspiration latent in them. The right time is now.[21]

Like other utopian visions, Mills's theory ended not so much in action as in frustration—which in turn led to further theorizing. If the established carriers of opinion were not to be trusted, then who could be? The question of the ontological status of truth then became converted to the question of truth's epistemological bearer. For a while, the labor intellectual seemed the perfect answer, but it was a response even Mills only half believed. He had collected too much data on labor bureaucrats not to know better. But once he made up his mind that organized business had as its chief enemy an independent and political labor movement, he was forced to conclude that the trade union movement itself was the last great wave of intellectual salvation. In some magic, spontaneous way, labor was to become the product of political opposition dragged into the future by its intellectual allies.

> The chief social power upon which a genuine democracy can rest today is labor. The political power of business indicates clearly that it is not enough for labor to struggle economically with business. Unless trade unions unify into an independent political movement and take intelligent action on all important political issues, there is danger that they will be incorporated within a government over which they have little control.[22]

In a paper which he prepared in 1945 for the Office of Reports of the Small War Plants Corporation on "The Middle Classes in Middle-Sized Cities," Mills could not resist returning to this theme of a labor-led revolution—a theme not uncharacteristically far removed from his research charge. By this time, he had become familiar with Lenin's theory of proletarian revolution, although it might be added that he drew the wrong conclusions about a working-class capacity for spontaneous development. He thought that white-collar people had an occupational ideology which was politically passive, and thus were not fit for a leadership role.

> They are not engaged in any economic struggle, except in the most scattered and fragmentary way. It is, therefore, not odd that they lack even a rudimentary awareness of their economic and political interests. Insofar as they are at all politically available, they form the rear guard either of "business" or of "labor"; but in either case, they are very much rear guard. Theories of the rise to power of white-collar people are generally inferred from the facts of their numerical growth and their indispensability in the bureaucratic and distributive operations of mass society. But only if one assumes a pure and automatic democracy of numbers does the mere growth of a stratum mean increased power for it. And only if one assumes a magic leap from occupational function to political power does technical indispensability mean power for a stratum.[23]

While his interests in white-collar people and in problems of stratification in general were strongly kindled during the Maryland years, long before the publication of his masterpiece, *White Collar*, Mills did not see such people as moving beyond alienation. From the outset, the bête noire of this debacle on the left was liberalism: liberalism in the form of the New Deal; liberalism in the form of leftist opposition; liberalism in the form of business rhetoric of the times. It seemed to Mills that liberalism, far from being a fighting credo, had become, pure and simple, the ideology of the American system as such. His early work on James and Dewey simply confirmed his strong belief that twentieth-century liberalism represented the opposition. And to this distinction, Mills remained firmly committed throughout his life.

Nineteenth-century liberalism in Mills's mind failed to take into account the changing economic foundations of political ideals. He asserted that a small-city, small-town assumption lay behind that liberalism, a failure to understand that we no longer live in a small-scale world. Early liberalism, he said, assumed an autonomy of institutions as if religion, education, and culture had nothing to do with economic ownership or political leadership. One after another, these values crumbled in the face of ongoing reality. The survival of liberalism was due more to the divorce from any realities of modern social structure than to the solution of these realities. It survived also because of an intelligentsia promulgating a kind of generalized rhetoric about ends and goals, ignoring means and methods. In what was Mills's earliest and perhaps clearest critique of liberalism, he wrote:

> As a kind of political rhetoric, liberalism has been banalized: note it is commonly used by everyone who talks in public for every divergent and contradictory purpose. Today we hear liberals say that one liberal can be "for," and another liberal "against," a vast range of contradictory political propositions. What this means is that liberalism as a common denominator of American political rhetoric, is without coherent content; that, in the process of its banalization, its goals have been so formalized as to provide no clear moral optic. The crisis of liberalism (and of American political reflection) is due to liberalism's success in becoming the official language for all public statement. To this fact was added its use in the New Deal era when, in close contact with power, liberalism became administrative. Its crisis in lack of clarity is underpinned by its use by all interests, classes, and parties. [24]
> I have always thought the source of creativity was in themselves, as individuals and as small self-selected circles; in their work and—above all—in the best intellectual and artistic traditions of the West. The sources of cultural endeavor seem to me international, the common property of civilized mankind, including historic Russia. [25]

Who were the unique carriers of truth over and against liberalism? Mills at one and the same time reaffirmed the eighteenth-century notion of universal man and that of individual creativity:

> The cultural prestige of nations is an attempt on *all* sides to exploit for nationalist interests what is essentially an international process. For the arts and sciences *are* international phenomena. Few indeed are the cultural and scientific products that are due to causes and traditions confined to

one nation, and by definition none of them become part of the grand tradition of modern man, unless they appeal to minds that know nothing of nationalistic boundaries.[26]

During the brief Maryland interlude Mills formulated his intellectual agenda. It was not yet a sociological research agenda, but a moral faith in the use of sociology to reach a brave new world. While his intellectual shafts established Mills as an essayist of some note and notoriety in the literary circles who read *Politics, The New Republic,* and *The New Leader,* they served a useful purpose beyond expressing his ideas. They made him quite well known in New York, the center of radical anti-totalitarian intellectual activities. And Mills's ambitions were no longer just to find another university post, but to find one in New York, where his imagination could be given full play. The center of culture fascinated him more than the center of power. In addition, Mills acquired basic ability, if not necessarily creativity, in techniques of quantitative research. The sort of "soft money" grants needed to sustain these activities were easier to come by in a major sociological department than at Maryland. All sorts of reasons conspired to compel Mills to seek a change. But however disenchanted he was with Maryland, Mills was not prepared to move to a place that did not meet his newly acquired sense of personal destiny.

In what must have seemed both a test and a tease, Merton wrote to Mills about an available but temporary position at Wellesley College in the Boston area:

> This is a position held by Mrs. Florence Kluckhohn, who will be aiding her country's weal by residing in Washington and doing war work. I don't just yet know what the salary would be, but I suspect somewhere in the neighborhood of $1,500–$1,800 for the semester. I have written to [Leland] Jenks suggesting that you might possibly be induced to consider it; should you be at all interested, why not write him directly.[27]

Mills did not write to Wellesley, but did take the opportunity to write to Merton at Columbia, reasserting his long-term interests.

> First, as I understand it, the opening is strictly temporary. That would not matter were I able to obtain some sort of leave from Maryland, but I can't. You see, despite the nonsense and the squeeze that goes on here, I do have, at least formally, tenure. And until I get something that is semi-permanent, I feel I should hang on here. Second, I feel the pressure of work pretty heavily, and even with my teaching load here, I do manage to get something done by routinizing the teaching.[28]

But despite these stated reasons for staying, the burden of his remarks was a reassertion of the need to leave. There were two additional reasons for leaving Maryland. Foremost of these was the dissolution of his marriage to Freya. Having created the fiction that he could transform an active worker for social justice in the Austin Young Men's and Women's Christian Association into a character from a D. H. Lawrence novel, Mills was finally unable to live with the realities imposed by an everyday relationship. It was during this period, too, that he met and fell in love with Ruth Harper, who was senior statistical analyst at Columbia's Bureau of Applied Social Research. Ruth provided Wright with sociological expertise no less than personal companionship—and at the very university where he hoped to be established. Leaving Maryland thus would mean putting some distance between himself and his first marriage, and, not incidentally, his first child, Pamela, with whom Mills could claim only a tempestuous if distant relationship.

Just as significant was the special need for an environment which could yield basic demographic and statistical information to substantiate Mills's growing passion for stratification analysis. His *White Collar* project neared completion while he was still at Maryland, except for the statistics needed to cement his argument and, where necessary, to correct his earlier crude formulations. Likewise, his growing interest in minority problems and class differentiation within the labor movement required the sort of sophisticated environment that Columbia uniquely provided and that Maryland lacked. With the sponsorship of Merton, and the support of such different sociological figures as Paul Lazarsfeld, Robert Lynd, and Theodore Abel, the appointment seemed to make sense to all concerned. Indeed, stormy though it became with the passage of time, Mills never brought himself to the point of relinquishing the Columbia connection.

But those who knew Mills personally were by no means uniformly delighted with the appointment at Columbia. Professional jealousy flared. Close intimates of an earlier period became manifestly hostile. Hans Gerth, the Weberian nonpareil of the Wisconsin years, made it abundantly clear to anyone who would listen that he felt himself to be the exclusive and not just the senior editor of *From Max Weber*. Gerth maintained that Mills, "an excellent operator, whipper-snapper, promising young man on the make, and Texas cowboy à la ride and shoot," insinuated himself into the Weber project only because he, Gerth, as a "fingerprinted enemy alien" needed to list an American citizen as co-editor for the book to obtain its legitimate publication.[29] He strongly implied that the move from Maryland was somehow illicit.

The Weber connection did have its origins during the Second World War. Gerth, who had been employed by the United Press Bureau in Berlin during 1937–1938, came to the United States early in 1939 as an alien and was confined to Madison, Wisconsin, for the duration of the war. There can be no doubt that this situation contributed greatly to Gerth's isolation from the mainstream of publishing and professional activities between 1940 and 1945. Clearly the translations of the Weber essays were prepared by Gerth, for the most part from versions he had produced for classroom use. It is also clear enough that even in 1945 Mills was a supreme stylist, whereas Gerth—whatever his émigré status was—was, to put it mildly, neither a graceful writer of English prose nor an adequate translator. Mills's primary role was in editing Gerth's work on Weber, and amplifying and interpreting the long, introductory narrative. Mills also helped place the extensive introductory essay on Weber within a meaningful American context. If the strictly biographical portions of the introduction were clearly the work of Gerth, the analysis of political implications is just as evidently the mark of Mills.

But Gerth never could quite let go. The more Mills's reputation grew, the more intense was Gerth's attempt to disparage his student and protégé. Upon the appearance of *The Causes of World War Three*, which made passing reference to the Gerth and Mills work on Weber, Gerth wrote to Merton asking rhetorically if his concerns about proper credit for the Weber materials should not become public.

> I wonder whether I could not try at long last to "stand up" rather than "lie low." I have become almost a habitué of the "horizontal" and I don't like the posture indefinitely. Besides, maybe my English is good enough by now to make myself clear, however imperfectly and unsophisticatedly. I don't like to be treated as an "informer" or "dirty little German refugee" or some such exploitable creature in the eyes of my betters and other operators indefinitely. . . . As I say, I can't take it any longer indefinitely to be walked over by "my betters." And I am fed up to be "culture fertilizer" and nothing else.[30]

Just what it was that Gerth expected Merton to do is unclear, since in fact Gerth had hardly suffered from his association with Mills. Indeed, he noted in the same letter to Merton that he had been promoted to full professor at Wisconsin, albeit he added bitterly that he was making several thousand dollars less than his colleagues.

Merton's response to Gerth could hardly have been reassuring. In effect, Merton simply reminded Gerth that from a legal and objective point of view, the issue of authorship had long been closed.

> What has happened is that this last episode [the promotional blurb for Mills's *The Causes of World War Three*] has reactivated for you the entire painful episode of a dozen years ago. It was then that you found yourself agreeing in print—both on the title page and in the preface—that these essays were "translated, edited and [put in print—RKM] with an introduction by HHG and CWM." Once that became a matter of public record, Mills can of course refer to it whenever he sees fit. It was then, not now, that the matter was publicly defined. . . . Once the book was published as a joint responsibility haven't you provided the right to refer to it as just that? This scarcely helps solve the problem, but to suggest anything else, would be to mislead rather than to help.[31]

Merton was not writing as an unalloyed defender of Mills. Indeed, by the end of 1958 Merton had clearly lost patience with, much less interest in, the sort of popularizing that Mills had embarked upon. But Merton, motivated by an admixture of moral balance, legal common sense, and perhaps a wish to preserve a colleague in his department from any undue harassment, behaved as he had throughout: a calming influence in a troubled departmental environment.

The Maryland years appear nebulous in retrospect because they were a period of personal movement and intellectual fermentation. Mills spent as much time in the District of Columbia as at College Park. He also spent each of his summers from 1942 through 1945 in New York City. This is not to say that the years at Maryland were without meaning. For while Mills continued to maintain a deep commitment to the great line of European social theorists from Marx to Weber, the wartime years convinced him that an empirical role for sociology was both possible and necessary.[32] It was this desperate effort to hold together research designs determined by societal needs and intellectual beliefs determined by philosophical antecedents that provided a dual, if inconclusive, legacy of the period.

If one keeps in mind the fact that by the time Mills left Maryland for the Bureau of Applied Social Research in 1945, he was only three to four years away from a total immersion in philosophical analysis and techniques, then the full impact of what superficially appears to be a transitional period without consequence can actually be measured. To be sure, Mills was never to resolve his dual loyalties to both philosophical sociology and empirical social research. He carried both elements with him to his next job. At Columbia University he was the empiricist; while among the literati in New York he was the historicist and critic of culture. Maryland provided an interlude—one that ended in a quiet acquiescence rather than a revolt against the dualistic tradition. This heavy baggage prevented Mills from ever becoming a systematic theorist or a methodological empiricist. He became instead a critic of both, and at the same time a captive of both.

REFERENCES

1. Hans H. Gerth to C. Wright Mills, January 5, 1942.
2. George H. Callcott. *A History of the University of Maryland*. Baltimore, Md.: Maryland Historical Society, 1966, pp. 330–31.
3. Wilson Record to Irving Louis Horowitz, February 20, 1978.
4. C. Wright Mills to Robert K. Merton, July 26, 1944.
5. Callcott, pp. 334–35.
6. C. Wright Mills to Eliseo Vivas, December 24, 1941.

7. Wilson Record to Irving Louis Horowitz, February 29, 1978.

8. C. Wright Mills to Hans H. Gerth, January 16, 1942.

9. Mills to Vivas.

10. *Ibid.*

11. *Ibid.*

12. C. Wright Mills to Hans H. Gerth, January 5, 1942.

13. Eliseo Vivas to C. Wright Mills, January 25, 1942.

14. C. Wright Mills. "The Structure of Events: 1917–1940" (unpublished manuscript, dated December 29, 1941).

15. Mills to Gerth, January 16, 1942.

16. C. Wright Mills. "The Personal and the Political." In *On Social Men and Political Movements*, pp. 12–23. (This collection has appeared in Spanish only, as *De hombres sociales y movimientos politicos*; Mexico City: Siglo Veintiuno Editores, 1968.)

17. C. Wright Mills. "The Political Gargoyles: Business as Power." In *Power, Politics and People*. New York: Oxford University Press, 1963, p. 72.

18. C. Wright Mills. "The Intellectual and the Labor Leader." In *On Social Men and Political Movements*, pp. 158–74. C. Wright Mills. "The Sailor, Sex Market and Mexican: The New American Jitters." *The New Leader*, June 26, 1943, pp. 5–7.

19. C. Wright Mills. "On the Old Left." In *On Social Men and Political Movements*, pp. 53–68.

20. C. Wright Mills. "The Politics of Truth." In *On Social Men and Political Movements*, pp. 43–46.

21. *Ibid.*, p. 43.

22. Mills, "The Political Gargoyles." In *Power, Politics and People*, pp. 75–76.

23. C. Wright Mills. "The Middle Classes, in Middle-Sized Cities." In *Power, Politics and People*, pp. 290–91.

24. C. Wright Mills. "Liberal Values in the Modern World." In *Power, Politics and People*, p. 189.

25. C. Wright Mills. "Power and the Cultural Workman." In *On Social Men and Political Movements*, pp. 148–49.

26. *Ibid.*, p. 152.

27. Robert K. Merton to C. Wright Mills, October 20, 1944.

28. C. Wright Mills to Robert K. Merton, October 25, 1944.

29. Hans H. Gerth to Robert K. Merton, November 16, 1958.

30. *Ibid.*

31. Robert K. Merton to Hans H. Gerth, November 30, 1958.

32. C. Wright Mills, ed. *Images of Man: The Classic Tradition in Sociological Thinking*. New York: George Braziller, 1960, pp. 12–13.

5

Marginality in Morningside Heights

The American university of today is best understood as a residual institution. What I mean by residual in this context can be gathered from what I have already said: the university is the last outpost of help, like the government of a welfare state.

Jacques Barzun, *The American University*

M ILLS DID NOT SO MUCH capture Columbia as inch toward it. He began to spend an increasing amount of time in New York City. Daniel Bell, whom Mills got to know while writing articles for *The New Leader*, which Bell edited at that time, helped him establish a summer residence in Greenwich Village during 1943 and 1944. It was through Bell that he made the acquaintance of such literary notables as Dwight Macdonald, Philip Rahv, and Irving Howe. These were already substantial figures in the New York literary scene. The war years permitted a broad anti-totalitarian intellectual common front to form, one that well mirrored the sense of political and cultural priorities during those special years. Mills's articles in such periodicals as *The New Leader* and *The New Republic* made him a welcome addition to this circle. He shared its revulsion for totalitarianism and its belief that the war would redivide power without redirecting energies; and quite apart from any beliefs in common, he came with a sense of frankness, even bluntness, and a polemical prowess that differed from but did not disturb the young notables of a wartime Bohemia.

Mills was writing occasional pieces for Bell and *The New Leader* during 1943 and 1944. This opened up yet further associations and friendships in New York. Perhaps the most important was his relationship with Dwight Macdonald, described touchingly in the "Afterword" to Macdonald's review essay on *White Collar*. This brief excerpt, clearly written after Mills's death in 1962, captures well Mills's sense of discovery in New York and his anticipation of a more permanent relocation to the literary center of the world.

> I first met Mills in 1943, a few years after he had broken out of his native Texan corral, like a maverick bull, to seek greener intellectual pastures up north. Our common interest was an antiwar monthly I was planning that materialized the next year as *Politics*—a perfect name that was his suggestion. We took to each other partly because we were isolated radicals in a wartime period and misery loves company but mostly because of a temperamental affinity: we were both congenital rebels, passionately contemptuous of every received idea and established institution and not at all articulate about it—he could argue about practically anything even longer and louder than I could. Also we had in common a peculiar (and incompatible really—but there it was) mixture of innocence and cynicism, optimism and skepticism. We were ever hopeful, ever disillusioned.[1]

Mills's relationship to Macdonald was to become typical of those he had established with others: a pattern of strong personal affinity followed by disenchantment and then drift from an old friend. In the case of Macdonald, the ostensible break came in the early 1950s, with the critical review he gave to *White Collar*. Mills always took criticism personally, and categorized friends and enemies according to their response to his work. In New York, with its contentious intellectual style, Mills did not end up with many friends. With a touch of wistful recollection, Macdonald notes that the relationship "was never the same again and we drifted apart in the fifties, he intensifying and expanding his radicalism, I losing hope, and therefore interest, in mine." The depth of that relationship can be gauged by the unique compassion for Mills that Macdonald shows in his self-deprecating comments.

Mills's sense of socialism was strengthened during this period by the fortuitous condition of having key members of the Frankfurt school on location at Columbia. The presence of Max Horkheimer, Theodor Adorno, and Herbert Marcuse added intellectual muscle to a sociology of the Left which was, at the same time, free of the Soviet taint. The linkage of the Frankfurt exiles with the Village bohemians made for a formidable environment.

Daniel Bell was most helpful in supporting Mills's claims for a position at Columbia, and Robert K. Merton and Robert S. Lynd offered their own support. However, the wartime expansion at Columbia was not in the small sociology department but at the Bureau of Applied Social Research. The research strength of people like Paul F. Lazarsfeld and Samuel Stouffer was readily harnessed to the national war effort. What began in 1941 as an arm of the sociology department soon evolved an independent focus and strength. Mills went to work there part-time in 1944 and full-time early in 1945. Mills's letters of the period indicate a certain foreboding about the new post—not so much about leaving Maryland, with which he had long since ceased to feel much kinship, but about what people would say in regard to his "selling out."[2] There was a certain moral posturing to his correspondence, but the quickness of his response to the Columbia bureau's offer and his simultaneous acceptance of a smaller War Plants Corporation contract from the government[3] left little doubt that Mills was pleased by the opportunity to move to what he felt to be the capital of the world and not just of the United States. The magnetic power of New York and its intellectual and research circles catapulted Mills to New York and out of Maryland. His interests were not simply in a university appointment elsewhere, but in an appointment, however marginal, in New York. His choice of Columbia represented a short-term prospect, and in that regard it was less attractive than his slot at Maryland, which was tenured.[4]

The move to Columbia presented Mills with a serious intellectual problem: On the one hand, his appointment at the bureau was a nuts-and-bolts affair. He was charged with supervising target projects in mass communications and public opinion polling under the overall direction of Paul F. Lazarsfeld, who, despite his own background in European socialist affairs, had developed a detached, almost antipolitical style of research and analysis once he came to America. Meanwhile, Mills's interests were becoming increasingly political and were swept by democratic socialist currents not unlike those Lazarsfeld had long since left behind. At first Mills valiantly tried to link the two styles of work—empirical and ideological.[5] In one research proposal, which focused on leaders of political opinion, he included some rather far-fetched statements about "false consciousness of political leaders." In reviewing the project Lazarsfeld was led to declare the entire report to be without redeeming sociological value. Not without a genuine sense of compassion, Lazarsfeld concluded "that Wright's training and the task at hand were at complete cross-purposes."[6] This was to become a continuing sore point, requiring the Columbia sociologists to either terminate his contract or move him into a regular teaching post.

As Mills settled into Columbia and the university witnessed a huge postwar surge in student enrollment, he was given a regular line appointment at Columbia College. It soon became apparent that partisanship rather than the value-free social science orientation preached by most of his colleagues was becoming a Millsian trademark. Even his projects at the bureau had a radical patina. A project on postwar engineering facilities ended with a gratuitous plea for greater social planning. He endowed Puerto Ricans living in the city with a strong sense of the special ways in which they were being exploited. Business executives were endowed with greater policymaking potential than politicians.

What Mills's Columbia connection meant to his Village comrades was difficult to ascertain. Many of his literary associates were not especially fond of sociology to begin with; they were probably even less inclined to accept as one of their own someone connected with the numbers-crunching Columbia Bureau of Applied Social Research.

Mills's early euphoria in New York soon turned to disquiet and frustration. He was once again a marginal figure: a literary outcast at the Columbia bureau and a sociological pariah in the Village. His marginality was particularly telling at the bureau, where he was paid to do research, not to preach ideology. Charges ranging from his manipulating data to achieve predetermined ends, to his being a statistical primitive became part of the common bureau lore. Fortunately for everyone concerned, Mills's appointment at the college in 1947 relieved him of much bureau work. The remaining work, which he nominally supervised, was completed by such able assistants as Rose Goldsen and Ruth Harper—who later became his second wife, and by Mills's own admission, a virtual coauthor on many of his projects.[7] The shift from bureau to college relieved Mills's anxieties about his more journalistic and literary concerns. What he lectured and wrote about was much more in tune with the thinking in *The New Leader, The New Republic*, and *Politics* than with his bureau work on the reconstruction of engineering education for a postwar environment, or even his study of reforming the social structure and personnel of naval research institutions.[8]

However, those early, formative years at the bureau were extremely important. They provided Mills with a solid foundation in empirical social research, which was reflected in such later works as *The Puerto Rican Journey* and *White Collar*. These publications earned him wide acceptability among social scientists who had seen him simply as a political philosopher. These years also gave him an independent vantage point from which to judge his more ideological friends. If marginality had a price, it also had its rewards.

Columbia University, precisely because of its diversity, permitted Mills to perform the multiple task of teacher, researcher, and even public figure. The absence at Columbia of centralized planning, and the power of its individual parts, like the bureau, made a marginal figure like Mills feel a good deal more comfortable than he had in the smaller worlds of Texas, Wisconsin, and Maryland.[9] It did so through its particular style of non-planning. This was illustrated in its management of Mills's problems at, as well as with, the bureau. In part because Mills failed to complete and deliver results on contracts for which he was directly responsible, or because he delivered unacceptable products, Mills was, as has been mentioned, removed from the bureau to the college. The trouble was that his teaching was also something less than legendary. In addition, in the late 1940s Mills still had not yet done the sort of outstanding work which was to be forthcoming during the next decade. Nonetheless, the Columbia department's belief in Mills's ultimate intellectual worth remained intact. It postponed for one year Mills's promotion from assistant to associate professor in 1947. How seriously the department viewed the postponement is attested to by the multiple drafts of the document transmitting the news to Mills, prepared by the then chairman, Theodore Abel, and revised by Robert S. Lynd.

We have all been disappointed by your failure to complete the Decatur study, for which you had assumed responsibility, and we are unconvinced by your explanation or reasons for your actions at this late date. This study was not a private arrangement between you and Professor Lazarsfeld, but deeply involved the whole department in the difficult problem of financing the Bureau . . . we are also somewhat troubled by reports that you exhibit impatience over student questions in class, and by an apparent casualness and diffuse presentation of class material . . . your teaching problem, to the extent that it exists, is perhaps a combination of an embarrassment of riches and an overextended work schedule. You have, we believe, the makings of a strong member of our Department; but it does not help either you or us to jump to conclusions, particularly in view of your own rather impetuous confidence in yourself.[10]

Mills's broad approach to data analysis simply did not work in the kinds of contract research that was the bureau's bread and butter. Projects which required careful attention to questionnaire responses left little room for discussion of large-scale issues. In his memorandum to Abel, Lazarsfeld described Mills's work at this level as "perfectly unsuccessful." On several occasions Lazarsfeld had indeed taken over the management of ongoing projects—more to bail out the department than to satisfy a client's wish. In the case of the Decatur Project, not only had all the money been spent, much of it by Mills, but a deficit of serious proportions had been incurred. The choice was either to go public with a fiasco or to make good on a weak project. The latter was the painful decision reached. Even if, as Abel was at great pains to make clear to Mills, the Decatur Project "was not a private arrangement" between Mills and Lazarsfeld, the solution reached had rested precisely on such a private agreement between the two.

The "squaring of accounts" Lazarsfeld worked out with Mills required him to supervise a study of Puerto Rican immigrants in New York virtually without pay, so that the balance in the Puerto Rican account could be used to offset the deficit on the Decatur study, which Lazarsfeld then completed on his own. That Lazarsfeld was no more equipped to study midwestern local politicians (the subject of the Decature Project) than Mills was to study Puerto Ricans meant little—the work got done, the books were closed:

Wright realized the difficulties into which he brought the office and myself, and he seriously looked for a way in which to compensate us. It was Wright who hit upon the suggestion that he take the Puerto Rico study off my hands, and short of having solved the Decatur problem this was the most constructive suggestion he could have made. It was very important for the bureau to get the Puerto Rico study. I could not possibly have conducted it myself. I do not know at the moment anyone else except Wright Mills who has the personality and the experience to undertake this task.[11]

While Mills was "director of the study, designed it, was in charge of its execution, and [was] the senior author [of *The Puerto Rican Journey*]," in fact he had a wide array of talent assisting him: Ann Lohmann was in charge of fieldwork and Rose Goldsen was in charge of statistical analysis and coding.[12] Clarence Senior was the only knowledgeable figure with firsthand information on Puerto Ricans in the project, and Ruth Harper [Mills] had background in the Social Security Administration, which fitted her well for the task of reviewing the data and making the final package work. By mid-1948 Mills had completed his own contribution to the project. In a letter to Mills, vacationing with Ruth in Yosemite Valley, California, Merton makes it clear that the completion of the Puerto Rican project permitted sufficient savings of money to pay all senior researchers and staff and to make good on the Decatur overdraft; it also helped the bureau generate money for a new study from the United States Public Health Service.[13]

By this time, both Mills and his bureau chief, Lazarsfeld, had had enough of this sort of contract research. The squaring of the accounts permitted a casual and relaxed separation of Mills from the bureau, and a delayed promotion to associate professor. The appointment settled, Mills was able to continue work on *Character and Social Structure* and *White Collar*, as well as a variety of articles far closer to his passions. As a parting shot, Mills worked over the final chapter of the Puerto Rican study, adding an opening paragraph which was unmistakably Millsian. Rose Goldsen once remarked that even though Mills had never seen the places described in the final report, remarkably enough he evoked the true meaning of life in Spanish Harlem and the East Bronx.[14] It was Mills himself, for example, who authored this finely etched portrait of race, sex, and ethnicity within Puerto Rican life in New York.

> The Puerto Rican journey to New York ends in the circumscribed worlds of Spanish Harlem and Morrisania. Neither these worlds, nor the economic transits to them, necessarily spur the migrants to take those identifications that form the classic pattern of American migration; it is as likely that they will continue to feel estranged, except for the few who gain solidarities with other thinned-out Latin American groups. In their slum dwellings, the migrants, especially those of Negro racial type, become pupils and victims of ethnic conflict. For the women particularly, models of adaptation to American life are not readily available or easily come by.[15]

But if the study put to rest Mills's problems with the bureau, those with the department had hardly begun. *The Puerto Rican Journey* was published early in 1950, closing out not simply a decade but a sociological work style that fitted the needs of neither the bureau nor Mills.

✍✍✍

Mills remained a Texan trying to break into the eastern establishment, and he did not have the easy success he initially envisioned. In a moment of self-realization, he wrote to Merton after reading *Social Theory and Social Structure.*

> Although in my distracted and benumbed condition it's hard to read anything with strict attention, over the last few days I have read all the new matter in your book and some of the older materials. It was very depressing. I hadn't realized (in fact I had for some reason been refusing to examine the point) how very far I had wandered from really serious work in our discipline.[16]

This "confession" and the rare self-knowledge it evidenced temporarily permitted Mills to normalize his relationship with the department. It permitted his transition from the bureau to the department to occur with minimum discord. This administrative shift did not, however, provide Mills with a sense of full integration. Mills was professionally isolated at the Columbia sociology department, confining his activities to the undergraduate level after 1954. This formula was simple enough: Mills would teach in the college, complete his research for the bureau, but not participate in the graduate program or begin new projects under the bureau's auspices.

To some extent, his relationships elsewhere offset the lack of friendship in the department. David Riesman remained cordial and supportive, at least until *The Power Elite* appeared.[17] Lyman Bryson was a figure to be reckoned with at Columbia, and he made it clear that he thought Mills had been "magisterial" in analyzing white-collar people.[18] Younger scholars like Kurt Wolff appreciated this anti-conformist strain in the American world. Wolff raised a set of disturbing challenges for Mills, who had staked a claim as a moral and political thinker. Wolff asks him: "What is your political position, and what is your philosophical position—including epistemological and ontological; and what is your explicit stand on the function of the social scientist? Having thrown the gauntlet, it would now in turn be strengthened by explicit statements on the topics mentioned."[19] Even though Mills did not reply in writing to these questions, Wolff's inquiry remarkably anticipated Mills's own later self-questioning and doubts. Many of his shorter essays and reviews written during the mid-1950s attempted to address these concerns.

But the answers Mills came up with increasingly alienated his Columbia colleagues. In quick order, as mentioned above, they assigned him to undergraduate teaching, which he incorporated as a badge of honor. His increasingly acerbic relationships with the wider Columbia community were not so easily converted into a modus vivendi. His ragings against the shortcomings of sociology meant little or nothing to the larger Columbia community. But when his criticism spilled over against Columbia titans and former friends like Jacques Barzun, Richard Hofstadter, and Lionel Trilling, his situation became ever more tenuous. All had been close to Mills when he came to Columbia in the mid-1940s, but all had been sorely tried and tested by the mid-1950s. Mills's isolation from Columbia deepened, his sense of scholarly worth was seriously injured, and increasingly he sought satisfaction from a small circle of friends and associates far from Morningside Heights. His outside lectures became more frequent, his vacations longer, and his sense of professional involvement in the affairs of social research curtailed.

Like many who came before and after, Mills was trapped by a certain innocence. He saw Columbia as the heartbeat of New York, when in fact in the 1940s and 1950s it saw itself as a veritable enclave of civilization amidst a sea of barbarism. It was not so much a matter of conservatism in its content—its administrators and professors were as liberal as any next-door university's—but rather a matter of conservatism in style, of good form. It was his style, even more than what Mills said or wrote, that gave him ceaseless trouble. His failure to observe the noblesse oblige of sparing one's colleagues in print was his most noticeable and probably most important blind spot—or perhaps this was an expression of revanchism by a man spurned and privately ridiculed once too often.

His criticism of departmental colleagues, university-wide associates, and his own university administrators—not for technical but for ideological reasons—ultimately became the root source of a deeply felt hostility toward Mills. It took a fellow Texan, and a departmental colleague, William "Si" Goode, to put the matter candidly. "There was no estrangement that occurred between Wright and me. We began estranged. Indeed, at the memorial services or meeting that was organized at Columbia University at his death, I seemed to be the only person who could not say: 'I used to be his friend, but we became somewhat distant.' It was rather the reverse."[20] Mills was caught in a cul-de-sac: antiprofessional in public utterance, quite professional in private desire. He coveted the status and the glory of elite institutions while despising their snobbery and style. At Columbia he more than met his match. He went to his death with this contradiction not only unresolved but largely unrecognized. He turned down offers at such new, innovative schools as Brandeis University in this country and Sussex University in England. Neither high salaries nor populist pretentions could lure him from his special lair atop Morningside Heights.

The 1950s were Mills's most productive and creative period. In those years he completed *White Collar, Character and Social Structure, The Power Elite*, and a variety of shorter works that identified him as a major figure in the sociological firmament. But for all of that, they were also years of growing estrangement from the local university environment and the larger professional environment as well. Mills was aware of this, and in public even seemed to take some pride in the contentiousness he aroused in others. Responding to a query in the above-mentioned letter from Wolff, who was then a deeply admiring colleague at Ohio State University, on why he wrote the way he did, Mills replied that he was not quite sure, but he did make a comment about his origins, which reveals that he was quite sensitive about his marginal status at Columbia, whatever the public reception to his work. He frequently alluded to the pain no less than the virtue of being outside the mainstream.

> My origins are all in this country. I have never been abroad, yet many people say I write as if I were a European about this country. It is no joke but a fact that my Texas grandfather has something to do with that. I am an outlander, not only regionally, but down bone deep and for good. In Orwell's phrase: I am just outside the whale and always have been. I did not really earn it; I just was it without intending to be and without doing anything about it except what I had to do from day to day.[21]

Just how far "outside the whale" Mills was in the 1950s is clear in a series of letters concerning T. C. McCormick's nomination of him for membership in the then elite Sociological Research Association. Of the three names suggested as sponsors of Mills, one wrote a letter,[22] a second neglected to answer,[23] and a third cited difficulties in Mills's "personal relationships with others."[24] It is hardly an exaggeration to say that within the sociology profession Mills had gained respect but little support. And the valued Columbia connection just did not travel well.

Typical of Mills's estrangement was the bitter exchange he had with Lionel Trilling. The controversy surfaced because of remarks Mills made about Trilling in a major essay, "On Knowledge and Power," published in *Dissent* in 1955. Mills went to work addressing the very issues Wolff inquired about. He lashed out at the "miscarriage of American civilization," especially as represented by the style of celebration he found in the work of Daniel J. Boorstin and his old friend Jacques Barzun. To Mills, it was the struggle for power and not the shared consensus about democracy which characterized American history. The attack on Trilling was thus a particular variant of animus for a consensualist vision as a whole. The episode so typifies the experiences Mills had with Columbia colleagues during the 1950s that it deserves more than passing attention. In its own way, it represents an entire host of relationships severed in print by Mills, never to be restored in private again.

In his essay, Mills noted in a testy and acerbic way that "Mr. Lionel Trilling [writing in *Perspectives USA*, No. 3] has written optimistically of 'new intellectual classes,' and has even referred to the Luce Publications as samples of high intellectual talent."[25] Trilling did not take kindly either to the reference or the hint of celebration. In the background to the statement was, of course, Daniel Bell, who had gone from *The New Leader* to *Fortune*, one of Luce's chief publications. This transition from "socialist" to "capitalist" press incurred Mills's moral wrath. Trilling's sense of intellectual outrage was evoked by Mills's handling of Bell. These next-door neighbors—Mills's office, like Trilling's, was in Hamilton Hall—were reduced to writing a memorable exchange. In this case, a breakdown of personal relationship became complete, with the two incapable even of passing civilities. But they left this vital exchange before the silence became complete. In responsing to Mills, Trilling noted:

> I have read over the passage in which I speak of the relation of the Luce publications to intellectual talent. It seems to me that I made it perfectly plain that my remarks about the desire of Luce publications to employ people of high intellectual talent were not to be understood as a favorable judgment on the intellectual quality of the Luce publications themselves. It seems to me that I made my intention unmistakable. But I'd much rather believe that I did not succeed in this, than that you willfully, for purposes of polemic, misrepresented what I said.[26]

Mills responded, first by expressing regrets if he had given Trilling personal offense; he said that this clearly had not been his intent. But he went on and cited chapter and verse from the offending paragraph in Trilling's essay. Far from granting any error of interpretation, Mills went on to recite the celebrationist presumptions behind Trilling's identification of intellect with power.

> The key points are two: First, the rise of the technician and consultant in all areas of modern America ought to be recognized, and is this not the burden of your essay, in such a way as to make clear the difference between the humanist ideal of intellect and mechanical rationality. That this distinction is not a real pivot in your piece, is a source of possible misunderstanding. Second, the most important fact about the intelligence of those who live long with Luce is the ease with which their intelligence is used in the bright, clever pattern without any explicit ordering and forbidding being involved. That is the beginning point for an analysis of the intellectual quality of the new technical intelligentsia which you seem in some rather oblique, even opaque, way to be celebrating.[27]

Mills's remarks evoked a four-page response, far more than the perfunctory one-paragraph reply his initial article inspired. Ripping into Mills's "feckless attitudinizing," Trilling granted only that Mills had no "conscious intention" of malice; he pointed out that the broadside against the Luce publications was wide of the mark on a variety of accounts. The very editor of *Dissent*, the journal in which Mills's critique of Luce initially appeared, Irving Howe, was someone whom *"Time* reached out for when he was scarcely known''; and Louis Kronenberger, for whom Mills expressed admiration in the very same paragraph as he critiqued Trilling, was ''an employee of Luce and a most valued one.'' Trilling went on to mention others like James Agee and Robert Fitzgerald who were ''intelligent people in the employ of Luce.'' Trilling added ''that the use made of their talents is another question''—to which Mills in his marginalia (he never did respond in writing to this letter) replied: ''But that's the whole point of talents—their use.''

The heart of Trilling's response to Mills concerned the uses of terms like ''technician'' and ''consultant,'' a rhetoric which, after all, was closer to Mills than to Trilling in their respective histories. Be that as it may, Trilling caught Mills off guard with an accusation of elitism and aristocratic preference far from the democratic premise Mills presumably started with.

> The meaning which you give to the words technician and consultant is a wholly pejorative one. What I had in mind was something at once more neutral and larger. I was trying to refer to circumstances which requires that masses of people have an intellectual training of some sort—school teachers, college teachers, social workers, physicians, laboratory workers, etc. All these people have considerable schooling and they are all touched with the pride of ideas. . . . I am not a priori charmed by ideology taking the place of principle and honor, as it tends to do in our culture. But ideology carries with it some principle and some honor of its own. And a culture in which ideology is dominant offers an opportunity for the intellectual. From the cultural point of view which you express in your essay, a point of view as it were aristocratic, very strict and traditional and ideal, there is nothing to be done with this new class; it is nothing but vulgar and outside the intellectual possibility. I continue to think that this is not so; a kind of cultural revolution has taken place, and like the industrial revolution, this cultural revolution creates a great deal of mess and vulgarity, but also brings with it many possibilities of revision and improvement.[28]

Here we witness the aristocratic literary critic defending mass culture and the populist sociologist defending elite culture. Mills did not quite know how to resolve this dilemma, and Trilling did not much care to resolve it. Living with a ''mess'' was quite acceptable to Trilling. For Mills, however, the problem of stratification and mobilization was at the heart of his radicalism.

Soon after this exchange Mills left Columbia on a sabbatical. His academic leave in 1956 took him to Copenhagen and London. In a special way, the leave extricated him from a personal morass and intellectual stagnation. Writing to his younger colleague, Dennis Wrong, who had recently emigrated from Canada to the United States, Mills sent his appreciation for Wrong's expression of distress over a review of Mills's *The Power Elite*. He asked Wrong not to worry unduly about harsh criticism. "It is difficult to find space nowadays for celebration, not just between you and me, but somehow as a whole group among us. Celebration that is not ironic has become almost impossible." He added a prescient statement about the potential impact of Europe on him. "God knows what changes the experience of it will make on what I write."[29]

✒〰✒

Whatever else the consequences of the European trip, the first of several, it did sever any organic sense of his being of Columbia University, even though he remained at the university. The college had been changing and the departmental curriculum was increasingly shaped and dominated by Daniel Bell, Mills's input notwithstanding. It is correct to note, as Seymour Martin Lipset did in a description of sociology during the 1950s, that Mills could no longer really be properly defined as being within the field of sociology; certainly he was not by the end of the decade.[30] As bitter and painful a judgment as this kind of excommunication by peers was for Mills, there was no gainsaying its accuracy. Lipset simply confirmed in writing Mills's long-brewing break from professional sociology, despite the fact that in the public imagination he was as closely identified with the field of sociology as Margaret Mead was with anthropology.

But before Mills gave up the ghost of professionalism, and before his intellectual distance from Columbia became complete, he offered one parting farewell, *The Sociological Imagination*. At its core, this was not just a statement about the rights and the wrongs of a field, but, as in so much of Mills's work, it was a summing up of, and settling of accounts with, his Columbia colleagues—and a few from Harvard thrown in for good measure. Lazarsfeld in sociology, Hofstadter in history, Trilling in English, and a host of others with whom Mills started out at Columbia became the object of critique no less than the subject matter of the study. This seminal volume not only settled accounts, but perhaps, for the first and only time in his life, gave Mills a sense of intellectual equality with his mighty associates at a university he could never quite bring himself to love or leave. Mills's sense of career prevailed: he stayed on at Columbia until his death. But his sense of honor, his intense individualism, compelled a final effort to completely distinguish himself from his comrades at the Ivy League outpost at the tip of Harlem.

Considering the intensity of the debate generated by the publication of *The Sociological Imagination*, it is in retrospect an astonishingly mild, gentle critique of the sociological profession. It is a hallmark of the academic conservatism characteristic of Columbia in the late 1950s that a book written in celebration of the social sciences should have aroused passions of a sort usually reserved for radical assaults on the field. The re-

87

sponse to the book may have reflected delayed reaction to the radical turn Mills had taken in his previous books, especially *The Power Elite* and *The Causes of World War Three*. Then again, by 1959 Mills had acquired an "aura" of heroic proportions, and he had done so without the benefit of the sociological establishment's imprimatur. But for the dedicated professional, nothing condemns more than popularity. Being a larger-than-life figure in a rather dull profession is itself enough to transform someone who is merely uninhibited into a mythic presence. The 1950s, in addition to being a period of intense professionalization in sociology, were a period in which the proper posture was deference, respectability, and self-assuredness in the face of "old-fashioned" humanistic criticism.[31] Lacking such a posture, Mills felt his colleagues' wrath.

The Sociological Imagination helped to make possible the penetration of a field by a new generation of social scientists dedicated to problems of social change rather than system maintenance. At a point when the gap between truth and purpose in sociology was extremely wide, Mills helped bridge that gap by discussing concrete issues of large-scale import in terms of what sociology could contribute. The book is written by an insider but it is for outsiders. Mills makes it apparent from the outset that instead of placing a field under attack (as others have done since, in *Sociology on Trial*[32] or *The Coming Crisis of Western Sociology*[33]), *The Sociological Imagination* has the goal of enabling ordinary people to grasp sociology as a new synthesis of history and biography and to understand the relationship between the two within society. The theme is consistently repeated and underwrites the work as a whole.

Although he does not, for the most part, acknowledge their influence, *The Sociological Imagination* reflects Mills's respect for the "other" Columbia—not the Columbia of the Bureau of Applied Research headed by Paul Lazarsfeld, but the Columbia of Robert Lynd, odd man out within the sociology department; of Jacques Barzun, who represented a humanistic assault intellectually and an organizational force to be reckoned with as academic dean; and of Meyer Schapiro, a foremost art historian and leading independent radical at Columbia. The combination of Lynd's concern with outrageous hypotheses,[34] Barzun's concern with the historical context of the intellectual imagination,[35] and Schapiro's emphasis on style as craft[36] underwrites this Millsian effort. Mills's connection with Columbia persisted even during his most traumatic period within the department of sociology. And even if he had deep personal troubles, his sense of the larger Columbia picture was clearly enhanced by people like Lynd, Barzun, and Schapiro, as well as by younger scholars who were beginning to make an impact on the university, such as Peter Gay in intellectual history.

The problems that Mills addressed himself to in 1959 paralleled the issues taken up by Robert Lynd in *Knowledge for What?* twenty years earlier. Mills asked us to consider the problem of war: how one can translate distaste for personal problems resulting from conflict into a movement to end international warfare. The problem of war at a personal level is how the individual can survive; but as a social issue the problem of war is how the individual can contribute to its termination, and generally manage or resolve conflict. Lynd made the same challenge just prior to the outbreak of the Second World War. He noticed that sociological influence shrinks from resolving the problem of war by refusing to translate its findings into programs for action. The conflict becomes inevitable as a function of the laws or evolution of society. This is precisely the reasoning followed by the German school of ''conflict theory.'' What has been must be. But Lynd saw such a social science as a way of insuring personal passivity.

Mills, too, asked us about the problem of unemployment. When unemployment is an individual problem it is a personal trouble, but when it becomes a problem shared by 25 percent of the employed class, as it was during the Great Depression, then one has every right to question the efficacy of a social system, or at least to postulate possible alternatives to that system.[37] In a broad way, this aspect of *The Sociological Imagination* also reflects Lynd's pessimism about private capitalism and its failure to ensure the level of welfare to which he felt the American citizen's technical skills and intelligence entitled him. Lynd went even further than Mills—arguing that a private enterprise system cannot accommodate the public welfare except perhaps through the ''leprosy of Fascism that is creeping across the present capitalist world'':[38] a very real fear in the period of German Nazism and Italian fascism.

Mills also asked sociology to consider marriage and divorce, not simply in terms of the personal troubles of man and woman, but as a social structural problem involving large numbers of divorces in relation to marriages attempted. The structural aspect of interpersonal relations is a key aspect of *The Sociological Imagination*.[39] A similar strain of thought is apparent in *Knowledge for What?* Marriage here is seen as one of the major obstacles to equality for human beings in American society. Behind Lynd's biological and psychological reasoning about marriage is an understanding of the tension involved in inequalities between the sexes.[40] Such inequities, instead of being dealt with publicly, are handled privately, by high suicide rates and incarceration in mental institutions. These are the pathetic responses to the quest for equality and serenity in an unjust social order. For both Lynd and Mills, the focus of problems remained distinctly sociological and American. Even their naiveté and tempered optimism seem unique to the American experience and to its interpretation of the sociological mission as meliorative and structural rather than intrinsic and instinctual.

Mills also shared with Lynd a kind of ambiguity about the Big City: calling it in turn horrible, beautiful, ugly, and magnificent.[41] Both responded to urban blight by asking, rhetorically, what should be done with the wonderful monstrosity. More than a hint of nostalgia for an earlier, simpler America is contained in their shared doubts about meaningful solutions. The earlier Lynd formulation, resting on a romanticization of his *Middletown* books, notes that since urban living tends to confuse and devitalize American culture, science needs to discover how to knot loose population masses into vital communities of interest, before the degenerating urban tendency renders culture impotent.[42] A love-hate relationship with the city is native to the American intellectual style, but beyond Lynd's and Mills's shared intellectual ambiguity about city living was the unique position of Columbia University within New York City. Columbia has always been more in than of New York City. During Mills's tenure, Columbia was close in spirit to a nostalgic fantasy of an Ivy League college and remote from the everyday lives of the black citizens below the bluffs of Amsterdam and St. Nicholas avenues, or the Irish working class bordering Morningside Heights on the opposite end of Columbia, or the Puerto Ricans to the south of the university. Mills, the commuter from West Nyack, did not know, any more than did Lynd, what to do or say about the City, not simply as a social problem but as a twentieth-century way of life. Mills's perceptive comments on Puerto Ricans in New York were unique, singular, and soon forgotten.

Both *The Sociological Imagination* and *Knowledge for What?* handle exploitation and degeneration pragmatically. Both draw their casts of intellectual characters primarily from American sources. There is even some overlap in intellectual heroes. For Lynd, they are Arthur Bentley, Harold Lasswell, Peter Odegard; while for Mills they are Kenneth Galbraith, Robert Dahl, David Riesman, David Truman, and, again, Harold Lasswell. The world of *The Sociological Imagination* turns out to be very much a universe or the American imagination: even if sharp differences between conflict and consensus as styles of thought persisted; the wholly American context of debate was evident. Mills repeatedly sounds the theme that the political task of the social scientist is the enterprise of the liberal educator as such: to translate personal problems into public issues. Problems are never seen in terms of simple masses or collectivities, but issues become public when they achieve the status of human meaning for a variety of individuals.[43] Lynd and Mills share an intense respect for individualism rather than a high regard for collectivism; a hallmark which typifies the essence of the American sociological tradition.

Even during the intense and ongoing political disaffiliation and disaffection of the fifties, Mills never asserted that America was a quasi-Fascist state. His harshest criticism was to suggest in an understated manner that "the social structure of the United States is not an altogether democratic one." His amplification makes it evident that he holds out a vision of America as democratic, and of social science as making America even more democratic.

> The United States today is generally democratic in form and in the rhetoric of expectation. In substance as in practice it is very often non-democratic, and in many institutional areas it is quite clearly so . . . I do not wish to give the impression that I am optimistic about the chances that many social scientists can or will perform a democratic public role, or— even if many of them do so—about the chances that this would necessarily result in a rehabilitation of publics. I am merely outlining one role that seems to me to be open and is, in fact, practiced by some social scientists. The political role of social science—what that role may be, how it is enacted, and how effectively—this is relevant to the extent to which democracy prevails.[44]

Mills shared with Lynd a special kind of nativism. Sociological influences of the European "classic" tradition were strong, but they should have been, given the overwhelming importance of people like Weber, Durkheim, Pareto, and Marx in the development of American sociology. Mills was not enamored of the "frontier thesis" of American ideas, but he always returned to it for want of any theoretical option. Like Lynd, he drew upon an outsider with a special kind of American vision, Kenneth Burke. Burke combined nativism with populism in a way that satisfied the urgings of both Lynd and Mills for social change and individual rights. The frontispiece of Lynd's *Knowledge for What?* includes the following statement from Burke: "In this staggering disproportion between man and noman, there is no place for the purely human boasts of grandeur, or for forgetting that men build their cultures by huddling together, nervously loquacious, at the edge of an abyss."[45] Mills tells us: "By all means, read Burke's *Permanence and Change*."[46] The purpose of doing so is knowing the universe—seeing experience as part of a larger world, and seeing experience as creating a world unto itself. This reliance on the observed and observable is typical of an American pragmatic spirit. Pragmatism incorporated a sense of experience as larger than reality, hence the need to return to sentiment rather than structure in analysis.

The differences between Lynd and Mills are not so much in terms of style as in what might be called the emphasis on psychologism in the former and sociologism in the latter. Almost like George Homans, Lynd wanted to bring people back into sociology, to move from the institutional to the individual. He reminds us that for the most part social scientists have lost the person below their horizon as they busily plow their respective research furrows.[47] He informs us of the dangers of the "relatively small volume of current research on the level of the rich and varied individual behavior with reference to a given institution"—a quantity that is directly related to the arduousness of such investigation.[48] Mills, on the other hand, tempered his individualism, first by translating the person into biography and then by considering biography an element in, rather than the essence of, the sociological imagination.

By connecting biography with history, and both with the social structure, the sociologist presumably can arrive at a meaningful sense of epoch. The essential unit of measure for Mills became epochal rather than individual.[49] In this sense, he shifted the ground of sociology from the small community to universal history, and hence from a democratic if limited scope to an apocryphal and unlimited vision. Everett C. Hughes caught this when in a review of *The Sociological Imagination* he noted that Mills seemed more indebted to the cultural science of Alfred Weber than to the more structural analysis of Max Weber.[50] Mills, in his annotated copy of the review, questioned this observation, because he was not aware of the work of the other Weber. Pragmatism rather than *Kulturwissenschaft* informed the Millsian universe; the use of history rather than the abuses of individuals ultimately captured his fancies.[51]

What created a special biting animosity toward Mills's work, in contrast to the widespread favorable reaction to Lynd's, resides more in the different epochs in which each wrote than in the contents. Anti-fascism helped Lynd; anti-communism hurt Mills. The automaticity of liberal assumptions within sociology for the most part dampened any severe critique of Lynd. Until Lynd, the Columbia critique of liberalism was Deweyan: pragmatic in nature and mild in substance. It was a critique of individual liberalism in the name of a new social liberalism. But though Dewey went a long way toward distinguishing between types of liberalism, he certainly had no intention of overturning the sacred canons of liberal doctrine itself. This was much more the intent of Lynd, for among the "outrageous hypotheses" that he introduced was the assumption that perhaps liberalism, old or new, did not have all the answers. Its very weaknesses ushered in a world of socialism. Lynd posed his critique in a series of questions; but they clearly went to the very marrow of the liberal imagination.[52]

Lynd ultimately argued that the problem of liberalism, new as well as old, was that it refused to make room for social planning and cooperative work. Its suspicion of cooperation led to a kind of piecemeal world view and an attack by separate disciplines on isolated parts of the whole. For Lynd, "the intellectual throttle" needed "to be opened wide." Opening that throttle specifically meant movement beyond constraints such as individualism and conservatism. The task of social science was to move beyond hypotheses, even fantastic ones, and the manipulation of people in human affairs. Social science was to become an instrument of progress beyond liberal inquiry into what people want and the changes necessary to achieve these desires.[53] There can be no question that MIlls was tremendously influenced by Lynd. His own later stinging criticisms of liberalism as a "banalized political rhetoric" clearly followed the channels charted by Lynd.[54]

Lynd's impact extended to professional matters as well. Mills cited, with great appreciation, his critical remarks on perhaps the most significant piece of collective, team-effort empirical research to emerge from the Second World War, *The American Soldier*: "It is a significant measure of the impotence of liberal democracy that it must increasingly use its social sciences not directly on democracy's own problems, but tangentially and indirectly; it must pick up the crumbs from private business research."[55]

It is not without irony that Lynd, a figure with whom Mills was to be most closely identified at Columbia, was also the senior figure most opposed to the retention of Mills in the department after the debacle at the bureau between 1945 and 1947. Lynd judged people and events from a moral—one might better say moralistic—perspective; and from such a vantage point he found Mills lacking. The only reason that Lynd accepted the departmental consensus was a parallel belief that since Mills seemed to be persecuted for his leftist ideas he could not be all bad. Still, throughout his career at Columbia, Lynd remained aloof from Mills. It was on the surface nothing more than a clash of morally centered individuals. But underneath there was a clash of two visions of sociology: Mills with his emphasis on power and executive manipulation of masses, and Lynd with his stress on status and the kind of democracy which results from the interplay of judicial and legislative forces.

✣✣✣

The pivotal wartime decade separating *Knowledge for What?* and *The Sociological Imagination* ended in 1949, and the problems posed by sociologists changed nearly as dramatically as the issues posed for them. Lynd was writing in an era of widespread disbelief about the capabilities of sociologists; indeed, most sociologists were probably less convinced than policy analysts that their earthly mission was unique. Much had happened during the forties: a bureaucratic work style had evolved that was distinct from departmental affiliation, and computer technology began to process information on a widespread scale. The endless needs of a nation in combat for both data and policy left their mark of social science—or better, consecrated tendencies which had been set in motion in the halcyon days of the New Deal. Under such circumstances Mills's endorsement of Lynd was viewed as nothing but a direct assault on Columbia and its Bureau of Applied Social Research.

The very successes of postwar sociology changed the nature of the problem. As the scientific efficacy of sociology became taken for granted, the political and moral values this new science of society should inculcate became the issue. The postwar years led American sociology into concerns with empirical detail, problems of milieu, and parceling of education to fit those with fragmented intelligence rather than an integral vision of the whole. In Mills's world, sociology as liberalism became its own enemy, taking as the norm what some people are interested in establishing, in contrast to considering alternative social possibilities.

Mills's world view ultimately rested on fusing subjectivity with objectivity, what people are interested in with what is in their best interests. Social science, presumably, is dedicated to the human interest and also has the capacity to distinguish true interests from false consciousness.

> If we take the simple democratic view that what men are interested in is all that concerns us, then we are accepting the values that have been inculcated, often accidentally and often deliberately by vested interests. These values are often the only ones men have had any chance to develop. They are unconsciously acquired habits rather than choices. If we take the dogmatic view that what is essential to men's interests, whether they are interested in it or not, is all that need concern us morally, then we run the risk of violating democratic values. We may become manipulators or coercers, or both, rather than persuaders within a society in which men are trying to reason together and in which the value of reason is held in high esteem. What I am suggesting is that by addressing ourselves to issues and to troubles, and formulating them as problems of social science, we stand the best chance, I believe the only chance, to make reason democratically relevant to human affairs in a free society, and so realize the classic values that underlie the promise of our studies.[56]

Concluding *The Sociological Imagination* on such an abstract note left Mills in a political lurch. Since social science itself serves as an interest group, in the very process of professionalization it diminishes both human compassion and scientific understanding. Despite this overwhelming contradiction, it was thoroughly within the Columbia University spirit to think of the social scientist as a vanguard of the intelligentsia, a sector apart, capable of bringing about social change and rendering social justice. Mills makes no appeals for organizing revolutionary parties, for guerrilla warfare or armed insurrection, and no appeals to bureaucratic or legislative reforms. Quite the contrary: he explicitly rejects all such external class attempts at change as a breakdown of the sociological imagination. And this imagination, decoded, becomes higher education, especially the classical and humanistic traditions.

If Mills opposes yielding social science to a higher form of bureaucratic technology, he also opposes abandoning the field in the name of social change and social justice. The intrinsic political benefits of social science underscore his conception of the field. He sees sociology as variety in human experience, rather than as handmaiden of political parties. In that sense, the book is a throwback to the Saint-Simonian vision of social science as creating possibilities for a world of thirty million Shakespeares and Newtons. From that inspiration stems Mills's assumption that social science should combat bureaucracy and ignorance alike. Ultimately, Mills offers an Enlightenment vision in which the intelligentsia once again perform a role as agents of social change and political criticism.

The fury in the responses to *The Sociological Imagination* undoubtedly rested on its second and third chapters. The second contains the well-known critiques of Talcott Parsons and "grand theory," and translates Parsons's statements in the *Social System* into "plain English." Underlying Mills's critique of Parsons was criticism of general theory. Mills had a root belief that the Parsonian approach is merely to catalogue while ignoring many structural features of human society.[57] When Parsons delineated the sphere of sociological interest as distinct from and beyond the reach of political science and economics, he made a number of assumptions about the nature of social order that were anathema to Mills. Beyond his suspicion of the conservative implications of the Parsonian approach, Mills was inherently antagonistic to systematic idealism. Just as Dewey had revolted against the philosophical formalism of Royce, so Mills rebelled against sociological formalism. The overwhelming repudiation of formalism is at the root of the pragmatic tradition; and the pragmatic tradition underwrites Mills's critique of Parsons.

The critique of Parsons was undertaken in seriousness but without bitterness. Mills graciously says that his literary-grammatical exercise is an attempt "to help out a little because these are very good ideas." In fact, many of the ideas in grand theory were standard to the field. Parsons never responded directly to Mills, although earlier, in 1957, he had written an extended criticism of *The Power Elite*. In it he pointed out that Mills spoke like a nostalgic Jeffersonian liberal, but failed to banish the inherent dilemma of the individualistic tradition in American thought—the need for both collective action and personal freedom.[58] Whether this critique can be called representative of Parsons's attitude to Mills is hard to say. We know that Mills appreciated Parsons's critique for its sobriety, so it is unlikely that his own comments were intended as intellectual revenge.

While Mills reflects a certain playful lightheartedness about grand theory, he is deadly serious about "abstracted empiricism." Chapter 3 is essentially a critique of a doyen of quantitative sociology, Paul Lazarsfeld.[59] Mills says that Lazarsfeld initially defined sociology as a methodological specialty per se and, that therefore he saw the sociologist as simply a methodologist, by tautological sleight of hand.[60] To Mills's way of thinking, Lazarsfeld's abstracted empiricism converts all individual behavior into social patterns. By definition, sociology implies collective work on large numbers of things or people. Mills contends that Lazarsfeld assigns sociology the task of converting philosophy into science through the method of methodology. An inversion occurs: methodology is transformed into method, and the sociologist is transformed into a person providing methodology for all other social sciences.

In Mills's view, Lazarsfeld no less than Parsons, albeit in quantitative rather than systemic terms, is advocating a kind of sociological imperialism—a world in which the sociologist is indispensable to the work of social analysis. He translates social theory into the systematic collection of variables useful in interpreting statistical findings. Mills's critique is also methodological in its essence; namely, that only a pluralistic vision is ample enough to cover all experimental conditions. No single method, quantitative or otherwise, can respond to all problem-solving needs. One must be concerned with social problems themselves, not just the problems of research.[61] Whether this critique fitted Lazarsfeld went unanswered. Mills's colleagues at Columbia seemed too stunned—or indifferent—to register any response.

Mills takes appreciative note of those sociological empiricists like Lazarsfeld who preface their work with summaries of previous work on the problem being discussed, but he does not feel that these gestures quite measure up to the needs of sociology as a historical as well as analytical discipline. Mills does not deny the need to do research with precision, for he is thoroughly aware that sociological work is usually presented in the form of careful and elaborate hypotheses, documented by detailed information. But he does argue for pluralization of methodology rather than a division of intellectual labor between sociologists who are methodologists and those who are theorists. For Mills, when it comes down to it, abstracted empiricism and grand theory alike represent two versions of the same polarity: both inappropriately separate method and theory. As a result, sociology is robbed of content on behalf of false dichotomies.[62]

Mills's attack on Parsons's grand theory may have irritated his supporters, but it was within the tradition of academic behavior. His review of Lazarsfeld was quite another matter. Here Mills had violated an unwritten rule. He had criticized a senior colleague in his own department. As much concern about form as content seemed to be involved in this aspect of the controversy over *The Sociological Imagination*.

Lazarsfeld made two comments about the matter: one in a letter to Mills, the other in a revised Foreword to *What College Students Think*, edited by Rose Goldsen and others. Both make it quite clear that Lazarsfeld was more annoyed by Mills than upset by the contents of the critique. His letter concludes with an air of resignation: "Well, I suppose that the damage is done." Whether the "damage" referred to is the publication of *The Sociological Imagination* as such or its unflattering portrait of Lazarsfeld is not clear.

> I was so harassed the last few weeks before my departure [Lazarsfeld wrote Mills] that I could not get in touch with you. I am leaving on Sunday, and

will be back at the end of September. . . . As far as your book goes, I could only read the chapter dealing with me. While I am still very eager to do some joint work with you on it, I am not as optimistic about that as I was before. I just don't know whether you select your examples for the sake of rhetorical effects or because you have not the time to follow other people's work in detail. . . . Well, I suppose that the damage is done and we might talk about it all over at the beginning of October when I shall be back in town.[63]

Mills took private pleasure at the irony of Lazarsfeld criticizing him for not taking the work of others seriously, then admitting that his own response to *The Sociological Imagination* is based exclusively on one chapter of the book—the one about himself.

In his February 1960 Foreword to *What College Students Think*, Lazarsfeld was no longer inhibited by departmental considerations or other constraints. He argued that *The Sociological Imagination* was in the same category as Pitirim Sorokin's book *Fads and Foibles in Sociology*; both spoke out against all empirical research. Lazarsfeld turned Mills's critique of empiricism into an assault on research. One need only contemplate how much survey research in antiquity would have enhanced our understanding of history to agree with Lazarsfeld that Sorokin's position is foolish. The commentary on Mills pointedly, even acerbically, linked Mills with Sorokin, as if the criticism on methodological grounds was not barbed enough.

> For the sake of completeness [Lazarsfeld wrote] I have to mention one more recent critic who seems to promote a kind of sophisticated commercialism. C. Wright Mills has objected to detailed studies of specific problems as exemplified by this book. His starting point is the fact that modern man is troubled. Someone must give the answers to all the problems we face. The sociologist is the one who should do it, with the help of a distinct quality, sociological imagination, "that journalists and scholars, artists and publics, scientists and editors are coming to expect." But, alas, today's sociologists are "failing to meet the cultural expectations that are coming to be demanded of them." We sociologists would all like to have and to satisfy such a distinguished clientele. (Incidentally, one cannot "demand expectations"; presumably, expectations are held and answers are demanded.) But how to do it? Unfortunately, Mills does not give very definite advice. He asks that sociologists have concern for the "human variety" and he is confident that "when we understand social structures and structural changes as they bear upon more intimate scenes and experiences, we are able to understand the causes of individual conduct and feelings. . . . Kings who have wanted to philosophers' stone or immediate cures for currently incurable diseases have usually advanced charlatanism not knowledge.[64]

The rupture between Mills and Lazarsfeld, which began a decade earlier at the bureau, had become serious and permanent. Lazarsfeld had sponsored Mills's arrival at Columbia from Maryland, and had spent a decade retooling him for the wonders of computer technology, sharing a considerable amount of work with him. In part because of this, Rose Goldsen, both a student of Lazarsfeld and a past co-worker of Mills, sought to soften the rupture when she sent Mills a copy of the Foreword. "I am enclosing a copy of this Foreword with my comments and a memorandum I just sent to him on the subject. I think both will interest you. I trust your judgment enough to believe that you will be more amused than irritated with him."[65] In point of fact, Mills was nei- ther amused nor moved to answer. He was far less tranquil about Lazars- feld and his research than was Goldsen some years later when she learned that Lazarsfeld had underwritten the National Broadcasting Corporation's whitewash of television violence and its impact on chil- dren.[66] Mills wrote to Goldsen:

> I have never—contrary to Professor Lazarsfeld's statement—objected to detailed studies of specific problems. On the contrary, I've done a few myself and I welcome such by others. In fact, I am just now in the middle of a quite empirical long-term job of work. I do not of course think such childish comment worthy of public answer. Such little backhand nonsense I've come to expect these days. But I do want you personally to know that I am very sorry that your book *What College Students Think* has now to be the vehicle for such dogmatic silliness.[67]

But that was not quite the end of the matter. Goldsen sent a carefully balanced appraisal of the Foreword to Lazarsfeld. Considering that she was once Lazarsfeld's secretary, no less than Mills's research associate, her comments on the Foreword must be reckoned as courageous. While chiding Mills's *The Sociological Imagination* for "missing the point by asking social scientists only to continue to observe agglomerations, fore- going the equally important need to say what the components of the ag- glomerations are," she argued with Lazarsfeld that Mills's point was not simply

> an assertion that sociologists must solve the pressing problems which con- front mankind. . . . This is *not* Mills' point. He asks sociologists to turn their attention to the problems which beset mankind rather than channel their energies into efforts which can result only in the recapitulation of de- tailed accounts of banalities. This is a reasonable plan. It makes sense. It says the sociologist is not the social bookkeeper; and conversely, that social bookkeepers are not sociologists. Mills does not urge that we dispense with the U.S. census. He says that census-taking is not sociology. And in my opinion he is right.[68]

Lazarsfeld had been the principal investigator for a number of im- portant research projects which were under the direct supervision of Mills, from the reformation of education at the University of Chicago in the post-Hutchins period to propaganda and its impact on radio listening habits. In the late 1940s, Lazarsfeld clearly perceived Mills as a major asset to the Bureau of Applied Research. From his viewpoint Mills in the 1950s was a prodigal son who had strayed from the field. Those who convert from one style of work or thought to another are more likely to be condemned for moving from virtue to vice than praised for exercising intellectual independence.

The intensity of feeling generated within the sociology department at Columbia over publication of *The Sociological Imagination* is an accurate barometer of the power of orthodoxy when the book appeared. Its publication had roughly the same impact as a critique of Thomas Aquinas might have had within Catholic circles in the post-canonization period. (Indeed, the struggles in Columbia's Department of Sociology had some characteristics of the schisms between Augustinians and Thomists at the University of Paris in the late fourteenth century.) Mills's book involved nothing less than an assault from within the academy on the basic assumptions of a department which had become the center of social research and the major producer of graduate students since the Second World War. The competition between Columbia and Harvard sociologists dated from the prewar period. But the internecine struggle represented a break within; a dissolution of a long-standing "gentlemen's agreement" that elevated positivism to the status of orthodoxy. This, more than anything else, explains the intensity of Lazarsfeld's reaction to Mills.

ᴄᴏᴏ

While *The Sociological Imagination* did violence to certain presumed rules of interpersonal department demeanor, in its general contours it continued a tradition of social criticism common to sociologists. The sociological critique has always been more intense than the criticism of sociology by outsiders. The work of Lynd and later of Mills is characterized by the most intimate concerns for sociological reformation. In this sense, their work differs markedly from the efforts of Columbia humanists like Barzun and Schapiro, who clearly held sociology in contempt, and who saw behavioral science as akin to phrenology. That members of the sociological profession, even outside Columbia, could not or would not credit his motives, much less his achievement, left Mills with a permanent sense of estrangement, not simply from his peers at the university but from the field as such. And it was an alienation from which he never quite recovered.

There was a definite difference between English and American responses to the book. For the most part, the English either thought the book irrelevant or took umbrage at its contents. The bluntness of Mills's language, the directness of his expression, the *American* qualities of the book, seemed to irritate even those English critics favorably disposed to Mills on intellectual grounds.

The review by Peter Willmott in *Universities Quarterly* is typical. He agreed that *The Sociological Imagination* offered a "powerful case," but Willmott simply could not abide Mills's style, the one aspect of the work which Mills placed most credence in. Like many British commentators, Willmott called Mills overly aggressive on the subject of social science and the United States, and found that he was "offensively rude about some of his fellow social scientists." He admitted that the book as a whole was clear and well argued, and that Mills's concern for American social science was a proper follow up to his earlier researches in *White Collar*. Speaking of Mills's first success, he added: "Even though his critical barbs may be fun, they make a mountain of speculation out of a small bit of evidence." Willmott concluded by urging a return to what Mills referred to as "abstracted empiricism."[69]

The Willmott review, while not especially distinguished, nonetheless exemplifies the British sense of style in contrast to the American sense of content. Even social critics like Richard Hoggart, writing in *The Observer*, could not resist mentioning, in an exceedingly favorable review, that Mills's prose was "coarse but direct, passionate and rhetorical."[70] Other British reviewers shared a distinct animosity for the rough style if not the substance of what Mills was offering. A. H. Halsey, writing the *Universities and Left Review*, observed that liberalism and socialism are more than explanations of historical conditions: they are in fact moral alternatives. But his essential point is that sociology in Britian was so delinquent that when the book appeared in early 1960, there was hardly a chair in a major university for sociologists, with most of the leading social ideas coming from people working in government and regional agencies.[71] As a result, *The Sociological Imagination*, reflecting as it does considerations of academic status and professional rewards, was hardly calculated to make a big impact on the British welfare-labor context. Charles Madge, writing in *The New Statesman*, perhaps best summed up the socialist sensibility toward sociology. "If sociology is imaginative, so much the better. But for myself I would no more put it at the summit of imaginative activity than, with Comte, at the summit of scientific activity."[72] Indeed, Mills's ideas are probably more relevant in Britain in the 1980s than they were twenty years earlier.

It was inevitable that more than a few British reviewers would miss the forest for the trees and see Mills's effort as a left-wing diatribe. One such reviewer, Julius Gould, writing in *The Socialist Commentary*, thought that *The Sociological Imagination* would intoxicate the devout circles of *Universities and Left Review* but have no impact on academic circles. Gould's remarks come close to expressing the marrow of British conservative opinion.

> Mills is a splendid self-appointed "outsider." He is full of rhetoric on all subjects—especially "power." He is deeply hostile to "mass society"; he

is an active user of the "alienation" ploy—that fashionable whimper of the expresso radical. And of course he depicts American society (and in this book American thought) in a light which endears him to the quarter-baked, the envious and the frightened. . . . The case for social science does not rest upon its power to rescue "alienated" man from modern perils. It rests upon the stimulus it gives its students and in its practical application in a variety of fields.[73]

The resemblance between the book Gould thought he was reviewing and the real book is so remote that one is hard-pressed to explain Gould's tone. A more subtle, indeed fundamental, criticism of the book was made by Terry Cliff in *Isis*. While sympathetically outlining the main tenets of *The Sociological Imagination*, he quite properly called Mills to task for equating armchair theorizing with conservative ideology, noting that such types of theorizing are just as compatible with conflict theory as with consensus theory.[74] But in the heat generated by Edward A. Shils's review, such meaningful critiques were, sadly, ignored.

Edward Shils's review in *Encounter* was the harshest attack on the book. Although he had met Mills only once, for "five minutes and ten years ago [1950],"[75] the level of Shils's animosity can hardly be attributed to simple intellectual disagreement.

> Imagine a burly cowpuncher on the long, slow ride from the Panhandle of Texas to Columbia University, carrying in his saddle-bag some books which he reads with absorption while his horse trots along. Imagine that among the books are some novels of Kafka, Trotsky's *History of the Russian Revolution*, and the essays of Max Weber. Imagine the style and imagery that would result from the interaction of the cowboy student and his studies. Imagine also that *en route* he passes through Madison, Wisconsin, that seat of a decaying populism, and that on arriving at his destination in New York, he encounters Madison Avenue, that street full of reeking phantasies of the manipulation of the human will and of what is painful to America's well-wishers and enjoyable to its detractors. Imagine the first Madison disclosing to the learned cowpuncher his subsequent political mode, the second an object of his hatred. The end result of such an imaginary grand tour would be a work like *The Sociological Imagination*.[76]

Mills's initial reaction, as indicated in the marginalia of his copy of the Shils review, was predictably angry: "slander, exploitation of select reality elements plus foolish stereotyping for defamation of my *person*." He wrote to Charles Page, editor of *The American Sociological Review*, who had assigned Shils to review the book in that official publication of the American Sociological Association.

> Shils does seem very busy, doesn't he? You know, I don't know the man, met him once I think for five minutes. Why does he hate me so? His re-

view is really the most vulgar thing I have seen of any book. Full of stuff about "the McCarthy of sociology" and "cowboys from the panhandle." Surely, this is not up to professional discourse. But then I suppose one must put up with this sort of silliness. Anyway, the thing to do is get on with the next one, and forget such a "profession" as this one.[77]

It is hard to know whether Mills meant Shils's profession of animosity or the state of sociology. In acknowledging receipt of the review from Melvin Lasky, editor of *Encourter*,[78] Mills responded by indicating that he would make no response to Shils, despite Lasky's offer to hold space in reserve for that purpose.

I think it best to make no reply. In fact, as an experienced editor it must be clear to you that no reply of any intellectual worth is possible to such silliness. In the first half of the review he simply abuses me personally and ignorantly (I haven't been in Texas for twenty years, except to lecture once or twice; I am rather frightened of horses and certainly wouldn't attempt to ride one, etc.). In the second half, he seems quite fully to accept his own paraphrase of my notion of the sociological imagination, after it's been put into his own pious cliches. This you call reviewing?[79]

The Shils review became something of a cause célèbre within American sociological circles. When Shils had been asked to review the book for *The American Sociological Review*, he had accepted the assignment without informing Charles Page of his previous assignment for *Encounter*. Mills felt that this was a serious violation of academic protocol: once over the coals was sufficient. Page agreed. In a series of letters to Mills, he helped to resolve at least one part of the Shils–Mills debate.

The Mills–Shils situation seems to be a fiasco. I had no idea that Shils had written a review for another journal; if this is the case, the established policy makes him ineligible as a reviewer for the *ASR*. Hence my letter to *Encounter*, a copy of which is enclosed. Personally, at this point I hope that *Encounter* intends to run his piece; finding a presumably suitable alternative reviewer will be a tough job but a delight in comparison with what has transpired on this matter to date. As you know, however, I am chagrined about the inordinate delay.[80]

At the same time he also wrote to the editors of *Encounter* asking for clarification of the situation. When such "clarification" came in the form of the review itself, Page, an exceptionally fair-minded person, again wrote to Mills assuring him that the book would be assigned to another reviewer.

I have just heard from Shils that he is indeed writing a review of *The Sociological Imagination* for *Encounter*. In replying to his letter and in response to his specific question, I indicated that you had informed me about the *Encounter* review. (I also assured him that you in no way suggested or implied that he should not review your book for the *ASR*.) I hope very much that this was not the disclosure of what you regard as a confidential matter. Under the particular circumstances, I saw no alternative. Of course, Shils is ineligible to review *The Sociological Imagination* for the *ASR*. I am now desperately trying to find another person.[81]

Although Mills decided to make no response to Shils, he did express to Lasky the hope that his "friends in England will write letters." He might have had in mind supporters like Tom Bottomore, Ralph Miliband, and Asa Briggs. He also added: "Would it not be a fine thing if my publisher buys an advertisement and rebalances the picture for the readers to interpret?"[82] Oxford University Press did in fact take a full-page advertisement in Lasky's *Encounter*. But that hardly closed the matter. In fact, only a direct response might have quieted Shils and the talk over the review. As it was, by the time the next round took place, this time over the posthumous *Power, Politics and People*, Shils was confronting a deceased adversary.

Why didn't Mills respond directly? To begin with, he envisioned himself as a poor polemicist. He responded to critics only rarely, and then, elliptically. But more important, by the time *The Sociological Imagination* appeared, and certainly by the middle of June 1960, his concerns had shifted dramatically. The inner light of professional sociology had given way to the beam of professional revolution, especially as it shone on Latin America and the Castro revolution. It was, then, a lack of interest rather than failure of nerve that was involved. Mills's refusal to respond to Shils's review represents his final disaffiliation from professionalism in sociology.

The generally severe reviews in the British media were countered by the generally favorable responses in the American periodical literature and newspapers. The American "celebration" of *The Sociological Imagination* was begun on May 14, 1959, in that most unlikely of places, *The Wall Street Journal*, and by that most conservative of men, John Chamberlain. He found it "one of the most exhilarating books of its kind," and thoroughly enjoyed the critique of sociology—both its grand theory and its abstracted empiricism.[83] Although he was pleased to see the book on the "dreary academic horizon," Chamberlain sensed that Mills's book, unlike Sorokin's *Fads and Foibles*, was not so much a condemnation of the social sciences as a special sort of quiet celebration. A studied, misplaced concreteness was characteristic of conservative support for Mills throughout his beleaguered career. Russell Kirk, already a key figure in the new conservative movement, writing ten days later in the *Chicago Tribune*, saw Mills as a forceful and lucid writer who made penetrating observations and tellingly denounced the bureaucratic ethic.[84] On the other hand, while recognizing Mills's appreciation of the humanistic literature, Kirk saw Mills as a descendant of Robert A. Nisbet and Sorokin. Yet the book was, in many ways, the antithesis of the sort of conservative critique provided in Nisbet's *The Idea of Community* or Sorokin's *Fads and Foibles*, offering neither panacea nor condemnation of human society.

Mills also received good notices in two erstwhile-liberal publications: *The Atlantic Monthly* and *Harper's*. The latter contained a review by Paul Pickrel which was particularly noteworthy for its observation that intellectuals have, strangely, become observers rather than actors in American society. His analysis of Mills was equally appreciative of the sociological and general audiences *The Sociological Imagination* aimed to reach.

> Mills' thesis is very simple: he believes that society exists and is worth taking seriously. Or, to put it another way, he believes that sociologists ought to be responsible people. Stated in that way, nothing could be more obvious; yet, what Mills has to say is by no means trivial, for he is combating major tendencies in contemporary attempts to portray society. He thinks that sociologists should be boldly pushing forward to try to understand and interpret and criticize society but that they are in fact pusillanimously taking shelter in two safe but insignificant shelters, which he labels with the words "psychologism" and "scientism."[85]

Given his mood of professional estrangement, the sociological reviews of *The Sociological Imagination* were far more sympathetic than Mills probably expected. In part, that was a consequence of the selection of reviewers. Everett C. Hughes, one of the great men of American social science, certainly a pioneer in the "Chicago school" of ethnography, reviewed the book for *The New Republic*. He viewed Mills's book as "primarily an essay on political philosophy." And while he considered Mills's use of *The Sociological Imagination* in analyzing what was going on among his brethren as "uncanny," he was not quite as pleased with the broadsides about Parsons and Lazarsfeld, because they "give comfort to those who welcome an excuse to attack social science from either a left or a right flank."[86]

The other notable sociological reviews were those by Wilson Record, in the *American Quarterly*,[87] and more significantly, by Dennis Wrong (a Columbia graduate and a student of all its people, mainliners and marginals alike) in *Commentary*.[88] Both struck the same note of positive ambiguity. Wrong's analysis of political bias in the social sciences is provocative enough to merit a discussion itself.[89] But from our point of view, the important element in the review is his appreciative but tempered support of Mills's critique of the styles and dominant schools of work in contemporary sociology. His nervous "clarifications" of Mills provide some rather sharp insights into Mills's weaknesses in carrying forth his own manifesto. Wrong appreciates how much Mills is in his métier as a critic, and how difficult it is for him to realize his program in scholarship:

> Mills has always made his most telling points when he is opposing a point of view that has been stated with sufficient clarity and intelligence to make it impossible to dismiss it in its least convincing form. In taking on Parsons and Paul Lazarsfeld, Mills chooses the most able spokesmen for Grand Theory and Abstracted Empiricism respectively. As a result, his own arguments are sharper and more probing and the frequent lapses into rhetoric and journalistic purple patches that mar his other books are less in evidence. Mills' gift is largely for synthesis, for sketching in the outlines of the whole, rather than for careful, close reasoning. His books are full of exciting vistas, imaginative suggestions pointing to overlooked connections in social life, but he invariably fails to follow these up in any rigorous fashion. For example, *The Power Elite* provides us with no more than a starting-point for the analysis of power in American society: Mills tells us *who* the decisionmakers and powerholders are, but, as I argued in the September, 1956, issue of *Commentary*, he neglects to discuss in detail *what* sort of things they decide and what *interests* they serve. He seems to hold assumptions about these latter dimensions of power that remain hidden.[90]

Wrong's comment reflects not only a sociological uneasiness, but also a traditional liberal discomfort. There is so much in Mills that is transitional between old Left and New Left, between old and new socialist verities. It was difficult, if not impossible, for sensitive scholars who identified with anti-communism, like Wrong, to cope fully with Mills as a pivotal figure in the transformation in the political life of America during the last stages of the Eisenhower decade. The task of "self-critical" social science had hardly jelled professionally, much less politically. The younger social scientists of the time were in the anomalous position of having to choose between newfound radicalism and professional respectability, between going into the political fray the way the intellectual ancestors of Mills had done or going into professional careers. It was not so much a matter of left or right as of fear that the kind of macrosociological emphasis Mills offered might disturb an intellectual equilibrium based upon functionalism that the field of sociology had come to rest upon. Yet people like Wrong, who themselves wished to play a professional role, could not but be enamored of and responsive to Mills's style, if not exactly his message.

Wrong's reaction to *The Sociological Imagination* is typical of the best criticism. He chides Mills for exhorting sociologists to think in historical and comparative terms while failing precisely to make historical observations (on fascism, capitalism) or comparative analysis (e.g., of power functions in Great Britain and the United States). The burden of his review is summed up thus:

> There is a striking discrepancy between Mills' own work and the admirable conception of what sociology ought to be. To begin with, his books are surprisingly diffuse and repetitive if measured against the altogether fascinating discussion of his methods of work . . . in spite of these exhortations I find his own studies of contemporary America lacking in historical depth and comparative perspective. . . . And yet *The Sociological Imagination* is incredibly rich in ideas. It is impossible not to feel a sense of personal gratitude to Mills for having dispelled the air of make-believe that clings to contemporary sociology, the dominating pretense that its practitioners are skilled scientists when their work so often falls below the standards of the most old-fashioned kind of scholarship.[91]

Wrong was echoing an oft-repeated complaint, that sociology simply was not living up to par, was not achieving its intellectual mandate—its self-declared mandate at that. While Mills later turned to a keener historical and comparative framework, when he did so the consequence was not so much the enrichment as the abandonment of the field. Thus Wrong's implicit question of whether sociology had the inner resolve or the outer reach to effectively deal with the moral demands laid upon the field in *The Sociological Imagination* was left unanswered.

The orthodox socialist had good reason to be concerned with this latent sociological orthodoxy in Mills. Sidney M. Peck, writing in *Studies on the Left*, a pioneer forerunner of postwar New Left magazines, sang Mills's praises in terms not unlike those of *The Wall Street Journal* review. He, too, was especially pleased that Mills had laid bare the emptiness of grand theory. He offered a loud "amen" to Mills's "revelation" that the academic structure was committed to the alienation of its most sensitive thinkers. But while Peck, a sociologist himself, was pleased with the critique of standard social science, he was mightily displeased by the last sections of the book, which, in fact, attempted to reconstruct sociology. Curiously, what has become the most universally praised part of *The Sociological Imagination*—the Appendix, "Intellectual Craftsmanship,"—was condemned as offering "paternal advice from one who has made it to young social scientists of radical bent who may also wish to become a success." He saw this Appendix as a fittingly flat conclusion of the "relatively weak closing chapters."[92]

In his own marginalia, Mills observed that this criticism was unfair. Indeed it was characteristic of the emerging New Left to interpret any form of advice in pathological terms. It is curious that Mills, at the height of his estrangement from sociology at Columbia, was nonetheless viewed by younger radicals as someone who had "made it," someone in the sociological establishment. Later revisionist sociologists who have made Mills a mythic forerunner of this New Left would be well advised to pay closer attention to the critics of his time. Peck's review harkens back to a line of reasoning which Mills had abandoned a decade earlier in *New Men of Power*. Peck argued against the mass-society hypothesis, which Mills held firm to, and for a class-society hypothesis of a Marxist sort. The workers, he asserted, constituted a highly organized public, and the "future of the sociological imagination" hung together or dissolved with the future of organized labor in the United States. For Peck, Mills had provided a manifesto without answers. The answers presumably resided in a working class that Mills had already abandoned as incapable of exercising a "vanguard" role.

The review by Arthur K. Davis, in *Monthly Review*, is very much in the same genre. An expatriate American sociologist who moved to Canada, and who indeed became a vociferous Canadian nationalist, Davis seemed pleased by the critique of the sociological profession. For Davis, Mills's book was a proclamation "in rolling periods that the emperor has no clothes." But while he was delighted by the condemnation of Parsons's "idealism" and Lazarsfeld's "empiricism" and found the broadside squarely on target, he was concerned that Mills did not follow the implications of his own belief that scientists must control their own means of research in some collective way. The problem for Davis, and for the Left generally, was less with sociology than with capitalism.

> First, it is scarcely conceivable that scientists could control, even indirectly, their own means of production except in a socialist society. Second, even though bureaucratic social science has great intrinsic limitations, as Mills makes exceedingly plain, this does not preclude its having socially useful roles within those limitations—provided that the bureaucracies it serves are democratically run for genuinely humanitarian purposes. There is the real rub. Science, both natural and social, is increasingly twisted in our latter-day capitalist society to anti-social ends, chiefly commercial and military. Does it not follow that scientists who would best serve their professional fields should join some progressive political movement to revise those anti-social policies and the institutions responsible for them?[93]

The Left generally was disturbed that Mills did not include in *The Sociological Imagination* an analysis of Marxism, or for that matter a manifest analysis of what was wrong with American society as a social system. Peck, Davis, and some of his colleagues at Columbia such as Meyer Schapiro found this lapse in the book particularly disturbing. Schapiro, for example, in reflecting on his own reading of the book, pointed out: "I read the typescript of his book on the sociological imagination and I remember something of our discussion of it, particularly his answer to my comment that the book lacked a consideration of Marxism as an alternative to the concepts and methods of Parsons and Lazarsfeld—'that would have to be another book,' he said."[94] While the American critics on the left were bemoaning the absence of an analysis of Marxism, George Lichtheim, writing quite clearly from the viewpoint of a Weimar German democrat, noted in *Commentary* that "the great advantage which Mr. Mills—notwithstanding a certain strain of naiveté in his political thinking—possesses over those liberals who stand further to the Right, is that he has read and assimilated Marx. This is not said in order to give offense, but simply as a statement of fact."[95] In point of fact, Mills had hardly even read Marx by 1959; and as for assimilating him, his earlier view of Marx's writings was so much through the prism of pragmatism that one might well argue that his understanding of Marx never really got beyond that of Sidney Hook and the American pragmatic tradition of the thirties. In Mills's world, up to and including *The Sociological Imagination*, Marxism was a remote input, at most—part of the radical tradition of native American life. The Left had solid grounds to be concerned with Mills's failure to take Marxism seriously. In a sense Mills always remained, politically, a child of populism, and intellectually, an offspring of pragmatism. Marxism was barely a whisper, much less a shout, which may explain why he found the special nativism of the guerrilla-led national liberation movements so attractive.

The upshot of *The Sociological Imagination* for Mills—whether as a result of the inner light he shed on the field or the external beams directed toward him by the profession—was increasing focus on problems of social change and political revolution, and decreasing linkage with the profession. The themes with which Mills concerned himself for his remaining three years were of little concern to his colleagues. This redirection of energies and a corresponding acerbic tone which crept into his work earned Mills the ridicule of his profession and destroyed the last vestiges of personal kindness or civility toward him that still existed at Columbia. Friendships that had endured for two decades crumbled. Mills insisted on becoming a man of the world, but in truth he was more like a man without a country. The man who coined the phrase "sociological imagination" soon became a man with an imagination devoid of sociology.

Mills never left Columbia. The opportunities were there, but the impulse to break the Columbia connection was never acted out. New York remained the American Mecca, the place sought by people living in all the other cities and states. It may seem odd, but this Texan "populist" was, by the early 1950s, converted into an "elitist." He not only wrote about those at the "top," but was quite content to be at the top professionally. A certain voyeuristic interest in the top remained characteristic of Mills. To move away from Columbia would have been to lessen his self-esteem. If he could never quite fit the mold, neither could he break that mold. *The Sociological Imagination* settled accounts with his Columbia adversaries; but through it all, the work, the voice, remained firmly those of someone quite at home in the world and the works of those he deemed it fit to freely criticize.

REFERENCES

1. Dwight Macdonald. *Discriminations: Essays and Afterthoughts, 1938-1974.* New York: Grossman Publishers/Viking Press, 1974, pp. 299–300.

2. C. Wright Mills to Hans Gerth, January 5, 1945.

3. C. Wright Mills. "Some Effects of Big Business and Smaller Business upon Civic Structure: A Report on Six Cities." Typescript submitted to John Blair, Director of Office of Reports, Smaller War Plants Corporation, Washington, D.C., May 1945. This project and its funds came with Mills from Maryland to Columbia.

4. C. Wright Mills to Robert K. Merton, October 25, 1944.

5. C. Wright Mills. "Leaders of Political Opinion [in Central City]." Typescript of discussion draft submitted to Paul F. Lazarsfeld, director of the Bureau of Applied Social Research, Columbia University, New York, May 18, 1946.

6. Paul F. Lazarsfeld to Theodore Abel, December 3, 1944.

7. C. Wright Mills to Robert K. Merton, April 10, 1954; Robert K. Merton to H. John Vincent, April 19, 1954.

8. C. Wright Mills. "The Study of the Social Structure and Personnel of Naval Research Establishments." Typescript submitted to A. H. Hausrath, director of Scientific Personnel, Office of Naval Research, Washington, D.C., February 1947.

9. See Seymour Martin Lipset, "The Department of Sociology," in *A History of the Faculty of Political Science at Columbia University*, by R. Gordon Hoxie et al. New York: Columbia University Press, 1955, pp. 284–303. Also see Daniel Bell, *The Reforming of General Education: The Columbia College Experience in Its National Setting.* New York and London: Columbia University Press, 1966, p. 296.

10. Theodore Abel to C. Wright Mills, final draft version, October 31, 1947.

11. Lazarsfeld to Abel.

12. C. Wright Mills, Clarence Senior, and Rose K. Goldsen. *The Puerto Rican Journey.* New York: Harper Bros. Publishers, 1950, pp. x–xi.

13. Robert K. Merton to C. Wright Mills, July 22, 1948.

14. Interview of Rose K. Goldsen with Irving Louis Horowitz, January 21, 1964. Also see her essay, "Mills and the Profession of Sociology," in *The*

New Sociology, edited by Irving Louis Horowitz. New York and London: Oxford University Press, 1964, pp. 88–93.

15. Mills, Senior, and Goldsen, p. 156.

16. C. Wright Mills to Robert K. Merton, October 5, 1949.

17. David Riesman to C. Wright Mills, January 3, 1952.

18. Lyman Bryson to C. Wright Mills, August 17, 1952.

19. Kurt H. Wolff to C. Wright Mills, April 1, 1953.

20. William Goode to Irving Louis Horowitz, April 25, 1976.

21. C. Wright Mills to Kurt H. Wolff, April 15, 1953.

22. T. C. McCormick to Robert F. Winch, March 29, 1951.

23. The "non-respondent," Paul F. Lazarsfeld, did send a letter to T. C. McCormick on May 21, 1951, explaining that he failed to respond only because of a trip to Europe. He noted: "I would of course be very eager to sponsor Wright Mills, whom I consider a valuable colleague and cooperative friend." But Mills's name had already been withdrawn in a letter from McCormick to Winch dated April 2, 1951.

24. John Useem to T. C. McCormick, February 27, 1957.

25. C. Wright Mills. "On Knowledge and Power." Reprinted in *Power, Politics and People*. New York and London: Oxford University Press, 1963, p. 607.

26. Lionel Trilling to C. Wright Mills, November 3, 1955.

27. C. Wright Mills to Lionel Trilling, November 7, 1955.

28. Lionel Trilling to C. Wright Mills, November 22, 1955.

29. C. Wright Mills to Dennis Wrong, September 23, 1956.

30. Seymour Martin Lipset and Neil J. Smelser. "The Setting of Sociology in the 1950's" (originally published in the *British Journal of Sociology*, 1959). In *Sociology: The Progress of a Decade*. Englewood Cliffs, N.J.: Prentice-Hall, 1961, pp. 1–13. [Note number 14 on Mills was written by Lipset; Smelser claims not to have known about it. In fact, the offending reference was deleted from the above compendium.]

31. For the best illustration of professional during this period, see the American Sociological Association–sponsored volume, *Sociology Today: Problems and Prospects*, edited by Robert K. Merton, L. Brown, and L. S. Cottrell, Jr. New York: Basic Books, 1959.

32. Maurice Stein and Arthur Vidich, eds. *Sociology on Trial*. Englewood Cliffs, N.J.: Prentice-Hall, 1963.

33. Alvin W. Gouldner. *The Coming Crisis of Western Sociology*. New York: Basic Books, 1970.

34. Robert S. Lynd. *Knowledge for What? The Place of Social Science in American Culture*. Princeton: Princeton University Press, 1939.

35. Jacques Barzun. *The House of Intellect*. London: Secker & Warburg, 1959.

36. Meyer Schapiro. "Style." In *Anthropology Today: An Encyclopedia Inventory*, edited by A. L. Kroeber. Chicago: The University of Chicago Press, 1953, pp. 287–312.

37. C. Wright Mills. *The Sociological Imagination*. New York and London: Oxford University Press, 1959, pp. 3–5, 9.

38. Lynd, pp. 221–22.

39. Mills, *The Sociological Imagination*, p. 9.

40. Lynd, p. 231.

41. Mills, *The Sociological Imagination*, pp. 9–10.

42. Lynd, p. 243.

43. Mills, *The Sociological Imagination*, p. 11.

44. *Ibid.*, pp. 188–89.

45. Kenneth Burke. *Permanence and Change*. New York: New Republic Books, 1936.

46. Mills, *The Sociological Imagination*, p. 215.

47. Lynd, p. 23.

48. *Ibid.*, p. 29.

49. Mills, *The Sociological Imagination*, p. 20.

50. Everett C. Hughes. "Can History Be Made?" *The New Republic*, June 22, 1959, pp. 30–31.

51. Mills, *The Sociological Imagination*, p. 143.

52. Lynd, pp. 224–25.

53. *Ibid.*, p. 250.

54. *Power, Politics and People: The Collected Essays of C. Wright Mills*, edited by Irving Louis Horowitz. New York and London: Oxford University Press, 1963, pp. 189–90.

55. Mills, *The Sociological Imagination*, p. 115.

56. *Ibid.*, p. 194.

57. *Ibid.*, pp. 25–49.

58. Talcott Parsons. "The Distribution of Power in American Society." *World Politics* 10, no. 1 (October 1957):123–43.

59. Mills, *The Sociological Imagination*, pp. 50–75.

60. *Ibid.*, p. 59.

61. *Ibid.*, p. 66.

62. *Ibid.*, pp. 74–75.

63. Paul F. Lazarsfeld to C. Wright Mills, June 8, 1959.

64. Paul F. Lazarsfeld. Foreword to *What College Students Think*, edited by Rose K. Goldsen, Morris Rosenberg, Robin M. Williams, and Edward A. Suchman. Princeton: D. Van Nostrand, 1960, p. 12.

65. Rose K. Goldsen to C. Wright Mills, April 1, 1960.

66. Rose K. Goldsen. "NBC's Make-Believe Research on Television Violence." *Transaction/SOCIETY* 8, no. 12 (1971): 28–35.

67. C. Wright Mills to Rose K. Goldsen, April 5, 1960.

68. Rose K. Goldsen to Paul F. Lazarsfeld, May 10, 1960.

69. Peter Willmott. Review of *The Sociological Imagination*. In *Universities Quarterly*, January 1960, pp. 92–95.

70. Richard Hoggart. "Nothing Like Leather." *The Observer*, September 6, 1959, pp. 3–4.

71. A. H. Halsey. "Sociological Imagination." *Universities and Left Review*, Autumn 1959, pp. 71–72.

72. Charles Madge. "The Politics of Truth." *The New Statesman*, September 5, 1959, pp. 281–82.

73. Julius Gould. "A Self-Appointed Outsider." *Socialist Commentary*, September 5, 1959, pp. 28–29.

74. Terry Cliff. "A Sense of Helplessness." *Isis*, December 2, 1959, pp. 29–31.

75. C. Wright Mills to Elizabeth Cameron, June 4, 1960.

76. Edward A. Shils. "Imaginary Sociology." *Encounter*, June 1960, pp. 77–80.

77. C. Wright Mills to Charles H. Page, April 1, 1960.

78. Melvin J. Lasky to C. Wright Mills, March 18, 1960.

79. C. Wright Mills to Melvin J. Lasky, April 1, 1960.

80. Charles H. Page to C. Wright Mills, April 4, 1960. See also Page's autobiography, *50 Years in the Sociological Enterprise*. Amherst: The University of Massachusetts Press, 1982, pp. 210–18.

81. Charles H. Page to C. Wright Mills, April 15, 1960.

82. C. Wright Mills to Melvin J. Lasky, April 1, 1960.

83. John Chamberlain. "The Job and Jargon of Sociology." *The Wall Street Journal*, May 14, 1959.

84. Russell Kirk. "Shrewd Knocks at Sociological Theories." *Chicago Tribune*, Book Review Section, Sunday supplement, May 24, 1959.

85. Paul Pickrel. "Images of Society." *Harper's Magazine*, June 1959, p. 88.

86. Hughes, "Can History Be Made?"

87. Wilson Record. "Of History and Sociology." *American Quarterly* 11, no. 3 (Fall 1959): 425–30.

88. Dennis Wrong. "The Failure of Sociology." *Commentary*, November 1959, pp. 87–88.

89. Dennis Wrong. "Political Bias and the Social Sciences." *Columbia Forum*. Fall 1959, pp. 12–15.

90. Wrong, ''The Failure of Sociology.''
91. *Ibid.*
92. Sidney M. Peck. ''Post-Modern Sociology.'' *Studies on the Left*, Fall 1959, pp. 71–74.
93. Arthur K. Davis. ''Sociology Without Clothes.'' *Monthly Review*, November 1959, pp. 256–63.
94. Meyer Schapiro to Irving Louis Horowitz, May 25, 1975.
95. George Lichtheim. ''Rethinking World Politics.'' *Commentary*, September 1959, pp. 249–57.

Sources

6

Pragmatism and the Revolt Against Formalism

[The pragmatists] were united in a common revolt against formalism which culminated in an emphasis on historical and cultural factors. . . . Their predilection in favor of history and culture as central concepts explains a good deal of their breadth.

Morton White, *Pragmatism and the American Mind*

IT HAS BEEN WISELY SAID that a man never really forgets his first love. This is true of intellectual matters no less than romantic affairs. Mills's first intellectual attraction was to pragmatism. When he was a young scholar, it was a way of life and a set of propositions about the nature of the world. From his first effort to his last unpublished writings he retained a lively interest in the social and intellectual values of pragmatism. Mills was the embodiment of Jamesian Man—complete with a heroic definition of self. Like William James, he invested his political beliefs with a highly personal content. He inveighed against American intervention in Latin America quite in the same way, and with the same motives, as James did in the Anti-Imperialist League. His faith in intellectual activity as the basic way out of the morass of power was articulated in a manner made famous by James's words: "Let intellectuals unite!" Mills's mistrust of narrow professionalism rings a familiar note to those acquainted with James's indictment of higher academicism. The similarities between Mills and James are so patently clear that it is disconcerting to see how thoroughly the critics have missed the connection.

At Texas in the 1930s, the pragmatic credo represented a strongly radicalizing set of beliefs in a fundamentalist environment. This was displayed in the central cast of intellectual characters with whom Mills came into contact. There was the naturalistic approach to religion, experimental views toward the learning process, experimental visions of scientific method, and the leveling of elites through citizen participation. The Chicago connection through Mills's mentors gave him a special sense of pragmatism—filtered through George Herbert Mead and onto the holy trinity of James, Peirce, and Dewey. It was Mead who first taught Mills the connection of communication to democracy. He noted that "the ideal of human society cannot exist as long as it is impossible for individuals to enter into the attitudes of those whom they are affecting in the performance of their own peculiar functions."[1] In other words, the larger picture of democracy is linked to the ways in which people relate to one another. Mills sought through pragmatism to connect the sociological imperatives of interaction to the democratic possibilities of naturalism. He sought to escape the arid formalism of European positivism; his early fascination with language issues certainly indicated an awareness of positivism.

Whether as a consequence of the dilatory procedures of his dissertation committee at Wisconsin, or simply because of a steady transformation of personal and professional priorities, Mills clearly lost interest in his dissertation on pragmatism after he left for the University of Maryland in mid-1941. This was so evident that Hans H. Gerth, Mills's principal adviser, feared that the dissertation would not be completed at all. He felt compelled to write Mills, as late as January 1942, urging him to finish his work on the dissertation without further delay. Gerth's letter clearly reveals streaks of paternalism, but the situation undoubtedly demanded such an approach. "It would be terrible if you could not come here in the summer. Try hard to write the thesis; come through with that stuff as soon as possible. Forget about the rest, we may have to go in due course, so first things first!"[2]

While Mills did provide Gerth with the necessary assurances, he wrote to another senior colleague at Wisconsin, Eliseo Vivas, saying that only the threat of losing his University of Maryland post prematurely was prompting him to finish his study of the pragmatists. Indeed, as early as December 1941 it is evident that Mills was more interested in getting on with what was to become *Character and Social Structure*, his Weberian statement coauthored with Gerth, than with paying any attention to the dissertation.

> I'm spending all summer in Madison [Mills wrote to Vivas]. I have to get the degree or lose my job. They make a great deal about that sort of thing here. Besides, just like you used to say about getting all stimulated and full of ideational matter in New York, well I feel that way about Madison—with you and Gerth. Gerth and I, you know, are doing a book—better not mention it, until he does. We signed up with a publisher the middle of this fall.[3]

In his later years, Mills rejected the liberal implications of pragmatism, seeing it as increasingly acquiescent and decreasingly critical of the powers that be. But even as he rejected pragmatic politics he held firm to pragmatism's naturalistic moorings. In a letter to E. A. Ross[4] during the time he was completing his dissertation, he enters into a lengthy assault on the twin evils of fatalism and mysticism, invoking the canons of pragmatism befitting a robust moral athlete. Mills spoke more like a pragmatist than an analyst of pragmatism as a system of thought.

> The pragmatic meaning of all this is that you become aware of where the bayonet is thrust from; you know the milieu across which it comes. You try to avoid being struck. But if you don't in fact know what part of the body to take the bayonet from, then you take it with eyes wide open. You make an *experience* out of it, even if it is your last. In desperate straits, the only frame of mind is: don't give a damn.[5]

The Maryland interlude, aside from affording Mills time to complete his dissertation, was essentially an opportunity for him to become aware of the Washington, D.C., political arena.[6] But still wrapped up in his dissertation, he saw pragmatism as a key element in this American political naiveté. The absence of a firm, clear foreign policy, the ad hoc characteristics of New Deal reform, and the absolute faith in experience as an adequate guidepost served to stimulate Mills's interest in alternatives. His initial contact with the Marxist tradition was either through Dewey's pragmatic criticism of Marxism or through German sociologists like Weber who were knowledgeable in, rather than affiliated with, Marxist doctrine. Mills showed not the slightest familiarity with the plethora of Marxian critiques of pragmatism which were not only available but in vogue prior to his own dissertation efforts on the pragmatists. Mills developed his analysis quite isolated from either communist or socialist criticism. As a double-edged consequence, his dissertation retains a remarkable freshness and freedom from dogmatism; but it also reveals a naiveté, posing issues in a vacuum, as if no one else had ever written on the subject of pragmatism.

Even Mills's earliest papers on the sociology of knowledge seem to owe more to the "apolitical" pragmatic Americans than to the "political" Europeans such as Marx and Mannheim.[7] That influence came a good deal later. For the most part, Mills's idea of the problem of language is "functionally linked to a system of social control," while the great dualism of European materialism and idealism is eschewed in favor of the Deweyan conversion of the "mental" as something "not understood apart from definitely social items." Mills's lifelong attachment for the sociologistic over and against the psychologistic derives from largely American sources.[8] This he makes quite clear in an early letter to Robert K. Merton acknowledging Merton's own efforts in the sociology of knowledge.

> I have been aware of your article in *The Scientific Monthly*. It displays a clear sensitivity to the problem controlling the ideas in "Language, Logic and Culture." I am very glad to receive independent verification from

you as to the genuine character of this problem. It may interest you to
know that it arose in my own mind before I had read any of the German
wissensozialogie. It came out of an examination of Charles S. Peirce and
John Dewey. For some two years now I have been engaged, on and off, in
extending certain contentions of American pragmatists in the direction of
a sociology of knowledge.[9]

In this same letter, Mills goes further in distinguishing and separating
himself from the European tradition, by claiming that his work "properly involves not only a typification of the intellectual sphere but a theory of social actions and of publics." This peculiar recourse to meliorative action of intelligent publics is clearly a pragmatic device to avoid the
pitfalls of a purely relativistic vision of the sociology of knowledge.

If Mills's support for naturalistic pragmatism was somewhat
hedged, even fudged, his opposition to an idealistic realism was crystal
clear. In a letter to Vivas, who did eventually abandon pragmatism for
spiritualism after World War II, Mills shakes his intellectual finger at the
older man.

Vivas, you have spoken of the higher life. I take it that the one chief component of such a special life is the readiness to bare one's soul and fangs to
another.

I don't go for the statement of god that you've given! . . . There are
too many men with their collars turned around who can point and say:
"see, Vivas believes in god." But they won't mean what you mean—because I know more about your other work and thinking that readers of
those two or three paragraphs don't.[10]

Mills was concerned not simply with pragmatism taking an idealistic
turn but with the tidal wave of theological absolutism such forms of the
pragmatic encouraged.

I feel that such shifts to the domain of religious terms at this time are tied
in with the general political revivalism that we are witnessing. Just watch a
flock of guys return from their flirtations with god after the war. I am analyzing several periodicals now, with a scheme to record certain shiftings,
making the thing more than an impression, objectifying observations on
intellectual movements. Now I do not say that your statement can be explained by the political revivalism. No. But I do think that there is a possibility that after the war, you might get grouped with writers whose work
can be so explained.[11]

Indeed, in *The Moral and the Ethical* Vivas so grouped himself—and
made clear a final break with naturalistic explanations.[12] Beyond that,
Vivas came to be aligned with precisely those conservative political tendencies in philosophy which temporarily buried the pragmatic movement
and its liberal sentiments.

In terms of space and structure, Mills's dissertation is more akin to a social history of American pragmatism than to an examination of the sociology of knowledge. The very choice of major and minor figures— Charles S. Peirce, William James, and John Dewey in the former category; John Fiske, Chauncey Wright, and Francis Ellingwood Abbot in the latter—follows the standard philosophic iconography of the prewar period. Indeed, the dissertation is on the institutionalization of professionalism in higher education, and the place of pragmatism in bringing this formal apparatus into being. In this, the dissertation is less concerned with the accuracy of pragmatic claims than with the efficacy of its powers in shaping policy.

Mills examines the major works of Peirce, James, and Dewey in an effort to explain their central conceptions in terms of their respective careers, publics, and general social-historical context. This is followed by a brief historical account of the transformation of higher learning and the professionalization of philosophy since 1860, which provides a social structural background for more detailed problems. Relevant features of the personal academic philosophy and the intellectual and biographical composition of the Metaphysical Club are presented to tease out problems of academic stratification. While many philosophic discussion societies flourished in New England, the most famous was the one Mills studied for his dissertation; the one organized in Cambridge, Massachusetts, in 1871 by Charles Peirce which included among its members William James, Oliver Wendell Holmes, Chauncey Wright, Nicholas St. John Green, John Fiske, and Joseph Warner.[13]

Mills finds the position of Peirce as a scientific technician and a philosophical outsider useful in reconstructing his own perspective. He examines the central aspects of Peirce's style of thinking: inquiry, doubt, belief, action, and sociality, the pragmatic maxim and logical realism. The publics and associates of William James are developed, and one of his key problems, the ''pragmatistic'' mediation of science and religion, Mills imputes to this system of analysis. The translation of the pragmatic maxim into the sphere of personal life-styles is considered in detail. From this vantage point it becomes clearer both how and why Mills internalized pragmatism as a way of life, even after abandoning it as a theoretically adequate system of thought.

Mills gives John Dewey's work the most extensive analysis. Four of his publics and several of his circles are presented; the foci of his attention from 1882 to 1939 are discussed and a full account of his career is given. Class, occupational, and demographic features of the American social structure are found to be relevant to an understanding of Dewey's generic perspective. All phases of his work are included in the analysis. Mills's major concern was with Dewey's theory of logic and its component conceptions. Significantly, the two works which Dewey wrote just prior to Mills's dissertation—*Logic: The Theory of Inquiry* (1938) and *Freedom and Culture* (1939)—had the greatest impact on Mills's early efforts to link language, logic, and culture.

Sociology and Pragmatism—as the dissertation was called when it was eventually published—contains so many elements of what Mills was at the time of writing and was yet to become that the act of sorting out these elements helps one resolve the puzzle of Mills. His dissertation is not simply dedicated to an understanding of Peirce, James, and Dewey, although admittedly the bulk of it covers precisely these three founding fathers of pragmatism. Rather, it is an analysis of the higher learning in America very much in keeping with the spirit of Thorstein Veblen.

The first part of the dissertation places the pragmatists in their university setting; it represents an attempt to develop a sociology of institutions. The second and third are the sociology of knowledge sections. That they were not yet meshed together is indicated by the fact that Mills himself remains ambiguous throughout about his own feelings toward pragmatism. So much is this the case that he felt compelled to prepare a commentary on the dissertation after its completion. This Postscript helped him not only to clarify his own assumptions about the world of pragmatism and the higher learning generally but above all to register his real doubts.

> This entire matter must wait upon an increase of the writer's knowledge of the political, economic, and social history of the United States since the Civil War as it may bear upon the conditions of the total intellectual life. The sort of knowledge really required can only come with a constant working of the facts over a considerable period and from many detailed studies. The lack of this sort of knowledge is a major reason for such deficiencies as these materials may have.[14]

While this exercise in self-criticism is candid and genuine, Mills failed to face another series of problems, equally genuine. The problems center around a thoroughgoing ambiguity as to what pragmatism meant sociologically: was it a commercialization of American culture or a democratization of that culture?[15] Both were, after all, varieties of the secular life. Such honest indecision about his intellectual underpinnings was to haunt Mills's formulations throughout his career.

His advisers' criticisms of the final draft of Mills's dissertation were of a perfunctory nature: they concerned Mills's atrocious spelling; his penchant for word invention, for example, "pragmaticism" rather than "pragmatism"; and general sloppiness in handling reference materials. Mills became recalcitrant on each of these points. He was especially vehement about the charge of word invention, quite properly claiming that Peirce and not he had invented "pragmaticism." While the dissertation could be subject to strong critique, the sorts of comments he had received represented, in his mind, pettifogging rather than analyzing.

In a sense, his powerful self-commentary represented his own evaluation of the weaknesses in the dissertation, a sort of back-handed final rebuke to his mentors rather than a concession to his dissertation committee.

Mills did consider publishing the dissertation, after he had completed his two efforts with Gerth, *From Max Weber* and *Character and Social Structure*. In a "publication agenda" prepared for Columbia University in July 1944 he includes: *"American Pragmatism: The Sociology of an Intellectual Movement*. With either Oxford, Vanguard, or the Columbia University Press. This will be delayed until all items above are completed, probably sometime in 1946."[16] Mills missed his timetable by twenty years. He did make some feeble efforts to submit his manuscript for publishing consideration, but after a distinct lack of response, he seemed more oriented toward forgetting the dissertation (and letting others forget it as well) than toward seeking a publisher. He had, after all, by the war's end become something of a full-fledged sociologist, and this unseemly expression of interest in pragmatic philosophy seemed out of keeping with his new Columbia image.

Mills's commentary on his dissertation appears as a Postscript in the published volume. It was written in part as a response to his dissertation committee, and in part to foreclose the need for a complete rewriting of the dissertation, which he could hardly have undertaken without digesting a great deal of new materials and methods. Yet the Postscript is not merely self-criticism, but also an implied critique of the sociological profession, or that portion of it which had not yet come to terms with pragmatism. It represents Mills's last thoughts on his dissertation as well as his first thoughts on an enterprise which remains open to future sociologists of knowledge. It is a noteworthy example of intellectual modesty, a characteristic infrequently associated with Mills's later and more extravagant literary mannerisms.

Mills openly acknowledges that his dissertation is incomplete, that he has failed to analyze George Herbert Mead, and that he has omitted a developmental scenario of how pragmatism has changed with respect to its phrasing of issues in the American social structure. He also admits his dissertation lacks any analysis of the idealist tradition within American thought, an idealism which is postclerical in nature. And he expresses his feeling, not unwarranted, that many of the important actors in American political life, from Henry Wallace to Rexford Tugwell, and in intellectual life, from Veblen to Mead, have not been properly accorded their place in the pragmatic world called the New Deal.[17]

But even at the end, having registered his self-criticism and acknowledged his last reflections on pragmatism, Mills remains terribly ambiguous about the pragmatic tradition. He observes that it is under attack from political as well as religious sources. Interestingly, he does not state whether those sources are conservative or radical—although he knew the literature well enough to realize that these critiques came from both sides. The Postscript is Mills's denouement with respect to philosophy; the final turning away from a philosophical literature to a sociological tradition. His summation is, therefore, not so much a prelude to more work in this area as a definitive statement of what will have to be done by others.

> There remains the present situation of pragmatism in America. Perhaps never before in its eighty years' existence has this style of thinking been so under attack as it has since the world crises which came to fruition in the late thirties. The attack has been in "spiritual" or "religious" terms and also on "political" grounds. No volume that in any sense could be called major has as yet resulted from these reactions. The personal and political reasons for such a course of events must be examined from a standpoint as removed from these reasons as is possible. To so examine it would offer the possibility of a fundamental understanding of the conditions for the future development of philosophy in the United States.[18]

Mills is arguing that pragmatism is part of the process of secularization in American life, specifically in American educational institutions. This secular process resulted from the transformation of American society from rural to urban, from small shopkeepers to large factory owners, and from elite to mass, as such changes pertained to education.

> The secularization of learning in America was not some vague mood and principle that was suffused through educational institutions. There was a set of rather specific social mechanics underlying and promoting the secularization, and they can be enumerated. . . . The secularization of the schools in the United States was not primarily due to any sudden or gradual turn *against* religion. It was due, negatively, to inter-sect conflict and, positively, to those middle class chances for ascent that were manifested by qualitative changes in the occupational structure.[19]

But secularization, over and against clericalization, was only one object of pragmatism. The second was specialization; that meant the development of the distinction between the expert and the amateur; the operational distinction between the place of technical learning and religious instruction, and finally, between the school as an adjunct to the Church and the school as an adjunct to state administration. Everything in American life, then, moved toward specialization, not simply as a consequence of the will to make a better living through higher learning, but because the state, rather than the religious institutions, had taken a central role in the education of the young. Pragmatism was the victorious banner under which this process marched forward.

> By the nineties science was part and parcel of large portions of the previous educational structure and had achieved its own institutions to carry its lore, technique, and mood. Not only was it privately endowed in new institutions, incorporated by endowments in older schools, but it was

publicly supported in state universities. The growth of science and its firm institutionalization were immeasurably facilitated by the Morrill Act of 1862 which bestowed thousands of acres of land in aid to those states which would set up industrial and mechanical colleges. Science was a steadily growing portion of the universe of education in which philosophers as well as businessmen moved. Science also became an established department of government. . . . Specialization means the development of a distinction between the expert and amateur. For medicine and law, and in America even for such occupations as journalism, it means an increase in the tuition period and it means schools and colleges to make possible and to implement professionalization. To make professions out of occupations you must have the specialist schools.[20]

Pragmatism was, however, more than a response to the needs of either secularization or specialization. It was also the underlying philosophy in the American educational movement that encouraged professionalization. It made it possible, through the Ph.D. system, to populate the university with American-trained personnel displaying a distinctive native regard for rugged self-improvement through measurable criteria. It was the final break with the medieval tradition in which the university or college was the center of learning. The emerging American division of labor made the university the center of social mobility. The graduate school in which professionalism was nurtured became the center of gravity. What became important was not teaching assignments but professional assignments. In this enterprise American pragmatism and American philosophy generally supplied the necessary antidote to European metaphysics. The early founders of pragmatism gave substance and shape to this newfound Americanization process by sharpening the distinction between professional and amateur.

The backgrounds of these men and their parents' backgrounds were primarily in law and not in theology. As a result, the connection between the state and educational network was made plain by the legal support of early pragmatism.

Sociology and Pragmatism is curiously restrained. It is an effort to outline the foundations of American liberalism and pluralism, and Mills at the time this was written was not quite certain of his attitudes toward either, or at least not certain enough to say whether their development was good or bad, necessary or accidental. This is not to deny the individuality of the work. The dissertation is undoubtedly a major effort in the sociology of knowledge and its relationship to institutional life. The work of Peirce, James, and Dewey concerns precisely the evolution of professionalism and secularism: areas in which these three giants of pragmatism pioneered. Mills no longer was working like a philosopher, but like a sociologist. Philosophical ideas became data for social investigation; they were not to be detached from empirical moorings. Background factors were taken seriously.

At the outset, Mills was neither critical nor negative toward pragmatism, or even toward the processes that he outlined. Certainly, later on, from the hindsight perspective of his analysis of power, the corporate system, and its cultural apparatus, one can see how critical this work was in intent if not in content. Yet *Sociology and Pragmatism* is remarkably hygienic from an ideological point of view. It is neither an attack nor a defense, but rather a statement of historical interest, and of the role of the technical philosopher in shaping American society.

This detachment was the inevitable result of Mills's ambiguous feelings. He shared Dewey's belief that science is power, and that the prestige of science derives from technology. On the other hand, he was less enamored of Dewey's idea of the canon of efficiency, of means and ends, of instrumentality and purpose in moral relationships. Mills had imbibed too much of the European tradition to accept a purely instrumental view. Mills's description of Dewey's critique of Marx and Marxism, despite his limited knowledge of Marx's work at that time, is well laid out, but one cannot help but detect that he had strong reservations about the Deweyan notion of intellect as involving community, and both somehow making democracy a reality. Dewey's Jeffersonian emphasis was a perspective Mills wanted to share, indeed sometimes was criticized for having. But he could not entirely accept it intellectually. It was the top of the ladder and not the bottom that fascinated Mills.

Mills's attitude toward James suffered a similar fate. He shared with James a psychological liberalism insofar as mind represented a window opening out to human action. Mills also shared with James an individualistic and moralistic pragmatism—which in political terms translated itself into an attack on American imperialism and empire building. He was nervous about James's individualistic piety, his puritanism, his intangible elitism. Nonetheless, the psychological viewpoint of James, which stresses action, accorded with Mills's increasing sense of the sociology of pragmatism and the role of the group, the collectivity. The trouble with James, for Mills at least, was the constant reduction of social structures to personal habits. Institutions, power, and authority were left out of James's reckoning. So again, the pragmatism of James, like the pragmatism of Dewey, seemed to cause Mills discomfort, but did not necessarily produce disenchantment.

With Peirce, Mills shared a keen sense of the importance of practical affairs, and hostility toward useless inquiries with no practical relevance. He needed to translate doubt into action, and thought into belief. The methodological structure of Peirce's thought was the most attractive part of Peirce for Mills, as it would be for any advocate of scientific method. His philosophical realism was also attractive, but it had a narrowness deriving from its reductionist bias toward consideration only of the biological. As a result, Peirce's undoing was that he could not fathom the social sciences. He could understand the intelligentsia but could not understand the publics who were required to believe in science, much less the need for a "science of man."

Above all, Mills could not accept the Peircean sentiment that the methods set forth by pragmatism were politically and socially neutral because they were based on the physical and biological sciences. In one of the few passages where Mills permits himself to criticize the founding fathers of pragmatism, he points out that the methods they espouse are by no means neutral. Fact and action become elements involved in stimulating doubt.

> The methods set forth by pragmatists are by no means socially, politically, or morally neutral. The difficulty of solving what turns out to be moral questions with a scientific technique is stated more popularly as getting the heart and head together in the face of intellectual publics who believe in "science."[21]

Mills was writing at a time when philosophical criticism of pragmatism was relatively weak and a sociological understanding of pragmatism was virtually nonexistent. With the exception of certain Marxist critics like V. J. McGill (who Mills apparently was unaware of), and a few sociological writings by economists like Veblen (who Mills knew quite thoroughly), the literature in 1940 on pragmatism was as poor in content as it was lacking in subtlety. Mills's achievement must be ranked as considerable. Yet, what was it in Mills that made him deal with pragmatism without regard to the Marxian literature? He has been accused of being a closet Trotskyist. In point of fact, his dissertation indicates a lack of knowledge rather than a disguise of Marxian wisdom. He is closer to arguing the case for a radical pragmatism, over and against conservative tendencies in pragmatism, than to making a full-scale social critique of main-line American philosophy. The fact that the Postscript was written in 1943, while the dissertation was completed in 1941, indicates Mills's growing awareness of a Marxian literature and legacy quite apart from the nativistic radicalism which motivates the dissertation. Ironically, it was Mills's inability to really use the tools of Marx that may have led him to write a "commentary," almost as a disclaimer, rather than undertake a new round of analysis of either pragmatism or education theories in America.

Toward the end of his life, Mills was intent on writing a volume on the cultural apparatus that would complement his earlier effort on higher learning in America. His very use of the words "cultural apparatus," rather than being propagandist, is indicative of the Deweyan tradition, in which culture is central and not at all subordinate. For Dewey and Mills alike the intellectual carrier of culture is not simply a reflection of a class system, but the very source of human power to communicate ideas. In this, too, Mills remained a child of the parent. Despite his constant references to reason and society, he never quite got away from experience and culture. It was experience, after all, that ultimately informed the pragmatic tradition, not rationality; not ideas per se, not systems or models of thought. Experiencing events, not generating a guide to the good or civilized life, was always the key to Mills. His first-person-singular theorizing had a fresh and at the same time naive quality. For him learning was always a firsthand experience, rarely a reflective derivation from other sources in the sociological literature. Ultimately, the pragmatic tradition informs his dissertation. It continues to be the spine which links the ganglia of topics covered in later writings.

Not the least tragic aspect of Mills's effort to arrive at a sociological understanding of pragmatism was that it remained largely if not entirely unknown to that growing body of scholars, such as Morton White[22] and Philip Paul Weiner,[23] who came into their own following the Second World War. As a consequence, in the climate of empiricism and functionalism prevailing at most major universities, at least in their sociology departments, too much emphasis on a dissertation about pragmatism was a detriment; in philosophy, the swing toward linguistic analysis and physicalism had the same dampening effect. Mills's dissertation proved to be out of phase with prevailing winds of doctrine, and that, rather than any negative sentiment on his part about the dissertation, led him to concentrate his publishing efforts in other directions.

The eventual publication of *Sociology and Pragmatism* did have the belated effect of providing Mills recognition from both the philosophical and sociological communities. The revolt against formalism in sociology clearly paved the way for a favorable critical response. Beyond this, of course, the later world view of Mills made a search for his critical roots of more than casual interest to those concerned with "what went wrong" in the past and "how to make things right" in the future. Because publication of *Sociology and Pragmatism* followed the writing of the dissertation by almost a quarter of a century, few sociologists knew of the work's existence, and fewer still had read it. Even those who had read the dissertation hardly knew what to make of it, since in fact the sense of the pragmatic tradition was much stronger in Mills than most of his commentators had ever imagined. For the most part, critics and crusaders alike saw Mills either as a Weberian, on the basis of his work in *Character and Social Structure*, or as a Marxist, on the basis of his later writings—or as a Paretian, on the basis of *The Power Elite* model. Mills himself did not help matters by locating the classical tradition in sociology almost exclusively in Europe. His background in philosophy tended to be sponged out, or perhaps self-expunged, by the irrepressible nature of the pragmatic elements in his work, as was clearly evident in the dissertation.

Mills died a few years before the publication of his dissertation. The characteristic animosity of critics was thus muted. The reviews tended to be highly favorable. Llewellyn Gross,[24] writing in *The Annals*, understood the book to be on the generic problems of the relationship between philosophical pragmatism and American social structure. He also noted that both are woven together with strands of educational history relevant to the growth of institutions and the professionalization of personnel in American philosophy. It is curious, nonetheless, that most reviewers, even those who liked the book, managed to ignore what it was about. The philosophic reviewers, in particular, could not quite fathom its subject matter, that is, the professionalization of a field, and saw in it a rather sprawling inquiry into the social-personal-cultural origins and consequences of Peirce, James, Dewey, and their doctrines. Critics saw the book as raising interesting questions and assembling interesting materials, but promising more than it achieved.

The most favorable philosophic review was that of Robert M. Barry.

> One cannot help but receive a clear view of many themes that are to be later expanded and made fruitful: the mind is rooted in social rationality; the importance of the social biography, the force of personalities; the fusion of craft, morality, and intellect; the balanced use of the European sociology of knowledge in a pragmatic context of social motives; and finally, the social (not sociological) grounding of scholarly motives, for the value of truth is ad hoc, as well as directional. I do not know a better way to introduce a student to some of the pressing issues of this century—of craft, morality, and intellect—than to have them read and re-read this book.[25]

By far the most influential review was published in *The New York Review of Books*, by Henry David Aiken.[26] Three full pages had great bearing on bringing the book to the attention of general readers. Like the other philosophical reviewers, Aiken tends to discount the sociology and promote the philosophy in the text. He argues that the first part simply represents "a desultory attempt to classify." He claims that Mills used puerile statistics in order to arrive at a definitive series of remarks upon the rise of the secular American university. In other words, Aiken's position is that Mills's book is good in spite of its sociological concerns rather than because of them. Aiken himself was a champion of modern pragmatic revisionism, and Mills's distance from pragmatism in later years tended to somewhat dampen Aiken's enthusiasm. He writes, for example:

> I am not convinced that pragmatism, either as a theory or interpretation or as a style of social and cultural criticism, is incapable of developing into a revolutionary philosophy where in context revolution is required for a deeper, more extensive amelioration of human practices and institutions. One of the things which Mills' own book shows is that none of the great pragmatists succeeded in defining the limits of pragmatic analysis and

prescription. In the nature of the case, pragmatism is an anti-essentialist philosophy.[27]

But, of course, Aiken is really arguing not with Mills's book, but with what Mills became in the last years of his life—a particularly harsh critic of American society, far harsher than a patrician at Harvard could accept.

Nonetheless, Aiken's balanced concluding remarks on the book can certainly stand without criticism:

> It is certain that Mills did not offer us a new synthesis; it is not at all certain that he would have wished to do so. Nonetheless, in an age of timid, anti-ideological neo-pragmatism which advances nowhere beyond the lessons of the masters, Mills at least makes a few moves toward a significant antithesis. Later on, he talks about the need for "structural" changes in the social systems, although I, at least, have no notion of what changes he really has in mind. Remembering our Nietzsche, we may perhaps say that Mills, like James, means to be a good "americano" even if not a good "norte-americano." And he perceives that any "viable" (horrid word), not to say any decent, consensus of the future must include more than the thin, brittle establishment that fancies itself to be "the free world." For this, in my opinion, he himself deserves a place of honor within the pragmatic tradition of which he has here proved himself to be an excellent historian and a trenchant critic.[28]

The irony is that it took such reviews to get the book a proper hearing. Despite Mills's fame, no major publisher was willing to publish the work after his death. Neither agents nor editors seemed capable of generating enough enthusiasm in the major publishing houses of New York to warrant a nibble, much less a bite. It was finally published by a small, independent firm, in a limited clothbound edition, and the strategy was to generate good reviews and hence trigger more extensive publishing interest. Somewhat astonishingly, the strategy actually worked, and the book went on to take its rightful place in Mills's corpus of writings.

After the reviews appeared, various publishers wanted to purchase rights to the book. Oxford was selected: first, because they had done his other major works; second, because they were willing to republish the book in a clothbound edition as well as bring out a paperbound one; and third, because they were willing to promote the volume as a basic Mills text rather than as a curiosity. The publishing history of this work is curious—not only for the lapse of almost a quarter of a century from completion to publication, but for the additional lapse of judgment on the part of the publishing community that prevented its wide distribution for several years after its initial publication.

The failure of this work to be published at the time of its completion led to an erroneous underestimation of the American context, as well as the native intellectual context, within which Mills actually worked. When it finally did appear, the volume came as a pleasant surprise to middle-of-the-road critics, and perhaps as an unpleasant surprise to those who perceived Mills as an extremist who merely had to work his way through the American literature to arrive at his European destiny. The truth was more nearly the other way around: Mills spent a lifetime celebrating European "classic" sociology only to arrive at his American destiny.

જાન્જાજ઼

It is the fate of significant figures that the size and extent of the caricature to which they are subjected is itself an inadvertent accolade. For his part, Mills was likened to Ernest Hemingway and André Malraux in literature, to Charlie Parker and Jack Kerouac in the world of marginal men, and to everyone who is anyone in the past history of socialism. In some circles it was fashionable to speak of Mills as the "Trotsky of Texas." The simple truth is that Mills was trained in philosophy and then in sociology; and that his mentors in philosophy were pragmatists. That his appreciation for the "classicists" in sociology—Durkheim, Weber, Veblen, Pareto, and Michels—among others, should have been so pronounced was in good measure a consequence of his philosophic criteria of what good sociology should contain.

His interest in Marx was a relatively late development. It came well after his working acquaintance with the orthodox movements within sociology, and it was stimulated by the iconoclastic group of sociologists (particularly Gerth) who had gathered at the University of Wisconsin after the Nazi rise to power, and reinforced by men like Theodor Adorno, Max Horkheimer, and especially his later colleague at Columbia, Franz Neumann. They made up the core of the exiled group which created the Institute of Social Research after having settled in the United States during the Second World War. These influences need to be properly located in time and space in order to highlight that the writings of the pragmatists, as well as Mills's concern with problems of social action and of political freedom in an industrial universe—plus his lifelong contempt for all forms of metaphysics—were brought to fructification in a unique sociological environment.

Mills's earliest published writings reveal a persistent reflection on pragmatic themes. The extent of his obligations to the pragmatic tradition can be adequately gauged long before the dissertation, in his study "The Language and Ideas of Ancient China." Here Mills tries his hand at explaining why a scientific tradition is stunted in the Asian East whereas it flowers in the European West.

> In America, this type of generalization from laboratory and craft facts has gone further than anywhere else. American pragmatism from Peirce through Dewey, and the core of Veblen, has been built squarely around

the technological laboratory and industrial domain of culture. The Chinese did not [do this]. Thus, although the means-ends, the physically technical logic, was no doubt implicit in the craft work of the Chinese, this logic was not raised to form part of the circle of official canons of truth and reality. The thinking elite were concerned with other domains of culture: the moral, liturgical, and political. The conceptions and structure of Chinese thought cannot be explained in terms of technological domain and experiences.[29]

Mills's judgments on the nature of Chinese scientific work, based as they were on the pioneering efforts of Marcel Granet, are subject to drastic revision in the light of the later researches of Joseph Needham and others. But the point is that Mills became convinced that what the European West called scientific was no less and no more than what the scientific tradition in America called pragmatic. It was the fusion of hand and head, of craft and intellect, which from the outset defined Mills's vision of the true scientist. "Intellectual craftsmanship" meant experienced participation in events, not the sort of nostalgic commitment to organic labor common to the English Edwardians and Victorians. The very emphasis on crafts rather than arts would indicate how close, in Mills's view, the pragmatist was to the populist.

An early paper by Mills, "Language, Logic and Culture," clearly reveals how deeply he was enmeshed with pragmatism not simply as a mode of philosophic discourse, but more importantly, as a philosophy which set forth the right sociological problems. The work of Peirce, Mead, and Dewey forms the warp and woof of his discussion. Language is seen "as a system of social control." Following closely Mead's *Mind and Society*, a symbol is defined as "an event with meaning, because it produces a similar response from both the utterer and the hearer." Communications is likewise defined operationally as the setting up of "common modes of response" in which the meaning of language "is the common social behavior evoked by it." The definition of mind as "the interplay of the organism with social situation mediated by symbols" likewise derives from Peirce and Mead. The capstone is the Deweyan definition of language and vocabulary as "sets of collective action" which are a consequence of social norms and values.[30]

This particular paper of Mills's reads like a digest of everything sociologically relevant which the pragmatists said about language and culture. By designating his work as "sociotics," Mills seeks to encompass all sociological phenomena involved in the function of language—especially the ways in which language channels, limits, and elicits thought. But as Mills readily acknowledges, sociotics as a concept derives from Charles W. Morris's *Foundations of the Theory of Signs*. It is nothing more than the relations of signs to their users—what Morris called "pragmatics"—seen from a sociological perspective. From this vantage point, rather than from Marx or Mannheim, Mills came to a study of the sociology of knowledge. This is why Mills emphasizes the social basis for the discovery of truth, rather than the economic basis for the location of error.

In his paper "The Methodological Consequences of the Sociology of Knowledge" Mills argued from pragmatist assumptions that the relativism of the sociology of knowledge is not necessarily an argument against that branch of sociology, since "the imputation of the sociologist of knowledge may be tested with reference to the verificatory model generalized, e.g., by Peirce and Dewey," that is, by probability and warranted assertions about the world. It was Dewey's *Logic* rather than Marx's *German Ideology* or Engels's *Dialectics of Nature* that led Mills to a full acceptance of the sociology of knowledge.

> The assertions of the sociologist of knowledge escape the "absolutist's dilemma" because they can refer to a degree of truth and because they may include the *conditions* under which they are true. Only conditional assertions are translatable from one perspective to another. Assertions can properly be stated as probabilities, as more or less true. And only in this way can we account for the fact that scientific inquiry is self-connecting.[31]

Mills fully shared Peirce's definition of a technical-intellectual elite, that is, those persons engaged in doubting, criticizing, and fixing beliefs. He had little difficulty in moving toward a sociological investigation of how beliefs are fixed, under what conditions doubt is institutionalized, and when criticism is tolerable. Beyond that, Mills criticized Mannheim for being inconsistent and ambiguous because, unlike Dewey, he confused factual examinations with the general relativistic aspects of knowledge.

> We need here to realize Dewey's identification of epistemology with methodology. This realization carries the belief that the deriving of norms from some one time of inquiry . . . is not the end of epistemology. In its "epistemologic function" the sociology of knowledge is specifically propaedeutic to the construction of sound methodology for the social sciences.[32]

On the other hand, Mills also employed Mannheim to criticize Dewey's notion of experiment as a form of scientific verification. In particular, he found Dewey's physicalism "informed by the failure to see fully and clearly the difficulties and the ambiguities associated with the physical paradigm of inquiry and particularly 'experiment' when applied to social data."[33] Mills felt that Dewey's concept of experimentation in a social situation does operate in accord with a reductionist model. As early as 1940 we find Mills using European *Wissensozialogie* to overcome empiricism; and the American pragmatic tradition to overcome rationalism. This was crystalized in Mills's *Sociological Imagination*, and in his collection of papers called *Images of Man*. The "classic tradition" was one which embodied a spectrum extending from Dewey to Veblen, as well as from Marx to Mannheim.

Throughout Mills's earlier efforts there is a dialogue with Dewey: sometimes direct and conscious, at other times elliptical and unconscious. Getting beyond Dewey generally meant moving from an epistemological to a sociological perspective, and not, as might be imagined, moving away from pragmatism as such. Motives are imputed or avowed as answers to questions interrupting acts or programs. But the model offered by Dewey is rejected by Mills for being "nakedly utilitarian." In fact, Mills writes, the choice of an action is determined not only by anticipation of different implications, but just as frequently by anticipation of the social consequences of the act. The trouble with Dewey's theory of valuation from Mills's standpoint is that "there is no need to invoke 'psychological' terms like 'desire' or 'wish' as explanatory, since they themselves must be explained socially."[34] To be sure, Dewey has the terminology of motives well in tow, but since "motives vary in content and character with historic epochs and societal structures," sociology is needed to locate the vocabularies of motives.

These early Texas essays, the solid core of Mills's early contributions to sociology, show that pragmatism was his tool for understanding the critical importance of society. Pragmatism provided a way to study social-psychological problems, a vein which was already being mined by George Herbert Mead. Pragmatism always remained for Mills "the nerve of progressive American thinking for the first several decades of this century"—even though it took "a rather severe beating" (which Mills did not quite bring himself to declare undeserved) from "fashionable leftism" and from "religious and tragic views of political and personal life." In fact, he defined pragmatism as the "emphasis upon the power of man's intelligence to control his destiny."[35] No matter how critical Mills was of Dewey's world, in which there was no final end to sustain life, he was far more critical of those, like Charles W. Morris, who abandoned pragmatism in a vain and empty effort to locate some providentially directed *telos*.[36]

For Mills, pragmatism was the doctrine which permitted a confrontation with theism. Whatever its shortcomings as a philosophy of American celebration it served well to offset religious fanaticism. The movement of people like Morris and Vivas from naturalistic to supernaturalistic approaches elicited Mills's harshest responses. He urged an emphasis on "remaking social orders which trap us" rather than intellectually surrendering to the frustrations of the moment by "dishing up messianic world religions." In short, not pragmatism but religion was the chief culprit.

In the long pull, Mills stood with a naturalistic pragmatism which could not be guaranteed over and against an idealistic pragmatism which sought legitimation in religion. The naturalism of a confused pragmatism was more appealing than the supernaturalism of an abandoned pragmatism.[37] Particularly in Dewey's hands, pragmatism had a Durkheimian emphasis on social contexts of behavior which in some way facilitated Mills's transition from philosopher to sociologist. The thought of abandoning pragmatism outright in favor of a religious vision was not possible without a corresponding abandonment of the sociological. And this step Mills was certainly never prepared to take. Thus, while Mills left philosophy, in part this was a consequence of the pragmatic prompting to confront the world in its hard social forms. It never became a "revolt" against pragmatism as such, the kind of open break which occurred in the cases of Charles Morris and Eliseo Vivas.

The kind of progressivism and populism with which Mills came to be identified was to some degree foreshadowed in *The New Men of Power*. The final chapter of the book is entitled "The Power and the Intellect," and it is essentially a plea for their fusion. The key phrase, and one which appears at least once in every subsequent work of Mills, is that "as the labor leader moves from ideas to politics, so the intellectual moves from ideas to career."[38] Precisely this bifurcation, this great dualism between theory and practice, is what the mainstream of American pragmatism addressed itself to. While pragmatism has often been accused of undue emphasis on action, it is more nearly the case that as pragmatism matured, its specific concerns became more theoretical, more attuned to preserving and institutionalizing the gains registered than to seeking new horizons to conquer. Pragmatists like James and Dewey were, from the outset, tied to educational reform and to intellectual functions.

Mills's high regard for "labor intellectuals" stems in some measure from a pragmatic base, i.e., the work context of learning. In *The New Men of Power* he says:

> Unlike many non-union intellectuals of more academic or journalistic types, the union-made intellectuals compete with each other in terms of the activity to which their ideas lead. They are not intellectuals for the sake of being intellectuals or because they have nothing else to do. They are union thinkers, with a big job on their hands. Such men are in themselves a link between ideas and action; this affects the healthily extrovert shape of their mentality. With them the gap between ideas and action is not so broad as to frustrate and turn their minds inward; they compete by having their ideas acted out, for better or worse; they are not just waiting and talking.[39]

What is so very interesting is this summary formulation is Mills's regard for action which is experientially derived, and his relative disdain for a general theory of action as such. He speaks of the "healthily extrovert shape" of the neutrality of labor intellectuals, not of theoretical moorings. Labor is a creative process. Labor intellectuals, those individuals who work but rise above union issues, are in the midst of this process. They have a "big job on their hands" in contrast to academic intellectuals, who are not at the same time significant social actors. Even though Mills had a longstanding interest in the sociology of knowledge, his separation from the European tradition is made clear by his total lack of interest in raising the problem of "interest-boundedness" and ideological aspects of an action orientation. For Mills, labor in the 1940s had a historic decisiveness which the middle classes could no longer claim. He had a considerably higher regard for their ideas during this period than any other. He speaks of "the main drift" rather than ideas. The good labor leader is one who has a sense of the main drift. What this main drift is at any given point remains vague.

Having already imbibed the lessons of Weber and Michels on bureaucracy and elites, Mills sought to fuse the sociological tradition to the pragmatic contours of American thought. The essential task of labor leaders in this fusion process was "to allow and initiate a union of power and the intellect." Furthermore, they were "the only ones who can do it." Perhaps the least euphoric aspect of this analysis was Mills's final cautionary statement: "Never has so much depended upon men who are so ill-prepared and so little inclined to assume the responsibility." In short, the fusion of actor and intellectual, of behavior and thought, was hardly inherent in the labor movement; rather, it was a desirable moral consequence of being a good labor leader. Even in Mills's most extreme expression of "sociological empiricism" there was a strong moralistic turn. The theme of reform through working-class participation was first expressed by Dewey in *Human Nature and Conduct*. Blue-collar socialization, said Dewey, had a therapeutic value in itself, independent of imagined long-range revolutionary potential.

The contest in which pragmatism arises in Mills's *White Collar* is of special significance. This work both marks the end of Mills's disenchantment with empiricism and introduces a more global view of social problems. It shows that he continued to view pragmatism as essentially a protest philosophy of the minority intellectual. Mills describes the Second World War period in severe terms as that moment during which intellectuals "broke with the old radicalism" to become "liberals and patriots, or give up politics altogether." He goes on to note how this act of betrayal was connected to a revolt against reason as such, leaving no doubt that he viewed the unconditional support of the war effort as an unbecoming posture for people of ideas. He sees this in philosophic terms as a movement in ideas from John Dewey toward Soren Kierkegaard.

No longer can they [the intellectuals] read, without smirking or without bitterness, Dewey's brave words, "every thinker puts some portion of an apparently stable world in peril." . . . Now they hear Charles Peguy: "No need to conceal this from ourselves: we are defeated. For ten years, for fifteen years, we have done nothing but lose ground. Today in the decline, in the decay of political and private morals, literally we are beleaguered. . . ." What has happened is that the terms of acceptance of American life have been made bleak and superficial at the same time that the terms of revolt have been made vulgar and irrelevant. The malaise of the American intellectual is thus the malaise of a spiritual void.[40]

In *White Collar* the pragmatic acquiescence of Archibald MacLeish and Lewis Mumford is seen by Mills as a betrayal of the optimistic, rationalist, and progressive picture of the world provided by the earlier pragmatists. During a period when Marxist philosophers were berating pragmatists as "philosophers of imperialism" and accusing them of other such ideological villainies, and when conservatives were in full search of essentialist modes of thought, Mills saw the plight of intellectuals, ideologically at least, as a global loss of nerve and a blunting of that cutting edge best typified in the thought of Dewey and Mead, as well as Marx and Freud. It was the fighting spirit rather than doctrinal irregularities which always captivated Mills.

However tinged with nostalgia Mills might have been, he was sociologist enough to know that "the liberal ethos, as developed in the first two decades of this century by such men as Beard, Dewey, Holmes, is now often irrelevant, and that the Marxian view, popular in the American thirties, is now often inadequate." They remained "important and suggestive as beginning points," but were nonetheless obsolete. Then what was to replace such views? Even if we grant that Mills adopts Weber's analysis of bureaucracy and Mannheim's description of social consciousness, the character of his social philosophy at the stage *White Collar* was written remains under a shroud. Already present were Mills's critique of the power elite, his condemnation of the political party system (which only argued over symbols and issues concerned with who gets what within the social order), and his appreciation of the function of anomie as a middle-class, as well as working-class, phenomenon. But there was no ready replacement of the pragmatic canons which initially shaped Mills. The very intimate and personal feelings expressed in the book reflect the work of a sociologist *experiencing* truth, rather than one structuring problems for future analysis. Mills was still linked to a pragmatism in which "rationality was formally located in the individual," and not to the "rationality of class" as in the Marxist system. He saw "fashionable Marxism" as giving "new life" to the major themes of liberal pragmatism. This was a view to which Mills held firm during the next—the last and by far the most hectic—decade of his life.[41]

The Power Elite, perhaps Mills's most controversial book but also his most enduring one, makes no mention of pragmatism. It does not have to. Implicit in the free-swinging critique of "mindlessness," of "machiavellianism for the little man," of "crackpot realism," is the sort of open-ended and tough-minded approach that made Mills distinct. Nonetheless, pragmatism became part of his definition of "the democratic man." It has been said in criticism that Mills's view of democracy was nostalgic, something which looked backward; that it was based not on the structure of social class but on criteria of personal experience. This is to some degree accurate. What is important is not so much the presence of nostalgia, since a backward glance or two is characteristic of even the most wild-eyed futurist, but the quality of this nostalgia. It was not the mimicry by the poor of the rich, nor the vicarious enjoyment of the powerless in the exploits of the powerful, which enticed and engaged Mills's attention. He was too critical of the stupefying ignorance of the poor to be much of a populist, he certainly sought to fashion no myth of the happy worker, and he was too concerned with the machinery and agencies of domination and control to have much faith in the power of reason to change society. Mills's "mass" was in contrast to "publics"—the mass had so little that a cultural apparatus even had to provide them with their "identity."

His vision of democratic man remained basically pragmatic. John Fiske's educated publics, which made policy in the town halls of America, were still at the seat of Mills's definition of responsibly exercised power. Mills had much more than a common-sense view of pragmatism. For him it did not mean mindless trial and error, or conscious anti-intellectualism. The concept of a pragmatic life meant tough-minded pursuit of democratic life-styles. This would give the "articulate and knowledgeable public" the help needed to keep leaders of society responsive and responsible.

That Mills's nostalgia is selective rather than a general motivating principle is indicated in an interesting note on the fashioning of American ideology by American historians.

> The "good" historians, in fulfilling the public role of the higher journalists, the historians with the public attention and Sunday acclaim, are the historians who are quickest to reinterpret the American past with relevance to the current mood, and in turn, the cleverest at picking out of the past, just now, those characters and events that most easily make for optimism and lyric upsurge. . . . In truth, and without nostalgia, we ought to realize that the American past is a wonderful source for myths about the American present.[42]

Ever fond of criticizing "liberal rhetoric," Mills nevertheless ends *The Power Elite* with this rhetoric. He wants a civil service linked with the world of knowledge and responsibility, people shaped by nationally responsible parties that carry forth open debates, people subject to a plurality of voluntary associations. In short, he wants the resurrection of social forces which the power elite have stamped out—but he does not explain how this is to be accomplished.

The Causes of World War Three is really an embellishment on themes raised in *The Power Elite*. From the point of view of political sociology, it does not represent any new theoretical principles. In this final pamphleteering period Mills retained a basic regard for liberal values, if not for the liberals who sought to carry forth such values; and a basic regard for pragmatic philosophies, if not for the pragmatists who acquiesced in the "conservative mood" of the "political directorate."[43]

ᵔᵔᵔ

Altogether new influences penetrated Mills's consciousness throughout the fifties. Beginning with Theodor Adorno, Max Horkheimer, and especially Franz Neumann, Marxism heavily textured with Freudianism became a central pivot. Even prior to this direct set of acquaintances, Mills benefited from his contact with European-trained scholars at the University of Wisconsin—especially Gerth. Furthermore, the profession of sociology made its own claims on the shape of Mills's thought—so that his early reading in James, Peirce, and Dewey was reinforced by trends within sociology to lead him to search out the origins and sources of scientific and academic institutions. However, contact with philosophy was not altogether absent, as is witnessed in his friendship with Charles Frankel of the Department of Philosophy at Columbia. The "classic" tradition in sociology nonetheless revealed increasing divergencies from the pragmatic tradition. This severance was particularly feasible, since few Europeans knew much or cared about American pragmatism, while men like Mills revered sociological ancestors like Durkheim, Simmel, Weber, and Mannheim.

Under these circumstances, one of two reactions might have been anticipated: either a full critique of pragmatism from a Marxist point of view, castigating the encouragement pragmatism rendered to European fascism and to American foreign policy, or a fading from consciousness of pragmatism. Neither was forthcoming. Mills was finally aware of Marxian criticisms of pragmatism by this time, and basically he thought them erroneous. The continued attention to pragmatism shown in *The Sociological Imagination* tends to call into question the second possibility. For Mills's final statement on sociological theory is still permeated with the attitudes he held as a young man. When he notes in *The Sociological Imagination* that the motivations of men, and even the varying extents to which various types of men are typically aware of them, are to be understood in terms of the vocabularies of motive that prevail in a society and of social changes and confusions among such vocabularies, he speaks very much as the pragmatist. The widespread use of Peircean semiotics in a chapter "Uses of History" is indicative of the voluntaristic position Mills took in relation to events in history. Even the phrase "events in history" fails to correspond to this view, since Mills would probably have said "history as experienced occurrences." If Weber and

Marx framed the essential contours of Mills's political sociology, Peirce, Mead, and Dewey framed his social psychology. "It may well be," Mills writes, "that the most radical discovery within recent psychology and social science is the discovery of how so many of the most intimate features of the person are socially patterned and even implanted."[44]

In Mills's view, human emotions take place with continual reference to "social biography," which in turn is part of an "experienced social context." This is neither a neo-Freudian language of genetic types nor a neo-Marxian language of alienated types. Mills was discontent with the "small-scale setting" of most varieties of psychoanalysis, the tendency to make values reside in the supposed needs of individuals in isolation and apart from a meaningful social context. In *The Sociological Imagination* we find him once more making an appeal to the pragmatic tradition to sanction his sociologism—this time to the work of George Herbert Mead: "The social element in the lens of psychoanalysis was greatly broadened, especially by what must be called sociological work on the super-ego. In America, to the psychoanalytic tradition was joined one having quite different sources, which came to early flower in the social behaviorism of George H. Mead."[45] The basis of a sound social psychology involves a linkage between the humanism of the pragmatic tradition and the exactitude of the psychoanalytic tradition.

One of the confusions extant with respect to *The Sociological Imagination* is the assumption by a number of critics that this work represented a theoretical work on the road to a "Marxist world overlook." This was simply not the case. Marxism always remained part of the social science tradition for Mills—and not the other way around. If anything, the final chapter in this volume, "On Politics," displays a powerful sentiment in favor of a "politics of exposure" rather than a "science of politics." Social scientists are said to be involved in "the struggle between enlightenment and obscurantism" the way Dewey held that all philosophers are involved in a struggle between living in an open, tentative world of experience and a closed world of dogmatism and certitude. Even if it is proper to note that Mills was touched by "nostalgia for the past," the nature of that "past" remains to be defined. Here it becomes perfectly clear that his faith in the will of enlightenment to conquer power makes it implausible to define him in terms of the neo-Machiavellian school of Franco-Italian sociology. The thought of power did not intoxicate or absorb Mills. If anything, the reverse was true: Mills was obsessed with the potential of reason to redirect the irrational rush of raw power. This is not Manicheanism, but old-fashioned rationalism. And if *The Sociological Imagination* reveals a declining reference to pragmatists as such, it is because in their modern form they became celebrators rather than critics of the American experience. In the vacuum created by the modern pragmatists, because of their increasing ideological stridency in political matters and their decreasing practical involvement in social and educational reform, Mills began to place a new emphasis on the radical aspects of the "classic tradition" in sociology from Marx to Mannheim. Thus, in his macroscopic work Mills moved away from a pragmatic framework, and into a more universal concern with contributions of radical European thought. The parochialism of pragmatic discourses on politics and society could not but have dismayed Mills as the years moved on. Pragmatism became an unsuitable vehicle for his global theories of power.

As Mills moved away from pragmatism as a theory, he moved nearer toward it as a way of life. He "internalized" the behavior of pragmatic man—at least Jamesian Man. This is plainly evident in Mills's one-man crusade to present the truth about the Cuban Revolution to the American public in much the same fashion that William James lectured up and down the Atlantic coast in 1898 in an effort to alert Americans to the dangers of the takeover in Cuba by American imperialism. James's efforts on behalf of the Anti-Imperialist League were perhaps as much inspired by his personal dislike of Theodore Roosevelt as by any real knowledge of Cuba. Mills's crusading zeal on behalf of the Cuban Revolution, particularly after the Bay of Pigs invasion attempt, was motivated by an equally personal (rather than political) dislike of John F. Kennedy. Personalities are important to the pragmatic mind, while the impersonal force of history is important to the dialectical mind. It is the difference between one philosophy which begins with personal experience and another which has its starting point in objective existence. In this sense, Mills certainly remained a firm adherent to the pragmatic canon of truth as involvement.

The portrait of Castro which emerges from the pages of Mills's *Listen, Yankee!* lends weight to this interpretation. For Castro is seen not as a model of theoretical acumen, but rather as the advocate of a tough-minded practicality. "Revolution is construction." The Cuban revolution is not so much a historic act as it is a creative act, a way of defining reality. "The revolution is a way of changing reality—and so of changing the definition of it. The revolution is a great moment of truth." And while Mills describes this kind of thinking as "revolutionary euphoria," he leaves little doubt that this is a euphoria which he personally takes great pleasure in, a shared euphoria. The Cuban revolution is a "connection." It becomes a therapeutic device for linking dreams and reality; an enterprise which has direct personal benefits. The Cuban economy is described as an almost spontaneous agrarian reform, a "do it yourself" type of economic development. Castro is said to have given a check to the *comandante* of agriculture, telling him to produce. The *comandante* in turn asked the peasants what they wanted to do. "Produce beans," was the answer. And so it came to pass that the agricultural sector of Cuba was socialized without the sacrifice of human lives, and without recourse to the rigorous planning characteristic of the East European Soviet bloc states. Spontaneity is everything. Say "Produce" and it is done. Say "Consume less" and it is done. Say "Defend the revolution against the insurgents" and it is done. All on a voluntary basis, and all with the sort of presumed spontaneity which characterizes the pragmatic criteria of truth as practice.[46]

The portrait of the Cuban revolutionary drawn by Mills is not much different from the picture of the good man drawn by Dewey in *Freedom and Culture* twenty years earlier.

> Our idea of freedom [writes Mills] is different from that of the reactionaries who talk of elections but not of social justice. Without social justice, democracy is not possible, for without it men would be slaves of poverty. That is why we have said that we are one step ahead of the right and of the left, and that this is a humanistic revolution, because it does not deprive man of his essence, but holds him as its basic aim. Capitalism sacrifices man; the Communist state, by its totalitarian concept, sacrifices the rights of man. That is why we do not agree with any of them. Each people must develop its own political organization, out of its own needs, not forced upon them or copied.[47]

The final words of Mills on this score, concerning his "worries for Cuba," would suggest that it is just these liberal values he thought might be subverted by a charismatic leader like Castro. "I do not like such dependence upon one man as exists in Cuba today." His view was that the United States had an obligation to assist Cuba in passing through its euphoric and essentially monolithic stage.

What is at stake here is not the factual correctness of Mills's position, or even the soundness of his policy recommendations. What is relevant is the constancy of the pragmatic thread in Mills's thought—considering pragmatism as an ethos no less than as a technical system of philosophy. His judgment was that the critics rather than the celebrators will, in the long run, be seen to have remained loyal to the basic philosophic and social commitments of the founders of American pragmatism. The fact that "fundamentalists" in the American education system have spent a decade attempting to displace pragmatism as a style of teaching and learning would indicate that the political potency and main drift of pragmatism is still toward mass democracy.

Who, after all, did the pragmatists influence? It most certainly was not, as Mills shows, the great unwashed. The impact of American pragmatism was popular only in the sense that the select publics who imbibed its lessons were concerned with social affairs and with demonstrating that public action can have public consequences. The muckraking tradition of Upton Sinclair, Lincoln Steffens, and Ida Tarbell was not directed toward the "overthrow of capitalism" but toward the exposure of the meat-packing industry; and it was not directed toward the "liberation of women" but toward universal suffrage and sexual equality. In this sense, early pragmatism was sociological and not philosophical. It paid scant attention to "fundamentals." Its theoretical energies were focused on the practical, the immediate, and the reformable. Winning games and not debating doctrines became its dominant motif.

That it should be educators and journalists who responded to the pragmatic challenge was thus something in the nature of an inevitability. It is precisely this strain that had the greatest impact on Mills. If, at the outset, Mills seemed anxious to use pragmatism systematically, by the close of his career he had begun to use pragmatism journalistically. The long trek from sociotics to muckraking involved many sociological improvisations. But there can be little question that the major theme undergirding these improvisations was remarkably constant. Mills was not a "half-baked" follower of Weber, Roberto Michels, or Marx. He was a fully developed pragmatic man. Seen from such a vantage point, much of the criticism directed at Mills has to be judged as largely irrelevant and off the mark. The reviewers of Mills's writings in the professional journals were unsympathetic and unresponsive, in the same way and with the same lack of comprehension as the reviewers were, fifty years earlier, toward Steffens, Sinclair, and Tarbell. The irony of the situation is that the "true reformer" (which Mills certainly was) suffered at the hands of the true believer turned true scientist, while at the same time he found himself celebrated by the journalists and columnists.

Mills was not solely formed by pragmatism. The chief personal influences on Mills—Clarence Ayres at Texas, who taught him the values of Veblen; Gerth at Wisconsin, who was responsible for Mills's initial appreciation of the German sociological tradition; the years Mills spent at Maryland, which instilled an appreciation of the economic factor in social history; his contacts at the Bureau of Applied Social Research at Columbia, which deepened his technical understanding—make it clear that Mills was something more than a pragmatist fallen among sociologists. His later appreciation of the critical role of Marx in political sociology and Freud in social psychology further removed Mills from the pragmatic position.

Reinforcing Mills's separation from pragmatism was the failure of nerve of younger practitioners of the pragmatic doctrine. Mills concluded that Vivas, Morris, and Mumford stood for acquiescence in the American social order; and they agreed with pragmatism's assumption that the evolutionary process requires a continuation of firmly etched commitments to liberalism. In Mills's view, the pragmatists also lost the urgency for broad communication with wider publics. As philosophy became professionalized, pragmatism abandoned its search for a public forum. The new pragmatism linked arms with logical positivism in its essential details. It turned its gaze inward, attempting to serve a philosophical justification for scientism rather than social reform. In addition, the increasing concern with technical problems of epistemology and ontology led pragmatism a considerable distance away from the social and reform impulses of its pioneers. As Mills himself realized, this process had already begun with the work of Peirce, and was completed during the decades Mills did his researches on the subject.

In *Sociology and Pragmatism*, Mills gives a resoundingly sociological examination of how philosophy in America became professionalized, and the role of pragmatism in the process, from the viewpoint of the sociology of knowledge taken in its most exact sense of how new social forces give rise to different intellectual styles. The variables in this study are sociological: the social origins of the thinker, the structure of the academic community, the requirements of the social context, etc. The philosophical criticisms of pragmatism are largely eschewed. This is not a study of the truth of pragmatism, but rather a study of its utility. The only comparable work in the sociological literature is Georges Sorel's *De l'utilité du pragmatisme*. But this latter volume is not genuinely of the same order, since its focus is ideological and sweeping, whereas Mills's is institutional and intimate.

It remains an ineluctable fact that Mills's early work on pragmatism was not simply a dissertation written to acquire a degree, with a simple or obscure topic chosen so that a board of academic advisers would certify it out of blithe ignorance. Quite the contrary: Mills had his troubles with the dissertation—first, the difficulty of convincing his advisers that the topic had merit; second, the absence of the sort of hard data usually regarded as necessary in dissertation topics; and third, the reluctance of the dissertation board to pass on it until after innumerable delays. It is reliably reported that with the exception of one adviser, the examination board did not even know of the work of Charles Sanders Peirce, and the rest had only a fleeting knowledge of Dewey's work. That Mills would incur such professional risks in order to do this dissertation must therefore signify a profound belief in its value and in the importance of settling accounts with one basic sphere of the American intellectual inheritance.

Even as he inveighed against the "American celebration," and spoke out in behalf of "plain Marxism," the mark of pragmatism remained too deep to be either bleached or expunged. His raw talent for common sense, an unrelenting suspicion of high-level abstractions, and a worldly versatility that made him feel at ease in all parts of the American social system ultimately stamped Mills as a pragmatist. There are times, in his writings as well as in his presence, when one felt he wanted nothing more than to shed this inheritance—to treat it as so much intellectual baggage. Even his various and sundry efforts to become Europeanized and Latinized ended in a dreary return. He would sheepishly smile and say: "It gets lonely without *The New York Times* every day." Which was as close as he could bring himself to admitting that he was the last hero of American pragmatism; or perhaps conversely, that pragmatism was the last hope of an American utopian.

REFERENCES

1. George Herbert Mead. *Selected Papers on Social Psychology*, edited by Anselm Strauss. Chicago: The University of Chicago Press, 1964, p. 282.

2. Hans H. Gerth to C. Wright Mills, January 5, 1942.

3. C. Wright Mills to Eliseo Vivas, December 24, 1941.

4. Edward Alsworth Ross was a minor but lasting influence on Mills. In *The Sociological Imagination* the dean of Stanford and Wisconsin sociology is described as "graceful, muckraking, and uptight" (New York and London: Oxford University Press, 1959, p. 6). A far harsher judgment of Ross as racist and reactionary is contained in Herman Schwendinger and Julia R. Schwendinger, *The Sociologists of the Chair: A Radical Analysis of North American Sociology, 1883-1922*. New York: Basic Books, 1974. For a balanced present-day view, see Roscoe C. Hinkle, "Basic Orientations of the Founding Fathers of American Sociology," *Journal of the History of the Behavioral Sciences* 11, no. 2 (April 1975): 123–28.

5. C. Wright Mills to E. A. Ross, December 12, 1941.

6. C. Wright Mills to Hans H. Gerth, January 16, 1942.

7. C. Wright Mills, *Power, Politics and People.* New York: Oxford University Press, 1963, pp. 423–38.

8. Robert K. Merton. "Science, Population and Society." *The Scientific Monthly* 44 (February 1937): 165–71.

9. C. Wright Mills to Robert K. Merton, January 23, 1940.

10. Mills to Vivas.

11. *Ibid.*

12. Eliseo Vivas. *The Moral and the Ethical.* Chicago: The University of Chicago Press, 1950.

13. Elizabeth Flower and Murray G. Murphy. *A History of Philosophy in America*, Vol. 2. New York: G. P. Putnam's Sons, 1977, pp. 507, 537, and 568.

14. C. Wright Mills. *Sociology and Pragmatism*. New York: Paine-Whitman Publishers, 1964, p. 465.

15. Henry Steele Commager. *The American Mind: An Interpretation of American Thought and Character Since the 1880's.* New Haven: Yale University Press, 1950.

16. C. Wright Mills. Memo to sociology department of Columbia University, July 14, 1944.

17. Mills. *Sociology and Pragmatism*, p. 467.

18. *Ibid.*, pp. 50, 53.

19. *Ibid.*, p. 47.

20. *Ibid.*

21. *Ibid.*, p. 53.

22. Morton White. *Social Thought in America: The Revolt Against Formalism.* Boston: Beacon Press, 1957; and Howard Zinn, ed. *New Deal Thought.* Indianapolis: The Bobbs-Merrill Co., 1966. This volume attempts to resolve precisely one area Mills felt his dissertation had failed to cover adequately. For a review of the more recent literature, see Bradford A. Lee, "The New Deal Reconsidered," *The Wilson Quarterly* 6, no. 2 (Spring 1982): 62–76.

23. Philip Paul Wiener. *Evolution and the Founders of Pragmatism.* Cambridge: Harvard University Press, 1949.

24. Llewellyn Gross. Review of *Sociology and Pragmatism*. In *The Annals of The American Academy of Political and Social Science* 359 (May 1965): 206.

25. Robert M. Barry. "The Pragmatic Movement and Intellectualism." *Transaction/SOCIETY* 3, no. 5 (July–August 1966): 46–47.

26. Henry David Aiken. "C. Wright Mills and the Pragmatists." *The New York Review of Books* 4, no. 3 (March 11, 1966): 8–10.

27. *Ibid.*, p. 10.

28. *Ibid.*

29. Mills, *Power, Politics and People*, p. 499.

30. *Ibid.*, p. 423–38.

31. *Ibid.*, p. 463.

32. *Ibid.*, p. 464.

33. *Ibid.*, p. 466.

34. *Ibid.*, p. 442.

35. *Ibid.*, p. 292.

36. *Ibid.*, p. 168–69.

37. *Ibid.*

38. C. Wright Mills. *The New Men of Power.* New York: Harcourt, Brace, & Co., 1948, p. 281.

39. *Ibid.*, p. 286.

40. C. Wright Mills. *White Collar: The American Middle Classes.* New York: Oxford University Press, 1951, pp. 142–43.

41. *Ibid.*, pp. 159–60.

42. C. Wright Mills. *The Power Elite*. New York: Oxford University Press, 1956, p. 358 ff.

43. C. Wright Mills. *The Causes of World War Three*. New York: Simon & Schuster, 1958, pp. 81–89.

44. Mills, *The Sociological Imagination*, pp. 161–62.

45. *Ibid.*, p. 160.

46. C. Wright Mills. *Listen, Yankee! The Revolution in Cuba*. New York: Mc-Graw-Hill Book Co., 1960, pp. 114–15.

47. *Ibid.*, p. 99.

7

From the Sociology
of Knowledge to the
Knowledge of Sociology

*For intellectuals, the exercise of freedom means to criticize error, to
unmask ideologies, to reveal the truth, and not to accept fatalisti-
cally the naked reality of power that denies the possibility of the exercise of reason. We cannot accept the present as an iron cage in
which the possibility for reasoned action is so rigidly prescribed that
the future becomes only the object of despair, an image that invites
apathy in the present and the acceptance of an even worse future.*

Hans H. Gerth, ''The Intellectual in Modern Society''

KARL MANNHEIM FUNCTIONED as the bridge which took Mills from the
darkness of philosophy to the light of sociology. Mannheim probably
served a similar role for dozens of other intellectuals. Mannheim's work
was introduced to America in the mid-1930s—a time of economic disintegration and academic crisis in philosophy. Mannheim's work was part
of a post pragmatic environment which reduced philosophy to Engels's
prophecy that philosophy would become little else than the study of its
own past glories. The late 1930s seemed to crystallize that crisis, while
also holding a glimmer of a way out. If philosophy was dead, or in the
hands of positivism and linguistic formalism, and all that was left to
study was a matter of science, the choices for younger scholars like Mills
narrowed.

The University of Texas, with its philosophically oriented departments of economics, sociology, and history, seemed the ideal place for
seeking a new synthesis; and Mannheim, with his eclectic flair for each
of these three fields, the perfect individual vehicle for the big transition
to the social sciences. Mannheim's relativistic view of history became the

median point between a materialist philosophy that was and a social science yet to be. Mills, in his lifelong belief that "history is the shank of any social study" which intellectuals "must study if only to rid ourselves of it,"[1] became the perfect expression and embodiment of the sociology of knowledge as a reasonable cross between empirical muckraking and a rationalist world view. For Mills, the sociology of knowledge offered exposé coupled with history. To show how this new symbiosis evolved is the purpose of this chapter.

Mills's self-imposed task of being, as Harvey Swados noted, "simultaneously a Teddy Roosevelt and a [F.] Scott Fitzgerald, a public figure—a man of action and an artist-thinker"[2]—was a constant source of both exhilaration and frustration. That he found it necessary to lambast the narrow world view of his professional colleagues and the public at large was reflected in a weltschmerz that would become painfully transparent in his late-period pamphleteering. However much Mills savored his role of lonely long-distance runner, approaching his daily work as if it were a proxy for military combat,[3] his mission was accepted with resignation. People who publish make themselves public;[4] thus, in the process, they produce their own biographies and, ultimately, a small chapter of humanity's history. In Mills's 1958 "pagan sermon," on *The Causes of World War Three*, he directed a question to the American clergy: "You claim to be Christians. What does that mean as a biographical and public fact?"[5] Change "Christians" to "sociologists" and we would not alter the spirit of the interrogation. The sociological imagination, Mills said,

> "enables us to grasp history and biography and the relations between the two within society. That is its task and its promise. To encourage this task and this promise is to mark the classic social analyst. . . . No social study that does not come back to the problems of biography, of history and of their intersections within a society has completed its intellectual journey.[6]

Just as sharp distinctions between theory and method were held to be contrivances, so were those between the sociological profession and the general public. Mills wrote for a public which accepted the Aristotelian ideal; the fear of sociologists and other members of the intelligentsia of appearing as "popularizers" partially explains why the public rarely took the time to seek out their work. In creating his own biography, Mills decided to distinguish himself in almost every possible way, personal and intellectual, from those whom he sought to reach so that they might come to grasp more easily the wisdom of his message. This created somewhat of a paradox: his self-image was that of a Great Man, but in the truly great society that he envisioned, his task would not be necessary to undertake.[7] In a sense, he was victim of the classic delusion of intellectual hubris that today's problems lie with the world who dares not take me seriously.

The Great Man theory of history is analogous to the theory of biological mutation. Periodically, an individual is born with attributes which vastly overwhelm those of his fellow human beings. As John Friedmann points out about such a person, able to grasp "unrealized forms of future history . . . he succeeds in wrenching society loose from its anchoring place in present equilibrium and turning it into the uncharted seas beyond the known and familiar lands."[8] A sociological interpretation of the Great Man—that is to say, in this case, a Millsian one—would hold that a person must at least seek to understand why people may feel themselves to be part of an abstract mass and thus be absorbed in personal problems, why they often perceive history as a series of unrelated, random events, and why they may perceive themselves to be acted upon, yet do not act.

It was not quite that simple, Mills's personal ego notwithstanding. Knowledge may be accessible to all, but only certain groups of persons can interpret it, and then only within certain epochs of history. If we can understand the conduct and motives of these groups and the individuals within them, we will be better able to interpret the content of knowledge. Mills argued that the prospect of a modern industrialized society, such as the United States, being governed by moral and rational discourse was becoming more distant with each passing year; he believed that individuals sought to examine interrelationships between concrete phenomena from the most narrow, parochial standpoint possible and often denied even the need for that. Mills believed that the individual's allegiance to a collective identity, whether it be social class, bureaucratic organization, nation, or party, usually distorts his or her constructions of social reality. It was to be the special role of the intellectual, spared by university life from the distorting role of masses and collective wills, to rise above partisanship into a true sense of history. The principal resource that Mills relied upon in overcoming this antinomy between interest and trust was Karl Mannheim. He was prominent during the 1920s and 1930s in advancing the frontiers of the sociology of knowledge—above all, in showing the relevance of Marxian categories, if not Marxian practice, to believers in the Western democratic tradition.

The position that the cognitive basis of rational thought derives from the thinker's social-historical context, the linchpin of any theory of the sociology of knowledge, animated Mills's work throughout his career. It enabled him to examine phenomena that shaped American social conduct; it provided him with a methodology to enable him to distinguish a social problem from a personal anguish; and, although in a manner somewhat different from that of Veblen, it crystallized and reinforced his near-estrangement from American mass culture and his professional peers. And while the sociology of knowledge as an intellectual tradition had decidedly European origins, because of Mannheim's own fascination with the Anglo-American traditions it expanded upon what Mills had learned in his earlier work on American pragmatism.

Yet what about Mannheim's conception of *Wissensozialogie* especially appealed to Mills? Marx had pointed out an organic connection between mental and social processes in his early writings almost a century before Mills felt at home with Mannheim for personal as well as professional reasons. Hans Gerth had been taught by Mannheim before both fled from Nazi Germany; it was inevitable that Gerth conveyed Mannheim's thinking to the younger Mills at Wisconsin. Mannheim gave Mills some of the ammunition he needed to overcome the psychologism extant in the sociology of the late 1930s and early 1940s.

From his studies of European thought since the Reformation, Mannheim concluded that knowledge is fundamentally a group or collective activity;[9] it "presupposes a community of knowing which grows primarily out of a community of experiencing prepared for in the subconscious."[10] Ideas are "situationally conditioned," or greatly influenced by the particular affiliations of the thinker—so much so that "the approach to a problem, the level on which the problem happens to be formulated, the stage of abstraction and the stage of concreteness that one hopes to attain, are all and in the same way bound up with social existence."[11] This does not mean that all knowledge is equally relative to various competing interests and therefore nonobjective. Such an interpretation would relegate *Wissensozialogie* to a circular and futile philosophical relativism. The antidote would be "relationism"—the view that in order for knowledge to provide a broad world picture those seeking to expand it must not only tolerate opposing viewpoints in the world of discourse but also embrace them. This would provide the guidance for the type of social change that lies outside the pitfalls of ideology—which is myopic, conservatizing, and "intensively interest bound"—and utopia, which, although it provides a greater measure of hope, could easily degenerate into chiliastic wishes for the transcendence of present societal conditions without giving any thought to what might replace it. As Mannheim argued in his last major work, *Freedom, Power, and Democratic Planning,* the individual must take a relationsist perspective "in the expectation of enlarging his own personality by absorbing some features of a human being essentially different from himself. Practically, this means that the democratic personality welcomes disagreement because it has the courage to expose itself to change."[12]

As ideas acquire validity by uniting more and more differing perspectives into a single one, they gradually shed situational specificity. By shedding or avoiding powerful biases growing out of ways of life that require allegiance to particular ideological or utopian positions, an individual can acquire a relational perspective. To overcome bias is simply a function of comparing as wide a variety of experiences as possible with respect to similar phenomena. This requires that we conduct our daily lives in a number of social circles that may overlap in style and in function: "Not only individual but also group experiences may become complementary, and . . . the roles which we live and directly experience may be in reality nothing but the inversion of the unknown roles in unknown individuals."[13]

It is impossible for any one person to exist within all these circles simultaneously. We do so on the margins of experience, becoming indirect mediators between viewpoints that would otherwise come into contact with each other only on the basis of presumed mutual hostility. The intellectual's role has always been to develop avenues of indirect discourse; to "contact the enemy," as MIlls was later to put it. Over time the intellectual has shed a Brahmin-like status and monopolistic control over knowledge. Modern intellectuals, drawn from a relatively classless stratum, do not so much belong to specific groups as "float" from one to the other; hence the term "free-floating intellectual" (freischewebende Intellegenz). This concept of marginality, heavily influenced by Georg Simmel, does not simply describe how intellectuals operate; but how they are *created* as a special class. The most marginal the intellectual is, the more likely to plant seeds of knowledge and learning. The very marginality keeps one relatively immune from ideological dogmatism and utopian messianism.

For various reasons, this general position reinforced Mills's wobbly self-image—which, one could argue, was an Americanized equivalent of a free-floater—more than his early pragmatist or other influences. Marx, for example, held that knowledge and social class were inseparable. Thus, any intellectual's version of truth would inevitably reflect his or her stake in the existing economic order. Mannheim posited that intellectuals might frequently exhibit certain class biases, but that no historical dialectic irrevocably defined these biases. This was one reason, among others, why as sympathetic as Mills was to Marxist critiques of capitalism, he could never quite come to consider himself a Marxist.

Max Weber argued that scientific knowledge was purely objective. It became subjective only when it involved personal value judgments. Mannheim stood this argument on its head; the content of knowledge he declared, depended on the subjective position of the thinker, while values themselves were objective, at least within the confines of a given epoch.[14] Mills, revealing the American influence of George Herbert Mead, emphasized the social-psychological relationship between the thinker and the audience he or she selects as defining the method by which to approach knowledge:

> From the standpoint of the thinker, the socialization of his thought is coincidental with its revision. The social and intellectual habits and character of the audience, as elements in this interaction, condition the

statement of the thinker and the fixation of beliefs evolving from that interplay. . . . No individual can be logical unless there be agreement among the members of his universe of discourse as to the validity of some general conception of good reasoning.[15]

Mills is here arguing with another, idealistic wing of the sociology of knowledge. Max Scheler, an aristocratic Platonist who held that a gulf existed between Being and Thought, held that while patterns of thought may differ by historical epoch and social context, they all spring from the perception of a universalistic absolute realm of ideas and value-ordering. By contrast, Mannheim held that truth is first and foremost a product of existence. Discourse may not lead to truth, but it can define and redefine truths within a given historical epoch. Truth is no "historical verity"; rather, it resides within our social life.[16] It was this latter standpoint to which Mills held firm.

The idealistic wing of the sociology of knowledge may have shared many assumptions in common with Mannheim, but they were committed to the sociology of knowledge as a culture and *opposed* the notion of sociology as a distinct branch of science. Instead of seeking an empirical basis, which would presumably relativize life into meaninglessness, Max Scheler, and, before him, Wilhem Dilthey felt that the function of sociology ought to be transforming philosophy from a metaphysical impasse to a temporal realm of consciousness and feeling.[17] Its place would lie in a larger *Lebendigkeit*. In short, Scheler and Dilthey did not seek sociological answers to everyday problems; Mannheim and his followers did. And it was to the place of ideas in ordinary life that Mills's work drifted.

One could go on with comparisons between Mannheim and Troeltsch, (Alfred) Weber, Meineke, or von Schelting, but at this pont we may be losing sight of the major point: Mannheim's sociology of knowledge, much more directly than others, gave Mills the raw material that would aid him in accounting for the intricate relationships between knowledge, belief systems, and power in an era when the latter two seemed to have increasingly little to do with the former. Mills integrated ideologies and institutions in a way that would give pragmatism an added dimension and would not require him to do anything more than float between collective affinities (although in the end he sought much more). Mannheim was that classic liberal who could simultaneously provide for Mills a bridge between his earlier encounter with James, Peirce, and Dewey and yet outline how a modern society could plan for a democratic future. Mills acknowledged his debt to Mannhein in the Introduction to *Images of Man:*

Karl Mannheim's essay on rationality contains the seeds of the most profound criticism of the secular rationalism of Western civilization. He did not work it out in just this way, but the passage given here is among the best writings of a man who is, I believe, one of the two or three most vital and important sociologists of the inter-war period.[18]

Even without such homage, one detects Mannheim's influence upon Mills, especially during the later years, when his use of decidedly Mannheimian rhetoric—"the main drift," "the big discourse," "the epoch in which we live"—bordered on the excessive.

A third and final reason why Mills picked up on Mannheim was that his German master was one of the very few *Wissensozialogie* theorists, at least during the 1930s, whose major work was readily available in English. Mills did not understand German, at least not well (Gerth handled all of the translations in *From Max Weber*), and, given that almost all the major thinkers in the field were German, the bulk of the literature was de facto inaccessible to him, except through the translations of Weber made by Gerth, and of Mannheim made by Louis Wirth of the University of Chicago.

The ways in which Mills used Mannheim as a resource, as numerous as they might have been, hinged upon three interrelated themes: (1) maintaining strong ties between philosophy and sociology that were increasingly in danger of being severed; (2) locating sources of power and their relationships to and control over knowledge; and (3) defining the apparent lack of a public sociology in terms of the malaise of American middle-class culture. The first could be seen most in evidence in Mills's early pre-Columbia writings, and later in *Character and Social Structure*; as well as *The Sociological Imagination*, and *Images of Man*; the second, about 1947 through 1956; and the third, from 1957 until Mills's death in 1962. Each of these themes, however, are readily detectable throughout his career; some may have been fleshed out more overtly or remained more latent than others, but they are in evidence throughout. His pungent criticisms of the consequences of political power guided by irresponsible conduct instead of open discourse are easily as applicable to the Bay of Pigs disaster as they are to *The Power Elite*. His clarion call in *The Sociological Imagination* to his profession to look toward classical thought as the principal guide for future research was heavily shaped by his Mannheim-created role of cultural gadfly-at-large. These categories should be seen as constituting a general outline, not a sharply delineated chronology.

◌◌◌

Mills's choice of a departmental major at Texas was for him an administrative formality, having little bearing on his choices of course enrollment, which were based upon course content and professorial reputation. He had absorbed philosophical and sociological traditions, among others, in a simultaneous fashion. Mills did not actually so much undergo a "transition" from philosopher to sociologist by way of Mannheim as he located in Mannheim's writings an approach, though not the only one, by which he could define pragmatism in sociological terms. Like the pragmatists, Mannheim was strongly imbued with political liberalism and relativism. He held a concept of truth as being defined through thought and action and of the use of indirect verificatory models as being the superior means toward developing ways of unmasking socially conditioned perspectives of truth. Mills made clear early on that he intended to build upon the American pragmatic and European naturalistic strains of thought, rather than to play them off against each other:

> Careful examination reveals no fundamental disagreement between Dewey's and Mannheim's conceptions of the generic character and derivation of epistemological forms. Mannheim's view overlaps the program that Dewey has pursued since 1903, when he turned from traditional concerns and squabbles over the ubiquitous relation of thought in general to reality at large, to a specific examination of the context, office and outcome of a type of inquiry.[19]

Mills went on further to declare an affinity between the other founder of pragmatism, Charles S. Peirce, and Mannheim in their approaches to verification.

> Peirce analyzed four segments from Western intellectual history. His comparative and quasi-sociological work was preliminary to his own acceptance of an observational and verificatory model which he himself analyzed out and generalized from laboratory science. . . . Mannheim's "total, absolute and universal" type of "ideology" in which social position bears upon "the structure of consciousness in its totality," including form as well as content, may be interpreted to mean this social-historical relativization of a model of truth, or the influence of a "social position" upon "choice" of one model as over against another. Mannheim's remarks do not contradict this more explicit and analytic statement.[20]

Mannheim's distinction between relationism and relativism had been one of the major stumbling blocks which he had never quite resolved to the satisfaction of those both critical and sympathetic toward the sociology of knowledge. Ziengenfuss[21] and Scimecca[22] concluded that it was ultimately "a play on words," while Phillips called it "far from clear" and "unconvincing."[23] Mills, too, found it wanting, although perhaps less so than others and for reasons far different than von Schelting or Speier, who viewed the sociology of knowledge as an encroachment upon the domain of philosophy. He felt that Mannheim had not taken his arguments to their logical conclusions; that he adequately defined neither the meaning of specific terminology nor its applicability to ongoing events. His dissatisfaction was nowhere made more explicit than in his review of Mannheim's *Man and Society in an Age of Reconstruction.*[24] Howard Becker and Thomas McCormick of the

University of Wisconsin served as book review editors of the *American Sociological Review* at the time, and no doubt they had personally solicited Mills's comments, given their student's great interest in Mannheim's *Ideology and Utopia*: Mannheim, said Mills, "does not evidence skill in deducing from large discourse specific hypotheses and constructing the means of their testing. His work loses in firm specificity to gain in novel conceptual optics."[25] Mills especially objects to what he perceives to be Mannheim's use of language, all the more troubling, since it had been Mannheim himself who had so lucidly explained at the beginning of *Ideology and Utopia* how members of collective social positions reinterpreting singular words in radically different ways could lead to an ideological morass such as that of Europe in the 1920s:

> This "mass society" is one of the least substantiated notions in the book. One wishes Mannheim had characterized it less with words like "emotional" and "national" and more with such indices as voting trends. . . . Repeatedly, the grossly unsociologic "we" is used. Exactly whom does this "we" include? Since he is not a magician, it cannot embrace others than those influenced in some manner by books of the kind he is writing. Who are these? They are the very ones whose decline in prestige and power he himself has traced.[26]

Mills saw in Mannheim a means for constructing working models of social structures in their totality in a way that would verify the pragmatic traditions. As represented by these passages, Mills sought to expand upon Mannheim's sociological conceptions of language, truth, and logic. Actually, Mills's pragmatic grounding had been one of the reasons why he found Mannheim to have only partially satisfactory answers in the first place. In this sense, Mills arrived at a study of the sociology of knowledge by way of pragmatism more than he used pragmatism to bolster his position on the sociology of knowledge.

Mills sought to develop sociological explanations for how ideological positions held by collective identities are interpreted by members within and outside them. In three articles he published during the Wisconsin period—"Language, Logic, and Culture,"[27] "Situated Actions and Vocabularies of Motive,"[28] and "The Language and Ideas of Ancient China"[29]—he emphasizes how language serves as a major catalyst for and inhibitor of social integration. Stylistically, his articles are often disjointed, even confusing, yet there is enough stimulation on a substantive level to make them of more than passing interest.

According to the first article, whether discourse assumes the form of the spoken or printed word, it is carried on by way of a language common to both thinker and audience. "Language" is not necessarily a given national or ethnic tongue, although this could be one example; rather, more generically, it refers to arguments whose symbols evoke common denominators of response. If language is interpretable in different ways, and if it determines the angle from which individuals approach a problem, it must also color how an audience interprets the motives of a thinker.

In "Situated Actions and Vocabularies of Motive" Mills holds that motives cannot be considered separate from either language or its social setting. Belonging to a given class or group in a mobile society permits individuals to acquire a set of motives whose interpretation will remain relatively stable. When a given member "breaks ranks," the character of the class or group changes. When we inquire into a person's real attitude or real motive instead of the stated one, we must recognize that we can do no more than to infer from linguistic habits what that person's socially conditioned behavior is at the time the opinion is stated or the act is committed. Mills was later to argue that this is not done in most opinion research carried out by sociologists. How, then, should sociologists work with such inferences? He answers that we can construct ideal types of vocabularies of motive that exist in constellations of situations.

> A labor leader says he performs a certain act because he wants to get higher standards of living for the workers. A businessman says that this is rationalization, or a lie; that it is really because he wants more money for himself from the workers. A radical says a college professor will not engage in radical movements because he is afraid for his job, and besides, is a "reactionary." The college professor says this [concern for truth] is because he just likes to find out how things work. What is reason for one man is rationalization for another. The variable is the accepted vocabulary of motives, the ultimates of discourse, of each man's dominant group about whose opinion he cares. *Determination of such groups, their location and character, would enable delimitation of methodological control of assignment of motives for specific acts.*[30]

To determine the identity of these groups would require the use of language placed in specified social contexts:

> What is needed is to take all these *terminologies* of motives and locate them as *vocabularies* of motive in historic epochs and specified situations. Motives are of no value apart from the delimited societal situations for which they are appropriate. They must be situated. At best, socially unlocated *terminologies* of motives represent unfinished attempts to block out social areas of motive imputation and avowal. Motives vary in content and character with historical epochs and societal structures.[31]

It was the linkage of Peirce's logic of language to Mannheim's sociological theory of knowledge that gave Mills a unique angle of vision. Even in his more familiar works this fusion shows. But increasingly it was Mannheim who gripped Mills's imagination. As Weber and Simmel had argued before him, Mannheim held that managing modern organizations with the principal emphasis on efficiency leads to a concentration of decision-making authority at the top. In his own way, Mills antici-

pated the "end of ideology" debate.[32] Solutions to problems are defined in relation to how well problems are eliminated from the organization so as to realize its objectives, instead of how the content of the
problems it faces can yield fruitful insights into the behavior of complex
social systems. There is an excess of functional rationality relative to substantive rationality. The results are conformity by the individual member to the organization's goals and a corresponding loss of personal autonomy, the dulling of individual curiosity about the world external to
the organization, the incapacity to develop one's own power of reasoning, and the dichotomization of work and leisure such that work becomes something to endure until leisure time arrives.

Mills would apply this argument to the way social scientists work in
relation to organizations whether they be academic departments, government funding agencies, or research organizations. Sociologists attracted to research, said Mills, are subject to strong organizational pressures. They confuse metaphysics with morality; in rejecting (rightly) any
realm of a priori judgments in their work they also assume (wrongly)
that research must be free of the tasks of addressing the meaning of
moral action and the place of knowledge. This position was honed in
fine detail in *The Sociological Imagination*. What may be less obvious is
that Mannheim not only "influenced" Mills in this respect, he predated
him by a quarter of a century in both tone and substance. In a 1932 article in the *American Journal of Sociology*, Mannheim, after criticizing
German sociology for its overemphasis upon speculation, observed:

> American sociology suffers from an excessive fear of theories, from a
> methodological asceticism which either prevents the putting forth of gen-
> eral theories or else keeps such theories as exist isolated from practical re-
> search. . . . This ascetic attitude towards theories seems to be based on a
> mistrust of "philosophy" or "metaphysics." Unwillingness to discuss ba-
> sic questions, however, does not benefit positive research. It is possible
> that many American scholars will admit the importance of theoretical
> construction. However, the main thing in the field of methodology is not
> to have a right opinion, but to act according to it. Now, it seems to me
> that the most valuable specimens of "empirical" sociology show a curious
> lack of ambition to excel in the quality of theoretical insight into phe-
> nomenal structures. They reveal a great anxiety not to violate a certain
> very one-sided ideal of exactness. One almost ventures to say, such works
> aim in the first place at being exact, and only in the second place at con-
> veying a knowledge of things.[33]

Mills would replace some terminology: "methodological asceticism"
would become "abstracted empiricism," while "realism" would become "the sociological imagination." What is central is that Mannheim
left unexplained the origins of these phenomena. Mills would thread together the two critiques; he would explain the preponderance of ab-

stracted empiricists in terms of their strong attachments to formal organizations that to some extent define the art form in social research. By the 1950s he had long since ceased debating the utility of the sociology of knowledge.

✑✑✑

There were several reasons why Mills lost his enthusiasm for writing on the subject matter of those earliest articles. The academic support for the general position he took was less encouraging at Columbia than it had been at Wisconsin. In early 1940, while still at Wisconsin, he wrote to Robert K. Merton at Tulane (the latter would begin his appointment at Columbia in the fall of 1941) soliciting his comments for a proposed revision of "Methodological Consequences of the Sociology of Knowledge." Merton responded some three months later:

> In general, I cannot accept the relativistic impasse to which I am forced to believe you (and Mannheim) are driven. Secondly I do not believe that the alternative is an absolutistic notion of "truth." Thirdly, I think it can be shown that the avowed epistemological consequences of a sociology of knowledge rest in part, if not wholly, upon a semantic confusion in the use of such words as "truth," "validity," "knowledge." Fourthly, I do not accept, of course, most of the other views of Mannheim with respect to the tasks of a sociology of knowledge.[34]

Neither relativism nor its variant, relationism, appealed as much to Mills in practice as it did in theory. He was more iconoclast than mediator. Whether during his undergraduate years at Texas[35] or during the latter period of his private life,[36] he displayed a temperamental, uncompromising stance in presenting an argument about almost any public issue he discussed—what could be called a bludgeoning approach.

But by far the most important contributing factor was that Mills sought to be more than a sociologist of knowledge; he wanted to be a sociologist of institutions—particularly those related to political power and cultural drift in American life—and the influences that intellectuals (and the sociology of knowledge) have on each other.[37]

Despite the reputation that Mills had garnered by the 1950s for his adversary relationship to the wielders of power in America, he made it clear that power in society could flow from Jeffersonian channels accessible to a decent intelligentsia, who could expose and express the choice of roles and conduct open to those with power:

> It's been said in criticism that I am too much fascinated by power. This is not really true. It is intellect I have been most fascinated by, and power primarily in connection with that. It is the power in the intellect and the power of the intellect that most fascinates me, as a social analyst and cultural critic.[38]

Mills held to Mannheim's premise that the modern epoch enables us to see with great clarity that opposing viewpoints in the political arena derive from specific social contexts and are thus potentially complementary. Intellectuals can serve as the unifying bond. They cannot readily instruct politicians on what the ends of society ought to be; they *can* instruct them to understand their opponents by unmasking actual motives and their historical social positions. Through this restriction the curse of elitism can be lessened if not lifted. Politics may be necessarily partisan, but partisanship itself is malleable and subject to unceasing revision and interrogation. Unlike Mannheim, Mills felt that the prospect for this "scientific politics," at least in the United States, was grim and remote. It had become increasingly so since the First World War and the advent of American participation in world affairs.

A common denominator that ran through all Mills's works on this theme can be stated as follows: There was a time in America when those who held political power were drawn from the intelligentsia. In the "overdeveloped society," however, men of power have abandoned the intellect as a reference point. In the process, liberalism as a political force, where it has not been spent, is readily employed by hirelings of the power elite to obfuscate the misdeeds committed by this elite in the name of higher morality. Just as it is true that knowledge seldom lends power to an intelligentsia, the inverse is also true: power seldom lends knowledge to an elite.[39]

The process by which Mills came to this position can be seem in several articles he wrote during his Maryland years. In an unpublished paper, "Locating the Enemy: Problems of Intellectuals During Time of War" (a title, incidentally, Mills was to use in describing his trip to Russia), he argued that the intelligentsia loses much of its capacity for autonomous conduct when it is called upon to perform services for its respective governments in times of war. For the sake of promoting national unity it is impossible to acquire plural viewpoints, since such viewpoints are likely to emanate from foreign nations and will thus be suspect:

> Liberal social thinking requires something of which to be "critical," and something to which to look as "promising." Liberal intellectuals are by their character as intellectuals in opposition. But during war, the opposition lies across national boundaries; aliens are the "enemy." All the social mechanics and situations connected with the tasks which thinkers pursue stand *against* the chances of the intellectual content of their thinking being otherwise than mentioned.[40]

Mills did not quite explain, however, why intellectuals would so readily perform these tasks—teaching, writing, editing, researching—in the hire of the state. The significance of the article inheres in Mills's implication that nationalism, like class, party, corporate, or bureaucratic affiliation, can serve as a hindrance to the validation of truth.

In another unpublished paper from his Maryland interlude, ''The Personal and the Political,'' he did seem to clarify why intellectuals would perform services for the state.[41] They have succumbed, he says, to an absurd dichotomy of intellect and politics. In the process, they have separated intellect and morality. Truth and power are handmaidens, and if those seeking, holding, or augmenting power do not make use of a sociology-of-knowledge approach to the truth, they risk being organized into the ''higher immorality.'' As Mannheim had earlier pointed out, intellectuals who are frustrated for want of power, or at least influence over those who wield it; must do the very thing that they have been avoiding: search for truth as a form of political activism, not as a contemplative sphere unpolluted by politics.[42] Yet as basically middle-class persons and jobs holders in organizations, they frequently succumb to the political psychology of the frightened employee. They employ self-censorship to select ''safe'' problems to approach, as opposed to those which might jeopardize their positions in the white-collar apparatus, knowing that they compromise their autonomy as well.

Mills sharpened this argument in a 1944 article, ''The Powerless People: The Role of Intellectuals.''[43] Politics in modern industrial societies everywhere, he wrote, is an enterprise whose prime currency is power—and secrecy, sham, dishonesty, bureaucratization, shutting off dissent, become the prime mechanisms for maintaining power. Yet the explanations for this situation are diffuse; it is more a question of an internal condition than an external enemy. The task of the intellectual is to determine the identity of these national sources and the people who set them in motion. Even during wartime conditions, Mills viewed as his central task the cleansing of the national soul. It apparently never dawned on him to inquire what the American nation would become in the absence of such a national soul.

> The shaping of the society in which we live and the manner in which we shall live in it are increasingly political. And this society includes the realms of intellect and of personal morals. If we demand that these realms be geared to our own activities which make a public difference, then personal morals and political interests become closely related. Philosophy that it is not personal escape involves taking a political stand. The independent artist and intellectual are among the few remaining personalities equipped to resist and fight the stereotyping and consequent death of genuinely lively things. These worlds of mass-art and mass-thought are increasingly geared to the demands of politics. That is why it is in politics that intellectual solidarity and effort must be centered. If the thinker does not relate himself to the value of the truth in political struggle, he cannot responsibly cope with the whole of live experience.[44]

This statement contains the germ of almost everything that Mills would write thereafter on the relationship between power and the free-floating intellect; indeed, certain sections were lifted verbatim for later use.[45] The preceding quote, in particular, reads like a statement of personal mission. In lecturing the clergy for avoiding politics, he maintained: "This world *is* political. Politics, understood for what it really is today, has to do with the decisions men make which determine how they shall live and how they shall die."[46] His stratification volumes could be better appreciated as missionary work exhorting secular and religious priesthoods to transform ideas into political action than as sheer empirical or descriptive studies.

The failure of modern liberalism, for Mills, was that whereas it had once relied upon reason and intellect for its leverage, it had become transformed into the language of functional rationality and institutional prerequisite.[47] The individual, within which the essence of liberal thought resided, had collapsed into political inactivism. Unable to account for the apparent decline of "competitive balance" between persons and organizations and the increased collusion of economic, political, and military orders, the individual was seeking refuge in apathy or ideological wish-fulfillment projected against some identifiable adversary.

Concurrent with the decline of liberal philosophy had been the ascendancy of liberal rhetoric. From Aristotle through Locke and Mannheim, one of liberalism's fundamental tenets had been that morality and freedom are to be found within the political process. But when the politically powerful use "morality" and "freedom" to justify behavior that consistently negates these ideals, they banalize the ideals of liberalism itself. Where liberalism had not become an obfuscatory device, it became the rallying cry for upward mobility and rising expectations within a mixed capitalist economy, a vehicle for private and quasi-private interest groups to press their claims upon a broker state that would give alms to each in the name of "fair play." The appeal of liberalism for the labor leader, bureaucrat, and businessman alike was its very bane:

> The ideals of liberalism have been divorced from any realities of modern social structure that might serve as the means of their realization. Everybody can easily agree on general ends; it is more difficult to agree on means and the relevance of various means to the ends articulated. The detachment of liberalism from the facts of a going society make it an excellent mask for those who do not, cannot, or will not do what would have to be done to realize its ideals.[48]

The charge that liberalism had become weak, soft, compromising, vacillating, mere rhetoric, and incapable of mounting an attack against political tyranny had also been made by ideologues of the Right and Left alike—although for different reasons. The response of the postwar liberal intelligentsia to their critics was a celebration of an "American century" and a championing of the "vital center." This was far removed from the narrow strain of the Left which Mills represented, and which was typified by the end-of-ideology theme established at the 1955 Congress of Cultural Freedom Conference in Milan. The late 1940s and the whole of the 1950s were the heyday of what Garry Wills called the "Bogart professor": the liberal tough-guy, who, given his manifold experience in the OSS, CIA, or better still, a brief, ill-fated flirtation with the Communist party, could meet the challenges of ideology run amuck.[49] With Arthur Koestler, Sidney Hook, and Arthur Schlesinger setting the general tone, the spokespersons for postwar liberalism, working under the assumption of providing a scenario in which traditional references to "right" and "left" would evaporate, opened up a primary front against the Left (susceptible to the temptation of blinding itself to Stalinism) and a secondary one against the Right (susceptible to the temptation of the corresponding McCarthyite overreaction). Thus, at the very time when liberalism became ideologically weakened, it evolved a "tough-minded pragmatism" or, alternately, "hard-headed pragmatism." Earlier criticism of the American social structure in its totality was considered at best "one-sided" and "utopian."

Mills thought this to be liberalism's great betrayal. It became a disillusionment with any real commitment to socialism, expressed more as a world-weary tone of voice than as an explicit argument. The very tough-mindedness lauded by the Congress of Cultural Freedom was paradoxically the confirmation of liberalism's impotence. The "end of ideology" was an ideology itself. In Mannheimiam terms, it was a particular ideology, not a total one, never going beyond incremental reform and oneupmanship over immediate adversaries into an examination of existing institutions. Mills wrote in 1960:

> "Utopian" nowadays I think refers to any criticism or proposal that transcends the up-close milieu of a scatter of individuals: the milieu which men and women can understand directly and which they can reasonably hope to change. In this exact sense, our theoretical work is indeed utopian. In my own case at least, deliberately so. What needs to be understood, and what needs to be changed, is not merely first this and then that detail of some institution or policy. If there is to be a politics of a New Left what needs to be analyzed is the *structure* of institutions, the *foundation* of policies. In this sense, both in its criticism and in its proposals, our work is necessarily structural—and so, *for us*, just now—utopian.[50]

Mills was arguing from the same set of precepts as Mannheim. The end-of-ideology ideologues, he said, had mistakenly aimed their guns at the entire utopian Left, when they should have properly aimed them at its chiliastic elements, who cannot project collective visions of structural change other than by completely transcending their existing social-historical context. Blinded by doctrinaire official anti-communist, those committed to the end of ideology seemed like chiliasts; the very reverse of empirical social researchers. To Mills, their very "hard-headedness" had prevented them from appreciating Mannheim's warning that "the liberal idea is adequately intelligible only as a counterpart to the ecstatic attitude of the chiliast which often hides behind a rationalist facade and which historically and socially offers a continual, potential threat to liberalism."[51]

ᴗᴑᴗᴑ

During the mid-1950s, Mills had become convinced that the power relationships in American life were less a matter of politics than of political culture, with "free-floating intelligentsia" becoming "cultural workmen." This shift in orientation, most noticeable in *The Sociological Imagination* and especially in the papers that constituted the unpublished *The Cultural Apparatus*, represented Mills's mature views of Mannheim. Mills's view of American culture was coterminous with his view of the impotence of cultural workmen to make a dent. In one major sense, it was very much attuned to many of the sociological and social-psychological observations of, and biases toward, the middle- and lower-middle-income families of the time. The 1950s were a period of organization men, pyramid climbers, status seekers, men in gray flannel suits, and lonely crowds. The Economic Man of *White Collar* led Mills to formulate a parallel cultural variant: "the cheerful robot." To such an anti-person, history was little more than a blind drift of incomprehensible forces, which, he mechanically reasoned, obeyed the classic law of Fate ("Whatever is, must therefore be"). This type of person was "cheerful" in the sense that his lacquered smiles masked his ulterior motive: getting ahead.

The central task of social scientists, at least of Mills's persuasion, must be to explain the components of historical drift to actual and potential cheerful robots alike. That they had not done so, said Mills, was attributable to their failure to recognize this constituency; social scientists were becoming highly educated cheerful robots themselves. As such they could not link up historical drift with human freedom.

> The ultimate problem of freedom is the problem of the cheerful robot, and it arises in this form today because today it has become evident to us that *all* men do *not* naturally *want* to be free; that all men are not willing or not able, as the case may be, to exert themselves to acquire the reason that freedom requires. To formulate any problem requires that we state the values involved and the threat to those values. It is that felt threat to cherished values—such as those of freedom and reason—that is the necessary moral substance of all significant problems of social inquiry, and as well as all public issues and private troubles.[52]

The pressures of increasing rationalization in modern societies not only separate daily and esoteric knowledge from each other, but also put distance between the groups that are in charge of them. Esoteric knowledge (intellect) and daily knowledge (common sense) stand at contrived opposite poles; intellectuals are said to have much of the former and little of the latter; the "mainstream" have much of the latter and little of the former. Whereas for Thomas Paine "common sense" meant an integration of personal life-style and political action, it has, for the cheerful robot, come to mean an ideal pretext under which "politics" becomes part of a public relations life-style. Self-serving cultural distinctions—"highbrow," "middlebrow," and "lowbrow" emerge. Freedom and security are increasingly indistinguishable. Threats to personal security are personified, with an assistance by the mass media, as "them," the enemies of freedom. Freedom is no longer a necessity, but rather an a priori assumption centered around vaguely defended notions of free enterprise and anti-communism. The extent to which both political freedom and private security are practiced becomes a general sociological concept. More importantly, this linkage permits us to clarify modern trends toward integral democracy. The struggle to secure freedom and security becomes ultimately the fundamental characteristic of the American political culture.

In eliminating it, however, there is a pitfall as well as a promise. Private lives and public issues may be integrated to make for a more "whole" individual; they may also be integrated by way of dictatorial fiats. The latter was the very drift that had been developing as a result of the power elite's coordination of knowledge and power. How could it be that in modern democracies, particularly the United States, the imposition of political, economic, and military authoritarianism upon private lives seemed a distinct possibility? Mannheim seemed to have an explanation. Although democracy is predicated on the faith in human reason to arrive at political decisions, it also allows for avenues of uninhibited emotional impulse. Democracy may foster the development of individual personality, but it also develops powerful mechanisms that induce the individual to surrender his or her conscience and "seek refuge in the anonymity of the mass."[53] A democracy of reason may become a democracy of impulse.

> Dictatorships can arise only in democracies; they are made possible by the greater fluidity introduced into political life by democracy; it represents one of the possible ways in which a democratic society may try to solve its problems. . . . As political democracy becomes broader and new groups enter the political arena, their impetuous activity may lead to crises and stalemate situations in which the political decision mechanism of the society becomes paralyzed. The political process may then be short-circuited so as to enter a dictatorial phase.[54]

Mannheim is here transposing De Tocqueville in terms of the sociology of knowledge. Mills appeared to follow Mannheim's argument insofar as he analyzed the willingness of the individual to withdraw from a political arena where power and intellect are mutually reinforcing. He differed as to which form of behavior this withdrawal represents. For Mannheim, who witnessed the ascension to power in Germany by the Nazis when he wrote "On the Democratization of Culture," the individual exercise of reason subverted by submission of the individual to a vulgarized, collectivized vitalism; for Mills, this was manifest in the individual's withdrawal from political participation altogether, except to cast a periodic and relatively meaningless vote. Authoritarianism is slowly consolidating itself in the West through default on the part of its potentially adversary forces.

The anxiety of the middle class throughout the century becomes a source and an outcome of its perceived impotence. The capacity for political action is held in check by predominating ideologies that are designed to prevent anxiety from becoming unmanageable. When these ideologies become multidimensional and conflicting, the individual turns inward and becomes blasé, failing to understand that feelings of being overwhelmed by public issues and personal problems are part of an interlocking trap. Intellect alone cannot permit an escape; it can only recognize the need to do so and suggest ways in which an escape can be fashioned. The actual task of springing the trap is the province of persons who publicly confront the question: "What must be done, personally and publicly, in order to get whatever it is we want for ourselves *and* . . . what must be done in and to the structure of society?"[55] The actors involved seem no longer to be found among intellectuals, but in a tripartite segment—intellectuals, scientists, and artists—each of whom must challenge the existing cultural apparatus established and maintained by the coordination of power. This apparatus consists of

> all the organizations and milieus in which artistic, intellectual and scientific work is made available to circles, publics, and masses. . . . Inside this apparatus, standing between men and events, the images, meaning, slogans, the worlds in which men live are organized, hidden, debunked, celebrated. Taken as a whole, the cultural apparatus is the lens of mankind through which men see; the medium through which they interpret and report what they see. It is the semiorganized source of their very identities and of their aspirations. It is the source of The Human Variety—of style of life and of ways to die.[56]

Cultural activities are subject to vocabularies of motive. Throughout the nations of the world, to experience a cultural event is to experience symbols of communication filtered through the dominant institutional order. A dominant cultural establishment develops through voluntary exchange between cultural workmen and ruling elites. The common bargaining chip is prestige. The cultural workman, as a yeoman craftsman, is co-opted every time he seeks prestige from the cultural apparatus; his ability to unite reason, sensibility, and technique to create beauty is thus compromised. There is a parallel here to the Marxian theory of surplus value of labor that was stated in Mills's 1944 *Politics* article: "The means of effective communication are being expropriated from the intellectual worker. The material basis of his initiative and intellectual freedom is no longer in his hands."[57] In this manner, the film star who accepts "$5,000 a throw" for a popularly demanded style even when he or she desires to break out of that style, the liberal intellectual or journalist who serves as a hired gun to obfuscate the Bay of Pigs affair, and the physicist who refuses to warn superiors of the dangers of thermonuclear war are each in need of developing a common collective consciousness, although one that is not class-biased.

By casting the social scientist in one of several social roles that can bridge the disparate cultural segments of the society at large, Mills's Mannheim-influenced person comes most into focus: sociologist-as-craftsman, sociologist-as-Great-Man, sociologist-as-autobiographer. Yet for all of the drama, ambition, and stimulation suggested by Mills's vision, it contains several weaknesses, beginning with the rather tenuous assumption that the activities of artists, scientists, and intellectuals are really all that much alike. Mills did not have extensive contact with the American cultural scene. His view of everyday life in America during the 1950s was bound to be considerably more pessimistic than the period was in fact. There may not have been a flowering of the Renaissance Man, but neither was there a cultural desert, interrupted only by a minute rumblings of creativity appreciated by an equally minute underground audience. Novelists such as Herbert Gold and Norman Mailer, as well as Allen Ginsberg and the rest of the Beats, may have been more talked about than read (and still are), but their work reached a sizeable audience notwithstanding; Hollywood produced a number of fine movies, some of which, such as Stanley Kubrick's *Paths of Glory* and Elia Kazan's *A Face in the Crowd*, were not only damning critiques of "crackpot realism" but box-office successes; Miles Davis, Bud Powell, and John Coltrane broadened the contours of jazz without causing undue atrophy to the music's audience or identity; modern art may have been "chic," but its popularity did not cheapen its creators—the brilliant crop of art critics saw to that. "Race music" became "rhythm and blues"; rock 'n' roll blew Patti Paige, the Ames Brothers, and *Your Hit Parade* off the pop charts. Like so many intellectuals of his day, Mills was not aware of the significance of this burgeoning native culture. Mills's European awareness had its price: European myopia to innovations not linked to high culture.

One could take a neo-Schumpeterian tack and argue that the mass media, so controlled and personified by the power elite, provided (via long-playing records, photographic prints, the cinema, and paperback books) the common fodder for that elite's very demise. This would be relatively close to Daniel Bell's later thesis in *The Cultural Contradictions of Capitalism*[58] Yet such an argument itself may not necessarily hold in the long run; and if it does, one must not assume that the net effect is harmful. Mills did not examine this possibility with respect to the mass media; he simply assumed that the mass media were primary agents of cultural drift.

Mills's view of the cheerful robot, while no doubt grounded in reality to a certain extent, is also a product of the limitations of both the mass-society literature and the suburbia-as-split-level-trap image one frequently encountered in his day. It was left to William Michelson, Herbert Gans, and Bennett Berger to develop counterpositions in response to William H. Whyte, John Seeley, Maurice Stein, and David Riesman. Mills's eschewal of structured survey research cost him dearly in this area. Unwilling to go out into the field, and working with a cheerful-robot hypothesis, he had to fall back on sorting out a collage of firsthand impressions, happenstance personal encounters, newspaper and magazine clippings, and other people's empirical findings to develop his own cultural critique. These devices may have been valuable, but they were so within severely circumscribed limits. Bennett Berger may have been pointing his finger at Mills when he concluded his study of a working-class suburb in California:

> The critic waves the prophet's long and accusing finger and warns: "You may *think* you're happy, you smug and prosperous striver, but I tell you that the anxieties of status mobility are too much; they impoverish you psychologically, they alienate you from your family. . . ." And the suburbanite looks at this new house, his new car, his new freezer, his lawn and patio . . . and scratches his head, bewildered. The critic appears as the eternal crotchet, the professional malcontent telling the prosperous that their prosperity, the visible symbols of which surround them, is an illusion: the economic victory of capitalism is culturally Pyrrhic.[59]

Because suburbia and mass man were so intertwined in the mind of Mills, it was not surprising that he failed to see authenticity and heterogeneity in both ideal types.

Mills's view of American political culture, a product of and a challenge to Karl Mannheim's approach to the integration of reflection and action within the intellectual, represented an incisive, but flawed, vision. The flaws were real enough, perhaps even crippling. Yet it was a credit to Mills's own qualities as a social scientist that he could provide working models for research, however damaging their nature. Their applicability extended well beyond American borders.

REFERENCES

1. C. Wright Mills. *The Causes of World War Three*. New York: Simon & Schuster, 1958, pp. 20–21.

2. Harvey Swados. "C. Wright Mills: A Personal Memoir." *Dissent* (winter 1963), p. 37.

3. Dan Wakefield. "Taking It Big: A Memoir of C. Wright Mills." *Atlantic Monthly* (September 1971), p. 65.

4. See *ibid.*, p. 70.

5. Mills, *The Causes of World War Three*, p. 156.

6. C. Wright Mills. *The Sociological Imagination*, New York and London: Oxford University Press, 1959, p. 6.

7. C. Wright Mills. "Two Criteria for a Good Society." In *On Social Men and Social Movements: The Collected Addresses of C. Wright Mills*, edited with an Introduction by Irving Louis Horowitz. (Unpublished in the United States. Published in Spanish only, as *De hombres sociales y movimientos sociales*; Mexico City: Siglo Veintiuno Editores, 1968).

8. John Friedmann. *Retracking America: A Theory of Transactive Planning*. Garden City, N.Y.: Doubleday, 1971, p. 228. Friedmann remains one of the few American planning theorists who incorporated into their writings the relationship between societal guidance and the sociology of knowledge.

9. Each of the following sources provides an adequate-to-excellent discussion or critique of Mannheim's sociology of knowledge. Among the briefer summarizations are: Friedmann, *Retracking America*, pp. 22–48; Scott Green, *The Logic of Social Inquiry*, Chicago: Aldine, 1969, pp. 5–6; W. Warren Wagar, *The City of Mass*, Boston: Houghton Mifflin, 1963, pp. 252–53; Hans Speier, *Social Order and the Risks of War: Papers in Political Sociology*, Cambridge, Mass.: MIT Press, 1969, pp. 190–201; H. Stuart Hughes, *Consciousness and Society: The Reconstruction of European Social Thought, 1890–1930*, New York: Random House, 1958, pp. 418–27; Benjamin Walter, "The Sociology of Knowledge and the Problem of Objectivity," in Llewellyn Gross, ed., *Sociological Theory: Inquiries and Paradigms*, New York: Harper & Row, 1967, pp. 335–37; Robert K. Merton, *Social Theory and Social Structure*, 2nd. ed., New York: Free Press, 1957, pp. 256–88; Kurt Wolff, ed., *From Karl Mannheim*, New York: Oxford, 1972, pp. xi–cxxxiii; Werner Stark, *The Sociology of Knowledge: An Essay in Aid of a Deeper Understanding of the History of Ideas*, London: Routledge & Kegan Paul, 1968; Jacques Macquet, *The Sociology of Knowledge: Its Structure and Its Relation to the Philosophy of Knowledge*, Boston: Beacon Press, 1951. For a discussion of Mannheim as a direct influence upon Mills, see Joseph A. Scimecca, *The Sociological Theory of C.*

Wright Mills, Port Washington, N.Y.: Kennikat Press, 1977, pp. 32–33; 50–51; Derek Phillips, "Epistemology and the Sociology of Knowledge: The Contributions of Mannheim, Mills and Merton," *Theory and Society* 1, no. 1 (1974); and Irving Louis Horowitz, "Mannheims Wissenssozologie und C. W. Mills' soziologisches Wissen," *Kolner Zeitschrift fur Soziologie und Sozial-Psychologie* 22 (1980):360–83.

10. Karl Mannheim. *Ideology and Utopia*, translated by Louis Wirth and Edward A. Shils. New York: Harvest Books, 1955, pp. 91–92.

11. *Ibid.*

12. Karl Mannheim. *Freedom, Power, and Democratic Planning*. New York: Oxford University Press, 1950, pp. 200–1.

13. Karl Mannheim. *Essays on the Sociology of Culture*, edited by Ernest Mannheim and Pual Kecskemeti. London: Routledge & Kegan Paul, 1956, p. 51.

14. Hughes, *Consciousness and Society*, p. 420.

15. C. Wright Mills. "Situated Actions and Vocabularies of Motives." *American Sociological Review* 5, no. 6 (December 1949):427.

16. Stark, *The Sociology of Knowledge*, pp. 333–46.

17. Irving Louis Horowitz. "Prehistoria de la Sociologia del Concimiento: Bacon y Dilthey." In *Cuadernos de Sociologia*, Facultad de Filosofia y Letras de la Universidad de Buenos Aires, Vol. XIII, no. 22 (1960): 189–214.

18. C. Wright Mills. Introduction to *Images of Man*. New York: George Braziller Publishers, 1960, p. 12.

19. C. Wright Mills. "Methodological Consequences of the Sociology of Knowledge." *American Journal of Sociology* 46, no. 3 (1940):456.

20. *Ibid.*, pp. 456–57.

21. W. Ziegenfuss. "Gesellschaftphilosophie." In Stark, *The Sociology of Knowledge*, p. 338. Stark himself levels precisely the same charge.

22. Scimecca, *The Sociological Theory of C. Wright Mills*, p. 50.

23. Phillips, "Epistemology and the Sociology of Knowledge," p. 65.

24. C. Wright Mills. Review of Mannheim's *Man and Society in an Age of Reconstruction*. *American Sociological Review* 5, no. 6 (1940):965–69.

25. *Ibid.*, p. 965.

26. *Ibid.*, pp. 967–68.

27. C. Wright Mills, *Power, Politics and People*. New York: Oxford University Press, 1963, pp. 423–38.

28. *Ibid.*, pp. 439–52.

29. *Ibid.*, pp. 469–524.

30. *Ibid.*, p. 448.

31. *Ibid.*, p. 452.

32. See Daniel Bell, *The End of Ideology: On the Exhaustion of Political Ideas in the Fifties*, rev. ed. New York: The Free Press, 1962, p. 24.

33. Karl Mannheim. Review of *Methods in Social Science*, edited by Stuart A. Rice. In *American Journal of Sociology* 38, no. 2 (September 1932): 273–82. Reprinted in Mannheim, *Essays on Sociology and Social Psychology*, edited by Paul Kecskemeti. New York: Oxford University Press, 1953, pp. 189–90.

34. Robert K. Merton to C. Wright Mills, April 16, 1940.

35. A. P. Brogan to John L. Gillin, February 2, 1939; Carl Rosenquist to T. C. McCormick, February 2, 1939; Henry D. Sheldon, Jr. to John L. Gillin, February 4, 1939.

36. See comments of Yaroslava Mills in Scimecca, p. 121.

37. C. Wright Mills to Hans Gerth, January 16, 1942.

38. C. Wright Mills. "A Preface to Political Morality." In *On Social Men and Political Movements*, pp. 5–11.

39. C. Wright Mills. *The Power Elite*. New York: Oxford University Press, 1956, p. 352.

40. C. Wright Mills. "Locating the Enemy: Problems of Intellectuals During Time of War." In *On Social Men and Political Movements*, pp. 134–37.

41. C. Wright Mills. "The Personal and the Political." In *On Social Men and Political Movements*, pp. 12–23.

42. See Mannheim, *Ideology and Utopia*, p. 104.

43. C. Wright Mills. "The Powerless People: The Role of Intellectuals." *Politics* 1, no. 3 (April 1944); also in "The Social Role of the Intellectual," in *Power, Politics and People*, pp. 292–304.

44. Mills, *Power, Politics and People*, p. 299.

45. See, for example, C. Wright Mills, *White Collar*. New York: Oxford University Press, 1951, pp. 59–60.

46. Mills, *The Causes of World War Three*, p. 155.

47. See C. Wright Mills, "Liberal Values in the Modern World." In *Power, Politics and People*, pp. 187–95; see also "Political Ideals and Vulgar Ideologies," in *On Social Men and Political Movements*, pp. 205–16.

48. Mills, *Power, Politics and People*, p. 189.

49. Garry Wills. *Nixon Agonistes: The Crisis of the Self-Made Man*. Boston: Houghton Mifflin, 1970, pp. 507–22.

50. C. Wright Mills. "Letter to the New Left." *New Left Review*, no. 5 (1960); also in *The End of Ideology Debate*, edited by Chaim I. Waxman. New York: Simon & Schuster, 1968, p. 134.

51. Mannheim, *Ideology and Utopia*, p. 226.

52. Mills, *The Sociological Imagination*, p. 175.

53. Mannheim, *Essays on the Sociology of Culture*, p. 174.

54. *Ibid.*, pp. 171–72.

55. C. Wright Mills. "Private Lives and Public Affairs: Life as a Trap." In *On Social Men and Political Movements*, pp. 38–47.

56. Mills, *Power, Politics and People*, pp. 406–7.

57. Mills, "The Powerless People," pp. 10–12.

58. Daniel Bell. *The Cultural Contradictions of Capitalism*. New York: Basic Books, 1976.

59. Bennett Berger. *Working-Class Suburb*. Berkeley and Los Angeles: The University of California Press, 1960, pp. 63–65.

8

The Protestant Weber and the Spirit of American Sociology

It was perhaps never before in history made so easy for any nation to become a great civilized power as for the American people. Yet, according to human celebration, it is also the last time, as long as the history of mankind shall last, that such conditions for a free and great development will be given; the areas of free soil are now vanishing everywhere in the world.

Max Weber, ''Capitalism and Rural Society in Germany''

ALL MAJOR ELEMENTS AND TENDENCIES in modern sociology take Max Weber seriously. Marxists appreciate his keen sense of historical specificity. Functionalists celebrate his capacity to stay close to explanatory variables. Traditionalists respect his sense of the place of religion and convention in social life. And liberals date Weber as the main source of their own commitment to a scientific standpoint over ideological persuasions. It is almost as if Weber provided not just a theory of status legitimation, but in his person was a special form of legitimation to the American sociologist. Parsonians identify with Weber's notions of bureaucracy and social stratification; Mertonians identify with Weber's concepts of career patterns of scientists and theologians and their stimulus to social change; and Millsians identify with Weber's concepts of authority and the dysfunctionality of raw power no less than the belief that at its source every problem is a moral paradox.

We know from Hans Gerth that whatever linguistic limitations Mills had in German, he nonetheless ''loved to pore over the Weber materials'' which Gerth had translated. If Mills never did quite make up his mind about Weber, it was less a response to Weber's writings directly than it was a mixed set of feelings toward those, like Gerth, who mediated his reading of the great German. Perhaps Marianne Weber, in her biography of Max Weber (a work which, by the way, Mills helped to support), best captured his essential spirit of dedication to freedom over tyranny, principle over expediency, and conscience over dogmatism.

> Weber always judged political events on the basis of one thing to which he clung all his life: Intellectual freedom was to him the greatest good, and under no circumstances was he prepared to consider even interests of political power as more important and attainable for the individual. Not for reasons of expediency, but only in the name of conscience does a man have the right to oppose the conscientiously held different beliefs of others.[1]

Weber was a European social analyst par excellence, but he traveled very well. He viewed events in grand world historic terms. Even when he came to the United States and saw "the Greek shining the Yankee's shoes for five cents, the German acting as his waiter, the Irishman managing his politics, and the Italian digging his dirty ditches," his real interests were focused not on the persons performing such roles but on the "Yankee" for whom the work was being performed.[2] True enough, this was circumscribed by his general belief in the waste created by capitalism. However, unlike the muckraking tradition that wafted out of the stench of the Chicago stockyards, unlike the studies of ethnic minorities, racial groups, and psychologically dislocated and sociologically deformed types, Weber's works uttered no cry for social change, for just laws, or for extending human rights. Such ideological posturing was simply foreign to Weber's legalistic style. Like the abstract "generalized other" of the symbolic interactionists, he saw only the "hopelessness of social legislation in a system of state particularism." Thus, Weber's totalism clashed with the reform instincts of Chicago-style sociology; with its personalistic emphasis on welfare and life-cycles.

Weber was concerned with power and authority: how they became legitimated, how status depends on authority. The world of the Chicago school, even of its conservative anthropological echelons, never could accept such a formulation, which seemingly denigrated status in deference to power and authority. It is small wonder that while Weber himself viewed his work as on a scale with that of Marx, the provincial sociology of the Midwest saw him as one more footnote to the power-and-authority school that could claim such an unlikely blend as Plato, Machiavelli, Marx, and Rousseau. From the American perspective it was indeed the case that what Weber conceived of as "world historic" trends were simply the decayed reflection of crumbling European intellectual edifices musing over their own past while taking a breather from war. Certainly that was the judgment from the American heartland: the one sector of sociology that was less than worshipful of Weber—and, not incidentally, the source of so many of Mills's early approaches.

Weber has little to say of the demimonde, of the underworld in which life is not "rationalized and bureaucratically structured" but basically unstructured, deviant, and marginal. Even the notion of charisma is directly related by him to political authority, rather than leadership styles in general. This reflects Weber's general neglect of the dysfunctional and personal elements in his system of social stratification—a theme which has been developed by many of Weber's American commentators. In sharp contrast, Mills's shorter essays are concerned with sailors in search of sex, prostitutes in search of respectability, and issues in deviance generally.

Weber was "discovered" by a special kind of American: the worldly eastern sociologist trained in Europe, or at least learned in the languages and customs of central and northern Europe. Learning about Weber was sifted through a filter called *The Structure of Social Action*.[3] The mood of the Chicago school in the thirties was analytic rather than synthetic, symbolic rather than historic. How was the Chicago school to know of Weber's interests in such things as the ecology of the city, property rights, the personal situation, and plebians and patricians when the Parsonian filtering process tended to minimize Weber's *Wirtschaft und Gesellschaft* precisely at those admittedly rare points where he ceased being systematic and grand, world historic and theoretic?[4] This was only to come at a later, postwar stage with the translations by Don Martindale of the University of Minnesota, which revealed that an entire layer of Weber's works lay undiscovered, unexamined in the Parsonian synthesis.

The American response to the European Weber is considerably more differentiated than prewar sociology allowed for—and for reasons not entirely trivial by any means. The East Coast developed styles of sociological research which increasingly became gentlemanly and remote in form and bureaucratic in substance. It was obviously easier to place Weber in this kind of professional context. In the postwar period, West Coast analysts rekindled an interest in Weber by shifting the emphasis from Weber as a theorist of social stratification to Weber as the political sociologist par excellence. There was also a clear shift in how West Coast thinkers like Reinhard Bendix and Seymour Martin Lipset operated with the data—even though many of these men were originally products of the East Coast or even Europe. There was an increasing emphasis on qualitative over quantitative findings. The basic valuational posture remained unchanged. Sociology on the East and West coasts retained an insistence on detachment over involvement, and pure research over applied research. In such matters, the newer western style was a perfect complement to the Columbia-Harvard-Yale approach to Weber. Generally, when the European Weberians examined the relationship of rich and poor, elites and masses, their personal sympathies were largely with the poor and the masses, but their professional interests were clearly focused upon examining the rich and the elites.

The role of Talcott Parsons in disseminating the spirit of Max Weber as a European orthodoxy can scarcely be overestimated. The design of *The Structure of Social Action* gives a critical anchor to a select cluster of Weber's writings. As translator of *The Protestant Ethic and the Spirit of Capitalism*, and later, with A.M. Henderson, of *The Theory of Social and Economic Organization*, Parsons set the tone for what was considered the essential Weber for a long while. The very idiosyncrasies of the Parsonian lexicon found their way into the corpus of those works of Weber he translated. If in the 1930s Parsons's definition of *Weber-studien* was rooted in the essay on the relationship of Protestantism to capitalism, by the fifties, when there was a much heavier number of translations available, the emphasis was shifting from Weber as illustrative of a "voluntaristic theory of action" to Weber as "illustrative of universalism and functional specificity." It was also Weber as the analyst of the "Western World" and of the "Anglo-Saxon" world to whom Parsons responded and resonated. He saw or created Weber in his own image: someone who understood both "the uniqueness of our social system" and "its precarious state of instability."[5] Weber *contra* authoritarianism was the political motif, and Weber *contra* traditionalism was the sociological motif.

The ways in which science can service the needs of totalitarianism and of modern bureaucratic structure tended to be profoundly minimized by Parsons. This is partially a consequence, hypothetically at least, of the Weberian tendency to minimize, although not ignore, the dysfunctionality of bureaucracy. The rise of fascism did temporarily shake Parsons's insular belief in conservative solutions and led him to emphasize, between 1945 and 1949 at least, checks upon authority rather than the rationality of authority.

It was not only what Weber stood for on specific issues that attracted Parsons, but also the sense that Weber (unlike Durkheim, Marshall, Pareto, or even Freud) made possible considerations of the social system within the framework of a general sociological theory. Inadvertently to be sure, Weber allowed for the evolution of a kind of sociological imperialism in which everything from family and personality to politics and economics could be viewed as a subsystem of sociology.[6] In introducing his first volume of selected papers, Parsons notes the existence of two big problems for social science: the development of a unified language, which is converted into a need for a conceptual scheme; and a theory of the relation of institutional structures and human behavior. On the latter score, Parsons identifies his view of function with that of Weber, since, says Parsons, only when human motivation is linked to the operations of a social system are generalizations about people "sociologically relevant."[7] Supplying a conceptual scheme and a general theory, Weber offered Parsons a way of transforming sociology from a parochial discipline, confined to local, small, and middle-sized issues, to a universal discipline dealing with large-scale issues, in which total systems proceed in Panglossian fashion always and everywhere toward increased rationality.[8]

To be a Parsonian became for a long time the only way professionals within American sociology could tolerably deal with big issues without being dismissed to Marxian marginalia. Parsons's own awareness of this undoubtedly accounts for his profound early animus toward Marxism and socialism. He adopted a cold, analytic stance with respect to any sociology which came within sniffing distance of a positive appraisal of "dialectics" or any other aspect of Marxology. This militancy differed markedly from his Olympian disregard of critics in general.[9]

Robert K. Merton, insofar as he represented a response to Weber, was not so much interested in systematizing as in secularizing the great European scholar. Weber became one of the classic father figures to whom the good sociologist turns for inspiration—specifically, for new ideas about old themes. The great theme of bureaucratization in modern society, for example, was for Merton not an illustration of universalist-instrumentalist action, but rather a challenge for further social science research into problems of professionalization. With some concern, Merton felt this approach provided an opportunity to "build a Solomon's House for sociologists"—with what telling effect remains to be demonstrated.

Bureaucracy as a theme enabled Merton to critically treat what Weber had failed to deal with substantively: the dysfunctions of certain bureaucratic structures; the administrative consequences of overconformity and maximum rule-boundedness; and above all, the possibility that Weber's pessimism, if not uncalled for, may have been slightly premature—since, as a matter of fact, "bureaucracy is a secondary group structure" oriented toward depersonalized achievement of "certain activities" only when primary group relations fail to solve problems and "run counter to these formalized norms."[10] The trend toward increasing bureaucratization in industrial societies raised for Merton a set of critical problems, which he outlined; many of his students in subsequent years filled in the intellectual crevices. But the overwhelming impression given by Merton's sociology is of problems to be solved rather than structures to be either applauded or overthrown.

Merton's use of Weber's sociology of religion is also dramatically different from that of Parsons. Instead of offering a propaedeutic review of Weber's position, Merton tried his hand at a slightly adjacent, related, but markedly distinctive problem: the differential tendency for German Protestants to pursue scientific career patterns more frequently than Catholics. The results of Merton's investigation were not particularly astonishing, nor were they intended to be. In a bibliographical postscript to his work *Social Theory*, Merton says that the results arrived at, at the empirical level, were "conceived as an effort to follow" and extend the "mandate . . . which Weber has opened up."[11] But the role of the "religious factor," even in a world of scientific discovery, is one that Merton placed great store by.

To underscore Merton's nonpolemical attitude toward the work of Weber, it should be noted that one of his most important papers, employing roughly the same analysis with respect to Protestantism and the rise of scientific societies in England, was published in *Science and Society*, which at the time was (and has remained) an avowedly Marxian journal. The problem of capitalism and its relation to the Protestant Reformation, particularly how it ramifies outward, is seen by Merton as a scientific problem bequeathed to modern sociology by Marx and Weber, stripped of its inherited ideological squabbling over whether economy or religion is the originating causal base of social development. The scientific problem in turn is seen as a social problem—an issue in the status of democracy.[12]

Merton responded to Weber as the sort of scholar who, above all, represented global considerations rather than some form of localism. Merton is no "easterner," but like Parsons, in this sense, a cosmopolitan figure entirely in touch with the world of European learning. Just how important Merton views this European context to be is reflected by his criticism of provincialism, rejected twice in the same sentence of his Acknowledgments to his omnibus collection *Social Theory and Social Structure*. Pitirim Sorokin is acknowledged as having helped him escape from the provincialism of thinking that effective studies of society were confined within American borders and from the slum-encouraged provincialism of thinking that "the primary subject-matter of sociology was centered in such peripheral problems of social life as divorce and juvenile delinquency." But since Sorokin had already gone off to "become absorbed in the study of historical movements on the grand scale," the search in Europe focused very heavily upon Marx, Durkheim, and Weber; and the problems selected for study by Weber—bureaucracy and the social structure, and the role of religion in social change—were uppermost for Merton over a long span of years. Even in Merton's more recent papers, such as "Social Conflict over Styles of Sociological Work," the impact of Weber upon Merton's liberal-heterodox view of the sociological field is noticeable. He argues for a Weberian middle position, against *Wertfrei* and *Partinost* alike; and for Weber's concept of a sociology which is *Wertbeziehung*—value-relevant. To the charge that value-relevance is a fuzzy halfway house, Merton responds much the way Weber did: that its very ambiguities allow for open debate and differing evaluations.[13]

⚬⚬⚬⚬

To be described as influenced by a figure is not necessarily a form of flattery. For Mills, as he was for Parsons and for Merton, Weber was a part of the classic tradition in sociology. But unlike either Parsons or Merton, Mills got his consciousness of Weber secondhand. It stemmed from German émigré sources. Mills learned about Weber from Hans Gerth, himself a German sociologist. But because of his Midwest intellectual links, Mills found his interest in Weber tempered by a range of considerations raised by other classic figures, such as Thorstein Veblen in economics, George Herbert Mead in social psychology, and John Dewey in philosophy. From the outset, Mills was uncomfortable with the role of interpreting Weber. What he did, in effect, was pragmatize Weber, as he was later to do in interpreting Marx. This is most obvious in the 1946 introduction which he and Gerth wrote for the translations of Weber's essays. Like Dewey and James, Mills saw Weber as "one of the last political professors who made detached contributions to science, and, as the intellectual vanguard of the middle classes, were also leading figures."[14] In the hands of Mills, Weber became the teacher and exemplar of intellectual courage, a moral rather than intellectual leader. It was not the refined pedagogic aspects of higher education that attracted Mills, but the moral infusion of politics that struck a responsive chord.

Aside from the introductory essay to *From Max Weber*, Mills wrote little about Weber which did not carry at least an implicit critical tone. In part this derived from ambivalences in his early association with Gerth at Wisconsin. This critical tendency was pushed even further and harder by Mills the further removed he was from Wisconsin. For it was Gerth who was responsible for the monumental projects of translating Weber's religion-sociology, and it was Mills who placed decreasing emphasis on the Weber legacy as such. After his collaboration with Gerth terminated, it would appear that his fascination with Weber diminished sharply.

Early in his career, Mills appreciated the fact that Weber was something less than a radical savior of sociology. He understood that Weber's kind of identification of charisma with irrationality was linked with totalitarianism, which, if Weber did not approve of, at least he had no intellectual defense against. Similarly, Weber's belief that bureaucracy would remain fairly stable throughout revolutionary shifts in power was a generalization that Mills felt did not obtain for twentieth-century bureaucracy.[15] It astonished Mills, even toward the close of his career, that this highly questionable formulation of the bureaucratic continuity should remain unchecked and uncriticized for so long among his professional peers.[16]

One aspect of Weber's thought that Mills picked out as potentially revolutionary in its consequences was the difference between Marx and Weber on the social organization of modern capitalism. Marx's idea that capitalism represents an anarchy of production was subject to Mills's jeering criticism. He saw this as one of Marx's basic generic errors. He stood with Weber in understanding that what made capitalism viable or at least durable is that in its statist form capitalism is rational and planned in the extreme.[17] Mills also learned from Weber that what made the development of a true revolutionary experience so difficult in modern capitalist society was that rationality had shifted from the individual and become lodged in the total institution. Because of this, the increased education of modern man had no revolutionary consequences; it only went to feed the needs of the all-encompassing institution for happy and well-educated robots.

Mills's positive linkage to Weber was based on several extrapolations: the role of capitalist political economy in the formation of the modern state, and the sacrifice of the intellect involved in outfitting the scientific soul for policy needs of the bureaucratic state. Weber's ambiguity on how to handle these relationships was translated by Merton as the need for intellectual heterodoxy, but as translated by Mills it became the need for intellectual commitment in combatting state authority.

Mills saw in Weber the need to connect intellect with power and not to shy away from the challenging dangers of possible corruption through power. The choice had to be squarely faced between what value element should rule: intellect or passion. Both Mills and Weber were contemptuous of fears as to whether intellect could be saved by avoiding problems of power and authority; neither quite brought themselves to appreciate the compromising and bargaining aspects of power. At the very root, one would have to say that this fierce devotion to intelligence is what Mills learned from Weber. Methodologically, Mills learned from Weber to deal with society as Parsons had done—as a complete social system—but he went a step beyond that, dealing with evolving social structures in a comparative context. It was Mills's hope to transform, via Weber, systematic sociology into historical sociology, without losing touch with empirical reality.[18]

The history of European sociology, and the selective absorption of that history by Mills and the radical tradition generally, represents an intense albeit symbolic struggle between the northern European, or Germanic, vision of the field and the Franco-Italian, or southern-tiered, vision. Without making too much of geographical distinctions (after all, Marx the internationalist was of German background), it can be said that each of these two broad-ranging macrosociological schools of thought had a distinct emphasis.

For Mills, as for Weber, authority was the linchpin of the social system. Every phenomenon stemmed from authority: legitimacy of a political regime, charismatic and bureaucratic forms of organization, the process of legalization of the social system, and the insinuation of cultural hegemony into a society. Authority resulted from internalization and absorption by the mass of superordinate and subordinate relationships. Over time, such political as well as economic inequalities became enshrined as norms. Ultimately, such relationships became values of the system. But Mills was much less confortable with a valuational approach than was Weber. He saw Weber as vaguely accepting and not just examining bureaucracy and power—a point others have made before and since. In this context, the alternative power model of Michels in particular served to rescue power analysis from normative theory.

The chief architects of the Franco-Italian school—Michels, Sorel, Pareto, and Mosca—were less analytically profound, but more to Mills's liking than their Germanic counterparts. For them, as for Mills, the key to political dominance was power. The imposition of power by one group over another made for authority, law, and the dominant culture. Michels, Sorel, Pareto, and Mosca presented the world as an arena of struggle. Yet the power of one person or system over another in some ironic way could never be legitimated, could never be internalized as Weber envisioned in his concept of authority. Underwriting the Franco-Italian school was the notion of mass behavior as a volatile source of change not readily harnessed to an elite ordering of events. Ranging from anarchism to socialism, the expression of the indomitable will of the individual could be suppressed, but acceptance of such suppression never could be internalized or legitimated as long as inequality remained a social fact.

The difference between authority and power, between Weber and Michels in particular, gave birth to other differences, which, when transplanted to an American context, led to sharp cleavages in the major schools of sociological thought. For the Weberians, the emphasis became consensus among the polity, bureaucratization in government, and legal norms. For the Paretians, the process was reversed: power determined the course of American destiny. The system somehow could never be legitimated given the existence of class differences and deep political antagonisms. As a result, the conflict model became dominant among the followers of this latter school. To do serious work in sociological theory meant coming to terms with this bifurcated inheritance.

Mills's own intellectual uncertainties with respect to authority and power, consensus and conflict, were shrewdly disguised rather than resolved. The notion of a "classic tradition" included Weber. By addressing himself to "big problems" and the "big picture," Mills obscured the core of these inherited sociological disputes but did not necessarily resolve them. Once the rhetoric behind the big picture was examined, differences of the most acute sort began to become manifest. It was simply no longer possible to hold the European tradition intact. Later conflict theories, like those of Lewis A. Coser, Ralf Dahrendorf, and Jurgen Habermas, made this clear. Mills himself, more out of intuition (or perhaps irritation) than sociological logic, also knew this to be the case. He was shrewd enough to know that theoretical disputations over the status of authority and power, or consensus or conflict, could yield either conservative or radical outcomes, depending on concrete circumstances. Hence, Mills was driven back to the results of analysis rather than any search for or commitment to general theory.

There is an air of ease and familiarity in Mills's writings about Weber; he incorporates him into his own corpus, rather than making distinct pronunciamentos about him. Mills does not show this same sense of ease in writing about Marx, and so it is hard to say whether Weber was more or less important in Mills's development than Mannheim or Marx. Given Mills's sociological eclecticism, it is best not to attempt a weighting of these "greats," but simply to examine what aspects of Weber helped to fill Mills's intellectual shopping basket. For if one cannot rightfully be a "Millsian" outside a wide tradition, this in part derives from Mills's own sense of employing theory for concrete research ends, rather than determining what these research tasks should be on the basis of completing or adding to a theoretical scaffold.

ೂ.ಲ.ೂ

Typical of Mills's theoretical eclecticism is the remark in *The Sociological Imagination* on the theoretical foundations of *The Power Elite*: "I had to take into account the work of such men as Mosca, Schumpeter, Veblen, Marx, Lasswell, Michels, Weber, and Pareto."[19] In that most Weberian of works, *Character and Social Structure*, Gerth and Mills nonetheless make much of the significance of the two traditions of Freud and Marx. But they will be perfectly content if for these two names, their readers prefer substituting Mead and Weber.[20] Mills later amplifies the methodological function as such a shopping basket view of theory—a view not at all out of character with Weber's open-ended approach to "theory construction":

> Sometimes I can arrange the available theories systematically as a range of choices, and so allow their range to organize the problem itself. But sometimes I allow such theories to come up in my own arrangement, in quite various contexts. At any rate, in the book on the elite I had to take into account the work of such men as Mosca, Schumpeter, Veblen, Marx, Lasswell, Michels, Weber, and Pareto.[21]

This helps to illustrate the arbitrariness of singling out the influence of any one sociologist upon Mills's intellectual development. Yet, insofar as doing so helps us frame Mills in an appropriate intellectual setting, the task remains marginally worthwhile.

This is not to suggest that Weber's work had little or no influence on the young Mills. It most certainly did, especially in the area of social psychology. Mills saw Weber as providing the necessary social-structure cement in an American world of individualistic psychology where minds were discussed without regard to bodies, where people were discussed without regard to publics, and in which interactions were granted without analysis of collectivities. Weber provided the intellectual sourcebook for collective psychology by giving strength and backbone to individual motivation. To quote again from *Character and Social Structure*:

> No matter how we approach the field of social psychology, we cannot escape the idea that all current work that comes to much, fits into one or the other of two basic traditions: *Freud*, on the side of character structure, and *Marx*, including the early Marx of the 1840's, on the side of social structure. . . . We have no objection, if the reader prefers, to use the names of George H. Mead and Max Weber, although of course they differ from Freud and Marx in many important ways.[22]

Yet, in the very next sentence, the "two basic traditions" become Freud and Mead, rather than Freud and Marx. "The reason we are drawn, again and again, to Sigmund Freud and George Mead is that they try, more effectively than the others, to show us man as a whole actor—instead of man as a set of traits, as a bundle of reflexes."[23] By the time of *Images of Man*, Mills had become even less specific, preferring the rhetoric of the "master trends" rather than the "master works." This constant shift in intellectual peerage reflects both intellectual confusion and a calculated eclecticism. In any event, Mills's casting about makes "influence tracing" just about impossible as an exercise in pure theory or doctrinal impact.

The fusion of sociology and psychology in a historical context was certainly Weber's lasting contribution to Mills's thinking. This contribution was made more important by virtue of the absence of a distinctive psychological orientation in the work of Marx. Certainly the mature Marx took a certain pride in the absence of psychological interpretations. His American followers, especially those politically active in the 1940s and 1950s, saw little problem with this. With the exception of Vernon Venable, Erich Fromm, and Herbert Marcuse, the psychologizing of Marx hardly had begun when Mills came to maturity. Hence, Weber loomed larger in Mills's thoughts than perhaps he might have in a later period of the 1960s and 1970s, when the early Marx of alienation had been rediscovered with a vengeance by psychologists and sociologists alike.

Mills grew increasingly disquieted by the impact of Weber upon American sociology. Weber's preemptive role with respect to functional structuralism certainly did not go unnoticed. If macrosociological tradition was described solely by the difference between Merton and Parsons, that in itself provided Mills with a prima facie reason to look beyond Weber for answers. Mills became uncomfortable with the legalistic and conservative bureaucratic tendencies manifested in American writings on Weber. Thus, without any overt manifestation of a rupture with Weberian theory, which would have meant a formal break with his mentor Gerth as well, Mills simply never returned to Weber once his relationship with Gerth was intellectually completed. *Character and Social Structure*, which was begun during the Second World War but appeared in print far later in Mills's career than he really wished, must thus be seen not as a work written "in between" *White Collar* and *The Power Elite* but as a long-delayed publication of the Wisconsin era.

Whatever else transpired on the intellectual journey of Weber's thought from Europe to America, it is an ineluctable fact that its cutting edge was lost in the process. In part this is because Weber's consistent enemies at home were right-wing nationalists. The struggle for scientific objectivity, value-relevance without ideological precommitment, was undertaken in a context of intellectual jingoism, Prussian manifest destiny, and the alarming bureaucratization of state power. Prewar (and wartime) America, the period from 1936 to 1946, from Parsons's early celebration to the Gerth-Mills collection, presented a somewhat different picture. Weber became an American "answer" to Marxism. It was the remnants of an old Left that was contested by the neo-Weberians. The roots of Weber at Columbia and Harvard, and later at the University of California (which in an odd way synthesized the conservative tendencies in neo-Weberian thought during the McCarthy period), offered an analytical framework of authentic power that did not overtly depend upon the Marxist tradition. Again, this became especially so in the postwar period, which became mired in Leninist and Stalinist orthodoxies. It was at the unique moment when new tendencies in Marxism had yet to emerge and old tendencies in Weber had crystallized and dissolved that Mills came upon Weber. The philosophy of pragmatism and the sociology of knowledge were behind Mills by the end of the Second World War. The sense that this was to be an American century had just taken root. Under the circumstances, all Mills could rightly do was extract those elements in Weberian thought that were serviceable to radical aims or were at least capable of dampening the chauvinistic implications of the American celebration of triumph. This was Mills's approach until the time came when Weber, too, could be treated as an element in rather than the essence of contemporary America social thought.

Mills made it clear that there were several important aspects of his relationship to Weber's legacy. First, *Character and Social Structure* was his least favorite book. He confessed to coming close to a public repudiation of this fine work. In part, he completed it as a repayment to Gerth for many past kindnesses, in particular, the co-editorship of *From Max*

Weber. By the time *Character and Social Structure* appeared, Mills's formal association with Gerth had long since ended. Weber came to be employed as a bridge to other theories of social philosophy:

> Max Weber defines motives as a complex of meaning, which appears to the actor himself or to the observer to be an adequate ground for his conduct. The aspect of motive which this conception intrinsically grasps is its social character. . . . Motives are accepted justifications for present, future or past programs or acts.[24]

But it was the way in which "social character" issued into "social structure" that proved most appealing to Mills: "Weber's use of the notion of structure enabled him to transcend the individual's own awareness of himself and his milieux."[25] It was Weber as the primary representative of the European macroscopic tradition, in contrast to the molecular tendencies in American sociology, that proved most attractive to Mills.

> Weber's analytic and historic essay on bureaucracy has not been repeated or checked in the same way (as the molecular), however much of it has been criticized and used. Macroscopic work has not experienced the sort of cumulative development that molecular work during the current generation of sociologists has.[26]

This sense of scope brought about the highest praise Mills was to tender to Weber: "The ethos of Max Weber was the climax of the classic German tradition."[27] However, even this praise carried with it an explicit criticism. Just as Ludwig Feuerbach was for Friedrich Engels not only the highest expression of classical German philosophy, but also its end, so, too, did Mills see Weber as the highest expression of classical German sociology, but also its end.

Ultimately, Mills's animosity toward liberalism, especially its sociological manifestations, led to a break in intellectual affinities with this highest expression of German thought. It was sociology itself that needed the closest critical scrutiny.

Mills had two specific problems with Weber's notion of rationality: first, its general linkage to the process of bureaucratization; second, its specific linkage to the structure of modern capitalism. There was simply no way Mills could square this circle. Even as early as 1946, he was critical of Weber's nostalgic liberalism, which empathizes with cultural freedom but remains relatively blind to economic exploitation.

> Weber identifies bureaucracy with rationality, and the process of rationalization with mechanism, depersonalization, and oppressive routine. Rationality in this context, is seen as adverse to personal freedom. Accordingly, Weber is a nostalgic liberal feeling himself on the defensive. He deplores the type of man that the mechanization and the routine of bureaucracy selects and forms. The narrowed professional, publicly certified

and examined, and ready for tenure and career. His craving for security is balanced by his moderate ambitions and he is rewarded by the honor of official status. This type of man Weber deplored as a petty routine creature, lacking in heroism, human spontaneity, and inventiveness: "The Puritan will to be the vocational man that we have to be."[28]

Since Weber identifies capitalism as the embodiment of rational impersonality, the quest for freedom that informs Mills and his other intellectual mentors is reduced to irrational sentiment and privatization. As a consequence, Weber's objectivity becomes "defensive."

> Weber represents humanist and cultural liberalism rather than economic liberalism. . . . Weber's own work is a realization of his self-image as a cultivated man concerned with all things human. And the decline of the humanist and the ascendancy of the expert is another documentation for Weber of the diminished chances for freedom.[29]

Mills's later defense of "plain Marxism," and his growingly strident attack on "liberalism as a dead end," must each be seen as an ultimate rejection of Weber; a final settling on Weber as the anti-Marx, rather than as the sophisticated "bourgeois-Marx" with which he had started his intellectual examination. By the time Mills produced *The Marxists*, his animosity toward liberalism and his rejection of this "creed" for Marxism was so complete that any further serious consideration of Weber was out of the question. It is clear that Mills came to consider the same cluster of figures he formerly admired—Weber, Mosca, Michels, Mannheim, etc.—as representative of "the firm ideology of one class inside one epoch; specifically the urban and entrepreneurial middle class." As a result any final settlement of accounts with the "classic tradition" became obviated.[30] What this polarization did to his earlier statements on the continuities between Marx and Weber, and on German sociological profundity as such, never did get resolved by Mills. Rather, sociology itself somehow became the enemy of progress; the source of the confusion was thus neatly externalized.

Mills had a peculiar relationship not simply to Weber but to European sociological doctrine in general. While Mills celebrated the virtue of large-scale macroscopic thinking and breathtaking analysis on epochal subjects, there was scarcely that fine attention to detail that characterized the more empirical and earlier aspects of his work. In this sense, Mills and Parsons were diametrically opposed. For Mills, the "classical European tradition" represented an unfurling of the banners of social research, a flag of legitimacy providing ideological fuel in times of intellectual turmoil. For Parsons, however, one got the distinct impression that the empirical world was served up to the theoretical construct of Weber's world view. The actual contents rather than the style of sociology became its "classical tradition' within Parsonian thought. As a consequence, the tone, not to mention the content, of Parsons's *General Theory* was diametrically in contrast to Mills's *Images of Man*. Parsons took the ideas of German sociology seriously. Mills took seriously only the sentiments—the underlying thrust, which took sociology into large-scale areas of historical and social analysis. Perhaps that is why, despite the severity of their differences, a peculiar sort of respect is manifest between Parsons and Mills.

The sense of discontent that Mills expressed about Weber in his later work stemmed in part not so much from any single proposition as from the amorphous theory of value neutrality. For Mills, such formal academic demands for nonpoliticizing of the classroom and lecture hall in practice represented bureaucratic support by Weber for Imperial Germany, or more gently, a denial of the overall policy considerations created by social research. Mills thought of Weber as a sociological Brahms; an old-fashioned medieval craftsman rather than a precursor of German Nazism. The absence of a cutting edge, the feeling that Weber was somehow removed from the social struggle, was ultimately more weighty to Mills than any single theoretical proposition. Whatever else Weber represented, he was the architect of academic freedom as academic responsibility. And Mills, whatever else he was, represented academic freedom as freedom from constraint. This philosophical gap between freedom as discipline and freedom as liberty could not be bridged—at least not by Mills. The disjunction between Weber and Mills on the public role of sociology is so wide and deep that in retrospect it is a tribute to Mills's personal loyalties to Gerth that he could restrain himself from overt criticism of Weber's work.

The identification of the neo-Weberians, such as Edward A. Shils, Seymour Martin Lipset, and Reinhard Bendix, with an increasingly conservative political posture also alienated Mills's affections from Weberian thought as such. The neo-Weberians from Chicago and California led the charge against Mills at that very point in time, circa 1956–1962, when older functionalist canons were breaking down in social science. This is scarcely the first time that followers of a major contributor to social thought have gone their separate ways. However, so uniform was the hostility to Mills among the inner circle of Weber's biographers, commentators, and translators that Mills can be forgiven if he somehow, albeit less than forthrightly, came to identify Weber himself as at least partially the intellectual source of his own professional miseries.

Nor were Mills's miseries merely intellectual. Personal resentments flared. Hans Gerth made it quite clear to all who would listen that he felt himself to be the senior author of the essays in *From Max Weber*; that in point of fact, Mills insinuated himself into the project only because he, Gerth, needed an American citizen to be listed as co-editor for the book as a passport to publication. It must be remembered that this collection had its origins during the Second World War and that Gerth as a German national did in fact suffer a certain alienation from mainstream publishing and professionalism. In truth Mills was, even in 1945, a supreme stylist, while Gerth, to put it mildly, was not a graceful writer or translator. The primary role of Mills was in editing the editor's work on Weber. In addition, Mills helped to place the extensive introductory essay on Weber within a meaningful American as well as English-speaking context. If the strictly biographical portions of the introduction are clearly written by Gerth, the political analyses and implications are just as clearly the mark of Mills.

These sorts of negative experiences with colleagues, with translations, and finally with Weber's corpus eventually led Mills to a personal review of where he wanted to go. It clearly was away from the history of sociology, and into sociology as a key to history. Yet, even at the end, when Mills's affections for sociology were at a low ebb, he could not bring himself to disavow a filial connection with Weber. Along with Marx, Weber was held supreme.[31] "Marx and Weber are greater than, for example, Mosca or Durkheim," since "every line they write is soaked in knowledge of history."[32] Weber offered clarity and profundity—and whatever "personal troubles" he occasioned, he was central to the public presentations of American sociology across the political and intellectual spectrum; a decent judgment which Weber himself might well have appreciated.

REFERENCES

1. Marianne Weber. *Max Weber: A Biography*, translated by Harry Zohn. New York: John Wiley & Sons, 1975, p. 120.

2. Hans H. Gerth and C. Wright Mills, eds. *From Max Weber: Essays in Sociology*. New York: Oxford University Press, 1946, p. 15.

3. It is not that the work of Weber went unnoticed or was unknown prior to the efforts of Parsons. But Parsons "internalized" or "operationalized" Weber. The working sociologist learned from Parsons how to use (Duncan might say abuse) Weber's work. See Talcott Parsons, *The Structure of Social Action: A Study in Social Theory with Special Reference to a Group of Recent European Writers* (New York: McGraw-Hill, 1937).

4. In this respect, Don Martindale's work rounds out our vision of Weber considerably. See the translation he and Gertude Neuwirth made of *The City* (Glencoe, Ill.: Free Press, 1958), and, in particular, his "Prefatory Remarks: The Theory of the City." See also Don Martindale, *The Nature and Types of Sociological Theory* (Boston: Houghton Mifflin, 1960, pp.

377–99). For a sound and impartial appraisal of the Chicago school, see John Madge, *The Origins of Scientific Sociology* (New York: The Free Press of Glencoe, 1962, pp. 88–125).

5. Talcott Parsons. "Introduction to Max Weber." In *The Theory of Social and Economic Organization*, translated by A. M. Henderson and Talcott Parsons, edited with an Introduction by Talcott Parsons. New York: Oxford University Press, 1947, pp. 82, 84.

6. Irving Louis Horowitz. "Introduction to the New Sociology." In *The New Sociology*. New York: Oxford University Press, 1964, pp. 14–15.

7. Talcott Parsons. *Essays in Sociological Theory Pure and Applied*. Glencoe, Ill.: Free Press, 1949, p. x.

8. On this point see Robin M. Williams, Jr., "The Sociological Theory of Talcott Parsons," in *The Social Theories of Talcott Parsons*, edited by Max Black. Englewood Cliffs, N.J.: Prentice-Hall, 1961, pp. 88–89.

9. See Parsons's unusual polemical reaction to Llewellyn Z. Gross's "Preface to a Metaphysical Framework for Sociology." *The American Journal of Sociology* 67 (September 1961): 125–36. Parsons's comment was carried in the same issue, pp. 136–40.

10. Robert K. Merton. "Bureaucratic Structure and Personality." In *Social Theory and Social Structure*, revised and enlarged edition. Glencoe, Ill.: Free Press, 1957, pp. 204–5.

11. Robert K. Merton. "Puritanism, Pietism, and Science." In *Social Theory*, p. 595.

12. Robert K. Merton. "Science and Democratic Social Structure." In *Social Theory*, pp. 560–61.

13. Robert K. Merton. "Social Conflict over Styles of Sociological Work." *Transactions of the Fourth World Congress of Sociology* 3 (1959). Reprint No. 286, Bureau of Social Research Publications, pp. 34–35.

14. Gerth and Mills, *From Max Weber*, p. 25.

15. C. Wright Mills with Hans Gerth. "A Marx for the Managers." In *Power, Politics, and People: The Collected Essays of C. Wright Mills*, edited by Irving Louis Horowitz. New York and London: Oxford University Press, 1963, pp. 54, 68–69.

16. C. Wright Mills. "Two Styles of Social Science Research." In *Power, Politics, and People*, pp. 557–58.

17. C. Wright Mills. "The Nazi Behemoth." In *Power, Politics, and People*, p. 171.

18. C. Wright Mills. *The Sociological Imagination*. New York: Oxford University Press, 1959, pp. 25–49.

19. *Ibid.*, p. 202.

20. C. Wright Mills and H. H. Gerth. *Character and Social Structure: The Psychology of Social Institutions*. New York: Harcourt, Brace & Co., 1953, p. xiv.

21. Mills, *The Sociological Imagination*, pp. 202–3.

22. Mills and Gerth. *Character and Social Structure*, p. xiv.

23. *Ibid.*

24. Mills, *Power, Politics, and People*, pp. 442–43.

25. Mills, *The Sociological Imagination*, p. 162.

26. Mills, *Power, Politics, and People*, p. 558.

27. Mills, *The Sociological Imagination*, p. 148.

28. Gerth and Mills, *From Max Weber*, p. 50.

29. *Ibid.*, p. 73.

30. C. Wright Mills. *The Marxists*. New York: Dell Publishing Co., 1962, pp. 27–39.

31. C. Wright Mills, ed. *Images of Man: The Classic Tradition in Sociological Thinking*. New York: George Braziller, 1960, p. 12.

32. *Ibid.*, p. 13.

9

Plain Folks and Marxist Dragons

There was nothing of the hack Marxist in Mills. He honored Marx by taking the ideas of the sociology of knowledge seriously, not slavishly. He applied it with true regard to the environment in which it operates. The real fabric of American life, not a textbook case of a "capitalist society," is the field against which he examined American institutions, culture, types, and in particular, his own profession and its failure in his eyes.

Anatol Rapoport, "The Scientific Relevance of C. Wright Mills"

AN OFT-REPEATED PIECE of hagiography is that Mills was a prophet of the New Left in America. This formulation offers the usual blend of myth and fact. They myth is that he was connected with the nascent Port Huron movement that led to the formation of Students for a Democratic Society. The fact is that he was casting about for new moorings in which to anchor the anti-nuclear movements in Europe and the revolutionary movements of the Caribbean. It is intriguing that Mills's work on Marxism predated by a decade the wave of neo-Marxian thought identified with "critical theory." One might argue with considerable justification that such renewed interest in the varieties of Marxian experience derived precisely from the failures of the old Left in the period immediately prior to Mills's death. Too much had already happened in practice—the Titoist break with Stalin; the emergence of revolutionary regimes remote from Soviet shores; the use of raw Soviet might to put down the Hungarian uprising (to name only a few examples)—to prevent a fundamental reconsideration of Marxism as a doctrine ossified by elites and restored by plain folks.

Mills's concerns with Marxism were consistent with his interests in Mannheim, Weber, and the pragmatic philosophers. Mills was less interested in American politics than in world affairs, as the global approach of *The Marxists* makes clear. Marxism became Mills's ticket to the world, his final break with regionalism and parochialism. The view from New York, from *The New Leader* and *Partisan Review*, was limiting. Theirs was a nineteenth-century Marxism. Mills was already in search of a twenty-first-century Marxism, a theoretical construct to match his new-found worldliness.

Mills's approach to Marxism should not be confused with the later work of the Frankfurt school in Germany, of the English group gathered about the *New Left Review*, or of the various clusters of neo-Marxists to be found in Rome, Paris, and various other Western European centers of learning. His argument for the sociological reconsideration of Marxism is all the more remarkable for its splendid isolation: the more traditional interpreters remained content with functionalist explanations. Socialism remained a utopian vision for Mills—worthwhile entertaining, but not central in an analytic sense. It was rather Marxism as an analytical tool that provided the initial point of entry for Mills.

From a practical point of view, Mills's flirtations with Marxism were exceedingly tentative. He held no Socialist or Communist party affiliations, and his voting preferences were simply nonexistent. Indeed, he made a point of boasting that his nonparticipation in the American party process extended to radical groups also. His self-declared political alienation was part of a deeply held belief that politicians, American politicians in particular, are corrupt. For Mills, the political process was not simply the realm of the powerful, but one of "crack-pot realism" much like the military realm which it supported. Not that Mills was waiting for the system to collapse or predicting that it would. He was too sober a sociologist to engage in fatuous speculation. But Marxism as analysis required setting no agenda or date for the collapse of capitalism. It was enough that Marxism generated intellectual excitement, political risk, moral commitment—the stuff of utopian claims on the present.

From the outset, Mills's affiliation with, and affection for, Marxism was rooted in his Jamesian sense of intellectuals being a class that existed for, as well as in, themselves. Marxism was an analytic device, a method for evaluating world trends. It is interesting to note that Mills had continuing affiliations with a number of independent Socialist periodicals from 1942 to 1955. At first, he wrote a considerable number of essays for Daniel Bell's *The New Leader*. This was followed by writing for Dwight Macdonald's *Politics*. After he arrived at Columbia, he wrote a series of pieces for *Labor* and *The Nation*, which in fact formed the bases for his book *The New Men of Power*. He next appeared in the pages of the most sophisticated student Socialist publication at the time, *Anvil*. This in turn was followed by a close identification with Lewis Coser and Irving Howe's *Dissent* during its formative years. He was consciously and deliberately careful to remain within the bounds of Socialist respectability and outside the bounds of Communist reductionism.

If anything, one senses a diminishing identification with Marxian publications as Mills matures. He began to perceive that too many Marxists were self-imposed exiles, cut off from widespread circulation of their ideas by elitist repugnance for mass society and mass culture. One might argue that Mills stayed closer to Marxist fundamentalism than did the "official" Socialist intellectuals who dominated the forties and fifties, but he certainly had only a peripheral connection to Socialist politics, and made only marginal appearances in its intellectual byproducts. Mills's socialism always remained a part of his social science tradition, and that fact clearly widened the gulf between Mills and his Marxian admirers and detractors alike.

The year in which *The Marxists* was produced was filled with ironic paradox and deepening personal anxiety for Mills. Economists, historians, and political scientists sang his praises, while sociologists rather loudly proclaimed that he was no longer part of the sociological community. While politically aware persons the world over hailed him as a rational voice in the American academic wilderness, policymakers in the United States tended to discount the sharp edge of his criticisms of foreign policy. This task was made easier by an increasing stridency in Mills's political writings and public lectures. Marxism as a weapon of the oppressed turned out to be a useful tool for intellectuals who were besieged.

Questions arose about the degree to which Mills had come under the influence of the dragons of Marxism. While Socialists from Latin America, Asia, and Europe claimed him as an authentic voice of Marxism, Socialists in the United States seemed convinced that he was anything but a member of the group. Such criticism of Mills intensified as a result of the publication of *The Marxists*. If anything, proprietary intellectual interests were piqued, and the critics became harsher. Donald Clark Hodges, representing Marxist orthodoxy, made a series of critical comments, the substance of which can be summed up as follows: Mills sees a convergence of capitalism and socialism in bureaucratic terms rather than the triumph of socialism over capitalism. He is essentially a military determinist rather than an economic determinist. Finally, Mills fails to distinguish between the rapacious nature of the capitalist economy and the generous nature of the Socialist economy, and hence understates the Soviet Union's "remarkable peace effort."[1] While Hodges's criticisms were severe, their form remained most cordial. Lewis Feuer reunited form and content in a critical assault on Mills's interpretation of Marx: "We should be guided, Mills says, by what Marx called 'the principle of historical specificity.' (Actually Marx never used this expression; it was introduced by his expositors, notably Karl Korsch.)"[2] The thrust of Feuer's remarks was that Mills was not really a Marxist. Daniel Bell, in *The End of Ideology*, also indicated that because he concentrated on elites rather than classes, Mills could not be identified as a

Marxist.[3] And with respect to Mills's "Letter to the New Left" urging a new moral crusade and utopian commitment, Bell wrote a response entitled: "Vulgar Sociology."[4] Such criticisms of Mills broadened out to include general political themes beyond the scope of Marxism as such. The New York radical scene, of which Mills had become a peripheral member, reviewed Mills's intellectual credentials and found them wanting.

While many of the criticisms of Mills's views on Marx were cogent and well taken, they presume a self-identification by Mills with Marxism as an intellectual system that simply was not there. If Mills had claimed to be a Marxist, and then emphasized military factors at the expense of economic factors, and elites rather than classes, the criticisms would obviously be compelling. But in fact, the distressing use of Marx as a touchstone for what is empirically right or wrong thoroughly enraged Mills. He intended *The Marxists* to assess how empirical events confirmed what was living and dead in Marxism. Mills adopted a critical stance to varieties of Marxism, but took sheer delight in the pluralization of Marxism as such. This very procedure condemned Mills to yet a further round of criticism as an inappropriate interpreter of the Marxian legacy. The orthodox were disquieted by their newfound advocate. But by 1961 Mills could hardly care less about self-appointed critics or defenders of the faith.

Mills was first and foremost a utopian. His assessment of Marxism was profoundly influenced by the continued deradicalization of Marx's thought in each of the self-proclaimed Socialist societies of the twentieth century—from the Social Democracy of Eduard Bernstein to the Bolshevism of Joseph Stalin. Mills had to "settle affairs" with Marxism to make clear the exact relationship between the radical utopianism of a mid-twentieth-century American sociologist and that portion of the "classic tradition" in social science carried on by Marxists.

In *The Marxists*, Mills spoke as a "political philosopher." He attempted to delineate the future humanity could expect. In the volume's fourteen chapters (seven written by Mills and selections written by Marxists from Marx to Mao among the other seven), the history of Marxian ideas was portrayed in present-day terms. Mills was no true believer; that which did not illumine the contours of present society was, from a pragmatic viewpoint, ballast, and was properly and unceremoniously treated as such. Mills reviewed conflicting modes of sociohistorical reality and had a healthy irreverence for the past. *The Marxists* set forth his standards for the sociological imagination: historical specificity and empirical predictability, living social doctrine presented in living language, and a meaning and impact of ideas that could match, if not outstrip, informed biographies and informing newspapers. The appearance of the book in a low-priced paperback edition, made possible paradoxically enough by capitalist mass marketing, reflected Mills's battle for a "public sociology" similar in intent, if not in content, to Walter Lippmann's "public philosophy."

As an overview of contemporary Marxism in the light of its intellectual antecedents, no single text then available covered the ground as extensively as *The Marxists*. To be sure, Mills's "historical specificity" borrowed more from Karl Korsch than from Karl Marx. But unlike Korsch's historicism, Mills's vision of Marxism is utopian with the dimensions of time included. With this method he portrays the interplay of social forces that created a number of Marxisms rather than a monolith "Marxist social science." Throughout, Mills distinguishes himself from Marxists and anti-Marxists alike. Rather than celebrating or bemoaning the fracturing of Marx's work by various competing factions, he sees in this very process of revision, reevaluation, and restoration the lifeblood of a social doctrine.

The thesis of the book can be stated simply: Marxists are important precisely because of their distinctive and different appraisals, whereas liberals are unimportant precisely because of the absence of such difference. Mills seems to be saying that liberalism is a perishing intellectual commodity to the degree that it becomes identified with the existing social establishment—in short, to the extent that it becomes monolithic. The pluralist, the person receptive to new ideas, the person interested in the social uses of social science—in short, the *classic* liberal—must perforce interest himself or herself in Marxism because it is within its confines that liberalism fulfills itself. The official liberalism of new and old frontiers is captive to statist dogma, whether on questions of academic freedom or foreign policy. As such, it has lost its capacity to move humanity. Mills was enough of a behaviorist to sense that ideas without consequences in public action have no consequence at all. Mills's volume is not an appeal to partisan passions. No Marxist could possibly be content with the relativism implicit in Mills's presentation of the contemporary panorama of Marxian ideas. It was nonetheless, for all its utopianism, a realistic assessment of contemporary political philosophy, and of what the free person should pay attention to in the realm of ideas if he or she wishes to carry on in the "classic tradition." In this, the book is an attempt to fuse the liberal imagination with the sociological imagination.

The Marxists is characterized by the same sort of sharp phrasing and barbed wit as appeared in Mills's critique of Parsons in *The Sociological Imagination*. Mills's hilarious characterization of the "law" of the "negation of the negation" is typical:

> One thing grows out of another and then does battle with it. In turn, the newly grown produces in itself "the seeds of its own destruction." Marx's texts are full of metaphors from the reproduction cycle and the hospital delivery room. Things are pregnant; there are false alarms; wombs and midwives abound. And finally, there is a "bloody birth."[5]

Mills asks us not to mistake metaphors for a method of thinking. He subjects Marxist analysis to this revulsion for the tendentious. The selections—from the writings of the Bolsheviks Lenin, Trotsky, and Stalin;

the Social Democrats Kautsky, Bernstein, and Luxemburg; the critics of Stalinism Hilferding, Borkenau, and Deutscher; and the new revisionists Khrushchev, Mao Tse-Tung, and Ernesto "Che" Guevara—thus make for lively and intellectually provocative reading. In this sense Mills intended *The Marxists* as a supplement to his sociological reader *Images of Man*.

✧✧✧

Mills's method of studying the writings of the Marxists constitutes a paradigm for the sociology of politics which is clearly intended to be considered alongside Robert K. Merton's paradigm for the study of the sociology of knowledge. Mills's approach has four articulated elements: (1) analysis of Marxist political philosophy in terms of ideology; (2) analysis of Marxism as an ethic, as a body of ideals and beliefs; (3) analysis of Marxist agencies of change, the instruments of reform, restoration, revolution, etc.; (4) analysis of Marxism as a social and historical theory, and of the assumption it makes about how people function in society. Mills thus offers a sociological analysis of Marxism rather than a Marxist analysis of society.

No claim is made by Mills for the sociological purity of inclusiveness of this paradigm for the study of political thought. Indeed, this distinguishes his approach from the exaggerated claims made by Parsonian sociologists. Writing as a social philosopher, he seeks to explain his own perspectives and beliefs in contradistinction to those of the Marxists. His beliefs are woven throughout the portions of the book written by others. A commitment to social science—of which Marxism is a very important part, both historically and in the present—is involved. The priority of social science as an empirical and historical whole, however, makes a dogmatic decision in favor of any one part of this tradition impossible. Indeed, Mills's volume closes with a set of questions for the serious reader. While he does not pretend to provide the answers, the long journey from cover to cover leaves us better equipped to answer questions about the nature and content of varieties of Marxism in the present world.

Mills's evaluative criteria are empirical and critical, but this is not the only level at which he operates. He is too sophisticated a thinker not to understand that the social importance of ideas may not have anything to do with how scientific or rational a system is. Hence, he tries to explain the widespread acceptance of Marxism in all parts of the world on the basis of ideological and moral fervor as much as on the basis of the truth contained in the doctrine. Himself a man of moral convictions, Mills was quite willing to stake his professional reputation in defense of these convictions.

Mills ever remained the man of enlightenment, a believer in the practical worth and in the consequences of ideas. His affinity with the writings of the Marxists lay in his belief in the human passions. He had no illusions about the cynical uses of Marxism in the Soviet Union, yet he could ask himself to what extent Marxism is usable as a political policymaking device. In short, Mills was himself a contributor to, no less than a commentator on, the dialogue raging within international Socialist circles after the collapse of Stalinism. The book fulfilled Mills's own conception of the role of the person of ideas in the real world.

The Marxists was first published in March 1962. Because the book was published only in a paperback edition, it failed to attract the critical attention given Mills's earlier works. From a personal point of view this hardly mattered, since Mills died that March, after having checked and cleared the cover design and page proofs. From the biographer's point of view also, it would be a mistake to make too much of this conjunction of events. There is always the tendency to attribute a metaphysical, transcendental significance to someone's last work, particularly when it coincides with the person's death. In Mills's case, the coincidence is irrelevant, since he had already prepared, or was well into, a number of other works at the time of his death.

Since Marxists often share with Kremlinologists a disdain for the "new boy on the block," the usual animosities toward Mills were compounded by a feeling that he did not know his subject well, that he invented his own Marxism without regard to the evidence, and that he introduced new categories, which were simply not to be found in Marx proper. Even those who, like Kenneth Winetrout, responded warmly to his half-essay, half-reader tended to emphasize Millsian rather than Marxist notions of what the book is about:

> *The Marxists* is an effort to counteract the ideological indifference to Marx. . . . Mills exhorts us to study Marxism, to study the present "as history" as a corrective to our ideological retreat. We are warned periodically that empty rice bowls cry for rice not democracy. It may be that an "overdeveloped" nation cries for surplus subsidies not ideology.[6]

Mills emphasized concerns for underdevelopment and overdevelopment. But he cared less about redistributing wealth than reinvigorating doctrine. He took seriously the end-of-ideology concept. But with the exhaustion of ideas in the West came a corresponding demise of their ability to generate excitement. The "action" was taking place within Marxian contexts, or at least within those nations professing a variety of socialism. At times it appeared that Mills cared less for the actual working out of socialism than for the clash of ideas generated by the emergence of a polycentric Marxism. Some of Mills's earlier concerns about the brutalities of totalitarian regimes were muted in favor of the clash of values as a utopian good. If he remained to the end a bitter foe of Stalinist and post-Stalinist Soviet terrorism, he nonetheless developed a strange fascination for the theoretical formulations of Stalin. Stalin was transformed from archetypical villain to quintessential theorist. Since he was a contributor to Marxism all else was forgotten, if not forgiven.

The Marxists is best seen as an intellectual holding action, a way-station on the road to more ambitious undertakings in the area of international stratification, cultural apparatus, and the study of the Soviet power elite. But whether this work reflected Mills's exhaustion or turn to the political Left is somehow meaningless, since, when all is said and done, it is the last work that was properly completed by Mills prior to his death. The rest is reconstruction and, partially, conjecture. One would like to consider *The Marxists* as simply part and parcel of an ongoing intellectual enterprise, but willy-nilly it assumes a magnified role by virtue of Mills's death.

Mills's critical attitude toward Marxism is easily documented; although his appreciation of Marx and Engels grew over time, he never conceived of Marxism as the fundamental standpoint guiding the social sciences. Marxism always remained part of the social science tradition—perhaps a nice wrapping, but never the entire parcel. His utopianism, along with his continued belief in sociology as a standpoint, informed his view of Marxism. Both elements prevented him from expressing or adopting Marxism as an orthodoxy. His fear of orthodoxy was even greater than his faith in the classic tradition in sociology.

If Mills himself resisted the temptation to claim he was Marxist, it is not particularly relevant to pursue such identifications. The more important question is what Mills found mutable and immutable in Marxism, and how it affected his own outlook on sociological life. The basic divide between the Marxist and the radical sociological traditions is whether social science is part of Marxism or Marxism is part of social science. This divide is no simple formalist exercise, for what is entailed is the primacy of evidence over partisanship—or vice versa. Mills is unambiguous about where he stands on this central point.

> There is today no "marxist social science" of any intellectual consequence. There is just—social science: without the work of Marx and other marxists, it would not be what it is today; with their work alone, it would not be nearly as good as it happens to be. No one who does not come to grips with the ideas of marxism can be an adequate social scientist; no one who believes that marxism contains the last word can be one either. Is there any doubt about this after Max Weber, Thorstein Veblen, Karl Mannheim—to mention only three? We do now have ways—better than Marx's alone—of studying and understanding man, society, and history, but the work of these three is quite unimaginable without his work.[7]

Mills mentions Weber, Veblen, and Mannheim, and reiterates the notion of the classic tradition, not simply as a litany of acceptable figures, but also as a statement that Marx presented only one part of the necessary world paradigm.

By the time that Mills wrote *The Marxists*, his estrangement from academic sociology, both imposed and self-imposed, had become virtually complete. His disenchantment with professionalism, coupled with a growing hatred of, no less than alienation from, functionalism as a dominant sociological ideology led Mills to redefine himself. He wrote *The Marxists* as a "political philosophy," and said that sociology should be confined to the study of "details of small-scale milieus." But his self-definition as a political philosopher extended beyond analysis of the structure of a total society (Marxism) in contrast to an analysis of partial frameworks (sociology). It also strangely recalls an earlier pragmatic theme: how to become "a bit closer to the experience of being full citizens."[8] The stated purpose of the book is precisely to urge citizen participation. This is hardly a Marxist formulation of the purpose of studying Marxism. Not the overthrow of social order, but a sense of the normative in Marx most attracted Mills.

For Mills, the central dialogue of the nineteenth century was the struggle between liberalism and Marxism. It embodied the assurances and hopes, and the ambiguities and fears, of what was for him the classical period.

> From the standpoint of modern times, the differences between the classic versions of these political philosophies are often less important than what they have in common. Above all they are animated by common ideals: the major secular ideals that have been developed during the course of Western civilization. Both marxism and liberalism embody the ideals of Greece and Rome and Jerusalem: the humanism of the renaissance, the rationalism of the eighteenth century enlightenment. That is why to examine liberalism or marxism is to examine the politics of this humanist tradition; to find either or both ambiguous is to find this tradition ambiguous.[9]

By the twentieth century, liberalism and Marxism exhibited more powerful differences than similarities because each had become identified with a state ideology. Liberalism and Marxism gave polarized expression to the twentieth century, the century of ideology, not utopia.

> In each case, as power is achieved, these political philosophies become official ideologies, become—in differing ways—engulfed by nationalism. In terms of each, the world encounter of the super-states is defined, and from either side, fought out. In the Soviet Union marxism has become ideologically consolidated and subject to official control; in the United States liberalism has become less an ideology than an empty rhetoric.[10]

The struggle between liberalism and Marxism became the struggle for preeminence within Western civilization or for the West itself. Mills makes it quite clear that he does not use the term "Western" or "the West" in contrast to "the Communist bloc," since major historical developments within Russia have occurred in its European, or Western, parts.[11]

What we have instead are two doctrines,[12] each having become the ideology of one class in one nation within one epoch. Liberalism, which by the last years became Mills's less-than-magnificent obsession, was said to link the American and Soviet blocs. Both were reformist regimes. But they were not simply co-equals; they were at different points on the developmental scale. Liberalism was drying up as socialism was becoming extensive. Capitalism was becoming smaller in scope while socialism was becoming larger in its areas of operation, so that even though each ideology was identified with certain nation-states, they were not of equal magnitude or equally compelling power in the twentieth century.

At this point Mills makes an interesting departure from orthodox Marxism. He neither criticizes nor celebrates the ascendancy of socialism and descent of liberalism. So much is Mills the liberal that he sees the pluralistic varieties of Marxism as themselves giving warrant to the essential worth of liberalistic pluralism, only this pluralism operates within the framework of Marxism rather than within the framework of liberalism. And the variety of experiences in Marxism, Stalinism, Trotskyism, Titoism—Marxism outside the Communist bloc, Marxism and revisionism within the bloc—all give him great hope of intellectual ferment and a practical opening to a more democratic form of government within Socialist societies. Thus it is that Mills, far from being fearful of the future, sees in every heresy a confirmation of the essence of liberalism, namely, free choice by free spirits.

Another way in which Mills reveals his pragmatic origins is in his continuing assertion of the critical role of the intellectual. Notwithstanding the Soviet experience, Marxism is seen by Mills as continuing the tradition of the free-wheeling intellectual. It is the "marginal and numerically insignificant body of scholarly insurgents," who Mills nostalgically refers to as "the kind of men we do not yet know well . . . but whose ideas have come to guide trade unions, political parties, mass movements, nations, and great blocs of States."[13] These political intellectuals become the vanguard of revolutionary movements. In the nineteenth century they could be located within the pragmatic tradition; in the twentieth century they are found within Marxism. But the role of intellectual as leader, as cutting edge, becomes far greater than that provided for in orthodox Marxism, since there is little appreciation of any vanguard role performed by proletarian or peasant. Whatever else, Mills remains true to his intellectual origins and goals. What we have is Marxism as utopianism, as criticism of the present, as a theory of intellectual justice. What we do not have is Marxism as a new orthodoxy or as an ideological justification for a vanguard party. For a nonpolitical participant as well as a nonbeliever, such as a *partinost* concept is unacceptable. Mills did, of course, have some very definite views on what Marxism was and was not. Above all, it was historical materialism; it was not dialectical materialism—or, at any rate, Mills had little regard for or interest in dialectics. He emphasized historicity, and, more specifically, historical specificity itself.

> Marx took the view, and practiced it, that history is the shank of all well-conducted studies of man and society. In his working model of nineteenth century capitalism, in which he designates the characteristics of each institutional and psychological feature, he states the historical function that he thinks each fulfills. He uses this model not merely as "an anatomy of civil society" but in an active historical way to indicate the changing relations of the elements and forces of which the model is composed. His work thus contains a model, not only of a total social structure, but also of that structure in historical motion.[14]

Mills noted that conceptions and categories are not eternal, but relative to an era in which they occur. Historical specificity is also, therefore, a theory of theoretical limits.

> As a theory of the nature of society and of history, the principle of historical specificity holds that the history of mankind may be, indeed must be, divided into epochs, each defined by the structural form it assumes. All we can mean by "laws" are: the structural mechanics of change characteristic of one epoch or another.[15]

There are many ways in which Mills parallels earlier efforts by Sidney Hook in the 1930s to pragmatize Marx: that is, to create a wide-open Marxism by denying its systemic properties. Hook announced that there is no one Marx. By generating an inventory of ideas that presumably define and determine the nature of Marxism there turn out to be seventeen major items in the dialectical shopping basket. This shopping basket itself defines the character of plain Marxism. Mills celebrated this broad-ranging populism. At the end, what we have in Marxism "is at once analysis, prophecy, orientation, history, program."[16] All of this is formidable and elaborate, but nonetheless it is not one thing, and therefore it is the property of no one person, group of persons, or party apparatus. The intellectual beauty of Marxism for Mills is contained in the capacity of revisionism to bring radical Marxism into line with new events.

> No sooner were its outlines stated than it began to be revised by other men who were caught up in the torment of history making. Then the intellectual beauty of its structure, the political passion of its central thrust began to be blunted by the will of political actors and the recalcitrance of historical events.[17]

Reality must ultimately limit moral choices; on the other hand, moral choice must always open up new possibilities for new realities. Mills engages in the beauty of dialectics. There are two kinds of Marxists, he claims: "vulgar Marxists," who seize upon certain features of Marx's political philosophy and identify these parts as the whole,[18] and sophisticated Marxists, who are mainly concerned with Marxism as a model of society, and with theoretical development through the aid of this model.[19] These false antinomies bear a striking resemblance to the abstract and grand theory and empirics found by Mills to characterize American sociology. However lofty were the themes introduced by Marxists, he found much of their analysis touched by scholasticism. He was simply not comfortable on any level other than the empirical. That the empirical tradition is the source of modern liberalism as well as socialism in no way disturbed Mills. He was willing and able to set aside his prejudices when risks to social science were involved.

Mills represents himself as a plain Marxist, and that means someone working within Marx's own tradition, but more specifically from a popular perspective. This redundant formulation is followed up by the assumption that many plain Marxists are also firmly grounded in the classical tradition of sociological thinking, and hence Marx becomes the law in their great nineteenth-century picture: little better than most perhaps, but part and parcel of the grand tradition. Plain Marxism includes a highly selective, almost eclectic group ranging from Gramsci and Sorel, in an earlier period, to Erich Fromm and Edward Thompson in the current period. One could argue that the tradition, even within this limit, is severely strained, since these people have in common scarcely more than what they have in contrast to each other.

The essential triad of Millsian doctrine rests on three sets of determinisms: economic, military, and political. He is not clear about which can be weighted most heavily. Throughout *The Marxists* he argues against a theory of power which is reductionistic, which seeks to settle metaphysical concerns rather than take the plurality of power at face value.

> Economic determinism becomes one hypothesis to be tested in each specific epoch and society. Military determinism and political determinism may also be tested. Given the present state of our knowledge, no one of the three should automatically be assumed to predominate uniformly among history-making factors in all societies, or even in all types of capitalist societies.[20]

The idea of economic determinism is attacked as illustrative of the labor metaphysic, which assumes that one class embodies all future tendencies, and makes terrible assumptions about political and psychological phenomena in relation to the corruption of the economic base. Mills comes close to saying that there is no economic base, but a mutual interaction between political, military, and economic factors.

> Behind the labor metaphysic and the erroneous views of its supporting trends there are deficiencies in the marxist categories of stratification; am-

biguities and misjudgements about the psychological and political consequences of the development of the economic base; errors concerning the
supremacy of economic causes within the history of societies and the mentality of classes; inadequacies of a rationalist psychological theory; a generally erroneous theory of power; an inadequate conception of the state.[21]

What we see, then, is the emerging sentimental attachment of Mills to
Marxism as he grows further alienated from the classical aspects of the
sociological tradition. But to the very end he remains true to his pragmatic roots. His notion of a "plain Marxism" has the effect of permit-
ting him to retain a sentimental attachment to Marxism rather than
turning him toward orthodoxy.

There is another sense in which Mills uses the notion of plain Marxism, and that is political: as a concept of criticism and marginality, and
even more as a definition of losers. Mills says quite plainly that the plain
Marxists have generally been found among the political losers. It is not
that they were theorists rather than actors; but that they were honest
rather than dishonest. As a result, humanistic Marxism tended to be
beaten by hack Marxism practiced by party bureaucrats.

> They have been "open" (as opposed to dogmatic) in their interpretations
> and their uses of marxism. They have stressed that "economic determi-
> nism" is, after all, a matter of degree, and held that it is so used by Marx
> in his own writings, especially in his historical essays. They have empha-
> sized the volition of men in the making of history—their freedom—in
> contrast to any Determinist Laws of History and, accordingly, the lack of
> individual responsibility. In brief, they have confronted the unresolved
> tension of humanism and determinism, of human freedom and historical
> necessity.[22]

Intellectual orthodoxy most invites Mills's animosity. It violates his
entire concept of plain Marxism. Whether it be historical specificity in
theory or marginality in political practice, his views end up as an attack
on official expectation, an attack on the qualifications of inherited ideas,
and an attack on determinism. It is the pragmatic volition of the individual in contrast to pluralist determinism that excites Mills's passion
and invites comparison of his view with other views of Marxism. Like
Benedetto Croce before him, Mills was concerned as much with what
was living and what was dead in Marxism as with converting the heathen
to sanctified doctrine. Mills offered more of an argument and a statement to the Marxist than he did a statement about Marxism to the unre-
pentant. And this fitted well with his characteristic individualism, his
inability to wear another man's intellectual cap.

Mills's ongoing belief was that the Soviet Union was not the unique
model of Marxism it claimed to be. It was a temporary aberration during
a period when monolithic views toward Marxism were being allowed to
crystallize until socialism got going elsewhere. Mills makes much of the

distinction between autonomy and dependency within socialism. Autonomy is good, and in countries such as Russia, China, and Yugoslavia the Socialist revolution can be considered a success. Where autonomy does not exist and a Stalinist regime has been installed, as in Albania, Rumania, Bulgaria, Poland, Hungary, East Germany, and Czechoslovakia, one does not have Marxism but the force of Russian arms. And at that point occurs the abdication of Marxism, not new beginnings.

Mills makes it perfectly clear that he views Marxism as both a transcendence and absorption of liberalism; it is a new pluralism dividing communism inside from that outside the Soviet bloc.

> The most serious error we can make in our effort "to understand communism" is to lump all the countries and doctrines that go by the name "marxist" or "marxism-leninism" together under some consistent evil called "communism." Although the Bloc is not splitting up it is far from homogeneous. It is neither immutable nor monolithic. The changes within it indicate neither the advent of communist society nor its disintegration.[23]

He considers the breakup of orthodox Marxism to be "a fact of the first importance." Without such a disintegration he would have been hard-pressed to accept any aspect of socialism.

As it turned out, Mills's last comments harken back to his earlier days at the University of Texas, and the remarks of Edward Everett Hale. For while his critique of the Soviet Union is severe, he points out that "however brutal the means have been, Stalinism has done the work of industrialization and modernization that was done by capitalism in other societies."[24] As Mills himself well understood, the question of whether coercion was the only means available is something Stalinism never came to terms with. Certainly Stalinism never postulated the possibility that humanistic forms might illustrate an industrial model of society.

The Marxists left Mills in the lurch. Like so many before him, Mills celebrated the questions raised by Marxism rather than providing many answers.[25] The book placed Mills in a quandary, or perhaps several quandaries. To push ahead with political philosophy necessitated his becoming a political actor. On the other hand, to move along with the task of creating a science meant to return to social science work, albeit within the Marxist tradition. Both choices were difficult, if not impossible, for Mills to make. The practice of social science was no longer something he could conceive of as a professional life-style.

Mills's own sense of exhaustion was generalized into a belief in the exhaustion of the social sciences, whereas his sense of exhilaration was similarly generalized into a belief that Marxism was a source of real, i.e., political, action. Mills had also come to believe that many of the questions he now felt required practical attention were insurmountable within contemporary social science proper. Rather than providing a rousing credo, an organizing premise, it was found to be intellectually wanting. It, too, had the same kinds of contradictions he had found in classical sociology. Mills's great strength had always been concrete observation. Yet his great desire was to become an abstract theorist. The inability to resolve his impulses toward research and theory, a paradox not unlike that faced by many others, ultimately led Mills into a *cul du sac* that he could not resolve, but that was resolved for him by his death.

Almost unwittingly, Mills could not entirely avoid the uses of Marxism as a pontifical device, a rhetoric of radical trends which permitted Mills to avoid any further Puerto Rican journeys or excursions into Chicano riot areas. The lever of history became the Great Tool that would instruct all oppressed to behave appropriately. Still, his sense of the actor in history was never entirely squelched. Tito and Castro, rather than theoretical or doctrinal wisdom, captivated his sense of practical purpose. If his was a Marxism with many faces, it at least included the utopian face, even though, in the end, he confused a cacophony of dogmatisms for a variety of options.

REFERENCES

1. Donald Clark Hodges. "The Fourth Epoch." *Philosophy and Phenomenological Research* 29, no. 3 (March 1969). See also my reply, "The Fifth Epoch: Postscript to an Epilogue to an Unfinished Social Theory of the Living and the Dead." *Philosophy and Phenomenological Research* 31, no. 2 (December 1970): 282–92.

2. Lewis Feuer. *Marx and the Intellectuals*. Garden City, N.Y.: Doubleday-Anchor Books, 1969; and *Ethics* 70 (April 1960).

3. Daniel Bell. *The End of Ideology: On the Exhaustion of Political Ideas in the Fifties*. New York: The Free Press, 1972.

4. Daniel Bell. "Vulgar Sociology." *Encounter* (March 1962). Reprinted in Daniel Bell, *The Winding Passage: Essays and Sociological Journeys, 1960-1980*. Cambridge: Abt Books, 1982. See my analysis of Bell on Mills, "From the End of Ideology to the Beginning of Morality?" *Contemporary Sociology* 10, no. 4 (July 1981):493–96.

5. C. Wright Mills. *The Marxists*. New York: Dell Publishing Co., 1962, p. 93.

6. Kenneth Winetrout. "Mills and the Intellectual Default." In *The New Sociology*, edited by Irving Louis Horowitz. New York and London: Oxford University Press, 1964, pp. 154 ff.

7. Mills, *The Marxists*, p. 11.

8. *Ibid.*, p. 9.

9. *Ibid.*, pp. 13–14.
10. *Ibid.*, p. 20.
11. *Ibid.*, p. 23.
12. *Ibid.*, pp. 21, 29.
13. *Ibid.*, p. 27.
14. *Ibid.*, p. 37.
15. *Ibid.*, p. 28.
16. *Ibid.*, p. 94.
17. *Ibid.*, p. 95.
18. *Ibid.*, p. 96.
19. *Ibid.*, p. 96.
20. *Ibid.*, p. 126.
21. *Ibid.*, p. 129.
22. *Ibid.*, p. 130.
23. *Ibid.*, p. 472.
24. *Ibid.*, p. 474.
25. *Ibid.*

PART

III

Substances

10

Proletarian Power and the American Dream Machine

By 1948 when C. Wright Mills published The New Men of Power *few Americans on the Left retained any illusion about the significant role organized labor had in fact played in sustaining the existing American System.*

Warren I. Susman, "Comment: I," in
Failure of a Dream & Essays in the History of American Socialism

W HATEVER PLACE ONE ultimately gives Mills in the sociological cosmos, one fact remains indisputable: he was a master analyst of stratification. His trilogy *The New Men of Power*, *White Collar*, and *The Power Elite* provides a fundamental analysis of the American division of labor between 1946 and 1956. During those years, all of them spent at Columbia University, Mills wrote and published these three books. They helped define the critical literature concerning American class composition and indelibly stamped Mills as a scholar of the first rank.

Sociology in the United States arose against a background of social change associated with industrialization and urbanization; its earlier practitioners were themselves from rural and religious backgrounds.[1] As a result, while early sociologists saw their mission as a struggle against social evil, they not infrequently identified that evil with industry and city life. The social formations characteristic of these newly evolving industrial and urban contexts were seen as rotting an integral American fabric. One serious consequence of this imbalance between the objects of study and their presumed saviors was the social pathology syndrome, in which the evils to be extirpated were identified with modernism and the good things were supposedly located in primary groups in rural contexts.[2] It is little wonder, given the prevalence of such backgrounds, that the sociological study of work was one of the least-mined fields in the discipline. Only the Depression and the Second World War made the subject of labor inescapable.

Mills had the distinct advantage of being at Wisconsin when Merle Curti in history and Selig Perlman in economic history were both in their prime; and the further advantage of befriending Richard Hofstadter, who, like Mills, taught at Maryland from 1942 until 1945, when both came to Columbia.[3] In its European incubation, sociology had grown up in larger social struggles, whereas in the United States the discipline emerged in universities.[4] The apolitical context of analysis poorly equipped the discipline for research into labor studies. In the postwar period, when the Bureau of Applied Social Research had funds to study work and workers, the intellectual cadre actually qualified to perform the research tasks was small. Thus Mills, for all his technical weaknesses in quantitative research techniques, seemed far and away the best choice to head up this subsection of the bureau's work. *The New Men of Power* was the first major result of this linkage of Mills with the bureau.

The decade after the Second World War was dominated by men and theories that sought a consensus, and viewed American society as the practical fulfillment of that consensus. Their claims about the fundamental unity of American social composition, even of ideological aspirations, veritably liquidated any sense of class differences. Richard Centers in psychology, Lloyd Warner in anthropology, and Kingsley Davis in sociology—brilliant scholars all—cast the die for a conceptualization of America as one great big middle class, grudgingly subdivided into categories of more or less prominent members. The social sciences did not so much liquidate the concept of class as vitiate it, by multiplying the number of classes to such a degree that class became a problem of measurement rather than a measure of the social order.

Mills's great and unique perception was that this "pluralist" vision of class not only abandoned the classical European tradition, but blotted out most important American social divisions. Social stratification became Mills's métier, the sociological turf upon which his critical skills rarely failed him. Mills's awareness of stratification derived in part from a healthy skepticism toward national societies generally, and in part from a sense of American society specifically. He had a canny instinct that things go wrong even in the best of all sociological worlds. If he had any grand unifying vision throughout his career (and one must doubt that he did), the closest he came was in describing the relationship between class, power, and the economy in American life, without any intellectual predeterminism. Mills's sentiments were explicit: he stood with citizens, for publics, and on behalf of the exploited. But his intellectual focus from the outset was more often centered on elites, policymakers, and exploiters. The moral and the empirical were joined in his stratification writings, where he made a unique effort to explore no less than expose these sectors. He rarely pulled it off, precisely because the *objective concerns* of his explorations were quite different from the *sub-*

jective feelings he had toward those he wrote about. Yet, if this unresolved tension led to personal inconclusiveness, it also created the basis of an intellectual achievement of high order.

The New Men of Power well illustrates this antagonism. It is not really about the working class in America, but rather is an investigation of five hundred of the most powerful labor leaders in American society. Mills did not study union rank-and-file decision making, but labor bureaucrats, who he envisioned as functioning like armed generals, political candidates and bosses, and business entrepreneurs. Even when Mills studied the working class, he regarded it as a fulcrum of power and not as part of a system of economic organization.

The book itself is formally divided into five parts, but its actual contents can more properly be divided into three parts, not especially well integrated, but each bearing directly on the nature of social stratification. Quite beyond that, the book is a study of American culture, of the role of intellectuals in the stratification system. This topic concerned Mills from his earliest days, and it was reflected in just about everything that he wrote. It was the way in which power connected to ideas, not the function of American trade unions, that gripped his imagination.

From this private agenda, Mills developed the first full-blown critique of liberalism to emerge in the postwar period. He did this bluntly, identifying liberalism with magazines like *The New Republic*, *The Nation*, and *The New Leader*, and considering them part of an ideological network. He argued that liberalism's very porosity of ideas encourages trade union leaders to dissipate their political energies actively campaigning for a great variety of issues and causes. Mills's antipathy for liberalism was intrinsic to his intellectual quest.

> The liberals want changes, but the means they would use and the practicality they espouse are short-run and small-scale. That is why their hopefulness and energy often seem so tragic, and that is why the left in general sees the liberals' activities as petty bourgeois screaming. . . . American liberalism, for at least one long generation, has lived off a collection of ideas put together before World War I.[5]

Mills's bête noire was not liberalism in general, but liberalism as the foundation of the labor movement's ideology. Liberalism was considered ''labor's home,'' the posture with which it is most comfortable. Mills implicitly joined liberalism as an ideology and labor as a pure economic movement as the essential testing ground of what is wrong with labor leadership.

In assessing political publics, Mills indicated his personal orientation toward the ''independent Left,'' far in advance, it might be added, of any concept of a ''New Left.'' He bemoaned the tendencies of the Left, as exemplified by magazines like *Partisan Review* and *Politics*, to "retreat from left-wing political life." In an implicit attack on Dwight Macdonald he accused the Left of "being tired of politics and even of life.[6] Just what these "little magazines" with limited circulation had to do with big labor leaders was never made very clear, but it was clear that they evoked strong sentiments Mills had in his private arsenal of affections and disaffections.

It was in publications like *Partisan Review*, *The New Leader*, and *Politics* that questions about labor and class consciousness were being examined. The Marxian prediction that working-class membership somehow yielded a working-class belief system had simply not taken place. Instead, workers developed a "trade union" consciousness, which accepted the premises if not always the outcome of a free market system. Into this theoretical void had stepped Vladimir Lenin, with his critique of working-class "spontaneity" and assertion of the need for a "vanguard party" which would compensate with its far-ranging vision for working-class myopia. The little magazines, with their collective fear and hatred of totalitarian possibilities of parties without classes, became the essential forum for an assault on Lenin, Stalin, and all the "isms" linked with their names. Mills's work on *The New Men of Power*, while at one level intended as an empirical survey of class consciousness, was at another a contribution to this anti-totalitarian rejection of vanguardism—of politicians telling workers what was in their best collective interests, instead of responding to those interests as they were articulated by authentic labor intellectuals.

Early in his career, Mills made clear the gap between him and the Communist movement—one that never closed despite the praise showered on him by the American Communists after the publication of *The Power Elite*. Of the Communist party he said: "It is very difficult to locate The Communist Party as a specific unit on any United States political scale. Its outlook and activities are those of a foreign national bloc within the lineup of United States politics."[7] Because of its commitment to foreign needs and its lack of independence, he dismissed it: "It is more an influence on one segment of the liberal center, displaying much of the smaller bourgeois psychology of this center, than it is a defined political public with definite U.S. roots and position."[8]

One might argue with these interpretations. Liberalism was not really as flabby as Mills made it out to be. It had, rather, made a realistic assessment that economic goals were the primary order of business in an American universe where political power had long ago been carved up. Mills's consignment of the independent Left to impotence proved to be true only of the particular little magazines he singled out, and it was hardly characteristic of the resiliency of left-wing politics in the years to come. Even his assault on the Communist party suffers from an absence of historical perspective, for whatever its commitments to Soviet objectives, even its most severe critics have recognized that American communism played a central role in the growth of industrial unionism in America. If that role was not always constant, neither was that of any other segment of labor leadership. Organizational efforts of Communists undeniably made possible a much more expansive vision of craft unionism in the 1920s, and a new kind of industrial unionism in the 1930s. But again, these expressions of Mills's private agendas were side issues and had little to do with the central subject of *The New Men of Power*; they had a great deal to do with his growing sophistication, as a New Yorker moving in heady intellectual circles. But his work indicates that he was not sure what to do once he penetrated these circles.

ののの

The majority of the book is taken up with information derived from a research project sponsored by the Labor Research Division of the Bureau of Applied Social Research. Mills directed this division in the late 1940s, and did so with characteristic élan, working with sophisticated quantitative data with an ease that belied his earlier philosophical training and lack of training in formal statistics. *The New Men of Power* would not have been written in the same way were it not for the resources of Columbia and for the Bureau of Applied Social Research. The information on labor leaders was gathered in the process of fulfilling the terms of a grant. In this sense, Mills represented a "new man" of sociological power—since the circumstances under which his work was conducted were a prototype of what would become standard research and publication procedure for postwar sociologists.

We may sometimes think that the penetration of women into sociology is a recent event. In fact, what is new is their visibility, not their penetration. In the preparation of *The New Men of Power*, Mills was assisted by a world of women: Helen Schneider prepared the essential empirical memorandum and the analysis of poll materials; Hazel Gaudet designed the preliminary tables showing the samples and was responsible for a considerable amount of the statistical work; Maud Zimmerman pretested several drafts of the questionnaire and integrated the interview material into a final tool of investigation; Ruth Harper was in charge of the preparation of the manuscript as a whole. Indeed, she probably had as much to do with the final research product as any single individual, even Mills himself. Finally, there was Beatrice Kevitt, who edited the penultimate draft and was involved editorially throughout the book. These women collected and analyzed the information that legitimated the theory behind the book. It is no exaggeration to say that they made Mills's general theoretical structure possible.

Much of that information, ranging from union membership to political party affiliation, is now dated by the organizational evolution of the labor movement. The 1940s were, after all, a time when a considerable gap remained between the American Federation of Labor and the

Congress of Industrial Organizations. Indeed, Mills calls his chapter on union competition "The Split Runs Deep." But even at the height of contradiction between the two master unions, Mills was able to say: "If these organizations were to unify organically, back of the alliance would be the most adroit and complicated political maneuverings ever to occur in our time and place." He added that in fact "the A.F.L. and the C.I.O. are united—in two separate blocs."[9] As the young men of the CIO grew older and leadership changes occurred in the AFL, and as emphasis on differences between the industrial and craft unions lessened and attitudes toward black and white differences became less pronounced, the reasons for the split evaporated.

When the gap was finally closed a decade later, it was replaced by other struggles, i.e., the AFL-CIO versus the Teamsters. It remains interesting to look back and remember how profound were the inner schisms between the two "liberal" national unions. The AFL hierarchy was guilty of everything from high pay scales to Republican party sentiments. The CIO was characterized by organizing drives to incorporate ethnic and minority groups, and lower pay scales for union officials. To Mills's credit, statistical differences did not lead him to overlook the similarities in the labor leaders' characteristics. He appreciates that labor leaders have their own agenda, whatever formal organizational apparatus they use.

When Mills wrote his book, labor racketeering was not acknowledged to be a branch of white-collar crime, as it is now. Indeed, only with Daniel Bell's three masterful essays on crime as an American way of life did a meaningful sociological literature on labor racketeering emerge.[10] The book does make an effort to capture a sense of the racketeering aspects of the labor movement, summed up in Mills's felicitous remark that just as "venture capitalism produces robber barons, in a somewhat delayed fashion, and on a much smaller scale, labor unionism produces its labor racketeers."[11] Like Bell, Mills viewed crime as an American way of life, taking different forms in different social strata.

Probably the most difficult data to analyze were on the subject of political party ties. There were definite differences between AFL and CIO party affiliations. Many AFL leaders were Republican in sentiment, even though the leadership of both the AFL and CIO were registered Democrats. Mills was writing at the height of the Henry Wallace movement and Progressive party activity, but this managed to capture only a small segment of the labor leadership's affections. The data clearly show that third-party politics were weak and scattered in the 1940s. One would have to add that this became even more so as the century progressed.

Mills attributed this political quiescence to uncritical devotion to the New Deal. The labor consensus was that since its organizing successes were highest during the 1930s, they could be attributed to the policies of Franklin Delano Roosevelt. Since Mills's purpose in doing the book, in part, was to forge a labor alliance through a third-party apparatus under the guidance of liberal intellectuals, the data gave him a problem. If an independent Left was in principle anti-Communist, and if the only sizeable third-party faction in labor at the time was Communist, then the human sources for a third-party formation were a priori impossible to locate or even manufacture.

The New Men of Power could not resolve this contradiction because, in fact, the period of time in which Mills was writing did not permit its easy resolution. Mills left no doubt as to his attitudes toward Communists, dismissing them as "U.S. Stalinists," people who make their judgments not in terms of the changing needs of working people, but on the basis of the changing needs of the ruling groups in Soviet Russia.[12] Given the absence of an independent Left, Mills's ideas about a new third-party formation ultimately came to rest on hopes and aspirations rather than facts and probabilities. Only if it could be proven that the established political system had failed labor would labor leaders be willing to admit the possibility of a new party. Unlike Mills, the leaders he studied did not believe that the established parties had failed them or that America had failed. This was, after all, the era of the American century: full employment at home and the Marshall Plan abroad. Mills was left with a critical posture toward the data he had collected. But that critical posture forms a basis of the theory which makes *The New Men of Power* of more than casual interest even now.

The theory segment of *The New Men of Power* is by all odds the most compelling. Here the essence of leadership as a sociological theme first emerges. What does Mills say about labor liberals that still permits thoughtful analysis? He points out that labor leaders perform the role of rebels poorly, and only during times of militant organization. What dampens the spirit of radicalism is that although labor leaders are in opposition to the received business system, they rarely fight power conferred on other types of organizations. Labor leaders seem to be incapable, by training and instinct, to locate labor issues in a context of state power, or the political system as a whole. As a result, the class struggles that labor leaders willingly engage in take for granted a mediating rather than a partisan role by the government.

The union, Mills points out, is a human institution, established to accumulate and to exert power. Hence the leader of a trade union is not a member of the money elite, but he is a member of the power elite. Here the concept of power elites enters Mills's thinking for the first time. The labor leader accumulates power and exercises it over members and the union as a whole. He is not simply a representative of workers, but a new participant in a world of powerful, contending elites.

As a consequence, the banner of class struggle in America becomes a foil disguising the struggle's pattern and the new claimants to the throne of power. Mills offered a conflict model of labor organization.

> Yet, in fact, all the time that he is the leader of a live and going union, the labor leader is in conflict with the powers of property: he is a rebel against individual business units and their unmolested exercise of the powers which property conveys. In his timidity and fear and eagerness to stay alive in a hostile environment, he does not admit this, and he often believes that he is not a rebel in the senses named, but the fact remains that he is. He is serving the function of a modern rebel by virtue of what his organization must do to live; modern rebels need not be romantic figures.[13]

Mills assures us that we are not dealing with a particularly religious person or a vanguard of the proletariat, but with someone of the same type, if not class, as an army officer, parliamentary debater, or political boss. This insight is of major importance. It helps to explain why the labor movement has never been a representative sample of those who work for a living. When Mills wrote his book, the CIO and the AFL had a total membership of 14 million; in the mid-1970s the AFL-CIO, now one organization, still had only a combined membership of 14 million, despite the fact that the size of the labor force more than doubled during those thirty years. Mills's great contribution was to present labor leadership without the conventional sentiments and trappings that in fact converted it to what it was not, the organized vanguard of the proletariat. He saw it, correctly, as a sector of the power elite.

His book is also concerned with the passivity of the masses, a lifelong concern. Always and everywhere Mills's pragmatism ultimately overwhelmed his Marxism. "The smaller alert public" rather than the "passive masses" are what really interested him.[14] He was interested in union leadership rather than rank-and-file membership, for he knew that only about one-third of the adult population of the United States either belonged to a labor union or lived in a family containing a union member. Even the one-third with a union linkage was primarily marginal to union activities. This was no way to run a revolution.

Unlike the management elite, or the military elite, the labor elite turned out to be social actors without a publicly defined role. They had power, but they were not entirely certain what to do with it. For this reason, Mills's "flabby liberalism" appeared particularly well suited to the union hierarchy. Mills worked hard to avoid using the rhetoric of the conventional Left in *The New Men of Power*. One finds no references to the bourgeoisie, imperialism, ruling classes, dominant ideology, and other familiar phrases of a rhetoric which numbs even the bravest heart upon sufficient repetition. One does hear phrases that were to become characteristically Millsian.[15] "The main drift," "alternatives to the main drift," or "the grand trend" were substituted for the rhetoric of the day. Mills sensed the exhaustion of Marxian language, if not the end of that ideology.

The price of freshness of language was often precision in meaning. It becomes something of a chore to determine what in fact a "great trend" or "great shift" really is, or what alternatives there really are. Yet, some definitions are hinted at, or can be intuited. Mills views labor as part of the main drift, first because its leadership joined with business and political leaders in what he claims is a tacit plan to stabilize the political economy of the United States. Here, too, one hears a suggestion of a "conspiracy" to maintain the capitalist system, a charge he leveled with increasing ferocity and decreasing caution as the great stratification trilogy unfolded.

In *The New Men of Power* Mills comes up short of claiming conspiracy, and instead says labor's ignorance contributes to the main drift. That drift, insofar as it is explicitly stated, means that the state has become the regulator of the national labor force, a task previously performed by individual employers. The new condition of labor is that free collective bargaining has become less a contest between business interests and the raw power of labor, and more an accommodation to political pressures and influence that unions, like management associations, are party to, but not always well informed about. This is a great insight by Mills. It permits him to appreciate the extent to which labor leaders maintain stability not because they share ideological attitudes with the bourgeoisie, but because labor amounts to so little apart from the interpenetration of state and economy. Labor's involvement in short-run decisions and responses to immediate pressures has led to an absence of appreciation for the big picture of state power. As a consequence, labor ideologists are able to provide few long-run answers to major political questions.[16]

Mills states his opposition to the main drift in terms of a call for third-party movements, which presumes a democratic consensus, and he acknowledges a political universe that is in fact responsive to alternatives to the major parties. One gets the impression that Mills's interest in a labor party were weak, even in the late forties. They were based more on his assumption that American society was incapable of solving its economic crisis, its cycle of "boom and bust," than on any positive program for an alternative Left-oriented third party. In the final, oft-quoted paragraph of the book, Mills revealed that he understood how little hope there was for a union of power and intellect within the confines of the trade union movement:

> It is the task of the labor leaders to allow and to initiate a union of the power and the intellect. They are the only ones who can do it; that is why they are now the strategic elite in American society. Never has so much

depended upon men who are so ill-prepared and so little inclined to assume the responsibility.[17]

By the end of the work a pattern emerges which was to become increasingly characteristic of the mature Mills: serious and profound criticism of the social system, accompanied by weak, even insipid alternative constructions to fill the void he helps us to understand. Mills well knew that most labor leaders, quite apart from the professionally trained intellectuals they used as staff assistants, were badly isolated from intellectuals, who were at the universities and in the research organizations. Labor organizations were probably among those who least used intellectual and social science efforts.

In the 1940s there was increased recognition by business and government of social science talent, but for the most part, organized labor remained hostile to these research-oriented intellectuals.[18] The struggle within the trade union movement—between its Right and its Left, between its Communist and non-Communist wings, between its orthodox democratic sectors and unorthodox political activist supporters—made labor leaders increasingly suspicious of and downright hostile to the very fusion of power and intellect that Mills called for. His sentiment overcame his sociology at this point. The Wobbly image of the effective intellectual as a member of the working class, and hence a link between power and ideas, took possession.

Within the union movement no more than 3 to 8 percent could even remotely be persuaded to a belief in the worth of ideas for the proper management of labor organization. Again, Mills's ideology, coming upon the harsh realities of his own data, ultimately determined that *The New Men of Power* would end on a note of monumental indecision. Only the "coming slump" of the American economy could salvage the indecision.[19] But that major slump did not occur. America entered a long cycle of scarcely unbroken upward growth between the end of the 1940s and the mid-1970s. Indeed, labor aristocrats finally came to realize the power of intellectuals, but they used them precisely as did business and government—as an ancillary service providing intellectual fuel for elite management of policy. This clearly was not what Mills had in mind when he spoke of the fusion of power and intellect. Nonetheless, *The New Men of Power* was a powerful contribution to the literature on stratification. It provided fresh—and for the time, brilliant—evidence that sociology could speak to, if not for, problems of labor. That in itself was no small achievement in the know-nothing atmosphere that prevailed in the ranks of labor leadership during the Truman presidency.

218

The response to the book was generally quite favorable. It was written with verve, and was well edited and accessible to a readership beyond the sociological community. The issue it addressed was of increasing significance to postwar Americans, and the book was without the conventional jargon or histrionic ideologies typical of writing on labor. Victor Riesel, writing in his *New York Post* column, called it "the most unusual book about labor I have yet read."[20] Joseph Loftus, at that time labor editor of *The New York Times*, writing in that paper, called *The New Men of Power* "a major project. The result is a collective portrait, not a series of personality sketches."[21] Even one of the magazines that Mills criticized for its flabby liberalism, *The Nation*, carried a positive review by Robert E. Nichols, who claimed: "What Dr. Kinsey did for sex and the American male, Dr. Mills now does for unions and the American labor leader. Although the subject is hardly as appetizing, the results should prove just as explosive.[22] But Professor Nichols's review also observes what was to be noted with increasing frequency—Mills's shrill tone. "He sometimes inclines to look at things too much in terms of black and white. But both his array of facts and his own views should jolt us into some fresh thought."[23] Aaron Levenstein, writing in *The Progressive*, described Mills as "a painstaking scholar, who has combined a study of the behavior of the labor leaders with mind-searching polling of their attitudes. He does not present his findings in clinical isolation but arrays them against the background of economic and political development."[24]

A singularly sharp and critical assault made within labor-intellectual circles was delivered by Mark Starr, educational director of the International Ladies Garment Workers Union. Writing in *The Labor Zionist*, Starr claimed that Mills's book profoundly underestimated the union's lively developing role as an autonomous welfare agency, giving individual workers a sense of belonging. Further, Mills basically urged political passivity, waiting for the next economic crisis in order for ideas to take new form; the role of workers' education was an area Mills vacated. Starr's final thrust was that if Mills were to sit in and listen to actual working-class educational activities in trade unions throughout the country, rather than to the New York intellectual elites and the discontented essayists who always presumed perfection as a critical starting point, he would be better prepared to write a book about labor.[25]

Mills's only defense of the book was made in response to Starr. Interestingly, he does not quite address himself to the specifics of the critique. He calls Starr a liberal obfuscator and a promulgator of official United States labor thinking. Mills refers to Starr as "a nice guy," and says "one really hates to slap him hard in public." But beyond this gratuitous comment, he goes on to say that "in the field of ideas we are enemies"[26]—a bluntness that was excessive, in print, even for Mills. Apart from properly defending himself against the ad hominem charge that he didn't know what was going on in the country, asserting to the contrary that "I feel that unions in Texas, Wisconsin and Maryland have gotten pretty close to the grass roots,"[27] Mills does not mind using some ad hominem arguments himself.

The questions Starr raised did haunt Mills. In rebuttal he chose to assert the right of social science research per se, rather than the absence of any real empathy for the people under investigation. He admitted that labor was too big and complex for one researcher to know it all personally. For Mills, research was organized and systematic experience, and unlike personal experience it was cumulative in the knowledge it yielded. However, saying this was not quite a response to Starr, since in fact Mills did not cover those parts of the labor process that Starr highlighted. Perhaps Mills could have answered that welfare features of trade unionism brought it close to the American mainstream and made it incapable of responding to radical thrusts.

Needless to say, *National Business*, *Financial Weekly*, and *Barron's* were not quite enamored with Mills either. In its own way, such critical attention provided legitimation for the book. *Barron's* argued that the meaning of the Depression of the 1930s was not its manufacture by the middle classes, but rather its prolongation by anti-business forces within the New Deal. The *Barron's* reviewer insisted that the Republican Eightieth Congress which sat between 1946 and 1948 did more to influence economic recovery than a Democratic administration had during the previous decade. He charged that Mills was a total romantic, since the absence of a Socialist movement in the United States resulted not from a private property ideology among labor leaders, but because labor had been so successful in grasping control of the Democratic party. The very power of trade union leaders in Democratic party politics prevented any third party from emerging.[28] And this is a significant point that Mills did not fully consider.

The academic response to *The New Men of Power*, was highly favorable paralleled only by the response to *White Collar*. Henry David, writing in *Public Opinion Quarterly*, claimed that the book "makes a genuine contribution to the literature of a field in which systematic investigation has been rare, and basic information is at a premium." However, he observed that "religious affiliation is not touched on, and this, it may be contended, is as significant as the place of birth of the fathers of labor leaders." He argued that the conservative orientation of the AFL was in part due to the predominance of Catholics in its union hierarchy.[29] This criticism seems off the mark precisely because the book does discuss, at least in passing, the religious factor in AFL and CIO leadership.

Irving Howe, in *Partisan Review*, also singled out for attack in the book, wrote an exceptionally favorable commentary. He saw this volume as being "in total opposition to such current inclinations as quietism, advocacy of preventive atomic war, and a truce with the right because of a fear of Stalinism." The politically alert publics designated by Mills were seen as usable categories for an independent Left. Howe made some shrewd observations about the situation of labor in America during the late forties. The favored international position of the United States, its dominant role as chief producer and creditor in the world, allowed it a considerable degree of maneuverability vis-à-vis the labor movement. "Temporarily, there is ample room for it in the American capitalist economy, for there are still vice-presidencies to hand out." Howe, as an early leader of the anti-Stalinist Left, was impressed by Mills's labor-oriented viewpoint, but less sanguine about Mills's inability to come to grips with the totalitarian impulses pervasive in the American labor movement.

> Perhaps the most serious obstacle to Mills' perspective is the atomization and demoralization of the anti-Stalinist left. The radical intellectuals have lately come to underestimate their powers, limited as those are. . . . The small failures of energy and will in New York have their repercussions in Detroit.[30]

Stalinist Russia had an inhibiting effect on democratic politics. The Cold War, as it dragged on, made for timidity and hesitation within the union movement and prevented any counterattraction to the pseudoradicalism of the Communists. Howe's comment is clearly a favorable amplification rather than a criticism of Mills—one which Mills appreciated.

Joseph Shister, writing in *Labor and Nation*, and head of the Labor and Management Center at Yale University at the time, also identified the book as an extremely important work dealing with a topic of cardinal significance. He uniquely appreciated the fact that the book is essentially divided between theory and data, and flawed by being carved up into five sections. He wondered if the trade union movement was quite as economic in its ideology as Mills made it out to be, or whether this inference was drawn not from the data but from Mills's general perspective. As a result, Shister was not quite convinced that a third party was a necessity; rather, it seemed to be a long-range possibility. While Shister appreciated the crisis of the intellectual in the labor movement, he saw Mills's work as being fueled more by clever intuitions than by scientific distinction. As a result, he urged more testing of the thesis of a third party as the only forum for moving the trade union leadership beyond strictly economic interests.[31]

Ely Chinoy, at the time a young instructor at the University of Toronto starting his research on automobile workers, wrote an excellent review in the *Canadian Journal of Economics and Political Science*. The book stimulated Chinoy's own interest in the sociology of work, and the follow-up research Mills sought. For Chinoy, *The New Men of Power* was a substantial contribution to social analysis that not only raised basic questions but suggested concrete alternatives. However, Chinoy was concerned about Mills's emphasis on "the main drift in the U.S." He found it debatable whether war or a slump would be the next phase of the cycle. Like Howe, he drew attention to the fact that foreign aid and defense spending might prevent a slump. Beyond that, Chinoy noted that after a war, labor leaders are likely to support any major reconstruction effort.[32]

A review of substance was written by Charles E. Lindblom for the *American Sociological Review*. Lindblom indicated that *The New Men of Power* was superior on all counts to Burnham's *The Managerial Revolution*. He found the work to be a careful examination of the facts, with an extraordinarily fruitful hypothesis as well as a provocative argument. Interestingly, Lindblom felt that the ideas of the book were more significant than its empirical findings. He probably empathized with Mills's own sense of the constraints of the data when he said: "In actual fact, a substantial part of the data, though useful for information, is unnecessary for Mills' purposes." As Lindblom understood, those purposes were a new diagnosis of power in the United States. Lindblom saw Mills's views on the nature of the next major depression as much oversimplified, and since they were essential to the development of some important parts of his thesis, Lindblom was inclined to consider these views an important weakness in the diagnosis of the main drift. "Slumps are not all of the same pattern, but Mills' estimates of how the next one will influence political alignments seem to rest on the assumption that like the depression of the thirties, the next one will come suddenly, be very severe, and will be allowed to continue for a long time without countermeasures being taken." Lindblom ended on an affirmative note: "It is always clear that Mills is a genuine democrat," and that his concern is, therefore, "for democratic leadership in the union movement."[33]

The New Men of Power was Mills's first work to reach a broad audience. Until then, his reputation had been entirely professional, but his association with the Bureau of Applied Social Research and his widening involvement with the New York intellectual milieus had given him an instinct for a wider world. Not only were there a wide variety of reviews of the book in the popular media, but his findings were reprinted in the press and he participated in the nascent genre of television round-table shows (which made a particular impression on him).[34] Mills even took an interest in the marketing effort by his publisher, Harcourt, Brace. He liked reaching the "publics" which exist beyond the reach of the "professions."

It is worth remembering that Mills's writings in this period attracted the support of the fragmented, independent intellectuals he was then appealing to for greater unity. As he moved away from analysis of labor and into the upper reaches of society, he also moved away from labor as an answer to chronic failures or problems within America. In so doing, he left behind a considerable portion of his own intellectual constituency. Mills never repudiated *The New Men of Power*, as he did *Character and Social Structure*, but neither did he ever return to the subject of labor directly. It was rather the cleavage, the schism, between labor and leaders, masses and elites, that became central for him. Mills's impulse and emphasis moved him in the latter direction: to the study of masses and elites, and ultimately to power itself as a crucial variable. Still, if it was the masses who gained his sympathy it was the elites who retained his research fascination. He left the trade union phenomenon behind in the first volume of the great stratification trilogy, along with his support for a concept of labor intellectuals who would serve as a *deux ex machina* for an emerging American consciousness.

The utopianism in Mills became apparent. He was to continue to search for a specific segment of the population who would be the bearers of the big news and the great truths. He started, at least, with a large social class, and ended, years later, with a small educated elite, the ministers and high priests of science. The utopianism inheres in the fact that Mills, while locating the "enemies" in society writ large, sought his "friends" in elites and would-be salvationists. Fortunately, he was, for most of the 1940s and 1950s, able to disentangle analysis from solutions.

REFERENCES

1. Roscoe C. Hinkle and Gisela J. Hinkle. *The Development of Modern Sociology*. Garden City, N.Y.: Doubleday, 1954. Edward A. Shils. *The Present State of American Sociology*. Glencoe, Ill.: The Free Press, 1948. Leon Bramson. *The Political Context of Sociology*. Princeton: Princeton University Press, 1961. Daniel Bell. *The Social Sciences Since the Second World War*. New Brunswick, N.J.: Transaction Books, 1981. These four monographs, read serially, provide a remarkably coherent framework for understanding the evolution of American sociological thought.

2. C. Wright Mills. "The Professional Ideology of Social Pathologists." In *Power, Politics and People*. New York and London: Oxford University Press, 1963, pp. 525-52.

3. See the following: Merle Curti. *The Growth of American Thought* (originally published in 1943), 3rd rev. ed. New Brunswick, N.J.: Transaction Books, 1981. Richard Hofstadter. *Social Darwinism in American Thought*. Boston: Beacon Press, 1944. Richard Hofstadter. *The Age of Reform*. New York: Alfred A. Knopf, 1955. John R. Commons et al., *History of Labor in the United States* (4 vols.). New York: The Macmillan Co., 1918–1935. Selig Perlman. *A History of Trade Unionism in the United States*. New

York: The Macmillan Co., 1922. There is no question that the efforts of the Wisconsin and Columbia historians had a great impact on kindling Mills's populism.

4. Pitirim A. Sorokin. "Some Contrasts of Contemporary European and American Sociology." *Social Forces* 8 (1929): 57. Cited in Bramson, *The Political Context of Sociology*, p. 81.

5. C. Wright Mills. *The New Men of Power: America's Labor Leaders*. New York: Harcourt, Brace and Co., 1948, p. 19.

6. *Ibid.*, pp.15–17.

7. *Ibid.*, pp.22–23, 200.

8. *Ibid.*, p. 295.

9. *Ibid.*, p. 83.

10. Daniel Bell. *The End of Ideology: On the Exhaustion of Political Ideas in the Fifties*. New York: The Free Press, 1962, pp. 127–209.

11. Mills, *The New Men of Power,* p. 131.

12. *Ibid.*, p. 199.

13. *Ibid.*, p. 8.

14. *Ibid.*, p. 31.

15. *Ibid.*, pp. 223, 291, and passim.

16. *Ibid.*, pp. 235–37.

17. *Ibid.*, p. 291.

18. Irving Louis Horowitz. "Social Science and Public Policy: Implications for Modern Research." In *The Rise and Fall of Project Camelot: Studies in the Relationship Between Social Science and Practical Politics*, rev. ed. Cambridge, Mass.: MIT Press, 1974, pp. 339–75.

19. Mills, *The New Men of Power,* p. 290.

20. Victor Riesel. "Inside Labor." *New York Post*, September 18, 1948.

21. Joseph A. Loftus. "Labor Leaders and Trade Unions." *New York Times*, October 3, 1928.

22. Robert E. Nichols. "The Leaders of Labor." *The Nation*, October 3, 1948.

23. *Ibid.*

24. Aaron Levenstein. "Labor's Leaders." *The Progressive*, November 1948.

25. Mark Starr. "Labor Through Polls." *The Labor Zionist*, March 18, 1949.

26. C. Wright Mills. "Dogmatic Indecision." *The Labor Zionist*, April 15, 1949.

27. *Ibid.*

28. G.S. (initials only given). "Books for the Businessman," *Barron's National Business and Financial Weekly*, December 13, 1948.

29. Henry David. Review. *Public Opinion Quarterly* (Winter 1948–49): 750–53.

30. Irving Howe. "Possibilities for Politics." *Partisan Review* (Spring 1949).

31. Joseph Shister. "Important Study of Union Leaders." *Labor and Nation* (January–February 1949).

32. Ely Chinoy. Review. *Canadian Journal of Economics and Political Science* (May 1949): 289–91.

33. Charles E. Lindblom. Review. *American Sociological Review* 13, no. 3 (June 1949): 432–33.

34. See "TV Spots: Court of Issues." *Newsweek*, December 20, 1948.

11

White Collar, Gray Flannel, and the Rise of Professionalism

A successful campaign for reducing economic inequality probably requires two things. First, those with low incomes must cease to accept their condition as inevitable and just. Instead of assuming, like unsuccessful gamblers, that their numbers will eventually come or that their children's numbers will, they must demand changes in the rules of the game. Second, some of those with high incomes must begin to feel ashamed of economic inequality.

Christopher Jencks, *Inequality: A Reassessment of the Effect of Family and Schooling in America*

T HE 1950s PRODUCED a remarkable literature in America on the "new middle classes." First, in 1950 came the publication of David Riesman's *The Lonely Crowd*.[1] The following year Mills's *White Collar* appeared,[2] and in 1956 William H. Whyte's *The Organization Man* appeared.[3] This trilogy was joined by a number of lesser, or at least less well publicized, books on the same subject.[4] What provided an impulse to the wide public absorption of this popular sociological literature was the coming of age of an intermediary class that could not find itself readily identified in the "classical" literature of the social sciences, or significant emotional content in the works of such novelists as Sloan Wilson and Louis Auchincloss. It is a measure of how potent this trilogy of books by Riesman, Whyte, and Mills was that fully a decade later Eric F. Goldman, the Princeton historian, could list them among the best eight books on the social and economic scene to mirror postwar American existence.[5]

If Mills's *White Collar* had one set of meanings for his audience, it had quite another for him. *White Collar* is the "swing book," the bridge between Mills's examination of the working classes of America in *The New Men of Power*, published in 1948, and *The Power Elite*, which appeared in 1956. In itself, *White Collar* established Mills as an important empirical researcher in the field of social stratification, and a leading theorist on that rare species *Homo Americanus*. Of all Mills's writings, only this book uniquely inspired a largely positive consensus. It satisfied the requirements of both the participants in and the critics of mass society. The book also pleased in equal measure representatives and critics of middle-range social science—those who saw problems in large-scale terms, but emphasized small-scale solutions.

"The white-collar people slipped quietly into modern society." Beginning with this opening statement Mills summarizes the character of the contemporary American middle class. "White collar" is the term he uses for a variety of groups broadly included in the middle class. This designation is occupationally descriptive, not intended to impose unity on such a wide-ranging group. White-collar workers perform nonmanual labor at better-than-average salaries, and in their social behavior and political attitudes they always "aspire . . . to a middle course." They are economically dependent on an employer class, fragmented into numerous groupings and interests, and constitute the bulk of the growing "urban masses." By virtue of these attributes, and because of the necessary connection of white-collar workers to a complex and frustrating society, they embody the psychological themes of our epoch. A majority are the "middle managers" of the administrative units of business and government which Mills refers to as "command hierarchies." They are salaried factory supervisors, inspectors, police and fire officers, salaried specialists—professionals of all sorts surrounded by technicians, sales personnel, and clerks of a thousand varieties. They are well paid at "the top" but less so in a graded descent to lower levels in offices, shops, and factories. Because they are so numerous and everywhere emergent, the contemporary literature of many nations draws on the experiences of this group to express modern dilemmas.

The most compelling dilemma is the waning of independent individualism as a life-style and as a social value, and the disappearance of social types and groups who made individualism a living reality. The "captain of industry," rugged, selfish, daring; the free speculator in land; the free small entrepreneur of a rural America, master of his own corner of the world—these gave way to the dependent and anonymous "little man" of the newer urban culture, a figure often examined and lamented in the literature of our time, and one whose "white collar" marks the shift of the middle class from older entrepreneurial groups to the mass of today's office dwellers.

With this idea Mills embellished a leading theme of the intellectual climate of the 1950s in the United States. In *The Lonely Crowd*, Riesman described the "other-directed" individual preoccupied with the consumption of goods, the new "typical" urban middle-class white American. The "lonely crowd" was alienated, often supine, confused in a rapidly changing world of ill-defined but seemingly endless opportunity, of amorphous power and economic groupings. Riesman gave touching testimony to the dilemma of economic growth without social or psychic meaning in *Faces in the Crowd*, his work on character and politics.

> Industrialization and leisure, higher education and a greater freedom in mores, allow us to make demands on family life and claims for personal satisfaction and growth that in the past were voiced only by a privileged few. We have, so to speak, democratized divine discontent. But while we know enough to be discontented with our human relationships, we do not know enough to improve them substantially, or even to know where to look for help.[6]

Ely Chinoy found the workers of the automobile industry more victimized by "the American Dream" than advocates of that dream. It was his assessment that bureaucratic social advancement through economic dependence rendered the values of labor and craftsmanship meaningless. The workers were further frustrated by a very limited "opportunity structure" of vast and centralized factories, where they were fed new versions of the old American Dream originating in middle-class success stories of a rise within the corporation through entry into a roughly white-collar social category. Their pride in work and craftsmanship was blunted by the technology-induced fragmentation of tasks as well as the middle-class ideal. Again, the result was disappointment and alienation. Two of Mills's friends added their voices to this growing search for meanings. Harvey Swados exposed "The Myth of the Happy Worker" and Erich Fromm declaimed against the new "manipulators of people and symbols." Each described a generation alienated from goals derived from meaningful labor, revealing the extent to which loss of work ideals and integrated occupational communities can breed psychological isolation and breakdown. Novelists such as Norman Mailer, in search of community, found it only in the subterranean world of "the Beats," whose withdrawal from crippling middle-class boredom and conventionality enabled them to make a community out of alienated souls.

Concern for the widespread isolation and alienation of the middle class was general, and Mills was greatly affected by this intellectual milieu. He took up his study of the American white-collar classes believing that their malaise derived from the decline of an aggressively libertarian, property-owning middle class and the emergence of a mass, dependent middle class. Mills made his study at a time when a freewheeling, radical critique of American society was likely to find only a few isolated representatives. Ex-radicals were busily naming names, recanting former associations. The American population was in a conservative mood in the decade which began with Senator Joseph McCarthy's crusade to identify social and political criticism with treason against the government.

ᴗᴖᴑᴖᴑ

Mills was expanding on two themes: one empirical and the other ethical. First, the term "middle class" has changed in content, and our perceptions must keep pace with this change. Second, this change, while tied to technological advances, has been achieved at great cost, which threatens the ideal of independence. Mills's analysis implies a critique because he could scarcely disguise his disenchantment with the consequences attendant on technological advancement. With the growing complexity and specialization of society, all issues before the public acquire a complex character. Public response and participation are hampered or made impossible as a consequence; hence the full exercise of social responsibility in national or community matters is seriously obstructed. But if individuals do not actively shape their own environment, how can they take pride in it, be informed about it, defend it? How can they surrender the right to make their own world without violating democratic principles? This is the problem as Mills sees it, and one which he raises in connection with "white-collar people." The surrender of the public sphere, the collapse of the political side of life and an active relation to it, is for Mills the outcome of the professionalization of politics, resulting from the concentration and centralization of property and organization. In this shift the earlier middle-class entrepreneurs, who politically shaped their world, have given way to an apolitical, white-collar middle class overwhelmed by the complexity and size of modern society. Because they have surrendered a part of themselves as people, white-collar workers in a regulated society are more divided within themselves and against themselves than the older middle class ever was by laissez-faire competition. This consequence can be overcome, according to Mills, only by the creation of conditions that enhance a high degree of community and at the same time maximize individual participation on a broad scale, so that individuals fully engaged in making their own environment may find sources of fulfillment in the civic virtues and need not search for substitute gratifications.

The origins of the American middle class were located by Mills in its early character as a stratum of broadly dispersed free farmers, as distinguished from Europe's narrow commercial stratum in urban centers. In the United States, because of the absence of aristocratic land ownership, the drive toward capitalism originated in rural areas. Unlike Europe, the United States achieved cohesion along capitalist lines in a rural context. The farmer became a speculator. Early businessmen were primarily "handicrafters" and small, independent tradesmen. Even the worker was not merely a factory employee but a skilled, hired mechanic. Business was not tied to the factory system. After the Civil War industrialization "took off," spearheaded by the "captain of industry," the "robber baron," the industrializing adventurer, who became established in the American mind as its ideal type of businessman, the pinnacle of success in old middle-class terms.

The openness of American society permitted mass identification with this figure, since it seemed possible to succeed in similar ways. This forward drive was unimpeded by international involvements. Small farmers, land and produce speculators, and captains of industry provided the success image for middle-class striving. What these groups had in common, and what is central for Mills, is that they were all independent and owned their own property, and therefore were consciously able to support and protect the ideal of self-sufficiency. The fact of independent property ownership became intertwined with the idea of liberty. The ideal of equitable distribution, which is potentially anti-wealth, was basically connected to the idea that each person was entitled by labor to a small share of the property. This share was to make people free because it made them "count." The old middle class was not only a success ideal but a model for achieving self-sufficiency and liberty. It bred an absolute individual, linked to other individuals by countless voluntary contractual transactions. Nineteenth-century America was a world in which laissez-faire was the principle of social life. Life was self-regulating, unguided by state authority. Individuals had the means to direct their own lives and could assume responsibility for doing so. In this context, competition limited excesses and goaded people on to achievement.

The old middle-class captains of industry declined because the property base for their existence was transformed. Democratic property, on which self-employed owners work in their own enterprises, gave way to class property, on which work is severed from ownership. The growth of the factory system and the expansion of industrial enterprises centralized authority. Both owner and laborer lost self-mastery. Great agricultural surpluses and a high-tariff policy enhanced capitalist growth. Although this was to shrink the farming population and the terms of production were to produce ruinous business cycles, the disappearance of the free market was especially responsible for reducing the farming middle class in size and economic importance. Foreign competition was increasingly a factor. The domestic market contracted. Monopolistic features of the economy became more apparent. The revolution in technology also brought periods of agricultural "overproduction." This process persisted, and gradually the systematic split between wage-earning cultivators and big commercial rural corporations became widespread. The industrial revolution tended to draw the family farm into its orbit and leave it stranded. The expansion of industry drove a wedge into the agricultural sector and transformed its property relations.

Despite this, small entrepreneurs were still mainly people on farms. Small urban entrepreneurs had never equaled their rural counterparts because big industrialization aimed more directly at their sphere of operations. The transportation network and the technological revolution, both organized by the city businessman, had rendered the small entrepreneurs in cities increasingly dependent creatures, compensating for their losses by clothing themselves in competitive, romantic images borrowed from those of the captain of industry. This "captain" had never been adequately replaced by other middle-classes success images because he was personally identifiable rather than an impersonal manager.

In the city business milieu, the small entrepreneur had a high commercial mortality rate; few survived compared with the number that initiated enterprises. The growth of great businesses absorbed the skills and markets formerly open to the entrepreneur, with the result that the business world was less homogeneous by the middle of this century than it had been at the close of the last century. Business concentration had become an ineluctable fact regardless of reaction to it and by whatever criteria business development was measured. The great fact to note, according to Mills, was the loss of independence throughout the middle class to business corporations as a result of property transformation, basically from small landownership to ownership by big factories. This constituted the ground for subsequent psychological and political transformations.

The heavy rate of small-business failure and the growing mentality of dependence produced what Mills considers the lowest form of human insignificance, the "lumpenbourgeoisie," the decayed group set off from the middle class in the way that Marx conceived the "lumpenproletariat" to be a degeneration of the proletariat. The "lumpenbourgeois" is the marginal middle-class man barely earning his way in the city or country. He exists from day to day, anxious, dependent, withdrawn into the frustrated family, dwelling in blank defeat and insecurity, forced into directionless thrift and subservience to those customers who patronize him. He is the last hurrah of capitalist heroism, although his persistence would seem to make him its very essence.

In this transition from rural to factory-based capitalism, the lumpenbourgeois rather than the industrial worker appears as chief victim. Mills so emphasizes individual ownership as a means to freedom and work satisfaction that the caricature of the beaten free entrepreneur, the lumpenbourgeois, is all the more pitiable or absurd in his blind, marginal persistence in the large-scale industrial world. So strong is the identification of the American mind with the free competitive capitalist that despite tremendous shifts in the direction of business concentration and propertyless mass dependency, the idea lingers on. Mills asserts that competition has in fact been narrowed and now occurs between existing industries controlling production. Individuals all seek to justify themselves in the light of the self-made ideal. Even where economic facts say otherwise, the competitive rhetoric lingers on. But, considering actual social behavior, Mills notes that small entrepreneurs do band together with others of their kind, pressing heavily for "fair competition." They do so because they have so little faith that it operates independently of their own pressures. Middle-class belief in competition has turned into a struggle to limit big business, and this class petitions government toward this end.

Since farm entrepreneurship has become so much like industrial and business concentration, the small farmer has also turned to political struggle, attempting to use the government as a support. In turn this old rural middle class can be politically managed only by enhancing its dependence on subsidies, which represent compensation for curtailment of production. This is as much as a means of managing small farmers' pressure as it is a way to cope with the growing monopoly of industry over rural life in the possession and distribution of goods and services. Independent farmers are no longer free producers for a free market, tied to their fellows by market relations, but are dependent upon a government policy of raising and maintaining agricultural prices to compensate farmers with public funds for the loss of that free market.

With the overall decline of the old middle class, and the consequent breakdown of community leadership and local loyalties, big businessmen have quixotically assumed the moral role of protecting democratic self-made ideals. Insofar as small entrepreneurs still play the role, it consists mainly of banding together and, through the Chamber of Commerce perhaps, exerting anti–big business leadership; or, where big business wishes to exert pressure against an urban project of some kind, small business may be mobilized by the bigger interests to provide effective pressure and give the proceedings a democratic appearance. On the surface small entrepreneurs lead the community, but they are usually participants on behalf of bigger business except at those times when they act to limit big-business encroachments. The prestige of the middle-class community leadership is maintained in various ways by other groups and only sometimes by the middle class itself. Since the myth of middle-class community leadership is so widespread, because of the old idea of independence it represents, community stability depends on its maintenance.

The small, traditional middle class is found by Mills to be everywhere, city and country, pressed from above by big business and from below by labor. This class smarts with resentment in both directions when it does degenerate into a lumpenbourgeois level. Its political heyday was the "Progressive Era," in the fight against plutocracy led by Theodore Roosevelt and then Woodrow Wilson. Yet, however politically vociferous the old small middle class may have been or may still be from time to time, its anti–big business spirit is a nostalgic harkening back to irretrievable times. Mills suggests that only a greater share of control "over that upon which one is dependent: the job within the centralized enterprise" points a direction for restoring economic security to political freedom.

The new middle class, "white-collar people on salary," constitute a majority of those people who work for 2 or 3 percent of the population. This middle class has steadily grown in proportion to the whole population, and this growth parallels the shift "from property to non-property" and from property to occupation as a new axis of stratification. The occupational shift had been marked by a shift from manipulation of things to manipulation of people and symbols: a shift to predominance of office, service, and technological rationalization over production. The wealth of produced goods must be distributed, and a high national "inventory" enforces the prevalence of a marketing, distributing economy. Furthermore, the government expands its bureaucracies to meet the challenge of increasingly complicated technological operations and concentrates a white-collar population on another front. State operations increase in specialization and depend on a complicated technology and expert personnel, which in turn are dependent on lower levels of these, and so on down.

The occupational structure is largely composed of nonproductive labor based on nonmanual skills, forming pyramids of prestige according to levels of power. Although at average and middle levels of income the white-collar employee often does not stand significantly above the wage laborer, society now assigns greater prestige to nonproductive skills, and the white-collar class measures significantly above wage-labor in prestige. As the means of administration of goods and services are enlarged and centralized in industry and government, the "managerial type" becomes more vital to the social structure. This supports the "managerial demiurge," which means that the society is impelled by the nature of its new primary work tasks toward a division between managers and the multitude who are managed.

Mills analyzes procedures in government bureaucracies and industrial organizations. He finds bureaucratization in the former loose and incomplete, despite the connotations of rigid lines of authority and efficiency in the words "government bureaucracy." The centralization of property and administration in public and private business and political operations accounts for this trend. What is problematic in the situation is that managerial authority in this complex is hard to locate. People hold positions on a hierarchical scale of prestige and income, but decision making seems to have no final authority. It is not lodged in an identifiable seat of responsibility for outcomes. Management simply becomes a way of life, a way of breaking down difficult tasks, a response to technological complexity that simply profilerates trained personnel and breeds a certain kind of behavior among the top ranks of an organization.

The characteristic managerial personality consequently seeks to belong in a managerial stratum rather than take command and assume responsibility. This style is reinforced by newer sources of recruitment of personnel. Few of the people who make up managerial staffs emerge from independent entrepreneurial experience; instead, they rise from inside administrative hierarchies, from circles of proven managers of smaller firms, and from the ranks of technical or business college graduates. Management of other people increasingly pervades work, involving transmission of orders to lower levels. The special amorphousness of "middle management" specialists, who do not execute orders at the bottom (like foremen) or make them at the top, but rather transmit orders and information at intermediate levels is a case in point. Technicians who join staffs because their special knowledge is needed become part of a chain of transmission and management of personnel relations without clear-cut tasks or responsibilities.

A new entrepreneurial type pervades the bureaucracies, greatly modified by large-scale unsentimental organizations. These are the figures selling insights into commercial research, public relations, labor relations. They link business with the world of advertising and communications. They specialize in "fixing" difficult, if not necessarily legitimate, matters, paving the way between firm and public or between firms. The old entrepreneurs advanced themselves by founding new enterprises. The new entrepreneurs compensate for the inadequacies of people in power. They must manage their situation shrewdly by underplaying their role, so as not to overstep top management authority and yet make their indispensabilty clear. They thrive on the slowness of bureaucratic operations, and their manipulation of anxieties and delays provides legitimation for an intermediate stratum.

Regardless of variations, managers of big business are the new economic elite of the twentieth century. Ownership has given way to management as the means of control and power in a business organization. Coming much closer to Burnham in 1950 than he had in 1940, Mills notes that concentration of property has given great power to its administrators. While owners retain legal rights, the powerful corporation managers have moved into the propertied class. Mills's point is that contrary to the usual argument that the importing of a top managerial class signifies the decline of property ownership, the ownership system and all its legal entitlements remain intact. This technique has expanded the ranks of the propertied class and delegated tremendous powers to the manager newcomers. Managers are not experts so much as they are executors of property. The point of it all is that the rift between ownership and management has led to greater concentration of power and property at one end of the stratification scale, and to the powerlessness of the small, independent sectors at the other. The ever-present danger of such polarization is undemocratic irresponsibility.

The managerial demiurge is a drift toward rationalizing all social units, brought about by the transformation of small, individually owned farms into great property concentration, which alters styles of administration and is compounded by technological complexity. The loss of initiative and seats of personal, identifiable responsibility leads to the fetishizing of organization life and the overshadowing of individuals. With an increasing conception of work as management of others within an ill-defined and shifting hierarchy, and an increased priority for skills involving technical consultation and persuasion, has come a drift from assignment of explicit authority in decision making to manipulation. There is thus a need to combat the impersonality of power be clearly establishing the limits of responsibility.

The technological revolution made necessary widespread training for new skills, but it was accompanied by a loss of independence on the part of the older professionals. Whether or not the latter owned their means of livelihood, it was directly under their authority and management. Their present-day counterparts merely manipulate a small part of a gigantic enterprise, within indistinct lines of authority, for a salary, and are utterly dependent on superiors or big owners. While free practitioners as high-style craftsmen are far from dead, they coexist with a broad new element: hired dependent professionals, absorbed by a great bureaucracy somewhere in the upper reaches of complex organizations. This also applies to physicians: compare free practice with dependence on a hospital and extreme specialization of skills within it. Lawyers are salaried and absorbed by business corporations, and law schools are converted into factories to serve the corporate system. The upper echelons of the teaching profession—college professors, who are generally from plebeian origins—are captivated by university status and learn, in their dependence on the university, to rise within its channels. Society may employ professors off-campus in its search for expertise, but their pattern of operations is tied to a campus and geared to special administrative tasks just as much as, or more than, it is tied to creative work. While the expansion of the ranks of the salaried professional has opened up opportunities for upward mobility to children of the lower classes, it is not a consciously democratic expansion, but simply the product of the dominance of a new technology.

The bureaucratic tendency to absorb the lower classes has gained strength in its passage through four phases. In the pre–First World War period, America boasted a pragmatic group of muckraking intellectuals who gradually gave way to the cultivated, hedonistic liberals of the 1920s. The 1930s brought forward the intellectual as a political agent, up to the years of the Second World War and a break with Depression radicalism. Since that war, a sense of tragedy and a loss of will have afflicted intellectuals. These are traceable to the commercial machinery which demands saleable novelty and standardized cultural products no less than to ideological demands for neutrality engendered by the bureacratic style. In this context, intellectuals seek connections to money and power through specialization of interests, narrowing their range so as to render themselves technicians. If they persist in free and unattached critical activity they are rendered powerless, if not meaningless, and their work mirrors their helplessness if they cannot stand up to the challenge. That is, the will of intellectuals to publicly communicate in freely critical terms may be overwhelmed by an environment that will then absorb them into its technical bureaucratic machinery because of their failure to persist. They may resolve their alienation in the objectivity of neutral technical pursuits, believing that relevance in a small defined sphere will compensate for a lack of control over society as a whole.

✍︎◦◦✍︎

The distribution of American manufactured goods has so preoccupied present society as to make the practice and standards of the market pervasive, and the salesperson a central American figure. The American business system is stitched into a network by salesmanship. Once the salesperson merely purveyed goods—which was effortless because demand exceeded supply. When supply and demand were balanced, the salesperson provided information by which to make purchasing choices. Now mass production has made mass marketing imperative and affluence demands a focus on distribution. Modern methods of distribution have gathered a great number of white-collar skills to bear on organizational tasks, especially the recruitment and training of sales personnel to compete for a limited market space and a satiated public. The economy has been pressed toward marketing in order to maintain its production levels. Salesmanship has been popularly elevated as a scientific ideology and a life-style, so that the country has become a vast salesroom preoccupied with the distribution of goods.

While American society has become less an association of independent small-scale enterprises and increasingly a complete industrial giant, the technological advancement and refinement of administration has proceeded. The "file" has become the nub of organization. The old office had few employees: the bookkeeper, the office girl, the typist, the office boy. But then the need for systematic arrangement of business facts (in a numerical file, an alphabetical index) created an army of clerks, divided according to specialized tasks. After this social group was

236

established, the cost of office maintenance grew and office machinery was sought to reduce costs. Since the First World War era, the technological revolution has intermittently been reorganizing offices and adding a tremendous assortment of specialized machinery. The spread of machines has prompted newer divisions of labor and further centralization of administration.

Surviving between the old office and the new centralized office is an intermediate business environment from which are drawn popular stereotypes about the female-dominated office world. Here a mass of women workers (and male bosses), drawn from the widowed, the single, and the young in search of independence, enter the office as a means of maintaining some middle-class identity. They have completed high school, taken a commercial course, or had a year or two of business school. They are ambitious enough to leave a small town and family to win independence in the big city. When frustrations or instability prove overriding in personal life, the office job becomes a career, and there, in a network of interpersonal relations, the women find a comforting community.

Technology and big-factory organization have conspired to fragment, narrow, and specialize work tasks; and, organized according to efficiency and production-level dictates, work has become separated from socially useful or self-expressive aims. It has become an unpleasant necessity. The white-collar employee does not even have a historic memory of the craftsmanly ideal as does the worker. For him or her there are no past or present models of work gratification, no status or personal touch connected to performing work. Office workers have no tradition of creating or owning a "whole product," and no former or present aesthetic satisfaction in either their work or their play. The pleasure element has given way to a standardization of tasks. As a result such people cultivate the trivia of hobbies or the pursuit of pleasure outside work. As people gradually accept the meaninglessness of the working life, they search for other frames of acceptance and gratification.

Given this condition, the employee has little beyond bald economic motives for work. Strivings after a secure income that will provide some measure of independence and peace of mind become intensified. While fear of unemployment or displacement may keep employees "thankful for any job," in general their concern for compensation through status intensifies. In lieu of satisfaction in the work process, pride is attached to high salary and status-bearing associates on the job or within the occupational structure of the country. Accompanying the tendency toward loss of individual power over the technical aspects of work is the elaboration of the exercise of power over people. Thus income, power, and status are pyschologically important in a newly elaborated way.

The problem of alienation from work has given the business world a need for self-justification. Studies of human relations in industry are as much part of this reaction as they are connected with planning for efficiency and productivity. But to date they have failed to create job enthusiasm. The split between work and living continues to be sharp. In an age when leisure is available to the mass, its pursuit outside a work life becomes a major preoccupation of the society. Mills adds that when older groups are outdistanced by new prestige-bearing groups or those newly connected to the benefits of the system, and status is as hard to identify and sustain as it is to attain, then search for status may turn into a virtual panic. This is particularly true among the white-collar population which has neither the status advantages of birth and money nor the frustrations of poverty. In this in-between state minuscule prestige distinctions within white-collar occupations and levels become important. The pressure for status differentiation and material acquisition increases as the historical basis for white-collar prestige dwindles. Once white-collar work was associated with greater ability and intelligence than was factory work. But this association has been dissolved; white-collar people now operate light machinery at a factory-like pace and in a factory-like style, and thus suffer in prestige. Further, the expansion of white-collar jobs and personnel has threatened whatever exclusivity this sector previously had, and therefore diminished whatever prestige was attached to such exclusivity.

With the widening circle of white-collar populations in expanding cities performing standardized, impersonal tasks, the status hunt becomes more frantic as it inevitably becomes more difficult. There are three reasons why the older sources of white-collar prestige are breaking down, making for this increased difficulty: (1) fragmentation of skills, which deprives individuals of the range of tasks attaching to a position, from which they derive prestige; (2) compensatory status-hunting outside the job, with increasing emphasis on acquisition of goods and on displaying a pleasing personality that will impress others; (3) diffusion of the sources of status in the environment, which by sheer multiplication reduces the ability of any one of them to satisfy status hunger. This is the irony of what Mills terms the "status panic."

The most striking feature of American success, as Mills sees it, is ambiguity. The "American gospel of success" has been a sort of realization of the middle-class gospel of progress. Post–Civil War American history is dotted with spectacular instances of "self-made," fabulously successful men who both verified and preached the success gospel. In the wide-open, laissez-faire universe envisioned in the literature on entrepreneurship, the way up was through daring independence, self-reliance, assertive acquisition of available resources, "right-living" sobriety, and a taste for competition. Success in this period was the product of personal virtues. The path ran from clerk to salesperson to entry into business on one's own. This entrepreneurial ideal of success and its inspirational ideology rested on a diffused economy of many small proprietorships.

Under the recent centralized system, where work is available through great corporate enterprises which hire armies of personnel, and where the working population is largely dependent on authorities they are unable to control, the pattern of success becomes a climb through myriad levels of status and income within organizational heirarchies. Only the presently propertied can continue to achieve success within this pattern. Newly acquired wealth is generally high-salaried wealth within the corporation, based on managerial skills and a climb to top administrative posts. The survival of free-enterprise inspirational literature—which had an early function of exalting a status quo—is explained by its present function of obscuring and apologizing for centralization and a system of dependency. The white-collar success pattern is ill-fitted to the exhortations of the entrepreneurial period. Yet its egalitarian appeal still persuades because leveling factors, such as education, support the idea of equal opportunity although the property and management structure do not.

The widespread availability of education and its modern orientation to practicality has strengthened feelings of status equality among all sectors of the population and has made people rely on the acquisition of education as a means of advancing themselves. It has become a primary instrument of social elevation into better middle-class occupations linked to expertise and technological skills. Schooling at all levels has become geared to produce and advance people trained for success in a white-collar, middle-class world. Whereas education once provided individuals with linkages to upper-class and political spheres, it now serves primarily to advance them occupationally, providing standardized requirements for, and means of entry into, the professions and semiprofessions. These effects do not generally extend to the lower classes of unskilled working people because there are great pressures on students from this milieu to leave school and accept unskilled jobs to help maintain the family. But upward mobility through education has become an American style. What is more, mass education breeds a peculiar anxiety in members of the old middle class, for they recognize that the means to social mobility is no longer small property but opportunity through white-collar and technological skills. Their anxiety is thus intensified with respect to the opportunities for higher education available to their children.

Mills claims to have uncovered an important contradiction. On one hand, equal educational opportunities for all become a widespread ideal and demand. On the other, educational requirements of lower white-collar occupations are tending to decline, thus leading to intensified competition for jobs at higher levels, which in turn undergo a process of loss of status by loss of exclusivity. While white-collar mobility has increased in scope and accessibility for the unskilled laboring class, countertendencies limit this pattern at the top of the white-collar organizational heirarchies. This cramps the success craze in America. While it is true that the children of lower-level wage workers have been able to rise to white-collar positions, those in lower- and middle-level white-collar positions have generally reached a peak beyond which they are not likely to go. The tendency of upper strata to rigidity, changes in birthrates and size of upper-strata families, and also an ever-narrowing number of highly skilled, high-paying positions hold the line against expansion or advance of middle-level, white-collar people.

Success through education and skill continues to be idealized in a postentrepreneurial era. When the upper point is reached for operation of both as mobility factors, the resultant frustration stimulates a widespread consciousness that something is wrong in middle-class life. Heavy turnover at the bottom of the white-collar ladder still allows for considerable ascent; but this does not operate all the way up the ladder. Contemporary inspirational and how-to-succeed literature mirrors rather than resolves these frustrations. Its success orientation no longer urges right-living sobriety; there is even less selling of self, Dale Carnegie style. In fact, it is hard to justify such literature as inspirational, since the costs, frustrations, and even corruptions of success are portrayed. Popular realism has tarnished the success image. The pressures to succeed become ends in themselves, no longer rooted in higher moral or national purpose. The older inspirational literature stressed individual responsibility for success and for failure. Ideas of chance—good and bad breaks—may soften the blows of failure, just as they hold open the possibility of success. But the contradiction in the ethos of success has become evident. Although the pressure to amount to something is still as great as it ever was, the image of success is so tarnished that it is no longer a challenge to everyone.

∽∾∿∾∽

Mills fully understands that the political expectations of orthodox Marxism have not come to pass. The capitalist system has not become a sharp struggle between workers and capitalists, with the middle classes driven into one camp or the other. The political directions of the middle class are sorted by Mills into several major possibilities. The continuous growth of this class has given it size and power, but not to the extent that it has become an independent force. Rather, it provides a broad stabilizing base for the society, balancing the political contents of different classes. Thus it provides for the continuation of liberal capitalism. The continuous growth of the middle class gives it the numbers but not the power for independent action. It will thus acquire the central function of running modern society, but not controlling what it runs. The coming period will belong to the "new middle class" only in a limited, bureacratic sense. This stratum of the bourgeoisie will thrust forward in a larger capitalist drive, and at times support reactionary or fascist solutions to threats to the system. But how this expansion of the middle class squares with a continuation of liberal capitalism remains unanswered by Mills. In fact, he fails to define the middle class as an intermediate strata or a decisive social sector. In this, he shares the dilemmas of definition with Riesman and Whyte.

The amorphousness of what actually constitutes white-collar work lends itself to a variety of conflicting theorizing about this sector or class. Mills considers and rejects the argument that there are no classes in America, only nebulous interest groupings in a complex environment. He argues in return that this does not disprove class notions. Still, the problem of defining class, or the character of the new white-collar population, is not simpler for that. Whether white-collar people are respectable and skilled upper-strata proletarians, new types of the old capitalist, a new class, or even a class at all, remains open. They are little inclined to revolution or even class cohesion, for their formation has been unaccompanied by political protest. The centralization of property and the reduction of the new middle class to dependency within bureaucratic hierarchies has been slow, painless, and barely perceived.

The conversion of many types of white-collar labor into factory-style jobs, in addition to the lower-strata clerical jobs, has pushed numbers of white-collar workers into a wage-worker type of class organization: the unions. Unable to sustain even a semiprofessional appearance at its lower rungs, a portion of the middle classes have even surrendered an attempt to present a professional appearance. With the decline of the small entrepreneur and the small office, the shared fate of economic dependence, and the great increase in number of employees constituting the modern centralized office, the middle classes have increasingly adopted union-style methods of struggle. At the turn of the century white-collar unionism was negligible. Today it is a significant portion of organized unionism, extending to transportation, communication, education, and even the Postal Service branch of the federal government.

The attitude of white-collar employees toward joining unions is influenced by the availability of union organization, the economic situation of the industry, the treatment of employees by employers, costs of production in relation to wages, and the extent to which the white-collar position is identified as a job or as a prestigious profession. The relation to the employer is often crucial, for if employees are hired as salaried professionals, they are not likely to view their interests as distinct. The political orientation of white-collar people also exerts an influence. If they are closely identified with the Democratic party or a third party, they are likely to be more pro-union than if identified with the Republican party. Frustration in "getting ahead" on the job may foster union sympathies. Mills concludes that personal exposure to unions, political party affiliation, and feelings about individual chances to climb predispose white-collar people to accept unions. Mills sees unionization as steadily increasing among white-collar personnel despite countertendencies. But unlike his feelings in *The New Men of Power*, Mills no longer supposes that unions provide a high sense of community or stimulate great ideological conviction. They are viewed quite instrumentally, as means to an end, rather than as providing strong new ties in other areas of life. It is not always the case that union organization strengthens worker solidarity or anti-management antagonism. White-collar ideology is still a middle-class striving to get to the top. The union is an impersonal economic instrument to compensate for an inability to get there. Union affairs may provide temporary relief from dull, routinized work. But basically white-collar unionists are more concerned with making their own position equal to that of other organized white-collar workers in the industry than they are with improving conditions among production workers in the same industry. This is in keeping with a general white-collar jealousy in regard to prestige and an attempt to hang on to some kind of professionial identity.

Unionization of the white-collar stratum, whatever the degree to which it has proceeded, occurs after both farmers and laborers have had their day of "insurgency" and have experienced action, assertive and united by a common will. White-collar people have come to unionism too late to share this experience or to create an élan on their own. They are thus sharing unionization in the period of its incorporation as an economic interest group into the "liberal state." Both Marxism and liberalism make the same rationalist assumption that individuals will perceive and act in their own interest. The Marxist idea of "false consciousness" is an attempt to cope with surrender of true interests. Both Marxism and liberalism preach an active relation to the social environment in which individuals are fully developed only by the exertion of their will in shaping their world. Political indifference, according to both viewpoints, is surrender of self-realization and responsibility, and inexcusable in a healthy society. But what actually exists is a state of political indifference to prevailing cultural symbols. Alienation from the inherited norms rather than new approaches becomes prevalent. Mills argues that there is a failure of response to the symbols of political culture, which is not compensated for by alternatives. Individuals are left unable or unwilling to participate in the making of their own world, and are consequently unrealized and thus alienated.

Individuals guided by the liberal model are overwhelmed by the complexity and fragmentation of work tasks, the centralization of property as an obstruction to entry into the ranks of the propertied, and the centralization of power. They occasionally seek an alternative in Marxism—which seems better suited to resist this new condition of dependence because of its efforts to achieve independence through class solidarity—but there are many individuals who feel a committed loyalty to the United States political system. Yet the main drift is toward surrender of the active relation to politics, toward apathy rather than loyalty. Perhaps white-collar groups do not feel more alienated than other sectors, and at the level of small-scale civic participation, perhaps they are even less so. But because of their inability to identify with a class-conscious model, because of their amorphous constituency, and because they are dependents, overwhelmed by the bigness of social organization and the complexity of issues, unable to keep the liberal model alive, the white-collar sector becomes a prime carrier of the modern mood of alienation.

Mills next turns to his pet theme of how culture and liberalism intersect. The mass media cater to and reflect the popular mood. They gear themselves to successful sales through simplistic formulas and are therefore unable to perform their function as bearers of information and insight. They specialize in peddling the bland and acceptable, reinforcing mass indifference. This functional limitation may be aided by the stake that owners and managers of the mass media have in the status quo. But public receptivity to the level and content of the media cannot be explained on that basis. Rather, it is linked to the structure and mood of the whole society. The increasing frustration of mobility at the middle white-collar levels, the pacification produced by great affluence, the loss of individual and independent relations to the world, the anonymity and dullness of a routinized work life, substitute gratifications provided by status, the fatigue of optimistic nationalism, immensity, rapidity, complexity, running ahead of individual capacities to keep pace—these all ensure that the media will have a mass following. This wedding of the popular media to the popular mood makes information transmission secondary. The result is that the media reinforce alienation by providing escape from and reassurance about a condition that needs intelligent criticism.

The most deadening outcome, for Mills, warming to his subject, is what he considers the decline of the political articulation of major social changes so that people may better shape their lives through conscious understanding. The American system has never known the kind of massive political movements that call the system into question. Its wealth and liberal style have perpetuated compromise and consensus. In times when basic orientations should be questioned and reshaped, they are instead dodged, out of sloth, indifference, or a false security drawn from past experiences. The present political period demands principled reexamination, in view of widespread alienation, and in view of the necessity of holding increasingly "invisible" seats of power in order to be responsible for policy. The country instead is slipping by on older techniques of politics and an ideology of compromise. The white-collar people are not likely to press this moral reorientation on the system. The base for independent liberalism has diminished. White-collar workers lack the cohesion to provide a class model. The result is that no one takes up the task of rejuvenation. Mills once again is left with a problem for which no solution is offered—except, perhaps, creative marginality: the very elitism he had come to discount if not dismiss in other work.

꘠꘠꘠

Nonetheless, the response to *White Collar* was both instantaneous and overwhelming. The book was done in a period of great American soul searching. It was the beginning of a psychological turn inward, at the very time worldly issues pertaining to the contours of America during the second half of the twentieth century were becoming increasingly vital. Since a similar trend occurred after the First World War, we can surmise how peculiarly guilt-oriented American society can be: external power combined with internal feelings of powerlessness.

There were the usual assaults from commercial quarters. *Business Week* said that "Mills' picture of America at mid-century borders on caricature; the weaknesses of the society stand out, the strong points are obscured."[7] But that did not stop *Business Week* from presenting the main points and findings of the book in an extensive and thoroughgoing manner. A more serious critique appeared in *The Management Review*, where Lawrence Stessin hammered at the theme that even Mills's friends were quick to sense represented the Achilles' heel of the book.

> I suspect that the principal shortcoming of *White Collar*, despite the solidity of its erudition and scholarship, is Professor Mills' own sentimentality. He yearns for those "good old days" when the nation was rooted in independent small businessmen and craftsmen, when they owned their own tools and reaped the benefits of their own acumen or handiwork.[8]

Then there were the usual mindless eulogies and attacks from daily newspaper sources. At least independent reviewers were in much greater abundance thirty years ago than at present. It is curious that even in the area of book reviewing there was much less "canned" material passing through syndicated hands than appears in newspapers now.

The Nashville Tennessean, which liked the book, claimed that Mills "attacks every problem in his new volume with both guns blazing from the hip."[9] Poor Mills was never able to live down his Texas background even though he had not the vaguest idea what to do with a gun or a horse. Max Lerner reviewed the book in *The New York Post*, noting that the passing of the old farmer and self-reliant businessman, and the emergence of the new white-collar sect or a sales personnel, clerks, intellectuals, and bureaucrats, were what the book was all about. He finished with a question—"Are we or they better off with this kind of class structure?"—as if anyone could do anything about the shift to begin with.[10] Lerner, like others, had difficulty seeing how class shifts implied such stringent moral lessons as those provided by Mills. Lerner's own later efforts to understand America as a civilization were an attempt to describe these big shifts without insinuating Mills's moral lecturing. But to Mills such objective analysis provided only a benign form of celebration of the American ethos.

The syndicated reviewer Sterling North took considerable umbrage at Mills's comments on book reviewers, especially his statement that "they have become members of a semi-anonymous staff governed by formula rather than devoted, professional work." North responded in outrage: "Sociological sausage! We say what we please, we write what we think, and we deeply enjoy our work."[11] The fact remains that the very syndication of North's column (in most papers his reviews appeared without his name) demonstrated the accuracy of Mills's charge. Much reviewing *is* done in a semi-anonymous context with formula writing that poorly represents the ideas of the authors.

But these were warmups for the reviews to come. The first major scholarly review was written by D. W. Brogan, professor of political science at Cambridge, and the *Saturday Review's* expert on the American character at the time. He found the book to be "stimulating and lively." Unfortunately, he spent most of his review expanding on his own considerable erudition about America. He did manage to say that the book was "free of sociological jargon" and was written "both clearly and plausibly." But Brogan was much more concerned about his own English interests than the American tragedy of class anomie. Nonetheless, his review set the tone for the weeklies and monthlies.[12] Horace M. Kallen reviewed the book for *The New York Times*. While generally positive toward it, he concluded on a shrewd critical note.

> I get the feeling that Mills has exaggerated what he hates in the class of which he is himself a notable figure and has ignored and minimized what is constructive and praiseworthy. Perhaps, like every caricaturist with a social conscience, he is employing exaggeration for the purpose of reform. Perhaps he desires, by bringing the most unappetizing features of his own class into sharp visibility, to generate the awareness that is preliminary to purposeful alteration.[13]

However, despite his reservations, Kallen found the book "worth reading and pondering if for nothing else, to alert the middle-class to their remoteness from ultimate salvation." One wonders if Mills thought the middle class was capable of pondering their condition in order to better their chances of salvation.

Liberal publications were generous to Mills, despite his attacks on liberalism. Ben B. Seligman, in *The New Republic*, found the analysis of the specific social behaviors of doctors, lawyers, and teachers to be "truly brilliant." In anticipation of *The Power Elite*, he would have liked "a more full discussion of the accumulation of power or of the new literature of resignation, and beyond that, of social hierarchies in a permanent war economy." Seligman was among the handful of people at the time to get a sense of the main drift of America in the 1950s, especially the relationship of war abroad and prosperity at home.[14] Irving Howe, in a review appearing in *The Nation*, struck a similar chord to that of Seligman. The sister liberal weekly called *White Collar* "exciting to read" and a book that was especially pleasurable for avoiding both "Stalinism," on one side, and "professional anti-Marxism," on the other, since both tendencies were much the rage in those unhappy days. But Howe was disconcerted by "Mills' occasional tone of tough, professional power-consciousness." He pointed out that after all, "white collars are worn by people, and when one sees how those collars tear into human flesh it would not be amiss to give into a little grief."[15] This lack of humanism was to distrub many of Mills's more intimate critics as the years wore on. It is curious how *White Collar*, the most "humane" of Mills's works, signaled this for so many of his critics.

Granville Hicks, writing in *The New Leader*, at the pinnacle of that weekly's power and potency, also found the book worthwhile in terms of making important contributions to the process of creating a new and viable philosophy of society. Hicks was nonetheless disturbed by the book's limitations, almost self-imposed, that derived from Mills "clinging to his image of himself as a radical." In a critique that was to ring time and again in Mills's ears, the question Hicks raised was: Does Mills have a plan, or, lacking that, a set of alternatives? It seemed to many of Mills's critics that he had a much clearer idea of what he was against than what he was for. He knew what was wrong with the present, but had little to say about what could be done to right the future. As Hicks wrote:

> The question to be raised is whether the radical stereotype isn't preventing good men, Mills among them, from contributing as much as they are able to contribute to the understanding and control of social processes. The broad tendencies of our society are fairly clear and altogether terrifying. If someone has a practical plan by which the evils of a mass society can be abolished or avoided, let him, by all means, announce it. But in the absence of such a plan, hadn't we better make the most of the advantages, the adaptations, the resistances, the loopholes, that have been found to exist or can be discovered? Why not drop the radical pose and get down to work?[16]

Many of the same people reviewed MIlls's major works time and again. The power of the intellectual gatekeepers was not just to make or break a book, but to begin to claim certain people as one of their own. Not a few of the academics reviewing Mills's works on stratification—such as Irving Howe, Lewis Coser, and Dennis Wrong—were later to be connected with *Dissent* magazine. The latter figure, writing in the *American Mercury*, clearly thought that *White Collar* was a superior effort, and that its exposition of the problems of the middle classes was probably the most balanced of any written during that period. Yet, while Wrong saw Mills as "having written a most serious book, one which tries to see where Hegel's angel of history is driving us in a period when, despite much ideological noise and glib chatter about atomic Armageddons, no one really seems to care," Wrong, too, was distrubed by Mills's "strident contempt for the white-collar masses." He shrewdly observed that "while Mills skillfully enumerates the reasons why such contempt is abroad, he himself drops into the little-man-what-now tone on many occasions."[17] However, this was not simply Mills's problem, but one common to the growing criticism of mass culture and middle-brow culture engaged in by the independent Left during the early 1950s. This was a disillusioned Left, taking its cue from the Frankfurt school of Max Horkheimer and Theodor Adorno. It was a characteristic of this form of continental radicalism that it condemned with equal ferocity the wrong created by a mass culture and the weaknesses of those who imbibed that culture. This ultimately proved to be a troubling position, since it left those academic radicals—from *Partisan Review* to *Dissent*—without a constituency, isolating them from both the powers that be and the masses who were never ready to be.[18]

By 1951 Mills had already earned himself a constituency among anti-Communist radicals and Socialists—especially the group coalescing around the Fourth International. They were paying much closer attention to Mills's work than he appreciated, or wanted. Being clustered in New York City, like the literary figures of the time, these Socialist linkages grew involuntarily stronger. The most articulate critic of Mills's work from this perspective was Gordon Haskell. While in full praise of the class analysis of the middle sectors provided by Mills, Haskell nonetheless viewed Mills as dangerously influenced by the same positivistic limitations that beset American sociology as a whole.

> American sociologists have done a tremendous job in developing and refinishing techniques for testing the attitudes of various groups in the population. They are very adept at discerning the way in which these attitudes, and the social and political instrumentalities which groups devise to meet their particular problem, change under the impact of changing situations. But they are grossly inadequate to explain violent, drastic changes in consciousness and behavior. As a matter of fact, both their po-

litical prejudices and the very refinement of their technique tends to make them shy away from the consideration of such changes which do not lend themselves so easily to precise measurement and documentation.[19]

Mills took this type of Socialist criticism seriously, at least as it reflected on his own changing literary and sociological focus. As the decade wore on and his writings became more tendentious, only the Socialists seemed responsive.

The sociological commentaries were themselves exceedingly important. While also highly favorable, they pointed out not so much the weaknesses of sociology as the shortcomings of Mills's use of data processing and social analysis. Paul K. Hatt, writing in *The American Sociological Review*, declared that *"White Collar* is a strong theme, well presented." But he also noted that "there is a breakdown in documentation. Actual data are reported primarily in relation to such things as occupational changes, unionization, etc., but the more significant bases of the argument too frequently rest on simple assertion and insightful observations."[20] If Socialists viewed Mills's book as too sociological, sociolgists tended to see it as too interpretive and, indeed, socialistic.

David Riesman, reviewing the book for the *American Journal of Sociology*, provided probably the most influential review of *White Collar*. This was a consequence not only of the journal's importance in professional circles but of Riesman's role as the senior author of *The Lonely Crowd*. He, too, revealed a knowledge of Mills and provided a generally favorable response to the text. But Riesman introduced a serious line of criticism that was to prove professionally telling over the long haul. Perhaps the basis of this criticism was nothing more than what Mills wrote in the marginalia of his own copy of the Riesman review, namely, that "Riesman was reflecting his own middle-class biases and pique." Nonetheless, Riesman's criticism were serious, and as so often was the case in Mills's career, went publicly unanswered.

Essentially, Riesman's critique can be reduced to three items. First, Mills "pays almost no attention to the ethnic coloring of attitudes to white-collar work. He does not discuss, for instance, how much it means to the Irish Catholic that he is able to leave the factory and enter not only the lower office ranks but the upper reaches of utility, manufacturing, and government bureaucracy, putting the seal of Americanization of his Catholicism on the way." The second line of criticism that Riesman launches is "a belief that the mass media are less exploitative and relentless than they appear in Mills' account." Since Riesman at the time was doing work exactly in this area, this comment proved to be exceedingly perceptive. Third—and a point that was to be empirically demonstrated later on by other sociologists—Riesman cast serious doubt as to whether or not the life of white-collar people was quite as drab and impoverished as Mills made it out to be. Riesman strongly implied that this critique was a reflection of Mills as outside observer processing his own private slogans and hidden agendas. Riesman was not quite as sure as Mills and the mass-culture critics that the middle class was as alienated as it was made out to be. Puttering about the private house and garden had its own values and payoffs for a war-weary America. Riesman shrewdly observed that Mills, by "robbing [a very strong word for Riesman] the white-collar people of any ethnic, religious, or other cultural dye," made the white-collar itself assume a more wan and celluloidal look than was, on the whole, probably warranted.[21]

Riesman's colleague and coauthor of *The Lonely Crowd*, Reuel Denney, writing in the *Yale Review*, struck much the same theme— even to the point of also declaring that "not all salesmen are Willy Lomans." One gets the impression that there was a greater concern to protect the middle class from criticisms than to analyze what Mills was saying about it. It was essentially Mills's dehumanization of the middle class that confounded Denney and was denied by most professionals. The absence of characterization and anecdote in Mills's writing was adduced as evidence of his ignorance of this class. Denney was also concerned about the Millsian dichotomy between "tough-minded and savvy tycoons" and "soft and naive" white-collar people.[22] In retrospect, one gets the feeling of distance on the part of those defending the middle class no less than those attacking this class. Something had gone wrong with the postwar American Dream even as it had just gotten underway.

Neither praise nor criticism moved Mills much. While there can be no question that he was pleased with the response, he accepted criticism passively. The one review which genuinely disturbed him was the savage critique proffered by Dwight Macdonald writing in *Partisan Review*. The various and sundry jibes MIlls made against that magazine were finally repaid in full by the review written by his old friend and co-worker on *Politics*. Macdonald, the literary bête noire of the 1950s, began with a confession—"I found his book boring to the point of unreadability"—and ended with a condemnation: "The book is a failure as descriptive sociology because Mills is forever getting in the way of his data, like the master of ceremonies who talks through the acts." Mills was accused of introducing, nay, smuggling, moral judgments and aesthetic impressions into his sociology. Although this was about the only weakness Macdonald actually articulated, he fired at will. What Mills did to Parsons in *The Sociological Imagination*, Macdonald did to Mills a decade earlier: reduce an entire paragraph to a few words. He took a paragraph from *White Collar* on the subject of prestige and claimed all it really said was that "ascendency is based on recognition of power." Quite beyond academic leaf raking, Macdonald accused Mills of "the apparatus of intellection without the thought process that sets it in motion." Macdonald made the point that the book "is like a great hard intricately convoluted seashell that encloses nothing living." To Macdonald, Mills was "a propagandist rather than a thinker." The evidence for this statement was that only five pages were dedicated to any kind of survey of political thought. Finally, Macdonald claimed that "even as propaganda or special pleading, the book is no good for the simple reason that the author fails to make clear what he is propagandizing for, who his client is. I think this is because he doesn't himself know, because he is himself drifting, confused, and, above all, indifferent."[23]

There can be no question that Mills was mightily disturbed by this review. It is hard to detect whether the disturbance was due to anger with the review and reviewer or concern about the professional injury such a review might have occasioned for his Columbia colleagues. To indicate how angered Mills was, he wrote to some of the key senior people at Columbia, specifically Robert K. Merton, Lionel Trilling, and Richard Hofstadter. He also sent the same letter to Hans Gerth and William Miller. Mills's letter is of great interest, not simply for its contents, but as an indication of how genuinely this review singularly incapacitated him.

> Yesterday I read Dwight Macdonald's review of *White Collar* in *Partisan Review*. As you probably have seen, it is completely thumbs down. Of course I know Dwight is an irresponsible reviewer, but I can't conceal the fact that it hurts. For if he is half right, the best thing for me to do is close up shop. Doubtless I'll get over it but the thing temporarily incapacitates me. There's only one kind of question that seems important to me, and I'd [be] very grateful if you'd answer it. Can I learn anything from this review? What does he say that I ought to take seriously, and what should I do about taking it seriously?[24]

Mills simply did not like doing combat with reviewers. He much preferred support from other colleagues, which he sometimes received. But in this instance, perhaps the personal responses to his pleas for support were as ferocious and hurtful as the review of Macdonald himself. It is hardly a secret that the response of Richard Hofstadter to this letter more or less terminated his personal relationship with Mills.

Hofstadter tried to be pleasant about the book and reassuring, but to no avail. For, after some pleasantries as to its style and substance, he said:

> My primary *feeling* about the book—and it is a vague and, as you would say, spongy feeling but nonetheless one I hold strongly—is that this book

is an excessively projective book, in the psychological meaning of the word. This is what Macdonald was getting at when he referred to a certain lack of disinterestedness in your thinking. You detest white collar people too much, altogether too much, perhaps because in some intense way you identify with them. There is a lot of human ugliness in the book—which is, I note, caught up in the jacket description of the book as a "merciless portrayal" of a whole class. There are some people and perhaps even some classes in society that may call for merciless treatment, but why be so merciless with all these little people? If their situation is characteristically as bad as you say it is—which I doubt—then in a book which candidly seeks to express emotion as well as to analyze, why no pity, no warmth? Why condemn—to paraphrase Burke—a whole class?[25]

Hofstadter hammered away at Mills's sense of entrapment and the projection of this doctrine of alienation onto the entire American middle class—a theory which he clearly did not share.

You have somehow managed to get into your portrait of the white collar man a great deal of your own personal nightmare, writing about him as though he must feel as you would feel if you were in his position—and indeed, as you do sometimes seem to feel in the position you have, caught somewhere in the midst of Paul Lazarsfeld's and Thomas Watson's white-collar machine. Look at your introduction: the words you apply to the white collar man: living out in slow misery his yearning for the quick climb, pushed by forces, pulled, acted upon but does not act, never talks back, never takes a stand, in a frantic hurry, paralyzed with fear, morally defenseless, impotent as a group, open to the focused onslaught of manufactured loyalties, turns to his leisure frenziedly, bored at work, restless at play, standardized loser, must practice prompt repression of resentment and aggression, etc. I don't totally reject this, but there is something else even in white collar life. You let yourself go too much in this passage, and it is one of the keys to the book. This is what I mean when I say the book is too projective.[26]

Hosftadter's final shaft, after again declaring his admiration for Mills as a sociologist, was his serious reservations about Mills as a compassionate being. It is a line of criticism that was to be increasingly potent as a decade moved along. Hofstadter concluded by noting:

What I miss in your work still is not the quality of mind, which you have in riotous abundance, but some human qualities, the absence of which is beginning to show *precisely because* you are trying to write humanistically meaningful books. You have not yet—I say this without too much complacency because it has been said to me and I believe it applies at home also—not yet humanized yourself, not yet got out of that Hobbesian nightmare. Macdonald was groping toward this, but doesn't seem to care about or understand you, which is probably his failing. His review is—yes, merciless. The hell with him. When everything critical has been said,

I find your book, the whole course of your work, your morale and your dedication as a man of learning, very inspiring.[27]

We have no record of Mills's response to Hofstadter, but one can hardly imagine that the kind but platitudinous remarks by Gerth really meant much to Mills, since by this time Gerth was far more wrapped up in his own world of German academicism than in Mills's Americana. Interestingly, although Gerth admitted that "Macdonald is a confused man," he urged Mills to feel grateful for getting some instruction and at least some information about matters of grave concern." Gerth felt that Macdonald was simply "ungenerous and resentful" and ended with an exclamation of "My God what shamelessness."

> After all what does he substantively dispute? Nothing at all. He does not say that the facts are wrong, he does not say that they were seen together by others in a more efficient way, he does not say that it is "old stuff," he does not say that the data, etc. are insignificant. He seeks to psychoanalyze you—i.e. he is more interested in the personality than the work—the work as a human document by a leaf-raking academician. He seeks to do that by looking at the book aesthetically and psychologically rather than meeting it on its ground: sociology.[28]

One gets the distinct impression from the rest of the letter that Gerth's sense of outrage has a flat and forced quality. Apart from contrasting with some really frothy communications earlier, there is the fact that more than three of its five pages are devoted to his own problems, and do not even indirectly address the agonies expressed by Mills in his own appeal.

Trilling did not write to Mills about *White Collar*, but they did meet on February 4, 1952. Ever a faithful recorder of events, Mills wrote down the sum of that discussion in a memo sent to himself. Despite its unflattering contents, Mills took the bit in his mouth and said nothing in reply.

> Too absolute a doctrine. White collar life also has pleasantries and gratifications. You obscure complexities and qualifications in this thought. Or is it style? Marxist anger isn't good anger, except in certain places, like working man's day in Capital. But you're too aggressive in your rush at the topic. Your pace is also too fast. Got to control it, by changing the pace. You don't have to worry about boring anyone! You must acquire a more chaste style; too much color in it now. Too much verbal invention. Too sloganized. Good color doesn't come by trying. Let color come when it does more casually. You've too much style, so that it seems mannered. Macdonald's point about use of metaphor is correct: use them only for vividness, not in normal communication; and when used they must be logically tight and consistent images. Knopf edition is best. See de Tocqueville on democratic style in America. By chaste style, one means that on the surface statements are casual and literal as possible; trust the fact to

come through on its own. Read Lecky, Newman's *Apologia*—elegant but immediate. Also read Shaw as model of expository writing; the debating style of the platform. Maybe can't get his wit, but forceful exactitude. His social indignation never gets angry. Destroy your illusion of creative literature and put in its place standards of exposition.[29]

One has the distinct impression that Trilling was not so much moved by the contents of *White Collar* as by its inelegant style, in the service of a critique of liberalism. For Trilling, style may not have made the man, but it certainly made the liberal scholar. He indicated a disconcerting feeling about Mills's style: the pace was too fast; the anger interfered with understanding. Trilling emphasized that "social indignation should always be elegant but immediate." The scholar "should never get angry." In a sense, Mills got what he asked for: a senior mentor slapping the wrists of an upstart schoolchild. His intimate and private self-critique is a revealing experience which makes plain how unsteady and unsure Mills remained in his Columbia University environment, despite the bluster, the *Sturm and Drang* style, in which *White Collar* was written.

There was in Mills a disjuction between the public and the private. The more strident and pronounced the writing effort, the more uncertain seemed to be the private assertions warranting that effort. It is hard to know whether an individual learns from others or simply resents them. There is no doubt that Mills did in fact take Trilling seriously. He went on to read De Tocqueville on the democratic style in America, and to imbibe nineteenth-century masters like Lecky, Newman, and Shaw. But the mannerisms Trilling would have imposed on Mills ran so counter to his growing displeasure with America that when Mills finally did filter these aristocrats of learning into his own world view, he only absorbed their criticisms of capitalist society, never their mastery of metaphor. If one is to judge by Mills's later writings, he did not so much try to overcome the objections of Macdonald, Hofstadter, Trilling, and the rest of his Columbia cohort as to come to terms with himself as a high-class journalist. He came to worry less about the style of literary performance and more about the substance of social policy.

In retrospect, *White Collar* is more interesting for the ways in which it reveals the ethos of the early 1950s than for its explanation of that ethos. Tautological reasoning overwhelms the empirics. The success of Mills's radical critique hinges on the very social psychology he disparaged in others. In the absence of any evidence that economic indicators were moving in anything other than an upward direction, he demanded moral purification. This was a period of the most intense rate of growth (including private earnings) in American postwar history. Yet Mills took comfort in and had recourse to the alienation thesis. It would seem that capitalism, while economically resilient, was humanly impoverished. The new wealth had ended in a wasteland of emotional impoverishment. As Bennett Berger was to show later in the decade,[30] it was by no means axiomatic that the new affluence of the new middle classes and their corresponding changes in life-style were either involuntary or a source of widespread discontent. And in politics as in culture, the swing to a middle ground spoke aptly for the rise of the middle class.

REFERENCES

1. David Riesman, Nathan Glazer, and Reuel Denney. *The Lonely Crowd: A Study of the Changing American Character*. New Haven: Yale University Press, 1950.

2. C. Wright Mills. *White Collar: The American Middle Classes*. New York: Oxford University Press, 1951. Unless otherwise stated, all references to Mills's work in this chapter derive from *White Collar*.

3. William H. Whyte. *The Organization Man*. New York: Simon & Schuster, 1956.

4. Daniel Bell. *Work and Its Discontents*. Boston: Beacon Press, 1956. Reinhard Bendix. *Work and Authority in Industry*. New York: John Wiley Publishers, 1956. Joseph A. Kahl. *The American Class Structure*. New York: Holt, Rinehart & Winston, 1957. Leonard Reissman. *Class in American Society*. New York: The Free Press, 1959. William Foote Whyte. *Men at Work*. Homewood, Ill.: Dorsey Press, Richard D. Irwin, 1961.

5. Eric F. Goldman. "Social and Economic Scene Mirrored." *The New York Herald Tribune*, January 15, 1961.

6. David Riesman (in collaboration with Nathan Glazer). *Faces in the Crowd: Individual Studies in Character and Politics*. New Haven: Yale University Press, 1952, p. 623.

7. Staff Report. "Portrait of Mr. Nobody." *Business Week*, October 6, 1951.

8. Lawrence Stessin. Review of *White Collar*. *The Management Review* (February 1952): 136–37.

9. J. G. Wharton. "Portrait of the Middle Class." *The Nashville Tennessean*, August 5, 1951.

10. Max Lerner. "Are You Better Off?" *New York Post*, September 6, 1951.

11. Sterling North. "This Pessimism Sounds Like Sociological Sausage." *The Journal* (Madison, Wisconsin), September 9, 1951 (and syndicated by many other newspapers affiliated with the *New York World Telegram*).

12. D. W. Brogan. "Rise and Decline of a Class." *Saturday Review of Literature*, September 15, 1951.

13. Horace M. Kallen. "The Hollow Men: A Portrayal to Ponder." *The New York Times Book Review*, September 16, 1951.

14. Ben B. Seligman. "The Briefcase Men." *The New Republic*, September 17, 1951.

15. Irving Howe. "The New Middle Class." *The Nation*, October 13, 1951.

16. Granville Hicks. "White Collar or Straitjacket?" *The New Leader*, January 28, 1952.

17. Dennis H. Wrong. "Our Troubled Middle Classes." *American Mercury*, January 1952.

18. A remarkable collective portrait of the New York radical literary scene, especially as it emerged in the late 1940s and early 1950s, is drawn by William Barrett, *The Truants* (New York: Anchor Press/Doubleday, 1982). The group gathered about the *Partisan Review*—Philip Rahv, Lionel Trilling, Delmore Schwartz, and Barrett himself—is probably the one for which Mills had the highest respect and yet felt deep resentment toward. If he assaulted "liberalism" with vigor during the *White Collar* period, it was because it took on a flesh-and-blood reality lacking in his earlier rejection of a more "classical" and less "ideological" liberal intellectual stratum.

19. Gordon Haskell. "The Middle Class in U.S. Society." *The New International* (September–October 1951):288–94.

20. Paul K. Hatt. "Review of *White Collar*." *American Sociological Review* 16, no. 4 (October 1951):727–28.

21. David Riesman. "Review of *White Collar*." *American Journal of Sociology* 57, no. 5 (1952).

22. Reuel Denney. "Not All Are Victims." *Yale Review*, Spring 1952.

23. Dwight Macdonald. "Abstraction ad Absurdum." *Partisan Review*, Spring 1952, pp. 110–14.

24. Mills to Hofstadter, Merton, Gerth, Trilling, et al., January 5, 1952.

25. Hosftadter to Mills, January 19, 1952.

26. *Ibid.*

27. *Ibid.*

28. Gerth to Mills, January 14, 1952.

29. Mills's recording of Trilling's words in a memo to himself, February 4, 1952.

30. Bennett M. Berger. *Working Class Suburb*. Berkeley and Los Angeles: University of California Press, 1960. *Idem.* "The Myth of Suburbia." In *Looking for America*. Englewood Cliffs, N.J.: Prentice-Hall, 1971, pp. 151–64.

12

Trinity of Power

C. Wright Mills' The Power Elite has become almost a bible for a younger generation of "new Leftists" who have a deep-seated need to attack a society which they fail to understand. Mills' serious scholarship means little to them; it is his Marxist-Populist image of American society which captivates them.

Arnold M. Rose, *The Power Structure: Political Process in American Society*

*T*HE *POWER* E*LITE* IS a work that was addressed to dangerous power tendencies at a time when few seriously thought it worthwhile to fuse sociology with moral commitment. The United States was emerging from a crippling cultural repressiveness amidst a world of plenty. One effect was to create a facade of government power that was unmistakably consensual. The critical evaluation of a great American celebration of its own power after the Second World War was needed. Mills's work attempted to throw cold water on national conceit and provide a warning that the possibilities of such power could lead to a reversal of the best democratic traditions in the American past.

Mills was less concerned with criticizing or defending specific agencies of power or institutions of repression than with holding the leadership of the United States answerable to its proclaimed democratic values. Sociologists who took this position looked to the classic tradition as necessary to the creation of important scientific literature. Mills emerged as a leading proponent of this point of view, which he and others believed would restore to sociology great historical perspectives and contemporary relevance. This sentiment of the mid-1950s was best captured by the young Tom Bottomore, who clearly bore the traces of someone influenced by Mills's efforts to hold class divisions historically accountable to class actors.

> The principal fault in many recent studies of social classes has been that they lack an historical sense. . . . Some sociologists have accepted that

there was an historical development of classes and of class conflicts in the early period of industrial capitalism, but that this has ceased in the fully evolved industrial societies in which the working class has escaped from poverty and has attained industrial and political citizenship. But this assumption is made without any real study of the evolution of social classes in recent times, or of the social movements at the present time which reveal the possibilities of future social change.[1]

Disheartened by the decline in significant concern about power issues, and by a style of small-range research that stood in perennial danger of becoming sterile and trivial unless its advocates moved on to larger generalizations, Mills and other sociologists, such as Robert Lynd and David Riesman, felt strongly that sociology should follow in the humanistic tradition that places science at the disposal of popular welfare. Their writings, and symposia of various kinds, upheld the significance of the uses of technology and power as a compelling subject for sociological attention. Arthur Kornhauser's anthology *Problems of Power in American Democracy*,[2] which included a contribution by Mills, reflected an array of big-range social science options. *Class, Status and Power*, edited by Reinhard Bendix and Seymour Martin Lipset,[3] collected past and present social science studies and opinions on stratification and power, their nature and exercise.

Two orientations developed among post–Second World War sociologists concerned with power analysis: they could be distinguished as consensus notions versus ''veto-effect'' notions. The former position was represented by Mills and the latter was best expressed by Riesman. The idea of power consensus is based on a conception of power involving groups of individuals who see in their command positions a source of common interest and who collectively guard their power, regardless of other differences, against the vast majority. The sources of their power may derive from economic wealth, personal or professional prestige, or control of political machinery, and may be practiced democratically or not. The fact that some individuals control vast power creates constraints on behavior, whatever the origins and sources of that power might be. In this, Mills remained true to his empirical approach to stratification at its upper reaches.

The Power Elite[4] helped formulate essential questions of power and liberty and restore them to sociological inquiry. Social definitions of power and stratification for Mills derived basically from the European tradition in sociology. Using Max Weber and his linkage of class, status, and power as chief stratifying elements in group life, influenced by Gaetano Mosca in his political definition of power (rather than by the Marxist economic emphasis), made strongly ''status conscious'' through the early influence of Thorstein Veblen on his thinking, Mills conceived *The Power Elite* as a practical application of these notions to the present

American scene. With a vigorous journalistic imagination, he "exposed" the issue in a manner not unlike American muckrakers of the early part of this century.

On the other side of the issue, and not necessarily completely distinct from Mills and his colleagues, were the veto-effect notions best exemplified in the sociological literature by David Riesman's *The Lonely Crowd*.[5] Riesman and Mills were considered the leading sociological "power theorists" of the decade of the fifties. Other voices engaged in the dialogue; Lipset[6] and Parsons[7] added vital contributions to the debate. But Mills and Riesman had a brilliant gift for summation, and for formulation of fresh terms in which to express social experience. Not surprisingly, the language and jargon of both men became widely popularized, and they are often considered archetypes of their respective points of view.

David Riesman's notion of veto effect was a theory of power which differed from a power-elite approach by viewing influential groups as interest elements whose power is limited by either psychologically felt or socially imposed limitations to power concentration. Riesman emphasized the high risks in the constant use of power. Like energy, power can run down (something Mills failed to note); hence the relationships of powerful groups are diffuse, distant, and limited. To see that a group has power is not the same as predicting accurately how and to what ends such power would be employed.

Despite their differences, the positions of Mills and Riesman reflect strong starting points in common:[8] Powerful persons are no longer highly individualized characters. The vast majority of American society—comprising a "mass," a "public," or the "other-directed" middle-class consumer—is a vague amalgam that has surrendered active defense of its own interests or active participation in serious political dialogue and organization. Both positions see the people as anomic, and the powerful who guide or dominate their lives as anonymous. The powerful may be a cohesive elite for Mills, or an amorphous collection of small, competitive groups making a unified "top stratum" impossible for Riesman, but neither characterizes the powerful as bearing any burdens of principle or responsibility. Both the power-elite and veto-group positions reflect the mood of the decade of the fifties. They reveal a utopian nostalgia for romantic individualism, courage, and the bearing of responsibility by a concerned and politically involved public. Both reflect a feeling of loss for the past and a dissatisfaction with the bland and seemingly uncommitted decade of the fifties.

The earlier work of the Lynds[9] had argued that power was institutionally located, and had emphasized its inherent tendency to concentration. They described this as the "energy" of a social order, and as such, inevitable. The environment in sociology supported the institutions of government and business as great power agencies and considered the small number of "chairs at the top" of these hierarchies as major repositories of power. Sociology saw the problem as how to "harness" power for socially humane purposes while maintaining the pluralist ideal of curbing its extension over an illegitimate range of purposes. In this context, Mills addressed himself to the social effects and desirability of power concentration per se, and found that the dangerous anonymity of decision-making behavior inherently tended to create irresponsibility, secrecy, and unsavory manipulation.

Mills was attempting to fix responsibility, and hence provide a moral dimension, for the exercise of power in large-scale decision making. He employed "structural clues" to identify the positions and decisions involved in the exercise of power in the United States, basically an inferential method of establishing the existence and range of a power elite. Mills rejected a notion that one sector, such as the military or the economy, was a singular source of power, and upheld instead the interrelatedness of polity, economy, and military, considering leadership in any of these sectors to yield power as such. The elite is one of power rather than of mere wealth or status alone; but it is enhanced by the abundant presence of the latter two factors.

ᕯᕯᕯ

Implicit in Mills's free-swinging critique of "mindlessness," of "crackpot realism," of "hard" decision makers, is an approach strongly flavored by the pragmatic style, as is his resort to "educated publics" as a countervailing force to irresponsible or secretive power administration and policymaking. But his division of the social order into a ruling minority and a vast, basically fragmented mass is drawn from the sociological thinking of the Franco-Italian school no less than the German-exiled Europeans. His decisive fusion of these European currents with pragmatic orientations, in combination, made a new sociology possible.

Mills saw liberals emanating only from the pragmatic tradition as powerless and nostalgic people, grown tired and acquiescent with age. As professional philosophers they were attracted to logical positivism with its love for technical and linguistic analysis, and were led away from a passion for applied research on social questions. But pragmatism had a popular dimension, the "journalistic" tradition of exposing social inequity designed to stimulate public action, and this was the liberalism which Mills looked for among his fellow academicians.

For Mills, the "muckrakers" set a radical liberal style. Upton Sinclair, Ida Tarbell, and Lincoln Steffens were not concerned with the overthrow or even an analysis, of the capitalist system. They were issue-oriented, concerned with moral advertisement of the unjust or corrupt practices of a given industry, not of industrialism in general. They pressed for reform of certain social practices, not of the social system. These were, in a sense, pragmatic sociologists, and their theoretical energies were directed at the immediate, the practical, the reformable. But Mills aimed not only at "exposure," but at the study of essential characteristics. His attention was directed primarily to social groups and secondarily to overtly political battles. Weber, Michels, Veblen, even Freud, became pragmatically useful rather than intellectually enticing. Mills searched various intellectual systems in order to make their many parts "operate" on the stuff of the social world, which is one reason why his legacy may seem so dubious on methodological grounds.

To counter the dangerous possibilities of an unchecked power elite, Mills sought to restore and protect, activate, and even lead an educated public to self-assertion. He consciously believed in the potential of reason, information, and public criticism as an answer to the pure Machiavellianism of James Burnham. Mills saw the "brake" on elite power as stemming from the political awareness of educated publics, which, tragically, became increasingly amorphous as the great stratification trilogy came to a climax.

The Power Elite seeks to demonstrate that a locally based scatter of power pockets, based largely on property ownership and solidified by upper-class families as property-owning units, has given way to a solidly compact and widespread network of power that resides in nameless, safely entrenched "top strata." Property ownership perpetuated through family inheritance has given way to the systematized management of corporate wealth, marking a great change in the exercise and maintenance of power in the United States. Starting from the romantic pluralism of Jeffersonian America, Mills sees fragmentation and dispersion of power reaching its climax and initial stages of deterioration in the nineteenth century. *The Power Elite* is a study of national patterns of power over a one-hundred-year span of American history. In this, Mills's work differs from kindred works like Floyd Hunter's *Community Power Structure*,[10] which never get beyond local or regional considerations.

The concentration of power occurred as a consequence of changes in the technological machinery for producing material wealth, which allowed for rationalization of social relations in the form of centralized management and control of social wealth. Locally based elites, when given holdings that made it logically in their interest to do so, entered into new combinations or allowed themselves to merge with large economic institutions and monopolies. This pattern of absorption and displacement dominated the life of the country until all competitive power groups were bypassed, absorbed, or crushed by a cohesive power elite.

Critics have said that Mills's power coherence scheme illustrates a highly exceptional circumstance; that in the main powerful groups compete with, fragment, defeat, or countervail one another and limit their spheres of influence. It is also said that Mills's exposé is little more than a naive discovery that power is not always and everywhere wielded democratically, even in a democracy. The nature of politics requires that the powerful exercise a certain amount of secrecy and manipulation, since that is the only way to keep power and use it. But Mills does not argue with either of these premises. Without denying the validity of the criticisms, it must be said that Mills's examination of a power elite does identify a worrisome trend in United States power patterns over half a century.

Despite the competitive groups that make up a power alliance at any given time, centralization of authority, as part of its rationalization around modern technology, has vested increasing power in heads of vast bureaucratic organizations, and in the informal and nonelective top strata of advisers surrounding the executive of the federal government. Mills emphasizes the increasing importance of the nonelective, appointed, powerful experts who back up executive decisions. Simply stated, whatever the competitive status of powerful and prestigious groups with respect to each other, all are losing a sense of responsibility to the public for whom they ostensibly make decisions. All are unable or unwilling to be subject to a popular will. All operate anonymously, without the mandate of election and without being obliged to give candid and publicly stated explanations for their acts.

The power elite is not a monolithic bloc, but rather a nameless, nonelected, and hence nonresponsible body acting without the support and knowledge of a vast public. The absence of enlightened public opinion and inquiry, jealously guarding its rights and exerting its influence, makes such an elite possible. It is in this sense that the power elite is made cohesive. Its consensus is not conspiratorial, but arises out of a need for a coherent policy despite certain class antagonisms. Mills seeks to restore public responsibility on the part of top decision makers, to restore the tension between an enlightened public and their elected officials. Beyond this lies a plea for restoration of an interest-bound public concerned with issues, rather than a gradual development of a frightened, nameless, and acquiescent "mass."

The Marxist position on power, aside from taking as its fundamental premise a class society dominated by an economic ruling class, is based on a concept of social battle or class struggle. This struggle, which is carried out by classes characteristic of a given mode of social production, is sometimes conscious, as, for example, in revolutionary periods. For Mills, power "stratifies" into a hierarchy. At each level in the hierarchy, power or interest groups may compete, but "upper" and "lower" levels are not set in combat against each other; one does not overcome the other in order to maintain and exercise power. There is a "rise" through the acquisition of wealth and prestige. Groups concentrate around the "means of production" and crystallize into status hierarchies, manifesting power differences. Social competition rather than class struggle is the norm—competition within the power elite and not between the masses and their rulers.

Once the social means of power are concentrated, competition for control begins to manifest itself in possession, delegation, and display of authority. Since such power inheres in the decision-making positions themselves, struggle for power replaces class struggles. Passage to the ranks of the powerful, accomplished initially through acquisition of strategic wealth, is a passage into a realm removed from the "people," the "public," or the "masses." The struggle for power is not consciously carried on to subdue and dominate mass society, but is waged in order to rise into another level of existence entirely, which is responsive only to a mobilized challenge "from below."

The looseness in Mills's use of the phrase "power elite" has made him vulnerable to his critics. The concept does fail to account for the property-distribution patterns and political character of a capitalist system as differentiated from a Socialist or other system. Some critics have argued that the implied universality of the power-elite scheme misses specificity about the social system in which elite groups operate and by which they are determined. For sociologists like Lynd, this was a failing in all analysis of elites, and he found political science distasteful because it held such analysis in high regard.

✧✧✧

In *The Power Elite* Mills set himself a clear task: concern with general conditions of "modernity" rather than with "capitalism." His approach blurred capitalism's line of continuity with the past as well as the characteristics peculiar to capitalism. Mills believed that modern technological rationalization and the concomitant centralization of authority were more significant than the uniqueness of any system; that they were, in fact, destroying such uniqueness. His unpublished writings attest to his belief that economic "systems" were giving way increasingly to a universal technological style. "Power elites" marked the Soviet Union as well as the United States. Their differences were increasingly ideological, and decreasingly economic.

In preliminary drafts and studies for unpublished works, Mills showed his fascination with characteristics of the twentieth century that were reflected on a worldwide scale. Influenced by the work of Isaac Deutscher and Edward H. Carr, Mills searched out shared characteristics of the United States and the Soviet Union which were the result of their convergent status as competitive giants, industrial complexes, and mass societies. He saw their patterns of stratification and social goals as providing a base for comparing similarities, especially because few saw these comparisons as valid.

Mills's intellectual energies were increasingly directed toward creating historically relevant political sociology which would get beyond a liberal rhetoric inherited from the "bourgeois" revolutions of 1789 and 1848, and a Marxology which was also useful only between 1848 and 1918. For Mills, liberalism disintegrated after the revolutions of 1848 because the middle classes could not deliver on their promises. Universal truth, free conscience, unfettered choice, all became disguised supports for capitalist systems and colonialist expansions. Likewise, official communism, while culminating in the deliverance of the Russian masses from capitalism, at the same time outflanked Marx's humanism and transformed proletarian rule into bureaucratic rule, political association into party life, voluntary association into terroristic cliques. Just as Anglo-American liberalism collapsed when socialism became a world rallying cry, so too did Russian Bolshevism collapse, intellectually at least. In his unpublished writings Mills treats socialism as larger than American or Russian nationalism. *The Power Elite* carries the ever-present implication that industrialism overrides systematic political differences to a sufficient extent to enable us to look for "global developments" as well as unique national differences.

His scientific "looseness" was intentional. He discarded traditional notions of ruling class domination, defining the powerful as those "who are able to realize their will even if others resist it." He was influenced by, but did not adopt, traditional Socialist approaches. For him, there were no impersonal "laws" of social movement; social movements created "laws." He departed strongly from the heavily felt influence of Pareto. For Pareto, there are clusters of elites around goods and values, and therefore many or at least several elites. But Mills holds that the interrelatedness of these groups yields a new unity, and a coherent concentration, which creates a passage from quantity to quality. Under new technological conditions, smaller and plural elites are transformed into a single elite, growing smaller in number as they acquire greater decision-making power.

Mills explicitly rejects a notion of a ruling political elite after the model of Mosca. Mills considers this concept of a "creative" or "tightly organized" minority to be tautological since it says nothing of the character of such an elite, and does not deal with sources of power. Even when it throws light on the crafts of rulership, it is not applicable to present conditions in the United States, which are always Mills's first concern.

Mills specifically disowns conspiratorial notions of power manipulation, although he has been criticized on such grounds. Daniel Bell's critique is a case in point. However, though Mills's analysis does verge on conspiratorial implications, these chiefly derive from his resentment of anonymous or nonresponsible authority. He does not ascribe to the prevailing elite either a conscious or a malicious determination to rule behind the backs of the people. Mills is concerned with the issue of which groups have how much power at the present time, rather than how such power has been acquired.

ᴔᴔᴔ

Mills begins *The Power Elite* with a broad look at the "Higher Circles," intended to capture the present power atmosphere. He distinguishes the upper power levels from the "ordinary" activities of most people. The crystallization of big power groups is based upon their social location. From this follows their other distinctions and ultimately their elite status. Appearance, education, and other "achievement" items separate people into various levels of prestige, but power underlies and upholds these differences and determines their level of importance. Such power involves the heaviest and farthest-ranging decision making in history. Command posts are at the head of the three major hierarchies: state, corporation, and military. Their interdependence in the present century has blurred the lines of authority amongst them, but has not resulted in any lessening of the concentration of power as a whole. The acquisition of wealth now occurs within these sectors, since nothing of import exists outside of them. And acquisition of wealth within their ranks is the first step to power.

Mills builds structures by means of architectural metaphors: top level, middle level, and public, mass level (which remains basically dormant). The powers of the last-named may or may not be exerted. The masses may exhibit a high state of powerlessness, even if it derives from unthinking surrender rather than imposed domination. Society, once led by competitive families and politicians at various levels of government office, now confines these to a middle level of power. To acquire great wealth, it is necessary to combine moneymaking with entry into a national elite, since its organs and instruments are necessary to such wealth, because conventional avenues have been blocked off.

Despite their secure positions as heads of corporations, the state, and the military, the power elite is not socially visible in the same way that older aristocratic elites were in Europe. The United States has never passed through a feudal period, and there is consequently less emphasis on conspicuous display of power than in societies with a feudal heritage. This is all the more the case because middle-class technicians are being raised to new heights of power in a society that is increasingly complex. What is more, a decrease of wealth in the hands of individuals makes the display of power more difficult to appreciate. This is not the case with state, military, and corporation commanders living in a democracy; institutions have no problems with egoism. Continuing this implicit critique of Veblen, Mills notes that their posts concentrate more power in the hands of a few than wealth could command—more than any individual could possibly amass in his or her own person.

Far from being "alienated," this relatively impersonal stratum comes to believe in its own worthiness, and begins to live an approximation of the qualities others impute to it. But contrary to the beliefs of a conservative and romantic humanism, the new power elite does not rise from people with superior personal qualities. Top positions shape personality, creating people equipped to serve their needs, which may not necessarily be those of leadership and intelligence.

Mills claims three major keys to understanding the cohesiveness of the elite. First, there is the psychological identity of elites with one another through a community of education, similar social origins, sharing the prestige that accrues to them, and social and political intermingling. Second, these psychological factors are backed up by the structure and mechanics of institutional hierarchies, in which organizational similarities and the fact of occupying command positions further shapes a conscious community of interest and personal similarities. Third, the mechanics of these hierarchies, the fact of intermingling, will produce a need for stricter coordination. This coordination intensifies the above features but is initially produced by the pressures for efficiency.

Prior to the shift of wealth and power to the metropolis, local control in America was what counted. The United States was a "scatter" of locally powerful elites in whose hands lay the wealth of the country. The class, status, and power systems of local societies were relatively equally weighted. The professional politician, whatever he was or was not in other respects, represented a powerful voice for these elite interests. The "new technology" brought into being a new group whose wealth no longer derived from property or "raw" goods but rather from technology, manufacturing, and industrial investment, and eventually monopoly empires were built.

Before that point was reached these new industrializing classes successfully engaged the "old local family" in battles for social eminence, wealth, and industrial potency. Manufacturing, the strategic source of wealth and power, soon overcame the old local society prestige and power system. The "old family" was overcome by "new money" derived from enterprises with which it had little or no connection. The "pedigrees" and status old families had acquired still lingered, but they no longer represented real power. The new manufacturing middle classes became national in the scope of their wealth; political representation, and hence power and prestige, were underwritten by the growth of the industrial metropolis. A great American fiction and nonfiction literature exists to illustrate this nineteenth-century social drama.

In the pre–Civil War years the big-city upper classes were a stable and close group, living on riches derived from landed wealth, inheritance, and speculative investments. After the post–Civil War boom in the industrializing North, these classes were overwhelmed with new money. The *Social Register* was, and remains, their chief source of socially recognized status. Graduates of those university institutions that keep the "top" supplied are likely to hobnob with this "Four Hundred," and through this association new wealth may acquire a certain distinction. Hence the Four Hundred are connected to, but not decidedly in, the power elite. Like local elites, they are the living reflection of another era, but their location and great wealth have given them the possibility of "hanging on."

The celebrity system creates another sphere of influence or means of acquiring it. Celebrities are, loosely speaking, "names" that need no further identification. They are not people of power, but they are people of wealth and considerable prestige. They are surrounded by prestigious accoutrements, and are identified in the popular imagination with power and influence. They are more a reflection than a part of a power elite.

Mills never makes his discussion of the celebrity explicitly relevant to *The Power Elite*. He seems to be interested in accounting for various patterns of success in an affluent society. However, he does not elaborate on, or solidly establish, connections between the "celebrity" and the "power elite" except to point out the new celebrity style of symbolic prestige. The very rich and consequently the very powerful of today rose from the ranks of big business. Their wealth came not out of their adventurousness (though this was a trait of some) nor out of greed or guile (though this, too, may explain certain fortunes) but rather out of what Mills calls the "structure of opportunities." No single person could have built, out of his or her own achievement orientation, the vast business empires and combines that manage and constitute today's industry. At one time America was a domain of untapped wealth to which millions of people migrated. Its population steadily rose, its land values increased, and its markets developed. Through the use or violation of existing legal statutes, and the passage of new ones protecting the rights of property in the form of the corporation, fortunes were accumulated. The state provided guarantees for the property-owning rights of great fortunes and in various ways protected the corporation. The corporation became a means to manipulate existing law to the advantage of industrial enterprises.

Behind corporate wealth, individuals continue to collect personal fortunes of unprecedented size. This class of people is called "the very rich." These people are not necessarily managers or caretakers of wealth, but they are recipients of the corporation's greatest monetary rewards. They hold its top seats and are its chief investors. Those who enter the corporate ranks without already possessing a considerable fortune find it almost impossible to acquire enough to climb to the top. The propertied family and the wealthy continue to supply the top ranks of corporate life, which in turn operate through a host of legal technicians and agents to protect their wealth. The corporation has made the very rich less visible than they once were, but no less powerful and no less wealthy.

Chief executives of the corporation are another component of the power elite. These new industrial captains are quite different from the entrepreneur of past epochs. They are not owners of corporate properties, yet they manage these complexes. They are not clearly distinguishable from the "very rich" who actually own the corporations, yet they constitute a distinctly twentieth-century group produced by the centralization and rationalization of private property. Corporate ownership breeds loyalties to industry as a whole rather than to the individual firm. Despite such corporate realities, Mills claims that the illusion of personal ownership in corporations is widespread. In reality, individual ownership is restricted, and management even more so. The top corporations are knit together by associations within their respective industries and regions, and by their common interests. This intricate machinery—that is, the technology of corporate management organized into profit-making centers—lends itself to central control. Management is increasingly becoming management of automated machines rather than people; and social problems are placed within an entirely manipulated context, one which emphasizes psychological rather than economic issues.

The executives of these top corporation posts are drawn from urban, upper-middle-class, Protestant, and entrepreneurial circles. Mills finds that in type and background, the factors that bind those chief executives are stronger than those that divide. "Free markets," "free competition," the fragmenting tendencies of the past, have given way to corporate consolidation. In this fact Mills sees the potential and the dangers of central control.

The rise of military commanders to the top strata of power is connected to the rise of the United States to international political preeminence. Military power in a big nation brings about the "return of the warlord" and a new military ascendancy. The national state has monopolized the "means of violence," and the new military is head of a heavily centralized organization which is increasingly vocal in national affairs. Formerly, armies in the employ of kings and nobles fought or conquered each other, but violence was limited and local, and power tended to re-create itself in localized areas and in multiple centers. Revolutionary periods may have created temporary "people's militias," but the "standing army" is the product of the modern nation-state. The military establishment is a thing apart.

In the nineteenth century the United States was preoccupied with making money and producing goods. Its middle class defended individual freedom, and the Constitution discouraged military preeminence in government. The early American elites were not a military caste or of a military temper. However, the increasing involvement of the United States government in the military and political life of foreign countries, the fact of recurring warfare, and the increasing United States involvement in colonial acts, in acts of "official violence," all demanded the maintenance and increase of military forces. As the American means of violence enlarged and became increasingly centralized, crystallizing into a major bureaucratic hierarchy, those in top military positions found themselves automatically in command of enormous centers of power. Increasingly, presidential policy has become informed by a military elite, particularly by a nonelected Joint Chiefs of Staff. And immediately below them is a high circle of generals and admirals exercising control over the far-flung military apparatus.

Mills traces the careers of military chiefs, establishing the overlapping training, religious affiliation, and psychological similarities of this new elite. Due to its honorable reputation, based on patriotic defense of the nation-state unit, the military is absorbed into the same status system that honors the corporate rich. The military tends to rely on industrial interests to produce its wares and weaponry. It underwrites, through funds granted by Congress, research employing industrial help and carried out in geographic locales of its own choosing. Just as industry has become bureaucratized, so the military man's managerial skill in a bureaucracy has become highly valued in industry. Hence military personnel have become a source for top industrial and corporate posts.

Because of the complexity of weaponry, the new types of military encounters, and the terrible dangers of modern means of violence, executive foreign policy is in genuine need of military expertise. The "middle levels" of power—Congress, special-interest groups, and so on— cannot provide adequate information for policy purposes, or are so fragmented as to be periodically incapable of influencing policy or counteracting undue military influence. Thus, the military fills a void rather than competes for power. Military commanders are not checked by popular will or elections; only executive resistance potentially checks military power. Because the military can act with fewer restrictions than other government agencies, their power is enhanced, and with it their conscious will and ability to press power to the limit.

Mills believed that America had never cultivated the art of diplomacy. It drew from both business and political circles, but it did not have a solid core of diplomatic professionals. The military, therefore, had the "space" to move into the higher councils of diplomacy. Production contracts between the military and corporate industry, overlapping directorates between the two, mutual absorption in the status system—all these brought industry and the military into a top-echelon consensus. Thus they became increasingly necessary for one another's policies and plans, and they are now enmeshed in a network of interdependent personnel and interests.

Like the other major hierarchies, the state has become enlarged, and the scope of its activities has reached unprecedented domains. For information and such influence as professional politicians are able to exert, they, too, have become dependent on the welter of government agencies. Their chief arena, Congress, is so swollen, complicated, and bound by local and state pressures that politicians can barely consider issues of national (much less international) import. Their prestige has always been insecure in a country suspicious of politics, and the party which brings them forward is increasingly like its rival. The big issues of war and peace are largely outside the sphere of influence of party politicians. The need for efficient solving of issues of national and international importance has forced a greater role on the executive, which surrounds itself by advisory bodies drawn from the military and corporate elites.

Professional politicians have given way to "higher politicians," individuals with policy concerns who may be drawn to their task through idealistic or opportunistic motives. The money received in such a policy-making capacity is of little consequence; but the power and status which accrue to these politicians are tremendous. In direct concert with the executive, and over the heads of Congress—the old politicians' battleground—the nation's most important decisions are made by the leading cadre of policymakers. There is little check on such decision-making power, and the freedom of operation the higher politicians enjoy is not matched elsewhere in political life.

Political institutions and politicians below the higher politicians have been superseded by the new "political outsiders." Party politicians in Congress are limited by responsibility to their constituencies and the political party sponsoring their career. "Bureaucratic politicians" are lodged in administrative agencies where they can work with or against the party politicians, but they are bound by the limits of bureaucratic mobility and a semiorganized array of agency organs. Political outsiders are neither party politicians nor bureaucratic politicians. They come straight to the top from the military and the corporation to advise the executive. They may cultivate helpful relations with elected officials, but they are freer than the elected officials to make policy, enforce influence, and extract prestige. The party politician and the party bureaucrat are essentially the middle level of power. The nonelected, presidentially appointed advisory official is an adjunct to the higher politician. In this way the policy process is brought inside the power elite.

Mills maintains that the rise of the "expert" in the United States was secured by the relative absence of a well-trained, informed, prestigious, and meritorious bureaucracy. The expertise and far-reaching view of the political outsider exists, in fact, in lieu of an efficient civil service. Thus Mills claims that the U.S. government has never maintained a genuine bureaucracy in which authority, rather than being wielded personally, is vested in the offices the bureaucrats occupy. The check upon development of an administrative bureaucracy is held to be the patronage system of the parties, which pays off party workers and supporters.

The old model of power assumed a plurality of independent, conflicting groups which settled into a social balance. Yet these represent, for Mills, the middle levels of power in which plural groups are hopelessly stalemated; despite occasional overlapping interests, they are essentially disunited. The emphasis of social scientists working in policy contexts is positivistic. They focus on appearance to such an extent that Mills claims "unseen" larger connections are simply not considered subject to scrutiny. Consequently, the emphasis on middle-level interest or veto groups has obscured a view of the structure of power as a whole, especially the top and bottom levels. The political sociologist has become a student of isolated political acts, of election behavior, and has thus lost the big picture. Because social scientists are a product of the professional middle class, their political activities and contacts are likely to be limited to middle levels of power, and they universalize this experience. Sociologists thus tend to bless the status quo, for the balance of power implies equality of power. What the social science observer often forgets is that a balance reached at a given moment seems fair only to those it favors. Hence the critic of a balance-of-power theory is likely to see a given balance as unfavorable and look to the larger structure of power in order to evaluate the sources of inequity.

Federal checks and balances have made the centralization of power in this country difficult, if not impossible. But for Mills, they serve more to check popular pressure than to accommodate it. "Divide and rule" prevents total power from centering on an individual or office, but it offers no justification for denial of a power elite. It rests upon the point of harmony between interests. But disharmony of interest is chiefly applied, in perfect sincerity, to public challenge rather than to political representatives.

Increasingly, political representation is deriving from monied groups, and the country is close to a dangerous decline in middle-class representation at the middle-power levels. Factors diminishing the political power of the middle classes lessen the effectiveness of the theory of checks and balances. Mills sees power at the top as relatively unchecked except for the convenience it finds in maintaining a democratic rhetoric. The fact of a power elite, of which the public is vaguely aware, anonymously and little restricted except by the pressures of competing strains within its ranks, overrides the traditional middle-class politics of America.

ᴼᴼ

The 1950s produced a pronounced conservative mood that pervaded the United States. Mills considered American conservatism far from a distinctive philosophy, bereft of a genuine class base or the possession of a classic tradition. Conservatism in its classic form, he said, involves some "natural aristocracy" suited for rule. The traditions it embodies are taken to be the cohesive element of society, responsible for its cultivated leadership and careful decision making. European conservatism has a philosophic bias in favor of an irrational "natural order" that reason must always exert itself to defend. The European conservative believes that real change is impossible, and consequently those who seek it can only bring chaos.

But in America there was no solid precapitalist class base to support a natural aristocracy. What is more, the competitiveness of American capitalism encouraged the ideal of the self-made individual and represented a constant challenge to a natural aristocracy. The European feudal order, its traditions and mores, the classes and viewpoints stemming from it, are prerequisites for a society wishing to bring conservatism forward as a political credo. Capitalism came clothed in the ideology of liberalism, and the official ideology of United States capitalism from the outset has been liberalism. By refusing to acknowledge the facts of present-day power, liberalism has become nostalgic. Its rhetoric is itself the chief form of a new American conservative policy. Periodically disgruntled middle-class elements respond to challenges to their prestige with a reactionary policy orientation. But this is rarely supported by the top levels of power. American conservatism is actually pluralistic: liberalism turned rhetorical, even fanciful. As a result, no serious opposition to ideological liberalism has crystallized. It has never shed its pretensions and continues to repose in absolute safety. The celebration of American life as supremely virtuous is seen by Mills to be the unfolding of the liberal rhetoric. This newer liberalism—and here Mills seems to have had in mind the young Arthur M. Schlesinger Jr.—has no critical edge and lives on in an America that was, creating a reality to suit itself.

Without a class base for classic conservatism, liberal conservatism sees the natural aristocracy of the United States in a scatter of morally superior persons corresponding to locally based elites and the quality of middle-level political leadership. While there is no aristocratic class, the aristocratic ethos settles upon the examplars of an uncritical liberal rhetoric. The petty-bourgeois Right has an appeal to status-frustrated individuals, but these political fragments cannot generally be lumped with the conservative mood. By implication it falls to the "political Left" in any given period to support real change in America or at least to provide some measure of criticism of the status quo.

The New Deal consolidated, even adapted, liberalism for the present day. Its victory between 1933 and 1945 effected a solid public loyalty to liberalism. The end of the Depression, brought about by the shadows of world war, consolidated this victory. Problems shifted from mass unemployment to mass culture. Most people seek status diversions and emblems. Defenders of what Mills called "Machiavellianism for the little man" stifle political criticism on a public scale, and challenge nothing and no one at the top power-levels of the society. The top leadership is thereby deprived of the most intelligent and sensitive elements and a mindlessness afflicts the top posts, because there is no critical public pressure to assure that the very best do rise to the very top. The separation of knowledge and sensibility from the top command posts and even from the middle levels of power, as well as the disaffection of the public from its critical responsibility, are reflected in and are the essence of the higher immorality in mass society. The result is organized irresponsibility.

ೋೊ

The Power Elite was the object of furious controversy that has hardly abated with time[11] When an American social scientist produces a book that attempts to evaluate the whole of United States society, such an effort is impossible to ignore. What is more, Mills wrote in a morally charged tone of indictment that invited challenge. Writing in *The American Journal of Sociology*,[12] Bell suggests that *The Power Elite* does not describe a specific instance of power allocation but a scheme for power analysis. For him, Mills is dealing with one aspect of the "comedy of morals." He holds that Mills writes in "vivid metaphor" surrounded by statistics, that he appears guided by Balzac's moral that "behind every fortune there is a crime." Bell sees *The Power Elite* as static and ahistorical because of Mills's disregard for the influence of ideology on sociopolitical behavior. *The Power Elite* is a hierarchy of "orders," rather than power organization in time. It is a "model" rather than a historical analysis.

Bell holds that Mills improperly interchanges terms: e.g., "institutions" for "domains," which is also confused with sectors, or orders. Therefore to speak of a priority of certain orders over others says little. It ignores how and why such a dominance of priorities is maintained, and also ignores the belief systems which perpetuate and influence its historical course. What is more, according to Bell, Mills lacks a working definition of power. For Mills it is nothing more than domination, but he fails to take up the norms, values, traditions, matters of legitimacy, and issues of leadership which would give the notion of power concrete substance.

For Bell the notion of a power elite at the command posts of institutions is a perfect example of argument by metaphor. These institutions, set up like granite blocks, with heads, have no identities or ideas. Even if their ideas and identities are not of primary value, their significance is still misunderstood. What people do and think gives them access to power, even within the major institutions. Locating a top stratum does not come to terms with the actual distribution of power. Bell complains that Mills is vague on what the "big decisions" constitute, or their meaning, and that he comes close to a conspiracy theory of history, and by implication, to the idea of perfect ruling class cohesion. Since he does not include or appreciate the role of ideas and issues, Mills cannot describe what unites or disunifies the elite. And ideas and issues for Bell are the "stuff" of politics. Thus Mills fails to see conflict of interests, and does not explain how centralization withstands disunifying tendencies.

Since Mills fails to distinguish prestige and honor from power and violence, he cannot trace how the former lead to the beliefs and patterns that produce the latter. As a result, the relationship between raw power and accepted status is all but eliminated. He does not tell us what constitutes honor, or when power will spill over into violence. He merely indicates the sources of prestige within the institutional hierarchy, not how status actually works. He does not explain why some values are brutally fought over and others are limited to political gaming—even within the same elite cohorts.

Mills's "big decisions" reduce themselves, according to Bell, to foreign policy and war decisions, rather than policies applied to domestic institutions, where more levels of decision making are involved. He accuses Mills of failing to recognize that the American Constitution centers war decisions on the presidential office, checked by Congress precisely to prevent a military elite from dominating top decisions. Presidential reliance on expert military personnel is hence not the equivalent of "military ascendancy," especially since decisions on violence are grounded in a world situation and not merely on military expertise informing foreign-policy making. Mills converts the obvious fact that leaders are responsible for decisions into a sensational discovery to suit popular resentment of power. His general neglect of concrete American experience leads to "obsessive oversimplification."

According to Bell, "power elite" is a slippery phrase that allows the social scientist to ignore the basic character of a social system. Mills does not differentiate the United States and the Soviet Union. He ignores the role of the Supreme Court. In sum, Bell sees *The Power Elite* as merely a polemic against those who say that in the United States decisions are democratically arrived at.

Critics, of course, have points of view in common and there is likely to be considerable overlap in criticism. Robert Lynd[13] simply and clearly raises the question of where the book was intended to go and then proceeds to criticize Mills in some respects as does Bell—but without his vitriol. Lynd had been developing a theory of power in democracy since the days of *Middletown*. For Lynd, power is a social resource absolutely necessary for the operation of society; like physical energy, it can be consciously harnessed for human welfare or corrupted by misuse. Determining democratic goals and tasks for a given social operation and figuring out whether such an operation enhances a democratic national life is therefore a responsibility for all power theorists. Lynd shares Mills's concern with the proper uses and applications of power, which he also found that elite groups abuse. Yet he chides Mills for failing to undertake an analysis of power that extends its meaning, especially for democracy. The chief task for the observer of power, says Lynd, is developing a theory of power for a given society. While Lynd is in basic sympathy with Mills's view of American institutional life, he is out of sympathy with what he sees as Mills's lack of commitment to a liberal democratic ethos. Consequently, he finds that Mills's ambiguous "exposé" lacks concreteness as well as meaningful goals.

Lynd also finds elite analysis generally limited, if not distasteful, because it obscures or ignores the basic characteristics of a given nation and social system. It breeds a careless or superficial "hit and run" analysis that amounts to a way out of dealing with capitalism, socialism, and class structure. Mills's pragmatism was far less attractive for Lynd in the mid-1950s, when he saw it as a poor stand-in for Marxist analysis, than when, in the mid-1940s, he saw it as a robust extension of philosophic analysis to include political issues.

Because Mills concentrates exclusively on power, Lynd claims, he overlooks the important continuities between present-day and nineteenth-century American capitalism. By focusing on "great changes," he fails to account for property as a power base. He treats the capitalist character of United States economic institutions as if it were a mere entry to the elite rather than the defining quality of economic life in the United States from the very outset of the Revolution.

Talcott Parsons[14] also raises meaningful criticisms of Mills, from a more conservative framework, although he grants considerable importance to *The Power Elite* because it attempts a major interpretation of the entire American society. Parsons begins by taking issue with Mills's use of terms, such as the economic meaning ascribed to "class" and "higher immorality." He considers that Mills is vague on relations between the power elite and other elements in the elite structure. But his doubts are more fundamental than terminology.

Parsons questions whether additions to the category of the "very rich" have occurred more through inheritance or self-earning, and he thinks Mills ascribes to them too much decision-making influence. Parsons holds that Mills erroneously confuses the "very rich" and the "corporate rich," making it appear as if they constitute a solid corporate hierarchy, when in fact they are distinct groups. He also argues that Mills's treatment of the "political directorate" is weak since he makes it appear to be infiltrated by business, leaving it little or no policymaking independence. Mills does allow independence only to the military, but on grounds which could just as easily admit the autonomy of the polity.

Parsons claims that government influence is great and very real, and hence its influence has considerable autonomy. It is not directed by business interests. This governmental influence makes the political directorate highly independent, precisely because of the United States's world position and its corresponding industrial maturation. The growth of power concentration appears pronounced only because nonpolitical decentralized patterns historically prevailed in nineteenth-century America, enhanced by a cultural emphasis on economic values.

Mills is said to look too nostalgically at Jeffersonianism, a doctrine incompatible with industrialization. Perpetuating the power of the local family elite, even if it would have preserved the "scatter of power," and thus competitive values, would also have impeded advanced industrialization, because it does not allow for differentiation of economic production in specialized organizations. Development brings specialization and structural differentiation, and more specialized leadership. There is specialization at three levels: (1) in organizations of economic production; (2) in functions within the economy; and (3) in class differentiation within society. Concentration is linked to the need to administer efficient production units while allowing for the numerous special tasks and skills needed to carry on production in a mature industrial economy. Parsons insists that Mills should have questioned whether this concentration has gone too far because of factors extraneous to development. Parsons claims Mills has provided no evidence that concentration exceeds the needs of efficiency and has contented himself with noting the fact of concentration. He further notes that the relative share of profits for the largest firms has been stable for more than a generation, suggesting equilibrium rather than excess. Parsons questions whether the power of managerial and executive classes has increased inordinately, and challenges Mills to demonstrate this.

Unlike Mills, Parsons separates the fortune-holders (very rich) from the executives (corporate rich). For the most part executives do not acquire fortunes that raise their status and position from the corporation. They are, rather, advanced by promotion, and decision-making control is in their hands rather than centered in family ownership. The original "captains of industry" failed to consolidate control of their enterprises. Executive responsibility was linked with competence in such a way that the ascriptive rights of property ownership gave way to the occupational functions of "professionals." There are two ways in which Mills obscures this shift, according to Parsons. He continues to speak of power within the economy as based on property, which is not substantively true; and he fails to appreciate the goal-oriented nature of industrial tasks. In old-style family enterprise, still predominant in the small-business sector, functions of management and ownership are fused in the same people. In the larger enterprise such functions have by and large become differentiated, serving as a system of checks and balances upon one another. Bonuses and large executive salaries should not be taken to mean control through property ownership. The power structure in business has been altered through the specialization process, not through control of property.

Contrary to Mills's contention, recruitment into the upper reaches of the economy operates almost entirely through relatively structured appointment. Mills insists that qualifications have little to do with this process. But the absence of formal entry procedures does not prove his contention. Given the nature of industrial society, Parsons indicates that the well-defined elite or leadership in business should be expected to develop. Power cannot be diffused equally in small units as small-business ideology would have it. However, Mills is right in showing that recruitment does derive largely from upper-class groups. The problem of an elite within the economy must be differentiated from that of an elite group ruling over the whole society. Parsons claims that Mills should have separated professions of high prestige within the upper classes from those who have power.

In a complex society the main locus of power lies in its political system. The early United States power system lagged behind its economic system. Since the end of the nineteenth century the mechanisms of political control have grown to control the economic sector. Mills mistakenly implies the reverse. He fails to understand the role of political organizations like parties in the power structure, nor does he see that the presidential office is the prize of party politics. The executive branch has extraordinary prestige as well as great powers that enable it to achieve political integration at a national level.

Parsons also insists that Mills exaggerates the importance of the military. While Mills sees the military as filling a decision-making vacuum, he is said to ignore crucial instances when it has been overruled. This criticism is meant to illustrate Mills's tendency to generalize short-term trends into essential features of the society. Further, Mills misunderstands the role of the courts and lawyers in interpreting, legitimizing, and translating the legal embodiments of power into the terms by which the members of the community agree to live. His conception of power is a "zero-sum" game, in which it is winner take all. But in fact power is not simply a facility for the performance of a function, but a basic, goal-directed social resource.

As a result, inequities aside, Mills is insensitive to what binds people to their positions, to their leadership, to their tasks. He focuses exclusively on distributive aspects: who has power, what interests are served. He ignores how it comes to be generated and what communal functions are served. The result is a partial and selective treatment. Mills foreshortens social processes, and the outcome is that short-run effects are taken for long-term factors. He also tends to think of power as "presumptively" illegitimate. In addition, on the basis of Parsons's schema of three types of philosophical utopianism, Mills is said to exhibit a Socialist mistrust of private interest and a utopian notion of public control.

Although criticisms of *The Power Elite* have had a wide hearing, empirically based studies have been conducted which implicitly or explicitly have sought to answer or broaden Mills's leading ideas. The most notable of these has been *Who Governs?* by Robert A. Dahl,[15] an examination of power and influence patterns in New Haven, Connecticut. This study not only implies that *The Power Elite* is oversimplified, but stands Mills on his head by reversing the conclusions reached in his work. Actually, neither Mills nor Dahl is specifically concerned with the nature of power and its relation to socioeconomic systems. Both focus on the distribution of power in a modern (rather than specifically Socialist or capitalist) context. Both are concerned with the effect of restraining norms on the exercise of political power. Yet Dahl seems to have deliberately decided that if Mills is right in the larger context it will be borne out in any community study. However, this is precisely what Mills's premises do not require. To reach the "nodal point" where decision-making power passes into the hands of a power elite, the range must be directly national in scope and ramification. To isolate the parts of the larger system is to focus on what is isolatable and not necessarily on what is essential.

Dahl draws richly and effectively on the history of the city and the backgrounds of its leading people. He begins with the premise that historically the exercise of power moved from a ruling oligarchy in a relatively simple and undifferentiated social context toward a pluralistic-democratic community in a complicated and highly specialized context. This movement occurred, first, as part of the growing complications and fragmentations imposed by an industrial society; and second, through yielding to pressures for dominance by advantaged ethnic, business, middle-class and lower-class groups. The breakdown of oligarchy was insured by specialization and mass pressure. The small, aristocratically oriented ruling group could not, and finally would not, resist these democratizing tendencies.

A proliferation of new claims was imposed on government by large masses. A fragmentation of areas of influence ensured. Politics could no longer be confined or defined by the interests of narrow and small upper classes. While it may be the case that lower classes remain without adequate political resources or high motivation to press their true influence upon government, the transformation of American democracy has been substantial. Political machinery is now largely manipulated by many middle-range groups whose various overlapping interests have brought about a political style of variously patterned coalitions involving larger numbers than ever. What is more, power and influence are primarily, if not entirely, centered in politics. And the political apparatus, however imperfect, does not operate through a guiding or covert directorate outside of government machinery.

Due to the dispersion of advantage and resources for middle-class groups and disadvantage for lower-class groups, politics is an interaction system with pockets of intense influence, gradually shading off outward. Influence crystallizes on issues rather than class lines, and the various interests an issue calls forth give a pragmatic coalition style to politics. This takes place in a context in which widely believed-in democratic norms impose limits on excessive concentration of power.

Dahl shares with Mills a feeling for the ambiguity of the sources and intensity of power. But aside from a few superficial resemblances, the similarity of their conceptions of power ends there. Dahl develops an elaborate structure, replete with detailed charts, to explain the nature of the public. This public is definitely not excluded from major decisions, and its removal from major issues is virtually self-willed rather than engineered "from above." From a set of interesting hypotheses, Dahl finds that this public is always courted as an electorate, and its temper and different interests are nurtured, appealed to, and cautiously accounted for in higher policy. Insofar as the public is ignorant or disinterested, this is a natural outcome of differences in leisure, resources, advantages, education, motivation, and interests. Opportunities are presumably always available to the elites, but, as in all societies, there are numerous other pursuits and interests that impose limits on, and attitudes toward, political participation. Consequently it is only to be expected that a concentration of political resources and influence will be in the hands of those who fully apply themselves to political practice, whether out of interest or personal suitability.

Dahl's shrewd analysis, in its community focus, is not unlike sociological analyses of the forties, which also considered the problem of class
definition from the standpoint of pluralism. This is the crux of the matter—the area of focus. By exclusive concentration on political machinery
and the ideology and composition of one city, whether typical or not,
other matters are sacrificed. For example, a "Millsian" approach would
have pursued the obvious economic ties of a middle-sized city like New
Haven to its neighboring giants, New York City or Boston. Furthermore, Mills did not deny popular effectiveness in local government concerned with local issues. His argument rested on the extent to which this
unit of power can suffice for the larger national picture. For example, he
would have attempted to gauge the extent to which any New Haven
mayor could achieve a significant political voice outside of his immediate electorate. For Dahl, this is not a serious question, for he is examining fluid interaction in one of its "eddies"—New Haven. For Mills, the
size of the terrain studied is an all-important question, since access to
power is based on acquisition of office in a hierarchy. Lower offices are
stepping stones to higher ones, entry into which is the achievement of
significant power. Mills would not have examined New Haven, to gauge
the mayor's power, but the "mayoralty" in a national context. Different starting points and not merely points of view account heavily for the
widest differences between Dahl and Mills. Far from providing an "answer" to *The Power Elite*, the "community" point of view was simply
evaluated as a special case limiting a "national" approach to political sociology.

Mills's *Power Elite* provided little in the way of theoretical innovation. Bottomore was right to note the absence of a coherent philosophical outlook.[16] But Mills did provide a sentiment which came to fruition a
decade later in works like Christopher Lasch's *The Agony of the American Left*,[17] Gabriel Kolko's *Wealth and Power in America*,[18] and G.
William Domhoff's *Who Rules America?*[19] It would hardly be news to
say that these were perhaps sounder treatises than that of Mills. They are
worked mightily to search for America through a coherent, but usually
European theory. However, Mills with his wide-open pragmatism left
his American passions on public display. His populism, sometimes rip-
ening into nativism, generated trust. Many of his erstwhile acolytes
stopped looking at the utopian prospects of an America growing in a
wide-open universe, and buried their passions beneath a rubble of socialist pieties. Their "improvements" upon Mills, tightening the vise of
ideology, may have improved theory but lost an audience.

Weaknesses and shortcomings notwithstanding, *The Power Elite*
still looks and feels less dated than the efforts of Mills's more sophisticated critics. While they are shrewd and knowing in their selective exposure of the nature, function, and division of power at a given time or

place, they do not explain the enduring character of *The Power Elite*. This durability has less to do with specific empirical illustrations of the use and abuse of power than with the utter transformation, in the second half of the twentieth century, of the relationship between economics and politics. The previous one hundred years, certainly 1848 to 1948, took for granted the economic sources of human behavior. Whether the motive was personal greed, corporate control, or military conquest, the answers were sought and inevitably found in economic drives. Nor was this economic explanation confined to the Marxists. Hobson on imperialism, Beard on warfare, and Keynes on monetary policy provided ample "bourgeois" formulas of the economic sources of everything from crisis to conflict.

What Mills did was cut away the debris of inherited doctrines by reversing the causal process. Power is not simply sui generis, but a response to political domination. It is this political element which determines the character of economic systems and even economic performance. Whatever the specific changes over time in Millsian formulas about who wields power and why, it has become an axiom of social science and public policy that the political process is the "base" and the economic network the "super-structure." Whether in the long run we are "dead or red" is of less consequence to Mills than the fact that in the short run the political process determines which of the two we become. It is not power but politics that is the source of the continuing fascination with Mills's work in this area; a fascination that has turned into a fixation as more and more decisions about economic matters are managed and manipulated by politicians—whether in the industrial or underdeveloped nations; whether by people of talent or just plain fools. This, then, explains the continuing passion for power: the realization by Mills that it has become a higher game than the struggle for wealth or status.

REFERENCES

1. Tom B. Bottomore. *Classes in Modern Society*. London: George Allen & Unwin, 1965, p. 77.

2. Arthur Kornhauser, ed. *Problems of Power in American Democracy*. Detroit: Wayne State University, 1957.

3. Reinhard Bendix and Seymour Martin Lipset, eds. *Class, Status, and Power: Social Stratification in Comparative Perspective*, rev. ed. New York: The Free Press/Macmillan Co., 1953, 1966.

4. C. Wright Mills. *The Power Elite*. New York: Oxford University Press, 1956. All references to Mills's work in this chapter will be to this book.

5. David Riesman, Nathan Glazer, and Reuel Denney. *The Lonely Crowd*. New Haven: Yale University Press, 1950, 1953.

6. Seymour Martin Lipset. *Political Man: The Social Bases of Politics*. Garden City, N.Y.: Doubleday & Co., 1960. esp. pp. 439-56.

7. Talcott Parsons. "The Destruction of Power in American Society." In *Structure and Process in Modern Societies*. Glencoe, Ill.: Free Press, 1960, pp. 199–225.

8. Todd Gitlin. "Local Pluralism as Theory and Ideology." *Studies on the Left* 5, no. 3 (Summer 1965): 21–45.

9. Robert S. Lynd and Helen M. Lynd. *Middletown: A Study in American Culture*. New York: Harcourt, Brace & Co., 1929, esp. pp. 478–502.

10. Floyd Hunter. *Community Power Structure: A Study of Decision Makers*. Chapel Hill: The University of North Carolina Press, 1953.

11. Bernard Rosenberg and Eugene V. Walter. "The Power Elite: Two Views." *Dissent* (Fall 1956): 390–98.

12. Daniel Bell. "The Power Elite Reconsidered." *American Journal of Sociology* 64, no. 3 (1958): 238–50.

13. Robert S. Lynd. "Power in the United States." *The Nation*, May 12, 1956, pp. 408–11.

14. Parsons, "The Destruction of Power in American Society," pp. 199–225.

15. Robert A. Dahl. *Who Governs? Democracy and Power in an American City*. New Haven: Yale University Press, 1961.

16. Tom B. Bottomore. *Critics of Society: Radical Thought in North America*. New York: Pantheon Books, 1968, pp. 63–64.

17. Christopher Lasch. *The Agony of the American Left*. New York: Vintage/ Random House, 1969.

18. Gabriel Kolko. *Wealth and Power in America*. New York: Praeger Publishers, 1962.

19. G. William Domhoff. *Who Rules America?* Englewood Cliffs, N.J.: Prentice-Hall, 1967.

13

The Causes of
C. Wright Mills

*Mills soon began to make up his mind, "to get his head together,"
and his stuff became rather too clear and one-sided: he judged capitalist America with a severity he didn't apply to socialist competitors
like Castro's Cuba. The double standard is as unattractive in politics
as in sex.*

Dwight Macdonald, *Discriminations: Essays and Afterthoughts*

HAVING COMPLETED THE great stratification trilogy, Mills, in the years
between 1957 and 1960, sought a wider turf upon which to exercise his
political imagination. The stirrings of a left-wing opposition to increased
defense budgets, stimulated by the successes of the Soviet space program, and the realization that nuclear parity was inevitable represented
the international background to Mills's new thinking. The rise of indig-
enous radical movements provided an additional postcolonial exuber-
ance that had restored a sense of innovation to the political process. This
emergence of a Third World, although not yet crystallized—Mills referred to its members in *New York Times* fashion as "Hungry Nations"—captivated Mills's imagination. These new nations represented
stratification problems at a global level. Finally, there was the problem
of the Soviet Union—of communism as an empirical entity—which became a matter of intense concern. Where Mills sought to position himself in the struggle between two world systems became a central element
in his last writings.

The Power Elite had brought Mills invitations for lecture tours
throughout the world. These years were filled with conferences in Scandinavia, the United Kingdom, Eastern Europe, and especially Latin
America. If the intellectual canvas had expanded, so too had Mills's
sense of the world. Mecca was pushed beyond New York horizons. But
along with objective changes was a subjective reorientation as well:

Mills's growing identification with world history, accompanied by his own belief in himself as a big actor on a big scene. It would have taken a person of extremely good judgment to resist the sort of blandishments Mills received from admirers such as Carlos Fuentes, a novelist already well regarded by the end of the fifties.

> We all admire and love you, not only as the United States' foremost intel-lectual voice, but above all, as a man and a friend. Can't these guys [re-viewers] see the writing on the wall? Won't they hear and understand the truth when it is as courageously and honestly spoken as you have done?[1]

Mills was not that person. The causes Mills began to write about became intense personal espousals. Events were no longer treated as objective events, no longer the tragedies of alienated shopkeepers or triumphs of people of power. Every event became subjective, i.e., the triumph of dy-namic revolutionaries defying all odds. Every description was tinged with personal beliefs and disbeliefs. Personal animosities were translated into public tragedies.

Monographs were transformed into pamphlets; sociology into the coaxial cables; the events of the world into the causes of the man. Mills was no longer just a strident critic of mass culture, but its engaging cap-tive. Being on the BBC, or on NBC in the United States, became a fo-rum for presenting the big picture as seen by the lonely warrior. The mass paperback replaced the class clothbound as a vehicle for presenting serious ideas. Verbal laceration became *au courant*, literary manners blunt. Mills began to think of himself as the special bearer of mass be-liefs; he became a movement unto himself. Armed with an Enlighten-ment faith that truth will out, he also became convinced that he was the bearer of the truth. He began to think that a readership of 400,000 cop-ies of *Listen Yankee!* was the same as a marching army of American sup-porters for Castro; or that a sale of 100,000 copies of *The Causes of World War Three* was the same as having launched a massive peace ef-fort. That ten times that number of people were reading or viewing Mickey Spillane went discreetly unnoticed. The utopian dimension en-larged to take on larger-than-life proportions: to be exposed to Mills was to be transformed into a marching army of devoted followers.

The correspondence from readers, his plain people, clearly buoyed Mills, indeed supported him against elitist critics. Celebrity status, which Mills was on the edge of attaining with the publication of *White Collar* and *The Power Elite*, became a quest, rather than a consequence of work done. Personal and objective factors became desperately, even dangerously, intertwined. He began identifiying himself with world his-tory and not just social reform. Politics became highly personalized. He saw himself as an actor in, and not just a writer of, great events. History and personality intertwined in a new way, to confirm his judgments on current stories. In this special context, Mills's overall commitment to a sociological profession was largely dissolved; and a certain frigidity set in between himself and former associates and colleagues in other disciplines as well. What in earlier years had been arguments among social scientists with a variety of Socialist and radical commitments became a hostile evnironment in which the nature of being an engaged intellectual was questioned. Mills's emphasis on viewing the powerful as a source of evil and not just strength led to his clear-cut rupture with his colleagues at Columbia.

An exchange in the mid-1950s with Trilling typified the widening gap between Mills and his fellow intellectuals. In this exchange Mills's attack on power and its intellectual kingdoms became crystallized. He saw power first and foremost in terms of technicians and consultants rather than politicians and militarists—or at least it was in this area that his passions were most obviously engaged. He wrote to Trilling:

> The rise of the technician and consultant in all areas of modern America ought to be recognized in such a way as to make clear the difference between this type of humanist ideal of intellect and rationality. That this distinction is not a real pivot of your piece is a source of possible misunderstanding. Second, the most important fact about the intelligence of those who live long with [Henry] Luce is the ease with which their intelligence is used in the bright clever pattern without any explicit ordering and forbidding being involved. That is the beginning point for an analysis of the intellectual quality of the new technical intelligentsia.[2]

For this part, Trilling epitomized the dominant liberalism which in the mid-1950s was quite certain of its own future. The vigor of Trilling's response is indicative of a triumphal rather than a retreating liberalism. Although the overt arguments between Mills and Trilling centered around their respective attitudes toward intellectual freedom, the covert debate was between a celebration and a critique of American scholarship in general. The particular discussion about Time-Life and intellectuals represented a personal rebuke and a defense of the liberal imagination. It is no accident that one of Trilling's major collections of essays was called *The Liberal Imagination*,[3] which in turn was answered by the phrase (and book title) *The Sociological Imagination*.

> The meaning which you give to the words technician and consultant [Trilling wrote to Mills] is a wholly pejorative one. I'm not *a priori* charmed by ideology taking place of principle and honor, as it tends to do in our culture. But ideology carries with it some principle and some honor of its own. And a culture in which ideology is dominant offers an opportunity for the intellectual. . . . The intellectual, by his ignorance of the state of affairs, is missing his opportunity for influence. From the cultural point of view which you express in your essay—a point of view as-it-were

aristocratic, very strict, and traditional in its ideals—there is nothing to be done with this new class.[4]

This sort of approach presaged the breakdown of Mills's humanistic academic constituency at Columbia, and not just his sociological cohort, which had collapsed much earlier. Whether by accident or design, Mills was led to search for an alternative constituency. He did this more out of a sense of tactics than principles, and he located this Archimedean lever in the Christian clergy, to whom he spoke from his bully-pulpit at Morningside Heights:

> I am on my own; you've got your God. It is up to you to proclaim gospel, to declare justice, to apply your love of men—the sons of God, all of them, you say—meaningfully, each and every day, to the affairs and troubles of men. It is up to you to find answers that are rooted in ultimate moral decision and to say them so that they are compelling. I hope your Christian conscience is neither at ease nor at attention, because if it is I must conclude that it is a curiously expedient and ineffective apparatus. I hope you do not believe that in what you do and how you live you are renouncing evil, because if you do, then I must infer that you know nothing of evil and so nothing of good.[5]

It is hard to say whether Mills was a Latter Day Saint or an early Moral Majoritarian. He thundered forth, not unlike Jerry Falwell, announcing the inviolable unity of politics and religion to the unregenerate and uninformed—and increasingly with a lecturing and hectoring style.

> The world is political. Politics, understood for what it really is today, has to do with the decisions men make which determine how they shall live and how they shall die. They are not living very well, and they are not going to die very well either. Politics is the locale of both evil and of good. If you do not get the church into politics, you cannot confront evil and you cannot work for good.[6]

But in fact, Mills was too good a sociologist to believe his own sermon. This is perhaps the reason why, tongue-in-check, he called it a "pagan sermon." His strong, instinctual reaction to religion comes out clearly in the following passage.

> As a social and as a personal force, religion has become a dependent variable: It does not originate; it reacts. It does not denouce; it adapts. It does not set forth new modes of conduct and sensibility; it imitates. Its rhetoric is without deep appeal; the worship it organizes is without piety. It has become less a revitalization of the spirit in permanent tension with the world than a respectable distraction from the sourness of life. Well settled among the nationalist spokesmen, the verbal output of U.S. religious leaders is now part of the defining of reality that is official, rigid, and in-

human. In a quite direct sense, religion in America has generally become part of the false consciousness of the world and of the self.[7]

The Christian religion and its clergy (here one gets the impression that Mills really means Protestant rather than Catholic) was an unnatural constituency. HIs naturalistic philosophy and secular outlook made this so. More natural and convincing was his appeal to the scientific community. The scientist, according to Mills, was a member of a cultural community which emphasized its secular linkages. It was this group which he knew best, or at least thought he knew best. Mills went so far in his neo-Platonist moment as to argue for the establishment of a civilian department of science and technology in which all scientific agencies of the government would be placed.

> To replace the present labyrinth and confusion of committees and consultants by such a centralized organization would increase the chance for a responsible public role of science and scientists. It would constitute a forum within which debates about science and policy debates by scientists could be made democratically open and responsible. And it would increase the chance that scientific endeavor would be removed from military authority and Pentagon decision.[8]

The longings after Saint-Simonianism, Comtean recipes, and a world inhabited by 30 million Newtons and another 30 million Shakespeares beat strong in MIlls. The noble savage turned scientist was to become the main obstacle in preventing the ''crackpot elites'' of the Soviet Union, the United States, and points in between from gaining control. J. Robert Oppenheimer, the martyr of McCarthyism, was to be the new saint of this scientific humanism as he and his colleagues did battle with the Science Machine.

But here again Mills was too shrewd a sociologist to believe in his own moralistic urgings and implorings:

> U.S. science has not developed a firm scientific tradition in the European manner. Here science has been virtually identified with its technological products, its engineering developments, its techniques; and it has recently become subjected to the corporate technique of the assembly line. It is in the use of science, and in the know-how of development projects, in the mass-production exploitation of its legacy, that the U.S. has excelled. This kind of industrial and military science stands in contrast to the classic, academic tradition in which individual scientific investigators or small groups are part of an uncoordinated cultural tradition.[9]

Mills repeatedly equated the academic tradition with scientific integrity, while on the other side of the ledger, he identified the technical industrial system with the evils of modernism. He began to identify with the forces of Jeffersonian ruralism he had earlier derided. His appeals, first to the ministry and then to the scientific establishment, were made on behalf of a nostalgia for a medieval, quasi-feudal world. Curiously, not unlike J. Robert Oppenheimer himself, with his notion of science and the open society, Mills found in the past a needed buffer against the present. In that sense Mills, like many other radical critics of the 1950s, talked forward while looking backward.[10]

This notwithstanding, the importance of *The Causes of World War Three* derived less from Mills's appeal to the past than from his reassessment of the concept of power. Mills did not move beyond the American national boundaries in *The Power Elite*, but in this considerably less substantial follow-up tract he began to flirt with the notion of an international power elite—not in terms of ideology but in terms of functions. In his own way, Mills accepted the idea of the exhaustion of ideology in existing political structures: Administrative decisions and the management of consent had replaced the existence of political innovation; political strife itself had become rountinized; both history-making and war-making were now monopolized by those who had access to the means of power. Mills laid great stress upon this latter point, as is seen in his comparison of Soviet and industrial American might:

> That is the point of immediate importance: Small ruling circles in both superstates assume that military violence and the whole supporting ethos of an overdeveloped society geared for war are hard-headed, practical, inevitable, and realistic conceptions. There are many other points of convergence and coincidence between these two countries, both in dream and in reality, and as the Soviet industrial complex is further enlarged the parallels will become more pronounced. In surface ideology they apparently differ; in structural trend and in official action they become increasingly alike. Not ideology but industrial and military technology, geared to total war, may well determine that the dreams of each will in due course be found in the realities of the other.[11]

Mills's argument becomes richly textured at this point. He does not assert the existence of a well-delineated international power elite—at least not the unity of elites as a simple reflection of political institutions—but rather that trends in institutional arrangements may lead to the development of transnational integrations which coexist and at times preempt the private economy of each major power. The exigencies of the marketplace create commonalities between the rich across national boundaries. But elite competitions remain prevalent. His own formulation of this fissure-fusion effect among world elites is both imaginative and at the same time surprisingly restrained:

> Their unity does not rest solely upon psychological similarity nor even upon the structural blending of commanding positions and common interests. At times it is a more explicit co-ordination. Such co-ordination is neither total nor continuous; often it is not very sure-footed. The power elite has not emerged as the realization of any plot. Yet we must remember that institutional trends may be defined as opportunities by those who occupy the command posts. Once such opportunities are recognized, men may avail themselves of them. Certain types of men from each of these

three areas, more farsighted than others, actively promoted the liaison even before it took its truly modern shape. More have come to see that their several interests can more easily be realized if they work together, in informal as well as in formal ways, and accordingly they have done so.[12]

Mills's notion of international power was strikingly similar to Weber's concept of an international bureaucracy. It was a phenomenon he envisioned taking place, but not with any pleasant anticipation. This international power structure turned out to be little else than an early form of anticipated détente between East and West. Mills saw such an arrangement of world order through world power as benefitting only the powerful blocs, not the hungry nations: the inevitable third force he was searching for as a moral alternative to a balance-of-power theory.

Mills's great worry was that both American and Soviet societies were characterized by the increasing integration of their functions into a bureaucratic state apparatus. The cleavage that existed between the private conscience, including the freewheeling intellectual, and the state apparatus deeply alarmed him. The only difference he saw between the Soviets and Americans in this regard was the formal institutionalization of Soviet life in contrast to the informal integration of autonomous and voluntary forces in America. Autonomous organizations in powerful states, like potent classes, operate behind the backs of individuals; "they ensnare one another." The elites work toward the maintenance of their own power without regard to general social values.

> In the U.S.S.R. and in modern totalitarianism in general the integration of autonomous forces is explicit; in the formal democracies it is much less so, and it is by no means a completed process. Yet it is well under way. Leaders of cliques, pressure groups, and associations maneuver within and between the organs of the democratic state and become a central part of that state. They discipline those whom they represent; their chief desire is to maintain their organizations, even if this requires them to lose sight of their ends in the effort to secure themselves as a means, even if it results in their loss of independent action. They ensnare one another; such history as they make is history going on behind men's backs, including their own.[13]

If this high level of integration is inevitable, then the very definition of advanced societies reveals a movement from the national to the transnational, from the political to the administrative, and from the powerless to the powerful.

The unresolved disjunction between what is and what ought to be presents itself as a continuous problem in *The Causes of World War Three*. Mills's constant appeals for the civilizing and politicizing of society lose much of their force in this utopian blast. For example:

> The goal and the means of world industrial development, and so of peace, are to replace the permanent war economy by a permanent peace econ-

omy. All private profit must be taken out of the preparation for war in the U.S. economy. The economic waste of war must be taken out of the world economies. Military personnel and the military mentality must be firmly subordinated to civilian and political men and purposes. Inside the U.S.A. we must become political again.[14]

Repeatedly Mills is thrown back to the private person who somehow will find the inner resolve to turn back the permanent war economy and create a durable world peace. We are told that the entire machinery of government is moving in a bureaucratic direction, but we are also implored to move all the machinery of humanity in a contrary direction. How this is to be operationalized remains painfully unspoken and unresolved. Presumably, Mills's standpoint is to be the rallying point.

The model Mills re-creates is once again the free-floating intellectual. It turns out that neither cleric nor scientist is really the answer. Mills reverts to the classical pragmatism of Dewey, an unyielding, undying faith in democratic culture and personal experience. The power of the intellectual has become potentially great.

> And because this is now so, to cultivate moral sensibility and to make it knowledgeable is the strategic task of those intellectuals who would be at peace. They should debate short-run and immediate policies, but, even more, they should confront the whole attitude toward war, they should teach new views of it, and on this basis they should criticize current policies and decisions.[15]

This is apparently what the intellectual should be doing. The person of sensibility has, albeit in a fragile form, the means of power—or at least the power to invest political meaning in intellectual work. To Mills's mind only such a person possesses the ability to speak in the name of peace, reason, and friendship between nations. The intellectual has become for Mills a special type of individual, the highest type, one interested in fusing knowledge and power. The "ought" is to act as a political intellectual, but the "is" is something else again. "In differing ways but often with frightening convergence, we now witness the rise of the cheerful robot, of the technological idiot, of the crackpot realist. All these types embody a common ethos: rationality without reason."[16] This is how Mills introduces some of the phrases with which he was to become most widely identified. He offers a Manichean encounter between good and evil, not just between two social systems or two kinds of economies, but the struggle between social systems and personal character within both the American and Soviet orbits. The showdown for Mills is ultimately moral in character, a reflection of differential expectations about what human beings can become.

❧

The Causes of World War Three was a painful exercise in exhortation, reflecting Mills's deep ambivalence about the intelligentsia even more than his loss of confidence in American masses and elites alike. The masses were inert, while the elites were duplicitous. A note of deep pessimism set in. Utopia turned to counter-utopia. An awful fate awaited the world: the death of the mind and universal control by a power elite that had become internationalized.

Such crudities notwithstanding, the volume struck a vital nerve in the literature of post–Second World War unilateral disarmament. Many of the issues that Mills dealt with distrubed wide numbers of people, for whom the Bomb took on ominous tones. The thawing of the Cold War after *Sputnik* gave added impetus to the disarmament camp. Mills spoke out with great eloquence about the need to convert military aid to economic supports, at least to various parts of the underdeveloped world. He spoke of the need for the United States, under the auspices of the United Nations, to take the lead in developing a world-class educational system. He strongly urged that all security and loyalty restrictions on scientific work and travel be lifted since these had a chilling effect on scientific production. But all was proclamation, little was explanation.

Long before it was popular to do so, Mills urged a cessation of the testing of nuclear devices. He foresaw a period of revitalization of the European role in world affairs at a time when, politically at least, Western Europe was still a basket case. Mills felt keenly that the future of world peace would be determined in large measure by European participation as a balance wheel between East and West. Mills also urged an embargo on all arms shipments to the Middle East in order to prevent that particular powder keg from blowing up simply because of the world's need for oil. Imaginatively, he urged an OPEC-like solution to Middle East economic problems. He offered a prophetic and dire warning that Western civilization had begun in the Middle East and that its ending could also occur there. Mills also urged that the United States provide an opening to China (as well as India) and recognize China diplomatically. That some of his policy proposals were foolish and others were ludicrously one-sided should not obliterate the fact that Mills did have a policy-oriented no less than moral message. We are still wrestling with many of the concrete issues outlined in his guidelines.[17] Mills might be accused of intellectual impatience, painting the political stage with a broad brush not easily transferred to solid policies. But few can doubt, even in twenty-five-year retrospect, his near-uncanny sense of the central issues of the historical epoch.

The central problem which Mills leaves us with in *The Causes of World War Three* is an abstract sense of good and a concrete sense of evil. The good embodied in individual heroics of individual intellectuals seems to be of small consequence when stacked up against the enormous military power of Soviets and Americans. Mills's deep and abiding suspicion of the Soviety Union increased rather than decreased over time. If he had far harsher things to say about the United States, it was only because it was a society with which he was far more intimate, one which at the same time offered more promise in some higher utopian sense. The charges and urgings of this extended pamphlet ended in frustration, a failure to indicate any sort of policies or programs to resolve the issues raised. Mills, like many of his literary friends, was reduced to waiting for the end—and worse, to identifying personal frustration with the termination of world history.

The Archimedean lever was still missing. Those who were to lead the children of paradise from its confrontation with disaster had not yet appeared. Hence, this remained one of the most unsatisfactory and unresolved of Mills's works, leaving both his defenders and critics unsure of where to proceed, and oddly enough, unclear about just what would be the essential causes of World War Three.

Writing in the pages of the *Chicago Tribune*, Russell Kirk saw Mills as a professor who has "dreams of setting this sorry old world aright by a few simple prescriptions of his own." His prescriptions "are not likely to take on reality." Kirk, to be sure, understood the quixotic nature of a book which on one hand condemned the power elite and on the other encouraged the formation of a new elite which would be "composed, naturally, of Mills and his chums."[18] In a syndicated review, Richard Massa claims that Mills's work offers an imbalanced picture of the Soviet Union and the United States. *The Causes of World War Three* "smacks of Neville Chamberlain, and it ignores the little man, the common man."[19] It was precisely the equating of the United States and the Soviet Union that offended the press reviewers.

Those who liked Mills's essays, such as Bryce Nelson, writing in the *Harvard Crimson*, also recognized that "the strength of Mills's thesis is lessened by the iconoclastic, irreverent tone that characterizes his writing. By now, we realize that he dislikes the 'Power Elite,' but making them into tangible villains often seems to be a perversion of reality."[20] Others saw Mills as a left-wing counterpart to Barry Goldwater, especially in his vision of the compulsory state of the economy of the people. Indeed, one reviewer frankly compared *The Causes of World War Three* with Barry Goldwater's conservative vision: "I am more fearful today of the loss of our freedoms through the establishment of super-government in Washington; super-business organizations in Wall Street, and super-labor unions in Detroit, than I am of Russian dictatorship conquering us by force."[21] And this observation of a conservative tinge to Mills's radical critique is not without merit, given his near-total despair about the American political system and process.

There was something of the radical conservative in Mills, the forward-talking but backward-looking intellectual. If this netted Mills some strong criticism, it also enabled him to pick up support from an odd assortment of populist types. But that support must have been as disturbing and unnerving to Mills as lack of support from the critics he had come to depend on. The Rev. Ralph E. Cousins, Jr., of St. Andrews Church in Ohio thought that the book "should be read by every clergyman in America." Another clergyman at a Methodist church in Michigan saw the book as an "incisive, discriminating, richly relevant statement." A rabbi in Boston viewed the tract as an in-depth "treatment . . . on the subject of world peace." A Unitarian minister in Illionis volunteered himself as a "missionary for its wide sale and readership."[22]

Mills's professional colleagues greeted *Causes* with criticism or stony silence. All of this must have left Mills feeling quite lonely. Even his friends on *Dissent*, pacifists like A. J. Muste, saw the book more as an argument than as an analysis;[23] while Irving Howe saw *Causes* as "characterized by a relentless thrust of assertion and a bludgeoning style, neither of which is much affected by complexity of argument or thoroughness of evidence."[24] The intelligentsia, the group whom Mills assiduously cultivated for many years, the very reason for his movement to New York City, simply ceased to take him seriously. It was not so much that they were critical of *The Causes of World War Three* as they were embarrassed by the book and for Mills. Oddly enough, Mills's new constituency, built upon ministers, students, and ultra-leftists, made him uncomfortable. *Causes* was a work largely passed over in silence by the right people. Nonetheless, it served to shed light on the transition of Mills from sociologist to moralist—the penultimate step on his road to self-immolation.

The academic year 1958–1959 was spent in Europe, largely in England. A cluster of British social historians and political scientists at the London School of Economics and the new University of Sussex gave Mills a reprieve. He gave a series of lectures on culture and politics to the British Broadcasting network which was well received. This putting together of his thoughts on intellectuals gave Mills a continuing sense of being a public man.[25] And at a time when relations with his fellow intellectuals in America had become badly strained, this overseas reprieve was deeply needed. The evolution of the New Left in England took place several years earlier than in the United States. From Asa Briggs at Sussex to Ralph Miliband at the London School of Economics offers of permanent posts came. But all were turned down. Mills, the ceaseless critic of American politics and society, remained the quintessential American. He was at home only in the place he was alienated from, among colleagues with whom he could engage in the good fight, face to face, man to man. Texas shootouts on Morningside Heights still seemed to him the natural activity for his final years.

ഗ‍ഗ‍ഗ

The Causes of World War Three was a negative book with a holocaust message: namely, prevent a war that nobody wants and that all will perish from. What eluded Mills was the positive forces of change.

He located this positive message with a vengeance in the Cuban Revolution. It came at a propitious moment. He was running out of time. Even the possibility of heroism within an American context seemed remote. Sociological analysis had failed to come up with the collective hero: neither the labor intellectual nor the inner-directed white collar worker nor undergraduate students nor Christian ministers would do. But this time Mills was not to be denied. The hero had come, the Messiah's name was Fidel Castro. Like the prophets of the Old Testament Castro led a crusade which seemed at first without hope (it was also without political dogmatism); and he led it to victory. By 1960, Mills wanted not just history, but victory.

Mills's love affair with the Cuban Revolution was many-sided. Initially, there was the personage of Castro. His identification with him gave Mills a sense of doing battle, first with Dwight D. Eisenhower and then with John F. Kennedy. In this way he was continuing his commitment to assault the bastions of power as he had in *The Power Elite*. The bête noire of his mind was to become President Kennedy, just as William James fifty years earlier had viewed Teddy Roosevelt as the quintessential imperialist. For Mills, Castro was the essential pragmatist, the quasi-Marxist who got things done without regard to Communist dogma or a Communist party. If there was a touch of mysticism in this view, then at least it was one that gave substance to Mills's sense of Third Worldliness; his love affair with an exotic place, and an unformed movement within a downtrodden nation. In *Listen, Yankee!* he wrote:

> You just have to come up with the facts about what kind of man Fidel Castro is, and what kinds of men the forty-or-so commandantes and the two-hundred-or-so capitáns of the Council of Ministers—all those who make up the revolutionary government of Cuba today—what kinds of men they really are. They have a real respect for the people and a real belief in the people. It's not some romantic idea. It's just something they know and something they are. These are the people—we revolutionaries think—and so you trust them. These are the people—and they can learn very fast what has to be done.[26]

The key to *Listen, Yankee!* is Mills's internalizing of the experiences of others. Mills writes manifestly and unabashedly as a partisan. The depersonalized "we" is really a generalized "I." This literary device was part of an ongoing effort by Mills to reach masses of people through the paperback medium. He never surrendered the eighteenth-century idea of Enlightenment: good ideas translate into a good society. He carried this vision one step forward and spoke as a partisan of those ideas—not unlike nineteenth-century advocates of the Socialist International.

> There is a world-wide competition going on, you know, and in this competition, we Cubans don't think you or your Government can avoid as-

suming that the advice and the aid we are taking from Russia, we are taking voluntarily. That happens to be the plain truth. We haven't done all this fighting to get from under one tyranny just to stick our necks into some other yoke—any other yoke. We're taking orders only from ourselves.[27]

Mills received a great deal of advice on how to do *Listen, Yankee!* from many people within the Cuban Revolution movement: above all Carlos Franqui, who as press attaché became a critical pivot in transmitting the Cuban message, and Juan Archocha, who served as translator to Mills. What began for Mills as a series of interviews with Cuban leaders ended as the internalizing of the Cuban Revolution. The revolution which Fidel made became one which Mills vicariously lived through. His volume contains some blunt reminders of an earlier era in which the United States was branded, often accurately, as the main if not the only source of Latin American miseries. The Cuban Revolution became, like the Russian Revolution, a harbinger of things to come: the inevitable end of the American presence in hemispheric affairs. The differences in size between the Soviet Union and Cuba, and the distinctions at the level of industrialization, melted in a tidal wave of words, a rhetoric quite widely believed at the time.

> Latin America is a great world region; it is a continent, long and repeatedly plundered; and it is in revolutionary ferment. That it is now in such ferment is a heartening testimony to the will of man not to remain forever an exploited object. For over a century Latin American man has been largely outside world history—except as an object; now he is entering that history—as a subject, with vengeance and pride, with violence. The unilateral Monroe Doctrine is part of the epoch of Latin American isolation. The epoch, and with it the Monroe Doctrine, is now coming to an end.[28]

The overview Mills offers, or rather voices, about Cuba with respect to the rest of Latin America now reads as high irony. Nations like Brazil, Venezuela, and Mexico are pilloried in *Listen, Yankee!* Argentina is said to have done "nothing of significance" to develop its wealth; Mexico's great revolution is considered stalled and "just a series of memories"; Brazil is simply a "dual society," whatever that was meant to convey. The possibility that these societies and all others would actually fare a great deal better than Cuba over time was simply incomprehensible to Mills. He failed to appreciate the meaning of Sovietization within a single-crop economy, or how an early rush to destroy the private sector served to inhibit the very expansion of the developmental groups in Cuba he was pinning so much hope upon.

Mills not only wrote about revolutionary euphoria in Cuba, he was a willing victim of that euphoria. Harvey Swados was correct in identifying the euphoria's source as the Cuban Revolution, which provided Mills with an "emotional home."[29] Seemingly, Mills had in mind a model French Revolution. The day the revolution triumphs, begins the world anew. The big clock in the sky both measures and determines the seizure of power:

> We're starting out with all the disorder that we've inherited, and with what amounts to No Culture in Cuba. To bring about real cultural and intellectual establishments is one of our greatest and most difficult tasks. It is linked, as we've said, with our need for administrators and technicians in the new Cuba. But we want much more than that. We want poetry as well as physics. And we know you can't plan for poets as you can for engineers. You can only plan and construct cultural institutions, and then hope that poets, as well as engineers, will grow in them and do great work.[30]

Throughout, we observe the theme of the society creating its poets and engineers, but little willingness to confront the way in which this Saint-Simonian dream was transformed into a Platonic nightmare.

Mills was reacting to the first years of a revolution whose structure had not yet crystallized. Hope against hope, he was affirming, not just describing, a movement without a party; a leadership born and bred in guerrilla activities and not just parliamentary cretinism; a nation seeking to carve out its own destiny apart from the American empire formerly inhibiting that destiny. It is to Mills's credit that *Listen, Yankee!* contains certain hesitations about events, even a cautionary spirit at the end. This helped him to put the brakes on the thrust of the work. The tract on Cuba reveals a curious dichotomy: When Mills spoke with his own voice, he did so as the political sociologist he was; when he spoke in the collective voice, he just as clearly summoned up the ideologist he had become.

The ideology which emerges in *Listen, Yankee!* is first and foremost a faith in populist Marxism; a polycentric vision of socialism breaking away from all orthodoxies. The belief rested on the fact that Cuba, at the least, represented a new Yugoslavia; like Tito's regime, Castro had earned his independence on the field of battle. In this way, the Cuban Revolution confirmed not only the end of American imperialism but the end of Soviet hegemonic control. It is not fruitful to speculate on how Mills would ultimately have come to view the utter dependency of Cuban society upon Soviet aid and support; one can only speculate that on the basis of his own commitment to pluralistic socialism he would have viewed the outcome as dismaying. Harvey Swados suggested that Mills's faith in Fidel had peaked by 1961. But Mill's interview "Listen Again, Yankee" showed only the reverse attitude: a pugnacity even less concerned with canons of evidence than it had been in the book.

Mills embraced the Cuban Revolution because it seemed to confirm his long-held pet theories about the decline of liberalism in the West and the growing embrace of democratic values by Marxist states. The do-it-yourself economics practiced by Cuba in 1960 was to Mills equivalent to the do-it-yourself pragmatism of the early New Deal days. In Mills's mind, the Cuban Revolution represented a victory for experimentation over and against the old American colonial yoke or the new Soviet ideological yoke. Even though he had moved far to the left of his earlier convictions, he remained adamant that the USA/USSR confrontation represented a singular evil—one best confronted by a "pluralized Marxism" rather than an "emaciated liberalism."

Mills had no doubt that Cuba would become a hemispheric model. Adopting the official tone of a Cuban spokesman, he shouted a warning:

> We're talking sense to you, Yankee; listen to us, please. What will happen, for example, when the people of all those South American countries realize their enormous wealth, both the actual and what could be, and yet find themselves poor? When looking across to tiny Cuba, they see the Cubans are not poor? What will happen then?[31]

The prospect that the rest of Latin America would do better economically than Cuba, that countries like Venezuela and Colombia would look across the Caribbean and see Cubans who were poor and a regime unable to exercise independence in foreign policy, simply never entered Mills's calculations. For him the course of events was clear: Since Socialist revolutions bring about nearly automatic new wealth and this largesse in turn is widely distributed, the Cuban nation would become a model for the hemisphere, and finally the whole hemisphere would engage in a thunderous revolt against its American masters. That this scenario did not play out—and, it seemed at the time of Mills's death, would not play out in the near future—failed to deter his enthusiasm. The love affair Mills had with the Cuban Revolution had no hemispheric antecedent. In fact, it became a mutual love affair on the part of Latin American intellectuals with Mills. He became lionized by everyone from Fidel Castro to Carlos Fuentes, receiving the sort of flattery his colleagues in American sociology, especially at Columbia, had entirely denied him. In Cuba, Mills's sense of a revolutionary movement unencumbered by Stalinism was fulfilled, as were his own sense of self-importance and larger-than-life ego needs. The only thing that began to unravel was the Revolution itself.

ᴑᴑᴑ

If the reviews of *Listen, Yankee!* were critical in the American press, the letters of support, especially from the Mexican Left, became thunderous. Arnaldo Orfila Reynal, at that time director of the leading publishing house of Mexico, wrote to Mills in strongly affective personal terms.

> In reading aloud your *Listen, Yankee!* with my wife, we were deeply touched with the greatness you show in your sheer understanding of the root of the problems of our Continent. It is the exact essence of the Cuban Revolution. I want to express to you the profound satisfaction I feel to be able to diffuse your beautiful message to the Spanish-speaking world.[32]

And a young scholar who had returned to Cuba to participate in the work of the Revolution, Armando Betancourt, wrote in a similarly effusive, mythologizing vein.

> Your name is already popular in all Cuba, to say Wright Mills sounds to say a friend. We thank you very deeply from the bottom of our hearts for having done that task, of telling our neighbors to the north the truth about this little island, little in size, but great in hopes, and spirit, and courage.[33]

To someone long denied what he felt were his just academic fruits, the enormous popularity of *Listen, Yankee!* was highly gratifying. Not that the correspondence was uniformly favorable. Indeed, the leader of the *Frente Revolucionario Democratico*, Salvador Ferrer, took umbrage no less than issue with Mills. That his statement could well have come out of the exile Cuban community in the 1980s, no less than in 1960, would have clearly disturbed Mills. Mills's marginalia proved that he was badly shaken by critical responses. Excerpts from Ferrer's letters are indicative of the polarizing impact, early on, of the Cuban Revolution—a development Mills, with his limited knowledge of the hemisphere, could hardly cope with:

> So Cuba was a "hungry nation" before Castro? We had Latin America's highest per capita production income and living standards. We were the Western Hemisphere's biggest producers of chrome, the second of nickel and manganese, the sixth of copper, ranked high in cattle raising, and led the world in sugar and fine tobacco. You say "only one school" was built in 58 years; our literacy ranked among Latin America's highest. . . . Our universities are barracks, with 750 professors ousted, and "students" drilling in uniform inside. Labor unions can no longer elect their leaders. The free, constitutional elections for which Cubans followed Castro—where are they? With Cuba's free press silenced, uncounted millions go for propaganda. In Havana for two years, thousands of Cubans daily have had the guts to defy Castro's guns to form four lines, in sun and rain, at the American Embassy. The fourth line is called the "life or death" line. Altogether, 300,000 have fled Castro, who says that only "the millionaires want to leave."[34]

In any final evaluation of Mills's work on Cuba it is important to keep in mind that however Mills may have idolized, sentimentalized, and pragmatized the Cuban revolutionary experience, he never accepted totalitarianism as the proper outcome of this regime. *Listen, Yankee!* is dotted by warnings and apprehensions about such a possibility. Cuba became part of Mills's final internal ideological struggle: his hatred of the American ruling class balanced only by his loathing of Soviet totalitarianism. Cuba was to be a third way, a new and independent variety of socialism. That his analysis failed to detect the utter impossibility of such a "Swedish" outcome within a Cuban context is less a reflection on Mills than on the backward state of hemispheric affairs prior to Castro's revolution.

The elemental decency of Mills (in contrast to Sartre's writings on Cuba) comes from the fact that Mills saw in Cuba practical, nonideological individuals—above all, people who admitted to confusion and doubt—whereas Sartre in his brief trip to Cuba saw only evidence of the Bergsonian *élan vital*. Sadly, as Régis Debray was later to make clear, it was mysticism, not pragmatism, which triumphed. The mystification of the Cuban revolutionary experience stood at the other end of the pole for Mills. His pragmatic view of the Cuban experience was played out without regard to either Sartre's metaphysical predispositions toward existentialism or the fanaticism of Soviet-type Marxism. The revolution from early on was locked into a world structure quite beyond national control. But Mills did not know that—or worse, pretended not to know. On the contrary, he accepted the views expressed by Carlos Franqui and other Left-critics of the Cuban Communist party that saw the Cuban solution as the ultimate proof that one can have a revolution without it becoming corrupted or perverted by Communist forces:

> The plain fact is, our revolution has outdone the Communists on every score. From the beginning up till today, always at every turn of event and policy, the revolution is always faster than the Cuban Communist Party, or individual Communists. In all objective facts, we are much more radical, much more revolutionary than they. And that is why we are using them, rather than the reverse; they are not using us. In fact they are being very grateful to us for letting them in on the work of the revolution.[35]

One must only wonder what Mills's response would have been to the triumph of party over movement, of collectives over individuals, and of Soviet domination over autonomous development. But even during Mills's life it was already evident that questions were being asked about forced collectivization. Jules Dubois, in his review of *Listen, Yankee!* on December 17, 1960, pointed out this fact bluntly. "When he states that 'the Cuban revolution, unlike the Russian, has in my judgment solved the major problems of agricultural production by its agrarian reform,' Mills is selling the American people a bill of goods that the facts fail to substantiate."[36] And in a much more sympathetic review, Hubert Herring, reviewing the book for the *Herald-Tribune* a month earlier, made his own set of rejoinders in a quieter mode, which Mills failed to address:

> The rejoinders to these points seem obvious. On Communism: the noises made by Fidel and Raul and Che Guevara sound like noises from the Kremlin—it may be pure coincidence. Rockets: those were mentioned by the master of the Kremlin. On the killing of thousands: no sober person has talked of "thousands" executed without fair trial, the figure is about seven hundred. On "democracy and freedom": we can point to the long list of patriotic Cubans who have left Fidel Castro and gone into exile—or to jail—because they saw no hope for democracy and freedom.[37]

The ideological climate in which Mills was writing must be kept in mind. There had emerged a widespread belief that the end of American civilization was at hand—or at least there was the absolute conviction that justice would be done only with the destruction of the American imperial enclave in the hemisphere. So incensed were Mills's radical Latin American supporters by the critical reviews he received that a group of leading Mexican cultural figures wrote a letter of protest. They reasserted the value of Mills's book and reaffirmed the absolute incorruptibility of the new Cuban order:

> "Listen, Yankee": We've been in Cuba. We've seen thousands of new schools, new hospitals, new roads, new housing, new symphony orchestras and theater groups, new popular priced books, new crops rising on the once-dead land of the huge estates. We've seen a people grown confident, proud, better off, consuming more than ever before—which accounts for the so-called "shortages" Dubois bandies about. We've seen the old order of privileges and exploitationary leaders. We've seen an incorruptible government at work. We've seen the wealth and the future of Cuba, for the first time, in the hands of the Cuban people. We've seen the hope of all Latin America in the faces of the new Cubans.[38]

As this manifesto makes clear, Mills became part of the struggle of ideas in the hemisphere itself: an outcome he and others did indeed anticipate when the book was being written.

Mills's quick response to the Cuban Revolution was not simply a search for a new heroism; it also expressed a sense of identification with Latin people. Since the mid-1940s, when he had written essays on Mexican barrios in Los Angeles (which were followed, later, with research on the Puerto Rican communities of New York), Mills had had a special at-a-distance love affair with Latin peoples. He did have some personal contact, however marginal, with Mexican-Americans during his Texas years, but aside from a passing mention of drinking with them in San Antonio bars, there is no other real evidence of face-to-face contact. Certainly Mills neither pretended nor aimed to be a Latin American specialist. Latin Americans for Mills seemed rather to represent the "ideal-typical" oppressed region, whether in Spanish Harlem or in Playa Girón.

Mills became the writer seeking world historic vindication, and he tried to achieve it by violating nearly every canon of the sociological imagination he had urged upon others. *Listen, Yankee!* ended up as his poorest effort in social analysis, a tract placed at the disposal of political forces he knew little of but cared much for. It contained banalities and hectorings which he personally loathed in others. From 1960 forward, his sense of self-doubt and failure overtook him. At the very point in time when the popularity of *Listen, Yankee!* was highest, his sense of self-esteem was lowest. Mills's desperate search for workable ideals came to an end in this wishful portrait of a nation embodying the perfect model of the perfect revolution. Swados summed this up touchingly:

> In his last months Mills was torn between defending *Listen, Yankee!* as a good and honest book and acknowledging publicly for the first time in his life that he had been terribly wrong. This would have meant not only caving in to the few whose opinions he valued . . . but returning to the United States and telling not only his enemies on the right, but the hundreds of thousands who had, so to speak, voted for him, that he was not a rough rider after all, but only a man of ideas who could be wrong, as men of ideas so often are. The tension was too much, the decline of the revolution, atop his personal pains, was too much.[39]

With the publication of *Listen, Yankee!*, and its earlier excerpt in *Harper's* magazine, MIlls achieved the celebrity status which had eluded him in the past. But the problem of Mills's limited knowledge of Cuba became dangerously apparent, especially when a debate on NBC television was proposed between himself and Adolf A. Berle, who, among his other talents in economics and diplomacy, had a lifelong commitment to hemispheric problems. Mills could scarely back away from the confrontation, not only because of a sense of purpose and mission, but also as a means to broaden his own commitment to underdevelopment as a global cause. Mills spent the month prior to the scheduled debate with Berle soliciting information from a wide range of Latin Americanists, including Frederick Pike, Donald Bray, Ray Higgins, Waldo Frank, Ronald Hilton, and others.[40] In each case, the letters asked for exact information on the hemisphere, on American military supports, and not least, on Berle himself.

Just how concerned Mills was about the forthcoming debate is indicated by the design of scenarios, i.e., what Mills would reply to queries and how much time each would spend on a variety of themes; Mills even solicited lists of individuals who might attend the debate, who could be called upon to ask the right questions at the right time. He viewed this debate as a career highlight, only slightly less significant than the publication of the Cuba volume itself. This contrasted sharply with Berle's downplaying of the event. But even Berle was caught up in the impact of a potential viewing audience of 5 million. "Mills's book, *Listen, Yankee!*, written after a couple of months in Cuba, where he had never been, was derived from interviews in Spanish, which he does not know, with refusal to ascribe identity to the sources thereof; really a piece of noisy propaganda and not even good, so I was ready to plaster him."[44]

But the debate never took place, at least not with Mills present. He suffered his penultimate heart attack just a few days before the debate was to be aired. Berle's response to the inability of Mills to participate was characteristically pugnacious: "C. Wright Mills has degenerated from being a capable though rather left-wing opinionated Professor of Sociology (Columbia) into a ranting propagandist. He was to have been the champion of the Castro regime, but he got a heart attack—partly I think because he was frightened—and had reason to be."[42] If Berle was relatively calm and benign about the debate, he remained bitterly angered by Mills's presumptions. Still, Berle's imputation of cowardice, of a feigned heart attack, was simply wrong. Mills had sustained a series of heart attacks dating back to his University of Maryland days. Mills's penultimate heart attack was not in any identifiable way connected with the proposed Berle television debate. Quite the contrary, such public appearances came to increasingly sustain Mills in his last days.

In place of Mills, Congressman Charles O. Porter from Oregon was chosen. "The result was a not uninteresting debate with a lot of questions from the audience, mainly loaded. But it did not allow for really good presentation of the issues and one always feels a sense of frustration."[43] And so ended this widely reported, incredible nonevent, occasioned by Mills's heart ailment.

Mills did an interview with the Mexican newspaper *Novedades* which in turn was translated into Spanish by Carlos Fuentes. The interview proved to be far superior in its command of Latin American materials and its sense of Cuba's place in hemispheric affairs. But it was also strident in its vision of American imperialism. Indeed, quite the reverse of expectations, Mills's view of the Cuban Revolution hardened rather than softened.[44] By 1961 his defense of the revolution had been elevated into a direct assault on American social celebration. He went back to older pet hatreds, weaving them into the fabric of his new love. Liberals became sheer obfuscators, right-wingers in hiding. *Times* became viewed as the "weekly fiction magazine." The Cuban Revolution became "the great unmasking of American liberalism." This revolution became not only a cause for Mills but a vindication of his prejudices. The frustrations of earlier years came to fruition with Cuba.

In the end, the revolution was a political act of a small Caribbean nation, which could contain neither Mills's intellectual ambitions nor his personal pretensions. Mills the political ideologist ultimately betrayed Mills the social scientist. He identified with a regime and with a position without ever investigating the social and political structure of the other side. There is no record, no indication, that Mills ever took seriously the critics of Castro—no indication except frustration that the regime could not manifest its self-professed independence even in the short run. In July 1961, only nine months before his death, Mills felt no need to update *Listen, Yankee!*, for he was sure that the events had vindicated him in every detail. He became more rasping, more convinced of the conspiratorial nature of the opposition and the institutional nature of the revolution. Increasingly, he turned his attack on the New Frontier, on President Kennedy, on Ambassador Adlai Stevenson, on all U.S. officials who would not listen to him. A number of Mills's commentators, like Swados, have tried to soften the blow by claiming that Mills was backing away from the more rabid of his statements in *Listen, Yankee!* But there is simply no evidence for this.

Mills became even more deeply enmeshed in what he saw as a one-against-one struggle with President Kennedy for the minds of Americans. Ultimately the revolution itself became a backdrop to a personal revivalism. The Bay of Pigs notwithstanding, what actually took place was neither the open warfare which Mills predicted nor the reconciliation between Cuba and the United States which he wanted.

Mills's great illusion about Cuba was that it could be a third way. It was an illusion he went to his grave believing. The Cuban Revolution today, after nearly twenty-five years of existence, with its initial leadership and inspiration intact, is the vindication of its own authenticity, as well as proof that Mills was correct in his perceptions of its importance. That the Cuban Revolution has failed to achieve its primary goal of political independence is an indication that what it achieved in authenticity it failed to achieve in autonomy. Hence one is left with an unhappy belief that Mills would have been confronted by Hobson's choice: to continue support for a revolution that had become bankrupt or to oppose that revolution and hence mock his own euphoria. One is reminded of Decoud's observation about Nostromo toward the close of Joseph Conrad's novel by the same name: "Here was a man that seemed as though he would have preferred to die rather than deface the perfect form of his egoism. Such a man was safe."[45]

REFERENCES

1. Carlos Fuentes to C. Wright Mills, December 27, 1960.
2. C. Wright Mills to Lionel Trilling, November 17, 1955.
3. Lionel Trilling. *The Liberal Imagination: Essays on Literature and Society.* Garden City, N.Y.: Doubleday/Anchor Books, 1950.

4. Lionel Trilling to C. Wright Mills, November 22, 1955.

5. C. Wright Mills. *The Causes of World War Three*. New York: Simon & Schuster, 1958, p. 157.

6. *Ibid.*, p. 155.

7. *Ibid.*, p. 148.

8. *Ibid.*, p. 164.

9. *Ibid.*, pp. 158–59.

10. Cf. J. Robert Oppenheimer, *Science and the Common Understanding*, New York: Simon & Schuster, 1954; and by the same author, *The Open Mind*, New York: Simon & Schuster, 1955.

11. Mills, *The Causes of World War Three*, pp. 18–19.

12. *Ibid.*, p. 24.

13. *Ibid.*, pp. 29–30.

14. *Ibid.*, p. 121.

15. *Ibid.*, p. 129.

16. *Ibid.*, p. 172.

17. *Ibid.*, pp. 96–111.

18. Russell Kirk. "Freely Given Advice on How to Avert War." *Chicago Tribune*, November 10, 1955.

19. Richard Massa. "Ism's in the United States." *The Chickasha, Oklahoma, Express*, October 30, 1960.

20. Bryce E. Nelson. "Drifting Quickly Toward World War III." *The Harvard Crimson*, October 24, 1958.

21. Ed Wimmer. "Goldwater-Mills See Compulsory State." *The Cincinnati Enquirer*, October 24, 1958.

22. Publicity release, Simon & Schuster, Inc., November 1958.

23. A. J. Muste. "C. Wright Mills' Program." *Dissent* 6, no. 2 (Spring 1959); 189–91.

24. Irving Howe. "C. Wright Mills' Program." *Dissent* 6, no. 2 (Spring 1959): 191–96.

25. Mills's "Culture and Politics: The Fourth Epoch" (1959), "The Cultural Apparatus" (1959), and "The Decline of the Left" (1959) all appeared originally in *The Listener* and were broadcast by the BBC. They are reprinted in *Power, Politics and People*, edited by Irving Louis Horowitz. New York and London: Oxford University Press, 1963, pp. 221-61.

26. C. Wright Mills. *Listen, Yankee! The Revolution in Cuba*. New York: McGraw-Hill Book Co., 1960, p. 124.

27. *Ibid.*, pp. 91–92.

28. *Ibid.*, p. 173.

29. Harvey Swados. "C. Wright Mills: A Personal Memoir." *Dissent* 10, no. 1 (Winter 1963): 42.

30. Mills, *Listen, Yankee!* pp. 140–41.

31. *Ibid.*, p. 29.

32. Arnaldo Orfila Reynal to C. Wright Mills, December 29, 1960.

33. Armando Betancourt to C. Wright Mills, December 9, 1960.

34. Salvador Ferrer to C. Wright Mills, December 14, 1960.

35. Mills, *Listen, Yankee!* p. 107.

36. Jules Dubois. "Apologia for Castro." *The Saturday Review*, December 17, 1960, pp. 19–20.

37. Hubert Herring. "American Spokesman for Dr. Castro." *New York Herald-Tribune*, November 27, 1960.

38. Fernando Benitez, Carlos Fuentes, et al. to Norman Cousins, December 28, 1960.

39. Swados, "C. Wright Mills: A Personal Memoir," p. 42.

40. C. Wright Mills to Frederick Pike et al., November 24, 1960.

41. Beatrice Bishop Berle and Travis Beal Jacobs. *Navigating the Rapids, 1918-1971: The Papers of Adolf A. Berle.* New York: Harcourt Brace Jovanovich, 1973, p. 720.

42. *Ibid.*, p. 721.

43. *Ibid.*, p. 722. This view was confirmed by Robert J. Alexander, the third member of the television panel on the show. Professor Alexander is a Latin American specialist who has written extensively on communism and democracy in the region.

44. C. Wright Mills. "Eschucha Otra Vez, Yanqui: 1961." Included as appendix to the third edition of *Eschucha, Yanqui.* Mexico and Buenos Aires: Fondo de Cultura Economica, 1961, pp. 211–59.

45. Joseph Conrad. *Nostromo: A Tale of the Seaboard.* Garden City, N.Y.: Doubleday, Page & Co., 1923, p. 301.

14

Postscript to Utopia: History and the Fourth Epoch

In "taking it big" Mills sometimes fell very, very hard, a risk that he understood and was willing to take. He appreciated other men who took the same risk.

Dan Wakefield, "Taking It Big," *The Atlantic*, September 1971

IN WRITING TO HIS DAUGHTER, the oldest of his three children, from whom he had been estranged for most of her formative years, Mills noted that "the worst thing in the world is pretension, especially cultural, intellectual and aesthetic pretension. The reason it is so bad is that it keeps you from learning anything. It keeps you from acquiring real sensibilities."[1] That Mills felt this proposition deeply is attested to by a life in which material possessions meant little and titles even less. But there are other forms of pretense which Mills was not so fortunate to escape: most notably, the effort to encapsulate and snare whole the meaning of the world. If pretension was the worst thing, then perhaps it might be claimed that for Mills ambition was the best thing. He tried to capture in one fell swoop the meaning of the modern world. That in this effort he crossed the line from ambition to pretension on many occasions might be forgiven; that he was less generous to others who did likewise is perhaps less easily overlooked.

Mills, in his last years, was in the process of producing three works that were to have been the capstone of his career. One leans to the formulation "had he lived," but in fact, the enormity of the tasks he set for himself, and the highly personal way he set about to achieve these tasks which sustained him in youth, betrayed him in the middle years. Poor health and bad habits combined to take their toll. Behind the facade of a powerful body was a man with a long-standing heart condition aggravated by excessive smoking and drinking. What remains is the significance of the fragments which he left behind.

The most complete, "Soviet Journal,"[2] was to have been a parallel to *The Power Elite*: namely, an examination of the Soviet power elite, including its intelligentsia. The second set of fragments were grouped around the theme of the New Left.[3] But this set, like the first, was larger in conception than its title indicates, since Mills's interests were no less than to settle accounts, once and for all, with the "cultural apparatus": the entire superstructure linking politics, ideology, and culture in high-, middle-, and lowbrow states. Finally, the least complete and most ambitious of the three projects was "Comparative Sociology."[4] This was to have been a multivolume program for studying the "state of the world," or more nearly, the play of forces which took into account American, Soviet, and Third World forms of power. These last writings, however impressionistic and incomplete, represented in nascent form a new and significant state in the evolution of Mills's work. That he was unable to realize these herculean projects does not diminish from the vision. Indeed, the fragments he left behind foretold in good measure the direction of scholarship in large-scale social science for years to come.

The Hegelian tradition recognizes that a vast gulf exists between subjective truth, or the truth of the private self, and objective truth, or the truth of historical judgment. In these last years, Mills moved away from a pragmatically dominated naturalism, in which vocabularies of meaning are infinite and irreducible, toward a dialectical vision in which such vocabularies are little else than the linguistic expression of ideologies and utopias. Historical frameworks replaced the experiential ordering of events. Mills moved from psychological terms to civilization-centered explanations. Despite Mills's increasing professional marginality, his deep skepticism about professional sociology, he remained convinced of the beneficial aspects of social science research as a whole. His practical no less than intellectual commitments underwent considerable transformation during the twenty years he worked as a professional, but it was an expansion within the "science of society" and never a repudiation of that "classic tradition." If any doubts remain as to the veracity of this claim, then the following examination of his steady preoccupation, even in his darkest years, with problems of culture and stratification within an international and comparative context should help dispel them. The intellectual continuities of his social scientific work helped give meaning to those final dark and despairing years.

Paradoxically, the study which Mills had most carefully constructed by the time of his death also has the least finished complexion. The tentative title Mills gave to this work, "Soviet Journal: Contacting the Enemy," was a product of his interviews with leading figures in Russian political, educational, and cultural life. The book is an attempt to go further in matters of political sophistication and literary form than he was able to do in *Listen, Yankee!* or *The Causes of World War Three*. "Soviet Journal" was going to be written in dialogue form, with a full spectrum of ideological-political types accounted for, ranging from a political conservative and a modern liberal to a Soviet Communist and a Socialist outside the Soviet bloc. All were to be queried by an independent American radical, a role Mills assigned to himself.

At the time of his death in 1962, Mills had reached the point of drawing a collective portrait from the various Russian officials he had met and talked with during April and May of 1960. These interviews were fully recorded; the answers Russian officials gave to his queries were set down with his own interpolations and interjections. The Soviet respondents offered up interesting remarks on the operations of life under the post-Stalin Bolsheviks, but certainly no "collective profile." Mills relied upon questionnaire techniques; the dialectical format was to yield up an ethnography of Russian political and intellectual behavior. Mills was anxious to carry forward his theory of political elites. While he speaks of the "Soviet elite," he mentions the difficulties in gathering information on that elite from interview data alone:

> The Soviet elite are closely identified with the Party apparatus, and feel their identification too deeply. This is quite understandably the case, because on some points it is simply the truth. Many of them are among the power elite, many others are closely connected with it, and most of them feel that they are connected with it. There are many lines of communication and lines to its centers open to them.

He concluded this point on the Soviet elite with a modest query. "It took me some thirty years of intellectual work to begin to come to an image of the United States which I thought reasonable and adequate. This is a country in which I have lived most of my life. Why do I think that in two or three years of study and one brief trip I can proclaim on Soviet society?" But proclaim he did. The Soviet regime had ultimately become for him what it had been for others in an earlier generation: the great betrayal of the utopian myth. His years of association with the anti-Stalinist Left in New York equipped him for this task.

Mills used the occasion of his "Soviet Journal" to clarify many points of sociological method. He was incisive in laying bare the essential fallacy of misplaced concreteness that doggedly pursues the empiricist. He made four points in his "Note on Method" which are characteristic and yet philosophically deeper than those expressed in *The Sociological Imagination*.

First, it is not possible to be concerned with empirical realities without the use of abstraction. One cannot empty one's mind and just see what is what. Even the most fanatical views are put forth in the name of fact or assumed to be self-evident. In selecting what one sees and what one makes of it, therefore, there are meanings, abstractions, and not mere events. Second, the suppression of abstractions only means that they will be smuggled in as general propositions among detailed observations and anecdotes. Third, it is not possible to render meaningful observations that are made or interviews that are held during brief visits without a sense of real history. What one sees is not just suddenly there. At least part of its meaning lies in its development. And all historical knowledge is abstract—inferences about past events from still-existing signs and reports. Fourth, in observing one society, or any specific features of it, one inevitably compares it with other societies one knows, especially one's own. This is not only a source of standards of perception, but also of self-perception.

It is crucial for interviewers to make clear to themselves and others just what comparative standards are being employed. Mills's summation of this point is crisp, strongly reminiscent of *The Sociological Imagination*.

> The appeal of first hand observation is merely a device of persuasion—of oneself and others. When someone says they changed their mind about Russian society because of first hand observations, this means that they have changed the abstractions, fanatical or not, by means of which they guide their observations. All observations of a country's life, save those of the insane or of the infant, are "second hand." It is the abstractions which guide observations that change, and this change is due less to any first hand observations than to many other and less tangible influences— including changes in intellectual and political fashion among one's circles at home.

The most fascinating portion of the "Soviet Journal" is the least elaborated: Mills's observations on Russian society, Communist politics, and guidelines for future American-Soviet relationships. Throughout, Mills repeats his belief in the "unattached intellectual." The advantages gained from not being involved with left-wing politics in the 1930s, or with American Communist literature of the postwar period, are repeated endlessly, as if Mills only half-believed what he was saying. However, he did take Mannheim's belief in a nonideological, nonpolitical sociology seriously. His vigorously independent political status is attributed to an accident of birth and belief, Texas and pragmatism. His manifest dislike of Communist literature in the United States he simply attributes to common sense. Mills's observations cannot be considered orthodox in any official Marxist sense of the term. But, perhaps because of the educated naiveté his work reveals, an extraordinary degree of freshness and individuality ensues. Mills took for granted the matter of sophistication in Soviet affairs. He felt that Isaac Deutscher and E. H. Carr and done the essential work and provided the basic insights into the nature of Soviet society: the role of the party elite, the changing nature of Russia under the impact of industrialization, the function of repression in the thirties, the dysfunction of the same sort of repression in the fifties, and so on. Nonetheless, it was not simply in confirmation of the work of others that Mills entered the sphere of "Kremlinology"; he was a student of power in his own right. His observations on the sociological aspects of Soviet power relations and prestige ratings are unique and arrived at with ethnographic detail lacking in the studies of others.

Mill's initial interest was in producing a monograph called "The Parallel: U.S. and U.S.S.R." This did not imply a mechanical inventory of similarities which both nations shared by virtue of their industrial-technological orientation. Mills was aware of the tremendous historical and cultural differences between the two giants. But he felt "that nothing is so clear as the speed-up of history in our time, along with the new shape of the world which often makes historical factors irrelevant to willful development." The "parallel" was "dialectical." The two great powers in contemporary life were now locked in combat with each other. But this very fact implied that their organization for total war compelled each of them to take on similar forms of military organization and produce similar weapons of total terror. Mills might be forgiven his excessive political relativism, which did indeed border on a deadening equalization of vices of the two superpowers. It was a time when few would admit a national right of the generalized "other" or a national wrong of the particularized "self."

Mills's evaluation of Soviet society was largely filtered through the senses and sensitivities of Soviet intellectuals. Discussing their own society, he found, Russian men of knowledge were optimistic; they saw the theory of future development running ahead of the facts and shortcomings of the present. Russians tended to lump present and future, actuality and potentiality. Mills's critical observations of how Soviet society functioned under Khrushchev, or had functioned under Stalin, always were met with a retort that problems such as shortfalls in agricultural production or the inhibiting impact of Stalinist repression would be met with, in the former instance, by a new plan and, in the latter case, by strengthening collective leadership. A recurrent set of criticisms Mills made about Soviet society concerned its Jesuitical emphasis on the collectivity, its denigration of individual responsibility or achievement, and its lack of real concern for events outside the Soviet orbit. These criticisms each emerged in a fast-clipped dialogue with a Soviet newspaper editor.

Mills: The Marxist questions; are there any since Lenin?
Answer: As a science, Marxism has always grown and will continue—
Mills: But give me an example?

Answer: At the 20th Congress: first, the struggle for peace, no fatalism about war; second, the thesis of peaceful coexistence.

Mills: These are policies, not theories. To drop a bomb or not is a policy, no matter who makes it. Anything on the theory of state power?

Answer: Policies are not just practical but theoretical matters, and debated as such.

Mills: Did this peaceful coexistence issue involve revision of Leninist views?

Answer: Not revision, but development. Lenin himself foresaw such a balance as possible. . . .

Mills: What do you think is the outlook for political action of wage workers in advanced capitalist countries?

Answer: I can't think for them.

Mills: Yes, but you are a journalist. Think about them, or stand naked of any theory.

Answer: Their progress will depend upon the development of wage-worker organizations and social consciousness. I can't solve those problems of Western Europe. I am not a specialist on the working class. You would know more than I do.

Mills: Yes, I do seem to know a good deal more. Moreover I am not so parrot-like in answering. In the Land of October, I want a greater and more various expression of opinion about such matters. What I get are answers about statistical size, a kind of giganticism.

The widespread chauvinism and ethnocentrism among Soviet leaders greatly disturbed Mills. He felt that too few Soviet scholars knew, much less cared to know, about alternative models of social development, the real status of the masses in advanced capitalist society, or even varieties of Socialist economics. Since Soviet society "abolished classes" by fiat and since only class problems were acknowledged as authentic, Mills in frustration and anger could never get his informants to intelligently discuss questions of stratification based on power, party, bureaucracy, and prestige.

In discussing Communist politics, Mills rarely missed the opportunity of twitting his hosts by introducing the name and writings of Leon Trotsky. Condemnations of Trotsky on the part of those who had not even read his works infuriated Mills, particularly since such condemnations usually came from high Soviet academic officials. He held the writers and essayists outside official circles in much higher esteem than the official political and intellectual cadres, and felt that they were "doing as much sociology as the sociologists." But he finally had to yield on a line of questioning concerning Marxist theory because there was so much blockage and static that he rarely got a useful set of responses.

If you attack Stalin, they will defend him. If you assume changes in principle, they will deny it. It is best to focus first upon new beginnings of two implementations of eternal principles: the one thing no one will criticize is the Party—it may make mistakes, but it is in their view self-correcting. Americans say the same thing of democracy, treating its institutions as above structural criticism. The Soviet slogan might well be: "My party, right or wrong, for in the end it will be right."

The Communist party apparatus was described in great detail. Mills noted that the Communist cadre was so committed to and emphatic about being responsive to popular pressures that it was indeed more circulatory and open-ended than the structural features of Communist political control might indicate from writings alone. The self-definition of the party apparatus as a guarantor of popular goals functioned, in the Khrushchev era at least, to reinforce the judicial safeguards of individual rights. But to his continued line of queries concerning Stalinism, Mills received carefully guarded replies on the "breakdown in legality" during the late 1930s and late 1940s. No one was willing to entertain the possibility that some sort of structural reform of the party machinery was necessary to ensure popular government in Russia. Just as in matters of Soviet society, so too in matters of policy, Mills's informants were too ready to say that the antagonism between the state and its citizens had been wiped out by wiping out the "bourgeois State." Problems between mass and elite, collective and individual, ruler and ruled, center and periphery were also eliminated by bureaucratic fiat. The Soviet "mix" always seemed to be resolved as a struggle between harsh present realities and a vision of an affluent and pleasant future. Mills noted with intense displeasure that there were few policy recommendations on how to get from here to there.

In establishing guidelines for a dialogue between intellectuals in the Soviet Union and the United States, Mills began to enter his individualist element. He was invariably more at home among intellectuals than any other group. For if Soviet optimism, buoyancy about the future, giganticism, and collectivism all genuinely went against his vision of the "Fourth Epoch," he nonetheless saw that optimism, buoyancy, and collectivism were positively functional with respect to Soviet agencies of power and goals for society. For Communist "hacks," both of a domestic variety and those imported from the United States (who also happened to be in Moscow during Mills's stay there), nothing could be done. They were declared to be insignificant in shaping policies either in the United States or in the Soviet Union. Mills held his chief fire for the intellectuals who did count. The serious Soviet intellectuals explained Stalinism, the limits of freedom under planning, and the political function to coercion in a way which strangely echoed Deutscher, E. H. Carr, and G. D. H. Cole in the West. The explanations were cool and reasoned—too hygienic for Mills's American tastes.

Mills moved beyond the frequently heard case for functional convergence between the two giants of the world. He wrote that "the differences between the two are very great. In my book on *The Causes of World War Three* and in the British Broadcasting Corporation lectures, I did not stress them [these differences] sufficiently.'' He accused both American and Soviet publicists of crude oversimplifications. He himself saw the master unresolved problem in terms of alternative visions as well as violations of freedom.

> In the first place, the very conception of freedom held in each is quite a different conception from the one held in the other. Second, the mechanisms and the forms of freedom, such as they are, are quite distinct in each. Third, moreover, the Soviet conception of freedom is held to be a state of affairs that is being realized more fully; that it has been violated during the Stalinist era is more and more admitted by Soviet publicists. Fourth, new beginnings, so far as freedom is concerned, means to the Russians a fuller realization of the ideals of communism. To the American publicist, it means a break with the regime, an ideological and political opposition to Marxism-Leninism. This idea is largely illusory. It feeds on incidents that are not seen as much of importance by Soviet intellectuals.

''Soviet Journal,'' then, was a report, an account of national reality which was a highly stratified reality. There is nothing rousing or shocking about it, nothing to indicate that Mills was either disenchanted or delirious with what he saw and the people he spoke to. He saved the sharpest jabs for dogmatists and sociologists, and his gentlest comments for women, children, and creative writers. If the Soviet Union telescoped the entire range of underdevelopment, steady development, and overdevelopment, the United States increasingly came to stand only for the last, for an overdeveloped ''affluent'' society pure and simple. The American intellectual slogan about the end of ideology was a reflection of opulence disguised as social science.

> The end of ideology has been talked about and assumed since the middle fifties. It means, first of all, a declaration of the loss of conception and faith in any form of socialism. Back of this are two facts: (a) the very poor quality and absence of political reflection in the United States and in the West generally; and (b) it means also the fact of political indifference and the absence of political movements or even demands on the parts of masses, especially wageworkers. These are provincial and lazy ideas, and from a worldwide view as well as from a local one it rests upon a very superficial notion about what is happening in the world and in the United States. It is not an analysis of political structure and trends or even of the character and trend of ideology. On the world scene, the problem is not United States ideology versus Soviet ideology, but rather the confrontation is: Soviet ideology versus United States ideology.

''Soviet Journal,'' while ostensibly a continuation of the popular line of journalism initiated with *Listen, Yankee!* and *The Causes of World War Three*, is more profoundly an extension of *The Power Elite*.

Mills saw the United States as part of the "overdeveloped society," a society in which the standard of living dominates the style of life, and a society in which the inhabitants are possessed by an industrial and commercial apparatus.

Precisely because of its backwardness, Mills found it difficult to put the Soviet Union into his picture of the Fourth Epoch. And, in fact, Mills tended to see Russian life as telescoping the problems of the underdeveloped country (in which the focus of life is still upon economic subsistence), the properly developing society (in which decisions about standards of living are made in terms of debated choices among cultivated life-styles), and the aforementioned overdeveloped society. This reflected itself in Soviet attempts to conquer outer space while leaving unsettled more practical tasks of political freedom and agricultural abundance. In the vast stretches of countryside, Mills saw enough to realize that for the mass of Russians, economic apparatus, the search for subsistence, remained dominant.

In the activities of the various branches of the Soviet cultural apparatus, Mills saw genuine effort at proper development in his sense: a widening of the options available for inspection, discussion, and finally decision. However, in the political apparatus Mills saw the nascent evolution of a bureaucratic machine huge in size, closed in mind, and far more frightening than the exercise of power in an open society. He did not therefore consider Stalinism, as many Western observers have, as illustrative of underdevelopment or of a Czarist continuum; interestingly, he saw it as illustrative of overdevelopment, of a society whose leading members were possessed by a technocratic mentality, and which would go to any lengths to protect the investment in the future—even if it meant darkness for the long present.

᳁᳁᳁

Mills's work on the Soviet political and social structure was to have set the stage for his larger-visioned works on the New Left and on comparative sociology. The collection of materials called "The New Left" was to have tapped many sources of Mills's past inspiration. One source was the work originally contemplated and designed as "The Cultural Apparatus." This work was to complete Mills's study of social stratification in the United States. It seemed logical that after *The New Men of Power* (on the working class), *White Collar* (a study of the middle classes), and *The Power Elite* (a study of the ruling classes) an examination should be made of intellectuals as a new class. Intimations of this were already plainly evident in Mills's concentration of educational levels among workers, the role of professionalism in solidifying the new middle classes, and the analysis of the cultural variables within the power elite. Between 1948 and 1956 certain broad theoretical formulations were made by Mills, chief of which was a global vision of the tasks of social science, and hence the world context in which ideologues, intellectuals, scholars, and policy advisers operate. As with Harold Lasswell earlier, opinion formation came to be seen as a generalized institutional expression of cultural forces and even of scientific formations.

Mills continued to place a high premium on the role of ideas in social life. In these final fragments he attempted to reconcile the classic tradition of sociology and new styles of industrial and technological organization brought about by socialism. Sociology and socialism, long at odds in the theoretical domain, were to be plugged into each other for the purposes of creating a more meaningful social practice. The purpose of "The New Left" was to locate the sources of this synthesis. Political sociology was to become a blood system through which the rising tide of world revolution would flow. A fact which Mills well understood was that there was no "New Left" in the late 1950s, only old futilitarians and young cynics. Mills's manuscript collection known as "The New Left" was an act yet to be staged, hence its premises remained inchoate. The resounding words of Mills can hardly disguise the unabashed moral prescription underlying his political descriptions.

> We cannot create a left by abdicating our roles as intellectuals to become working class agitators or machine politicians, or by play-acting at other forms of direct political action. We can begin to create a left by confronting issues as intellectuals in our work. In our studies of man and society we must become fully comparative on a worldwide scale. . . . We must do so with all technical resources at our command, and we must do so from viewpoints that are genuinely detached from any nationalist enclosure of mind or nationalist celebration. We must become internationalist again. For us, today, this means that we, personally, must refuse to fight the cold war. That we, personally, must attempt to get in touch with our opposite numbers in all countries, above all those in the Sino-Soviet zone. With them we should make our own separate peace. Then, as intellectuals, and so as public men, we should act and work as if this peace—and exchange of values, ideas, and programs of which it consists—is everybody's peace, or surely ought to be.

This direct appeal recalls William James's rousing call for *Les Intellectuelles* to band together against the War of 1898. But more importantly, one can see in retrospect that "The New Left" was to be a bridge from "Soviet Journal" (whose subtitle, "Contacting the Enemy," is exactly what Mills meant by getting "in touch with our opposite numbers") to "Comparative Sociology," which is no less exactly what Mills intended: to get sociology "fully comparative on a worldwide scale."

The title "The New Left" may first strike one as strange, because, as mentioned above, there was no such animal on the American scene in 1960. This, furthermore, seemed to be a peculiarly sectarian formulation for a work intended as the key to Mills's effort to forge a political sociology. But both types of objections were forcefully parried by Mills. In the first place, the New Left was already a significant political factor, especially in Latin America, Asia, and Africa: the nascent Third World. And the fact that the United States and its persons of learning were so tardy in recognizing this world force only indicated to Mills a delinquency, an American failure of nerve. The rising tide of a Third World, a stagnation of official liberalism in the Western capitalist world, the breakup of the Soviet monolith in the Socialist world, the polarization of economics along "have" and "have not" lines, increased possibilities of growth in new forms of thought and culture no less than in new styles of economy and society—the whole picture heralded the rise of a New Left.

In the second place, the New Left was not sectarian, because for Mills the radical tradition embodied the mainstream of Western democracy. Very much in the spirit of J. L. Talmon's *The Origins of Totalitarian Democracy*, Mills identified Marxian socialism, with all of its historical deformities, as the theoretical embodiment of the impulse to achieve equality and parity. What he did not appreciate is the near-complete linkage, in the Soviet experience at least, of the drive for economic equality with political repression.

> Marxism consistently embodies the tradition of the West. It contains its ideals, and moreover, in it these ideals are stated in close connection with one set of conditions under which it is held they might be realized. That is why it is much more worthwhile and difficult to criticize Marxism than to criticize liberalism. Marxism contains what is most valuable in liberalism: the secular humanism of the Enlightenment. But at the same time, Marxism as theory is much closer to and more directly relevant to the realities of our time. There is more reality and less obfuscation in its theory—although, of course, liberalism and Marxism contain considerable dosages of both.

The notion of a New Left was not an effort at political mobilization. Mills was just as removed from political participation at the end of his life as he had been in the beginning. But he did attempt to characterize the master trends in the political-social complex by picking out their central features. Insofar as he existed, Political Man was a "Left man" for Mills. It was precisely the nonpolitical individuals who remained under the weight of traditional rhetoric, who allowed their thought to deteriorate into empty slogans about the good life as the private and egotistic life. The threat to an honest Left, in the late 1950s at least, did not stem from a conservative renaissance, but from a collective ennui which had gripped our affluent society.

> We cannot smash our own little routines and become political in the larger manner that integrates political consciousness with everyday life

and into the very style with which we live ourselves out. But we do not seem able to take the initiative. The way in which we live has whittled away our capacity for exasperation. We have become tired before we have done anything and before anything was done to us by an enemy we could make explicit. We've really never declared war as a truly American left. There is no American left.

In nascent form a great deal of "The New Left" can be found in the seven chapters Mills wrote for *The Marxist*: the nature of ideologies and ideals, causes for a decline in the old Left, the collapse of liberal ideology into liberal rhetoric, the absorption of Marxian elements into liberalism, the absorption of liberal elements into Marxism, the theoretical strengths and weaknesses of Marxism as a tool of modern revolutionary movements, and the vacuity of liberalism in relation to problems of the emerging nations. There is Mills's critique of the end-of-ideology thesis; his view of the decline of the old Left, and the rise of the New Left minus the dogmatism of Stalinism and the flabbiness of social democracy. The special character in social development in Asia, Africa, and Latin America began to occupy his attentions. The Communist model, the capitalist model, and the independent forms evolving in Scandinavia rounded out his sense of potential sources for a Left revival.

Mills's intellectual energies were increasingly directed toward a political sociology of historical relevance, something which would get beyond a liberalism that had been useful between 1732 and 1848, or a Marxism that had been equally useful from 1848 to 1948. Liberalism disintegrated after the revolutions of 1848 because the middle classes could not deliver on their promises. Universal truths, free conscience, unfettered choices—all became disguised forms for capitalist statism and colonialist expansion. Likewise, official communism, while culminating in the deliverance of the Russian masses from capitalism, at the same time outflanked the humanistic portions of Marxism and transformed proletarian rule into bureaucratic rule, political association into party discipline, voluntary associations into terroristic cliques. Just as Anglo-American liberalism had collapsed when socialism became a world rallying cry, so, too, Russian Bolshevism would collapse when democracy became a world rallying cry. What Mills erected in his unpublished manuscript on the New Left was an architectonics of socialism as a political ideology, as a democratic ethic, and as an institutional agency for promoting change. He was, strange to say, a godfather of Eurocommunism, of a cosmopolitan movement which is larger than Russian nationalism, and capable of transcending the rhetoric of planning commissions or the rancor of terrorism.

Mills, in near-mimicry of Lenin's "What is to be Done?", asked: "Where do we Stand?" His reply was indicative of the spirit with which he approached the herculean task of producing a major tract on social science and political philosophy.

I try to practice the politics of truth. That means to me that I determine by my own standards what I think is true, what I think is false, and what I think is just and unjust. It means also that I do not give unconditional loyalty to any institution, man or state. My loyalties are conditional on the politics of truth as I determine the politics in each and every case.

In relation to "The New Left," this meant, in the first instance, getting beyond the Cold War rhetoric of East and West. And while Mills had few answers to his own questions, the authenticity of social science as a standpoint outside of politics was never doubted.

We stand without any political philosophy that is adequate to meet the political strategy of Bolshevism, the Ideological Message of Marxism, the economic aid of the Soviet Bloc. We have not known how serious the crisis of a political philosophy is because it has not been really felt as a crisis within the advanced capitalist world. For due to a number of geographical accidents and historical good fortune, not to mention exploitative relations with less developed countries, especially in Latin America the United States has not experienced any crisis in political philosophy. Liberalism has been good enough. But if it is good enough to outcompete communism inside the United States, and most of Western Europe, that is not where the competition is going on. The hysteria about that rather pitiful competition, and about the long-distance rhetorical interchanges between the United States and the Soviet Union have obscured from us the real locale of the competition, of the world encounter. That locale is to our south and to our east—in Latin America, Asia and Africa. It is there that we now begin to see the results of the crisis of our political philosophy. If we value the ideals of Western Civilization, then we must see that it is a crisis not only of our political philosophy but of political philosophy itself.

But this politics of truth acquired a metaphysical air of certainty, something which stood outside of space, time, and ordinary mortals and their claims on the political process.

What had intensified the crisis while at the same time disguising it, said Mills, was a reward system based upon power, not ideas: i.e., the betrayal of intellect. Anti-communism was merely negativity. "The chief function of anti-communism amongst Western intellectuals is to make them happier with present society, to turn them from political to cultural concerns, and to make them content with the provincialization of their interests." Mills viewed the growing privatization of intellectual life, the identification of sophistication with the private life, as the perfect status symbol of decline. Nor did he consider socialism as antipolitical, socialism as virginal American morality, to be a true confrontation with the dirty problems of social life meant to move beyond rhetorical excess into applied politics. Mills considered socialism in the United States to have deteriorated into a "rather cowardly posture" enabling the American intellectual "to assume a noble and rather saddened moral stance, which does not require that one confront the real moral dilemmas of the world." Mills saw moral socialism as the height of immorality because it never confronted thought with the need to act, and in fact denied the need for action through an inhibiting process: i.e., that which doesn't meet the standards of doctrine is by definition an evil in the world.

> Socialism is merely a holier-than-thou moral doctrine, and does not require attention to the means of action, to a usable rhetoric or ideology, or to a theory of society. It is the intellectual and moral dead-end of the futilitarianism of the old left. Anything that might be called a new left will have to be a great deal better than that. Otherwise it would be more honest to forget about the whole thing and take up some other line of work.

One need not be reminded at this point that Mills was scarcely able or willing to take his own advice.

The policymaking apparatus, by virtue of its meliorism, had deprived itself of the mechanism of political options. Mills did not explicitly work out the mechanisms through which this phenomenon was registered, much less the ways in which it might be overcome. Nor, for that matter, did he account for the judicial limits upon coercion in a democracy. He did not explain the relation between the "need for commitment" and "the politics of truth," or why culture replaces politics, or how status replaces class in the affluent world. Presumably, the unwritten portions of "The New Left" were to have filled in such gaps.

Mills's description of the functional components in the decline of politics in the West still offers significant guidelines for his sense of rectifying matters. In a section designated as "The Collapse of Ideology," Mills did not see the "end of ideology" in "celebrationist terms of a non-ideological-welfare-state-free-from-problems"; rather, his was a far more sober analysis. Mills sensed that to speak of the end of ideology was not only to describe the exhaustion of general theory; the terminology itself described a theory—rather, a "half-theory." Everything depended on where one proceeded from this acknowledged state of affairs in the West.

Mills pointed to four concurrent events leading to the collapse of liberal social thought. The historical agencies of change in democratic capitalist societies have been an array of voluntary associations which came into focus in a parliamentary or congressional system. These voluntary agencies functioned for each social class and each subgroup within a class. At the present time, however, these have dried up, and elitist policymaking from the top has replaced generative activities from below. Along with the collapse of the historic agencies of change there has taken place a hardening of the structural arteries of former times. Old structures come to be viewed, and to view themselves, as eternal precisely to the degree that they remained unchallenged. In his sphere, liberalism, with its theories of a state-imposed harmony and balance, provides the ideological cement for the status quo. Mills draws from earlier formulations made in *The Power Elite* in noting how clear it is that to talk about the collapse of agencies of social and political change is not to say that such agencies do not exist. On the contrary, the means of history making, of decision and the enforcement of decisions, have never in world history been so enlarged and so available to such small circles of people on both sides of the Cold War. A potential independent agency for initiating social change, the intellectual, has either been absorbed by the Establishment (the Crackpot Scientist) or alienated from politics as such (the Mass Society Critic), or else functions in a nonpolitical way—even when politics are central (the Higher Academician).

It is not that the "crisis in liberalism" in the West lacks any counterpart in the East. The "Soviet Journal" makes perfectly plain that Mills sought in vain for independent agencies promoting social change that would or could break Establishment modes. Nonetheless, Mills felt that if it were a matter of the Soviet Union versus the United States, the former had authentic advantages. First, it had a rational and rationalized economy based on planned growth. Second, it had a dedicated intelligentsia oriented toward future tasks and future victories. And third, it had a political science and a political ideology based on large-scale industry and not on small-scale enterprises and voluntary associations. If the "Great Contest" were exclusively determined by American capitalism and Russian communism there was little question that communism would emerge victorious. Mills did not say whether he approved of this outcome—only that it would occur.

He indicated, however, that it was not likely to occur, since the American consensual society was not able to raise the general level of the world economy any more than the Soviet coercive society was able to raise the general level of world democracy. The Third World was precisely that empirical feature which transformed the New Left from dream to reality. The emergence of nations and social systems calling themselves Socialist and at the same time "unaligned" politically represented for Mills "new kinds of social structure having new kinds of ideologies and innovative forms." Mills had no doubt that Marxism would proliferate yet new strains and varieties. Paradoxically, Marxism as pluralism would preserve the root content of a liberalism purified of its statism. How this was to take place, given the propensities of Marxist regimes to accentuate state power, was again not clarified. Mills might have added on this score that in the West, too, new forms had taken shape. Nations as advanced as Sweden and England showed deep divergencies from the American pattern, despite their general economic incorporation into the capitalist bloc nations. But Mills's hostility to the West had grown too deep to cope with varieties of capitalism or libertarianism. Mills's expectation was focused on the preindustrial countries outside either bloc. Even though some leaned toward capitalist democracy and others toward communism as a political economy, they showed a capacity and a will for independence and experimentation which reflected itself in the whole political posture of nonalignment.

This process whereby the Third World becomes a third way intensified during Mills's final years. In the Soviet bloc, there was the schism between China and the Soviet Union. In the West, the schism grew between Western Europe and the United States. Meanwhile, in the Third World there was a general disengagement from practices and premises of advanced powers as such, a willingness to endure the costs as well as the benefits, at least in some nations, of authentic changes in social structure.

What troubled Mills, and what remains unresolved in "The New Left," is the symbolic function of such nations as Venezuela and Cuba. He saw Venezuela as the perfect embodiment of American foreign political and economic policy, and Cuba as increasingly faced with the need to make pragmatic decisions in favor of a less-than-reliable Soviet ally. Mills fashioned his doubts into a series of dilemmas which remained largely unanswered. The first dilemma Mills saw harkens back to his early interest in the sociology of knowledge. In a prescient statement, he pointed out that there was a "distinction between what men are interested in, versus what is to men's interest according to their ideals." Mills felt that a central problem in both classic liberalism and classic Marxism was that both were in favor of what an elite considered human interests to be.

> Both resolve the dilemma by an expectation, by acting in ways that are to men's interests. One expects that in due course, or in the long run, these men will come to be interested in it. This is the expectation implicit in Marx (and John Stuart Mill!): that a class-in-itself will become a class-for-itself. What Lenin did was speed up the process, help it along. In fact, his "voluntarism" is based upon a belief in its "inevitability." He took part in history (a) a increase its tempo and (b) to counteract the lagging of counterforce, primarily the efforts of social democracy to wait a while.

Mills considered the root problem of political sociology to be profoundly ethical. In an earlier essay, "The Problem of Industrial Development," clearly earmarked for expansion in "The New Left," this emerged in terms of the expectations people have. People are interested in the fruits of industrial growth. Political actors must perforce be interested in the costs of such growth. Whose work is to be invested, at what tempo, with what kind of outside assistance, and at what costs to personal liberties—all of these are root questions for political sociology, and no less for a political morality.

At the time of his death Mills was giving this matter considerable thought. His reading interests in Gunnar Myrdal, John Strachey, Paul

Baran, and all of those mining comparative economic development attested to his growing belief that the ideology of the New Left would emerge as the practical ideology of the developing areas. The task of intellectuals in the advanced areas of the world was to assist in the herculean job of providing ideology by supplying a scientific theory of social development: an undertaking which, at the time, it seems Mills was prepared to take on singlehandedly. The United States, he said, had worked itself into a bind: sacrificing growth to the maintenance of a decaying political and economic structure. The Soviet Union's bind was that it had sacrificed political freedom to get a plentiful supply of economic goods. It was outside these blocs that a social synthesis was really possible. Little wonder, with such theorizing, that Mills became more tolerated than respected in places of intellectual power.

This analysis did not mean that there were no tasks for the Left in the Untied States. Mills was very much the American. He attempted in the penultimate, and least developed, chapter of "The New Left" to offer two agenda items with which any future left-wing movement in America would have to come to terms conscientiously and honestly—communism and pacifism. His observations on American communism completely discounted the possibility that it would be a significant political force in the years ahead. Yet he did not exclude the possibility that as a New Left emerged, this might increase the size of the Communist faction and necessitate a reconsideration of such problems as a united front and the need for a solid phalanx against congressional witch hunts. Surprisingly, Mills did not consider the possibility that "old Bolsheviks" would absorb the "young Turks," as indeed they have done in those countries where a Communist seizure of power has taken place. He thought that such a consolidation of the Left would be a consequence of rather than a prelude to a truly democratic revolutionary social upheaval.

Mills's distance from the American Left is most interesting, given the frequent criticism that he was a man obsessed by power. He indicated, not unlike the preachments of A. J. Muste at the time, that nonviolent resistance was not merely a set of values or a set of techniques, but a new method for making history, perhaps the most radically innovative one yet evolved. It could be adhered to and practiced as a principle or merely selected as a tactic where one believed it would be effective. However, Muste's impact notwithstanding, Mills raised a significant objection to pacifism as an exclusive or sufficient principle. "But: how reconcile pacifism as a principle with the right to revolution in the Cubas of this world. Under a tyranny such as Batista exercised, I do not believe anything would come out of the Gandhi type actions—only death without meaning or effect."

Striking a predictive note of considerable acumen, Mills addressed himself to the relation of pacifism and violence in the American South.

In a statement important not simply for its content, but because it is one of the very few times Mills dealt with the ''Negro Question'' as central for Americans, he said: ''The same problem of violence and the New Left will come up in connection with the Negro sit-in movements in the South. Within a year or two, what will Negroes do, what should they and those who sit with them do? What should we do if white hoodlums actually shoot up Negro slums?'' While he offered no answers to such questions—indeed, he tended to subsume all issues of race into class analysis—his concluding remarks make plain a generalized moral empathy for human rights that was not evident earlier in Mills's career.

> We are free men. Now we must take our heritage seriously. We must make clear the perils that threaten it. We must defend civil liberties long enough to use them. We must attempt to give content to our formal democracy by acting within it. We must stop whining about our own alienation long enough to use it to form radical critiques, audacious programs, commanding views of the future. If we do not do these things, who will?

The two most revealing items in ''The New Left'' from the standpoint of Mills's personal development as an intellectual and a man of social science come in the preface and in a postscript. Both statements are highly relevant: the former, as an indication of the long trek Mills made from *The Power Elite* to ''The New Left''; the latter, as a statement of ultimate intellectual moral intentions quite beyond the analysis of power.

> It has been said in criticism that I am too much fascinated by power. This is not really true. It is intellect I have been most fascinated by, and power primarily in connection with that. It is the power in the intellect and the power of intellect that most fascinates me—as a social analyst and cultural critic.

Underscoring this point at the very end is a brief description of the intellectual terms of the current crisis in human relations.

> The most revealing intellectual terms of our crisis are the theories and practices of social inquiry and reflection, in particular the abandonment of the classic tradition in sociological thinking. There is much fruitful discussion these days of the humanities vis-à-vis the natural sciences (in the Soviet Union it is taking the shape of a controversy between physicists and poets over what type of Soviet Man). But in the West, and certainly doubly so in the United States, there has not been an appropriate discussion of the social sciences as a political problem, as a problem for policymakers. The simple fact is that if we do not develop more adequate sociological theories of the character of present-day varieties in social systems, of the ways in which history is now being made and extended, then the varieties of Marxism will fill the vacuum by default.

Mills did not intend these remarks as some sort of anti-Marxist crusade. Yet he deeply believed that while Marxism was a fundamental part of the classic tradition of social science, it was only a small part, and not the whole. As such, he felt an ever-deepening need to move beyond Marxism. He had "settled accounts" with *The Marxists*, and he had offered an account of present political realities in the East and West in "The New Left." What remained was a telescoping of scientific knowledge about the world. And in a projected multivolume effort, "Comparative Sociology," he aimed at a magnum opus that would raise social theory to science. The work of G. D. H. Cole on Socialist history, E. H. Carr on Russian political history, and Joseph Needham on Chinese civilization convinced Mills of the need for a big format if his global vision of stratification was not to be viewed as superficial and unconvincing—a charge he was hearing with increasing frequency and irritation during his "pamphleteering" days.

√∩∽∩√∩

"Comparative Sociology" was a handle which Mills gave to a projected "six to nine volume comparative study of the world range of present day social structures." Mills never got beyond a few select scenarios of this panorama. Critical as he was of the oracular tradition of Toynbee, Sorokin, and Spengler, he appreciated their underlying global vision: to account for the individual in society by accounting for the individual in history. What led Mills to believe that the enterprise was worth the energies necessary for its realization was a concurrent tradition, basically British, which managed to weave the same patterns of social history within a firm ethnographic stitching. Mills was still empirical enough to avoid the grand manner of theorizing, which, however congenial in abstraction, proved unwieldy as a concrete expression of social realities.

A series of lectures which Mills gave at the London School of Economics in 1960 provided him with the jumping-off point for "Comparative Sociology." Especially significant to him were the distinctions between the "modern era," or the "Third Epoch," and the "postmodern era," or the "Fourth Epoch." The Enlightenment was symbolic and yet symptomatic of the Third Epoch. Out of it came the ideas of economic rationality (or socialism, broadly speaking) and political libertarianism (or democracy, speaking with equal scope). But the Third Epoch gave way to the Fourth Epoch because of the seeming incompatibilities of the two master ideological notions. Rousseau, Marx, and Weber seemed to offer the paradox in stark terms: increased rationality may not be assumed to make for increased freedom. The existence of mass estrangement among workers, anxiety among professionals, and anomie among middle sectors invalidated the "modern" period. The price of rationality is nothing short of a suspension of freedom (bureaucratized socialism and capitalism), while the price of freedom is nothing short of rationality (the balanced, developing society).

Thus, in the West—Mills never quite made up his mind whether or not the Soviet Union was part of his "West," and if so, specifically to what extent—there is a common cluster of issues which are "epochal" in character. Mills saw his multivolume work as entailing a multilinear rather than a unilinear theory of history. Each major world region has its own historic and irreducible form of development. Just how extensive a departure Mills makes from the theory of historical materialism or unified world systems can be seen from the following comment:

> In the course of studying the historical contour of each world region, the impact of extraneous world states will be stated, but to quite varying extents. For my contention is that the need for historical analysis varies greatly in importance according to the nature of the social structure that we are trying to understand and explain.

Harkening back to the much-maligned *Character and Social Structure*, history was to be seen in terms of macroscopic social systems, rather than social systems being seen in terms of history, as one finds in historicists from Marx to Toynbee. This distinction emerges in two root questions which Mills feels should be asked by the sociologist:

> What is the nature of our epoch and how best can we define it for study? In short, what are the tasks of a theory of history and how can we best use it to delineate the structure of the present world's social structure and how best can we define them? In short, what are the tasks of a comparative social science and how best can we set up a comparative accounting?

Mills next was confronted by the problem of just what items are truly comparable; and no less, what constitutes the basis of selection? For a solution to this problem, he turned to the work of the new "Chicago school" and primarily to Sylvia L. Thrupp, who was a founder of the journal *Comparative Studies in Society and History*. The idea of comparative sociology, borrowed from the science of anatomy, brought new enthusiasm into the kind of social science which Mills came to see as necessary if a parochial and debilitating nationalism was to be overcome. This fitted in well with the kind of Weberian historical analysis of social character offered by Hans Gerth in an earlier period of Mills's intellectual formation.

What was needed was some way to break the arbitrariness not simply of ethnocentric accounts of history based on national prestige, but of explanations of history that in their high degree of abstractness and generality were at best "ideal-typologies" with strong subjective biases. The reason for the multivolume character of "Comparative Sociology" was to avoid making ideal types which are of little scientific relevance, but are at best heuristic devices for making people act in a certain way. Mills's comparative analysis of stratification would begin by taking selective variables (demography, economic output, forms of social control, etc.) and would provide an exhaustive account of these variables, rather than covering a far-reaching geographic area with a selective account as was characteristic of the oracular historicist tradition.

The first volume was intended to provide information on all that could systematically be said about the external factors of world regions. Exhaustion of the statistical and systematic knowledge was a necessary prologemena to setting forth key classifications and master trends. Mills intended to deal with no fewer than one hundred nations in terms of an "area code" not unlike that provided by Woytinsky in his masterful demographic researches. This "area code" was to be reinforced by a study of two phases: the transformation from ruralism to urbanism in each area, and the revolutionary pivots and main drifts in each area. What would make this kind of exhaustive account of development possible was the theoretical premise that what happens in one nation powerfully affects immediately surrounding nations within the common region. Presumably, Mills believed that the statement "When France sneezed Europe coughed" is susceptible to enlargement. Thus, when China flexes its muscles, the Southeast Asian countries do more than just observe. The coalescence of geographic, ethnic, and linguistic clustering is one which needed considerably greater amplification before its analytic utility could be established; and Mills had simply not gotten around to doing so at the time of his death. But the worth of the attempt, whatever the outcome, is incontestable. It would have been, in Mills's mind, the first real breakthrough from ethnocentric "Western" or "American" sociology into a "world" sociology.

The cultural relativism of Malinowski and Benedict in anthropology was a primitive effort in the direction of a nonethnocentric social science. But for Mills, since their relativism remained encumbered by ideological and intellectual commitments to liberalism, the breakthrough was only partial and inherently restricted; for example, the study of kinship relations in a small Amazon town was exhaustively taken up, while the entire northeast of Brazil in revolutionary ferment was unexamined. The frequent penciled allusions to the work of Ralph Linton, Alfred Kroeber, Clyde Kluckhohn, and other anthropologists in his copies of the major anthropologists of the time indicates that Mills was not unaware of the possibilities which cultural anthropology opened up in the study of world regions. Likewise, his growing interest in geographic, demographic, and especially economic problems emphasized Mills's belief that a comparative international sociology was at least possible, if not inevitable.

The only other segment which Mills had sketched out even in preliminary form was one which would take select sociological issues as they manifested themselves in the "four epochs" (ancient, medieval, industrial, and postindustrial) in terms of "regional codes" (by continental areas, and by the power blocs: Western, Communist, and Third World) and economic development (underdeveloped, developed, and overdeveloped). The precise variables which he envisioned as necessary for further study are: symbol spheres; ascendant modes of communication; public help and social services; world horizons, e.g., manor, nation, cosmopolitan, international; reaches of power; societal self-images, e.g., ruled by God, Reason, Bureaucracy; public relevance and the role of intellectuals in developing types of personality; forms of legitimation; and finally, types of anxiety and psychological problems. One can only conjecture just what Mills would have done with his "epochal sociology." One might argue with some credibility that the magnitude of this self-imposed task, coupled with its unrealizability, finally served to do him in; it was the final, self-created *cul de sac*.

The idea of an epoch is a construction. It is a suggested way of thinking about contemporary society and about the place of this society in the course of history. It is a far-reaching idea, for if taken seriously it requires the social scientist to summarize the pivotal events and decisive trends which characterize contemporary society—and more than that, to do so in such a way as to make plain just how this society differs from other societies. This permits the construction of an epoch to be located within human history as a whole.

> External events and historical trends are not enough. To make our point that we are indeed being moved into a new epoch of human history requires, first, that we show a shift or a change in the psychological bearings of the individual's biography and character; and second, intellectually, moreover, we must show that the very categories of explanation which served to orient men in past epochs no longer are satisfactory in the present epoch. It is this fact that is perhaps most central in defining an epoch. For the explanations on which men lean set up for them what they expect and what they hope for. And it is by means of the "hoped for" that we can most readily enter into the meaning of an epoch for human and psychological values.

The concept of human expectations entered into Mills's most advanced sociological thinking. His earlier work tended to take psychological potentialities and longings as raw data on opinions. The place of ideas in the definition of an epoch in Mills's final writings recalls the work of Wilhelm Dilthey rather than Max Weber on the function of general ideational categories in defining the *Geisteswissenschaft*, and the work of Karl Mannheim on "styles of thought" rather than Karl Marx on "material foundations" in defining the *Zeitgeist*.

> An epoch may be defined in terms of a set of principles that permeate an entire society, that define it as a totality, and that more or less persist. How long they persist sets the historical limit of the epoch; how far they permeate the society sets the structural limit of the epoch. By principles, I

mean a way of explaining the episodes and events that make up the historical content of the epoch, as well as the types of integration, the moods and feelings, the aspirations of the individuals. Above all, an epoch may be defined in terms of that feature which is most powerful historically, the center from which changes arise; the center of sociological initiative. When what is happening in the social world as well as what is widely felt and widely thought can no longer be satisfactorily explained by the received principles, then an epoch is ending and a new one needs to be defined.

The lifelong interest Mills had in the sociology of knowledge, in the study of the ideological and utopian apparatus that leads to consciousness of society and consciousness of interests, is strongly reflected in his final discussion of the maximum problem in social history. Mills reaches both sociological and literary heights, which inspires conjecture as to just what he would have produced in his magnum opus. Even as a fragment, it stands as a powerful description of the relationship between social change and human consciousness.

Men become acutely aware of historic change only when it occurs within the short span of a generation or two. But even when the conditions of everyday life change swiftly, even when they come to see that their children face a world which they as children never faced, they come only grudgingly to a consciousness of epochal change. The pace of change, however, need not be revolutionary, although in our generation is has been. It need not be violent or sudden, although in our generation it has been. More than the mere fact of rapid change is needed. Most men do not feel deeply and completely affected by the fact that since World War II, Asia has again stood up in world affairs, that since World War I, Russia has demonstrated to the world an alternative form of industrialization—the first since the seventeenth century—that the long ascendency of the British has decisively ended, as well as the score other pivotal facts of the present world. It takes a certain imagination and a certain memory to grasp something of the meaning of these shifts before the meaning comes into your daily life and you are carted off to war or thrown into an economic slump, or urgently asked to believe new beliefs or to hate new enemies. More than mere eventful changes, even those as fast and prolific and almost total [as] in our generation, [are] needed for the consciousness of epoch.

This represented the last point which Mills reached in his description of the public tragedy known as society. In so doing he also reached back to make one final desperate attempt to link that public tragedy with private anxiety, stratification with personality. In a blaze of passion he wrote his own sociological requiem.

Some men have longer memories and more imagination than others. They are aware of a wider range of everyday milieus, and believe that they understand more of their own times. Such men are likely to become more puzzled beyond the mere shoulder shrug, when historical change is fast paced. They become puzzled because their explanations break down; then it is that their expectations collapse and sometimes they become more [than] puzzled: they become disoriented. This means that those who had expectations, those who thought they could explain what was happening in the world came to see that they could not, and hence to sense on every side a new epoch arising. It is in terms of ideology that such men become aware of crisis; when these crises become more than merely partial, when their whole view of life becomes upset, they experience anxiety. It is out of such anxiety that epochal consciousness arises.

Beneath anxiety of men with ideology, and the everyday fetishism of men without it, there is more than personal troubles and there is more than ideological confusion in the face of change. Troubles and confusions there may be, but they, in turn, do not spring from the biographies of individuals. These biographies themselves, the plan of life and the ideological view of how things are, in various and intricate ways are an intrinsic part of the structure of society. Beneath the consciousness of epochal change, beneath an anxiety and confusion and bewilderment that indicate it, there are changes in the very structure of whole societies inside the entire modern epoch.

At the end, he finally perceived the great truths of Ibn Khaldun, Vico, and Rousseau: development involves real social costs; every penetration of the fog of ideology creates new forms of social anxieties; and every beatific vision of world peace is bought at the price of new social upheavals brought about through change.

ஒண்ணன்

In these final and personally agonizing years, Mills addressed himself to the open secrets of society. He pointed out the rise of a Third World in nascent form; he revealed the shortcomings of American deterrence policy; he saw the horrible truth that only the Soviets seemed endlessly in need of emulating the American dream of consumer affluence; he showed that the breakup in the "classic tradition" occurs when people of knowledge become subservient to people of power. Alexander Herzen once wrote that "one has to have great courage to speak out loudly, to say the things secretly known to everyone." Mills had that sort of courage. His audacity stemmed from a capacity to organize and clarify the obvious, rather than seek out a unique rhetoric. Hence it was easy to underestimate his insights. The final and unfinished writings of Mills must be seen as a part of the ongoing scientific struggle between clarification and manipulation, or if one prefers, the Faustian struggle between moral tribulation and immoral treason.

Mills's ethical perspective was more open to inspection than that of any other American sociologist. He developed a notion that public performance and public worth were to become the touchstone of any social science. If sociology lacked this active dimension it was worthless. Like psychoanalysis, which attracted Mills, sociology should make no bones about both its therapeutic goals for the individual and utopian goals for the society at large. A combination of therapy and utopia defined the worth of social research, pure or applied.

Issues of freedom and organization, autonomy and hegemony, are difficult to answer in the abstract. Mills reacted against private magnates because he saw them as profiteers, and against government bureaucrats because they stifled initiative. His utopiansim drove him to strange linkages. He was a pragmatic anarchist, and no less a conservative radical. He was against the Second World War but never surrendered his claims on the usefulness of violence. He had a touching rural town hall approach to settling political disputes, and yet advocated cosmopolitan life-styles. He was for rugged individualism and yet opposed a social system fostering and advocating such an ideology. He never so much as voted, yet he offered political advice to anyone who would listen. He opposed the civic culture as profoundly antipolitical, yet he rejected political participation because it destroyed the civic culture. These contradictions define Mills as a human being. His attempt to resolve these contradictions helped to define him as *auteur* of the big picture.

Whether Mills possessed the architectural skills to pick up the diverse images that form the big picture of the modern world has to remain a moot point. Death at the age of forty-five decrees that no answer to this can be given. But speculation whether he would have been able to rise to the heights of social analysis and historical synthesis is less important than his willingness to make the attempt at a synthetic system. We can only judge a life that is lived, not an afterlife or a life that might have been. In this regard, Mills remains both a harsh taskmaster and a reassuring figure in helping us map our social world in the act of evaluating his private world.

Coming to the end of our story does not mean exhausting a sense of the man. Mills's ambitions at the end were of the same cloth as his earliest efforts: to implement the Enlightenment ideal of universal knowledge through the practice of human reason. As Mills himself early on learned from Kenneth Burke, the vocabulary of motives is infinite. Those who disliked Mills saw in his effort arrogance and moral fanaticism. Those who liked Mills saw in the same effort a dedication, selflessness, and moral grandeur unmatched by his colleagues in the social sciences. It would be false to the sense and purpose of my work to claim that the truth is to be located on either side of this ethical judgment. Even if the answers to the "real" Mills could be found, they hardly matter. Posing the issues in this way falsifies his own sense of purpose.

Mills is ultimately best characterized in terms of seriousness: the achievement of enlightenment through the classic tradition in social science. His brief years coincided with an epoch in social research in which the findings of social science mattered a great deal: both to society as a whole and certainly to its practitioners. If discourse and debate often turned personal, even bitter, it was not just because Mills was possessed of or because his enemies were lacking in human worth. Rather, it was that driven by a willful sense of purpose, of seriousness, Mills became a prophet and a fanatic. His celebrators became absorbed with the truth or falsity of his prophesies, while his detractors developed strong antipathies for his fanaticisms. In a young discipline such as sociology, desperately searching for scientific respectability and professional standing, it is little wonder that his critics walked in an air of triumph, while his defenders saw themselves as bitterly engaged.

Mills remains an engrossing figure for the social sciences and for American letters less because of any uniquely inspiring concept or well-turned pithy phrase than because of his persistent belief that the qualities of intensity, purpose, and judgment must be brought front and center into the discourse of social research. That the boundaries of social science were often breached only led him to defy those professional structures rather than doubt his own moral and political imperatives. If we look back at the great utopians of the past, we find them uniformly breaking empirical barriers to create, in their mind's eye at least, a better future. That America was Mills's essential laboratory for testing, teasing, and thundering was an accident of birth, but one which gave special meaning and a cutting edge, albeit a blunt one, to his search for the Fourth Epoch—the utopian longing within all ideologists and, I daresay, all sociologists.

REFERENCES

1. C. Wright Mills to Pamela Mills, May 12, 1960.

2. C. Wright Mills. "Soviet Journal: Contacting the Enemy." (Unpublished manuscript.) Written and prepared from interviews gathered in the USSR during April–May 1960. Given the condition of these materials, exact page references will be omitted.

3. C. Wright Mills. "The New Left." (Manuscript containing both published and unpublished materials.) Among the published fragments, see "The New Left," in *Power, Politics and People: The Collected Essays of C. Wright Mills*, edited by Irving Louis Horowitz. New York and London: Oxford University Press, 1963, pp. 247–59; and "On the Old Left," in *De hombres sociales y movimientos politicos: Ensayos de C. Wright Mills*, edited by Irving Louis Horowitz. Mexico City and Madrid: Siglo Veintiuno Editores, 1968, pp. 53–68.

4. C. Wright Mills. "Comparative Sociology" was a tentative title that Mills settled on for his multivolume project, which he hoped that the Rabinowitch Foundation would fund. He passed away without completing a unified draft, but left a folder entitled "State of the World: Propositions and Policies" on the "underdeveloped group of nations." Here again, very few fragments were published representative of this final form of his thinking. The two most important are "The Problem of Industrial Development" in *Power, Politics and People*, pp. 150–56; and "Consciousness of Epoch and Self," in *De hombres sociales y movimientos politicos*, pp. 297–303.

Index